DEMOCRACY AND SLAVERY IN FRONTIER ILLINOIS

DEMOCRACY
AND
SLAVERY
IN
FRONTIER
ILLINOIS

THE BOTTOMLAND REPUBLIC

James Simeone

Northern

Illinois

University

Press

DeKalb

Library of Congress Cataloging-in-Publication Data

Simeone, James, 1960–

   Democracry and slavery in frontier Illinois : the Bottomland Republic / James
Simeone.

      p. cm.

   Includes bibliographical references (p.) and index.

   ISBN 0-87580-126-3X (alk. paper)

   1. Illinois—Politics and government—To 1865. 2. Slavery—Illinois—History—19th
century. 3. Illinois—Race relations—Political aspects. 4. Whites—Illinois—Race
identity. 5. Whites—Illinois—Politics and government. 6. Social classes—Illinois—
History—19th century. I. Title.

F545 .S56 2000

977.3'03–dc21   99-089566

TO MY PARENTS,

WHO TAUGHT ME TO DOUBT WHAT I LEARNED FROM READING BOOKS

CONTENTS

ACKNOWLEDGMENTS

This study is the result of a decade-long preoccupation with American political thought and development. Along the way I have accumulated intellectual debts too numerous to detail. I would like, however, to acknowledge some extraordinary sources of support and inspiration.

Illinois Wesleyan University (IWU) awarded me a Junior Faculty Leave during which the work was finally revised. I also received an Artistic and Scholarly Development Grant from the university, which financed additional archival research in Springfield, Chicago, and Indianapolis. Provost Janet McNew provided a generous grant to fund the final stages of the project. Tari Renner, my department chair, has been a model of support, as have my political science colleagues Kathleen Montgomery, Frank Boyd, and Greg Shaw. The faculty at IWU have created a remarkably supportive and open atmosphere of intellectual exchange. I have profited immensely from conversations and contentions with Paul Bushnell, Mike Weis, Bob and April Schultz, Mike Young, Chris Prendergast, Brian Hatcher, Julie Prandi, Bob Bray, Irv Epstein, Seth Crook, and Carl Gillett. I gratefully acknowledge Patra Noonan's graphics work in producing the maps.

My interdisciplinary approach was encouraged early on by members of the Department of Political Science at the University of Chicago. I thank especially Lloyd Rudolph for his overall support and perspective on interpretative social science. Cass Sunstein, Nathan Tarcov, and Gerry Rosenberg mentored me at crucial moments along the way. I first learned the habit of disciplinary poaching at Chicago, where I was able to study the English Civil War with Mark Kishlansky, the common law with Charles Gray, Latin grammar with Nancy Helmbold, cultural theory with Richard Schweder, republicanism with Ralph Lerner, and hermeneutics with Jay Schleusener. These scholars inspired me with their brilliance, but their unswerving commitment to a student outside their disciplines impressed me in a more fundamental way by shaping my view of critical inquiry.

I must also mention two other people without whom my time at Chicago would have been less fruitful, Adam Stephanides and the late David Greenstone, my dissertation adviser. I thank Adam for keeping the conversation going in ways only a polymath can; and as professor and mentor, David embodied the best of the Chicago tradition as I know it. He used to say that Perry Miller and Ludwig Wittgenstein were the greatest minds of their generation, save Albert Einstein. Before I met David, I didn't know any political scientists who took the work of historians and philosophers seriously: in this work I offer my contribution to the interdisciplinary political science he pursued along with Michael Rogin and Ira Katznelson.

Within the Illinois Historical Society community, I have benefited from discussions with John Hoffman, Bob McColley, Kay Carr, Richard John, Ellen Eslinger, Ed Ferguson, and Robert Webb. I thank Richard J. Ellis and Andrew R. L. Cayton for their thoughtful criticism on earlier drafts. I am grateful as well to Martin Johnson, my editor, who repeatedly showed the rare ability to mix gentle encouragement with incisive criticism.

Finally, I offer my warmest thanks to Kathi, who has made this wild ride a most enjoyable one.

DEMOCRACY AND SLAVERY IN FRONTIER ILLINOIS

INTRODUCTION

HOW THE PEOPLE
BECAME THE WHITE FOLKS

Early in the morning on December 9, 1823, a mob of protestors gathered at the home of Illinois Governor Edward Coles. As the governor's straw effigy burned brightly in the darkness, the mob cried out "State House or Death." The night before the state house had burned to the ground, and the townspeople reacted with alarm. The crowd was harassing Coles because he refused to pledge to build a replacement structure. When he advised waiting until public funding could be secured, the protestors decided he had not fully appreciated the crisis facing the town. They feared losing the state capital designation and with it their fortunes.

Mobs and fire in the night were becoming routine in Vandalia, the new state capital; the gathering in front of Coles's house now confirmed the tradition. The previous spring a mob had marched through town yelling "Convention or Death." Before that, in January 1823, a fire damaged the town's bank and land office. Because these buildings held deed and loan records, rumors of arson proliferated. Adding to the townspeople's worries, the bank was robbed in March 1823. Although the residents believed the robbery and fire were unpreventable, the new fire meant the town would face another investigation. The editor of the *Illinois Gazette* at Shawneetown gave voice to their anxieties: "This misfortune following so closely the burning of the banking houses and the subsequent robbery of that institution, seems to stamp a kind of fatality upon the place, as prejudicial to its character as a seat of government, as it has been to the interests of the commonwealth." In the morning, supporters greeted Coles. Relieved to find him safe, they gave assurances that "the mob was composed of the lowest class of the community."[1]

The governor's troubles did not end there. Within the month arsonists burned 400 fruit trees and some outbuildings on his farm near Edwardsville. Then the county commissioners of Madison County sued him for emancipating his slaves without posting the requisite bond.

Coles understood that these "defamations and persecutions" originated from his political enemies, "the factious Conventionists."[2] This was a group of legislators who had opposed his effort to end de facto slavery in the state. They instead passed a Convention Resolution allowing the people to decide the matter. What Coles did not understand was the profound resentment he created in his opponents by articulating anti-slavery sentiments without excusing his wealth and privilege. Like the protestors at Vandalia, the conventionists suspected that the governor, recently arrived from a plantation in Virginia, did not recognize the hard times in Illinois. They viewed his large farm with envy, not merely because of its size but because hired hands worked its fields and orchards. While most settlers cleared their own farms, Coles employed a battery of laborers, among them one of his freedmen and a cook who was still his slave.

The class prejudice faced by men such as Edward Coles was brought to Illinois by the wave of emigrants flooding the state after the War of 1812. The new arrivals, who came mainly from the southeastern and southwestern states, had been inspired by Andrew Jackson's victory over the British at New Orleans. They looked forward to a future of importance in the nation. They expected to be treated with respect in the Illinois Territory, then situated on the western edge of the American frontier. When Illinois joined the Union in 1818, they took hold of citizenship as if it were a personal belonging. They refused to accept the degraded status of "settlers and inhabitants," as territorial residents had been designated by the Northwest Ordinance of 1787. Nor were they satisfied with the subordinate status they had previously suffered in their home states. They claimed Illinois for the New West and, so, hoped to leave behind forever the embarrassments they endured as poor whites among men such as Edward Coles in the Old East.

Nothing unified the generation that came of age with statehood as much as a distant, haughty leader—and Coles could be both. With characteristic western optimism, the postwar emigrants to Illinois Territory expected to build a society that included freedom and prosperity for all settlers. The democratic revolution they led embraced social as well as political equality. They united behind a powerful version of western "republicanism," the early American equivalent of democracy, but their unity was tested when the pursuit of equality turned into the pursuit of slavery. For the 18 months between February 1823 and August 1824, they debated the power of the people to make Illinois a slave state. That a free people could contemplate instituting slavery was not an aberration; it was the inevitable consequence of their republicanism which stood for the belief that the power of the majority, without more, granted legitimate authority to rule.

The view of the convention controversy as an egalitarian social revolution in full bloom has been obscured. Previous studies have emphasized the injustice of slavery while leaving the issues of social and political authority unexplored. The standard history of the convention controversy by Theodore Calvin Pease illustrates the trend. Pease worked on the *Illinois Centennial Survey,* a taxpayer-funded effort employing a team of historians, from 1907 to 1920, that produced five authoritative volumes covering the state's first century. The "complacent smugness" of the conventionists disgusted him. But he allowed the disgust to eclipse his portrait of the movement, quoting with obvious incredulity a conventionist who argued that "our state would be more republican" if slavery were allowed. So outlandish a remark, Pease let it stand—"a caricature" of the movement—in place of serious examination.[3]

Contra Pease, this study examines the convention controversy not in spite of its many contradictions but because of them. The conventionists insisted on social equality, but flirted with introducing chattel slavery. They desired easy and open prosperity for all, but hoped to get it by unlocking the competitive forces of the market economy. They praised the West as the nation's haven for outsiders marginalized in the East, but chauvinistically refused to recognize the claims of many local minorities. They decried federal tutelage, but were dependant upon favorable treatment from the national government in areas as diverse as public land prices, Indian removal, and postal service. They claimed to want freedom and equality for all, but the majority were in fact concerned only with the rights and status of one class, race, and gender: poor white males. After the controversy, even the first contradiction was not fully resolved, for slavery was not legally barred in Illinois until 1845.[4]

Precisely because of its contradictions, the convention movement reveals the distinctive grain of antebellum American politics. The conventionists believed that their legacy, stretching back to the Revolution, embraced the most progressive elements of liberal democracy. Yet the movement they led exhibited almost every breach of liberal democratic principles a republican government could make. In effect, all the fears about the role of factions in government and communal passions in society so often tied by Federalists to direct rule by the common people came true in Illinois. The case for the Federalists can be made even stronger, since the Convention Resolution and associated projects like the State Bank were never considered illiberal by those who supported them. Ominously, just the opposite occurred; conventionists claimed to defend "a liberal policy" that treated debtors with great leniency and, in the convention case, returned government to the people.[5] Had they planned on it, they could not have more accurately confirmed the social pathologies that Federalists predicted would develop in small, intensely participatory democracies. Conventionists placed liberal democracy in a precarious condition by trammeling property rights, violating the rule of law, and curtailing the reach of equality. When on August 2, 1824, the convention was finally rejected 6,640 to 4,972, by the slim margin of 1,668 votes, the much maligned 1818 constitution played a large role in the defeat. Its separation of powers and mandated waiting period for amending the constitution allowed tempers to cool and countervailing interests time to mobilize. The story of the controversy to this extent confirms the Federalist genius for designing institutions able to check and balance power in state and society effectively.

This is more than a story of a pro-democracy movement that threatened the stability of democracy, however. The conventionists also set out to change the meaning of "the people" in Illinois. In this effort, they pioneered patterns of political development that reshaped the very essence of democracy in Illinois and ultimately America. From the start, the identity of the people in Illinois was contested. If the conventionists acted as if they knew who the true people were, a complex social reality belied their confidence. For the state contained a motley assortment of human residents: Native Americans from several tribes; old French *habitants* and their African slaves; recent English settlers; and two generations of American pioneers of varying ethnic origins. Among this last category, a cohesive identity was created by those who referred to themselves as "the white folks." This name is reported in a story by Christiana Holmes Tillson under circumstances that confirm the idea that political identity is constructed "in the recognition of difference, in the opposition of self and other."[6]

Tillson, who traveled to Illinois from Connecticut in 1822, recounted her experience with "an old Tennessee woman, who had a terrific opinion of the Yankees." The Tennessean, reflecting on the increasing number of northern emigrants to the state, remarked: "I am getting skeery about them 'ere Yankees; there is such a power of them coming in that them and the Injuns will squatch out all the white folks." It was a telling comment; so telling the woman soon regretted it. As Tillson notes: "Nothing afterwards would exasperate them more than to have a Yankee call them white folks." The exasperation may be explained by the fact that, as ex-governor Thomas Ford noted, "the very negroes of the rich call such poor persons 'poor white folks.'" The phrase was offensive, then, because it suggested that certain blacks had a higher social status than certain whites. This violated the norm of racial distinction in the South, "based on the fact" (to use John C. Calhoun's terms) "that no domestic servants were ever white." The white folks, in other words, were defined and defined themselves in terms of their position in the American pecking order. Economically, they were the class below the wealthy whites; racially, they were the race above the blacks, both free and slave, and the Native Americans. Conceiving themselves as an endangered "middle class," the white folks brought a sense of urgency to the state's politics. As the Tennessee woman saw it, the "Yankees" threatened on one side, the "Injuns" on the other; she viewed her own social position as tenuous. Upon the fact of social perceptions such as this, the conventionists constructed their political platform.[7]

The convention movement served the white folks' class interests by neatly attacking what they perceived as threats to their civic standing, whether from wealthy whites and Yankees or from blacks and Indians. It undermined the African-American bid for equality and disputed the white elite's claim to rule by virtual representation. This curious double strategy was always present during the convention controversy, yet only the second half was acknowledged; the first half was blocked from consciousness and for the most part remained unspoken. The conventionists defended "limited slavery" as a way to lift the white folks from obscurity. Their plan would do so not merely by providing labor to improve farmland but by enforcing a clear social separation between white owners and black slaves. The implicit underside of the convention struggle was real enough; and when no black folks were available to deride, their defenders among the white folks were attacked.

With the double strategy of attacking the class above and the race or races below, politics in Illinois departs from the classic pattern of the "white settler state" whose "*herrenvolk* democracy" is "democratic for the master race but tyrannical for the subordinate groups." Illinois produced instead a pattern of democracy that made white supremacy implicit, while class warfare was sublimated into cultural warfare. However much the conventionists may have dreamed of being slave masters, they first had to prove themselves as political masters. This required battling the elite, and it was this, their publicly avowed struggle, that brought about the institutional changes needed to refocus the purpose of republican government around the interests of the poor white male. Grandiose claims of the master race and odes to white supremacy they would leave to the elite. Until their own "whiteness" was secure, the white folks would be preoccupied with the battle for elite recognition and respect.[8]

This larger pattern of political development was reinforced in the United States by a political system geared, as Louis Hartz pointed out long ago, to luring the colossal "American democrat" into a party's coalition. The social character of the American democrat excluded the slaves but indiscriminately combined the peasant, proletarian, and petit bourgeois classes of Europe into one broad social class in America. An entity with so broad and deep a reach was bound to dominate America's two party politics. Once the Federalist and the National Republican elites were overthrown, and beginning at the state level, American political culture was free to develop its enduring antebellum pattern, in which the political pressure of obtaining a majority redirected conflict from the fight over class hierarchy to fights over ethnocultural and religious differences. To adopt the terminology of E. E. Schattschneider, the "scope of conflict" had been widened. By adding issues sponsored by poor whites to the political agenda, the nature of the conflict and what people meant by politics changed fundamentally.[9]

The minting of the American democrat in the form of the poor white male forged white racial identity, marked African Americans and Native Americans for separation and exploitation, and created a political ideology that revolved around cultural—not class—issues. Previous studies have drawn the broad outlines of this political development. On the class front, studies ranging from presidential rhetoric to familiar discourse have argued that the social pitch of language in United States was lowered during these years. With regard to race, scholars such as Alexander Saxton have documented the rise of a "white republic" in the first half of the nineteenth century. Other works have examined the impact of race on American political development generally. But studies of how the people became the white folks in the context of state politics are surprisingly rare.[10]

Elitism in Illinois was personified by Ninian Edwards, the powerful patron of the territorial governing system. Edwards served as territorial governor from 1809 to 1818. Like Coles, he was thought to have excluded himself from the people merely on account of his "aristocratic" political style. Another elitist, Jesse B. Thomas, who in 1818 was elected to the U.S. Senate, was also tainted by his association with the territorial government. But he had opposed Edwards for so long that some of the conventionists viewed him as one of their own. Conventionist Thomas Sloo, Jr., senator from Hamilton County, indicated as much in a letter written from Vandalia on January 12, 1823: "We had our election for senator. . . . Our friend Jesse B. was re-elected on the first ballot, notwithstanding every exertion was made to defeat him. His triumph is the greater, as he had a great portion of the big folks against him; but no matter we beat them, and I hope we shall always beat them."[11] By opposing themselves to "the big folks," the conventionists substantiated their claim to represent the white folks. Beginning with statehood, this localist faction in the legislature articulated the egalitarian sentiments of the white folk majority. They painted Governor Coles and all the nonconventionists as big folks who had violated the norms of western republicanism by precommitting themselves to an anti-slavery policy.

The unified social and political identity of the white folks was bolstered by a cohesive ethnic identity as well. They made up one of the "four British folkways" that settled the American colonies during the seventeenth and eighteenth centuries. David Hackett Fischer identifies the four as the Puritans, in New England; the Quakers and Pietists, in the Delaware Valley; the Anglicans, in Virginia; and the northern British "border people," in the "backcountry." This last group, arriving between 1718 and 1775, moved to the western edge of the original colonies throughout the Appalachian Mountains but concentrated mainly in Pennsylvania, Virginia, and North Carolina. The white folks were those members of the backcountry who had migrated to Illinois. They found there a plethora of bottomland, the kind of fertile, rock-free land their families had failed to secure back east. In Illinois they set about building a society suited to their egalitarian ideals, a bottomland republic.[12]

Although at the margins of the American republic, Illinois nevertheless stood at the center of the fundamental change in politics that was required by the dissolution of elitism. In the East the change was experienced as a loss of deference. But the old, entrenched political order still had to be torn down, and a new one built up. In the West, by contrast, the Federalist elite was never firmly established in the first place; the republican elite in the territories suffered politically simply by being federally appointed. The backcountry's egalitarian political culture thus encountered few restraints in Illinois. Once the big folks were defeated, poor white male interests (or at least their leaders' sense of them) were able to monopolize the political agenda as nowhere else. With time, the assumptions of white folks' democracy became embedded in Illinois political culture, and if they developed elsewhere, they attained a clarity in Illinois that makes the state an ideal candidate for a case study.

The importance of the changes Illinois pioneered in the nation is suggested by contrasting the image of "the people," employed in the letters exchanged by John Adams and Thomas Jefferson, with the one shared by Stephen A. Douglas and Abraham Lincoln in their famous Illinois debates some 40 years later. When Adams restarted his friendship and correspondence with Jefferson in 1812, one of the first topics he raised concerned the rise of millennial prophets. Dismissing zealotry in religion as credulous and dangerous, Adams noted that "Virginia produces prophets, as well as the Indiana Territory," and these he considered "not much more irrational" than the advocates of "universal Republicanism" in France. It was perhaps a vestigial aristocratic impulse in Adams to lump together and dismiss all such prophets, but in his formulation, the American people are indistinguishable from the Indians and the French. The closest Adams comes to "us versus them" thinking is in preferring Americans over English.[13]

Jefferson was, of course, no friend to John Bull, but in his response to Adams's letter, one begins to see the emergence of a different view of the native Indians, one that views the us of "the people" from inside the particular identity of the white settlers. Jefferson insisted on a distinction between the "Richmond and the Wabash prophets." The former (millenialist Christians) were "too inoffensive" and "too honest to be molested," while Tensquatawa was "a very different character." What made the Wabash prophet different? Jefferson offered only this explanation: Tensquatawa was "a visionary, enveloped in the clouds of their antiquities, and vainly endeavoring to lead back his brethren to the fancied beatitudes of their golden age." One suspects that Jefferson's distinction remains inchoate because he at least partially shared Adams's view that Tensquatawa's perspective was too much like his Christian and French republican counterparts to amount to a fundamental difference.

Contrast this with the uniform identification of "the people" with "the poor white man" by both Douglas and Lincoln in their famous debates. Scholars categorize Douglas as a utilitarian and an individualist defending freedom of choice because of his rejection of Congress's power "to force a good thing upon an unwilling people." From this perspective he is contrasted with Lincoln for his "moral relativism" and his approbation of governmental neutrality on the issue of slavery. Yet throughout the debates he repeatedly articulated a value that defined popular sovereignty in an absolute fashion: "I hold," he asserted, "that this Government was made on the white basis, by white men, for the benefit of white men and their posterity forever, and should be administered by white men and none others. I do not believe that the Almighty made the negro capable of self-government." "The people" assumed by Douglas's doctrine of popular sovereignty were white men.[14]

This aspect of Douglas's position is certainly not a revelation. What needs to be emphasized is that even when Douglas framed his position in more universal terms, he still assumed an angle of vision that represented and targeted the poor white voter. One of Douglas's "cardinal principles" was the idea that all the states were equal: "I hold it to be a fundamental principle in our republican form of government that all of the States of this Union, old and new, free and slave, stand on an exact equality." As abstract and individualist as this sounds, it was in fact motivated by the egalitarianism often found just under the surface of western political thought. The western states resented Congress's meddling with them as territories; they bristled at the sign of inferiority implied when representatives from eastern states suggested that the West ought to take direction from the East. Douglas's "popular sovereignty" was, from this perspective, nothing more than a confirmation of the ability of poor white males in the West to control their local communities. It defended "the right of every people"—that is, every local majority—"to decide for themselves the nature and character of the domestic institutions and fundamental law under which they are to live."

Popular sovereignty was Douglas's way of courting the West's poor white males without having repeatedly to say so explicitly. The Little Giant's use of coded language represents the dominant Jacksonian approach. The Republican Lincoln, though he shared many of Douglas's assumptions, took a different approach in courting the poor white voter. Slavery was, as Lincoln argued, a "moral, social and political evil." His absolute emphasis on the moral side of the issue provided the basis for a universalist interpretation of the "all men" clause of the Declaration of Independence. But no less important, at least in terms of Republican Party appeals to the voters, was the social evil of slavery. This was that the extension of the institution of slavery deprived, as Lincoln put it, *"free white people everywhere . . .* Hans, Baptiste, and Patrick," of the op-

INTRODUCTION / 1 1

portunity to settle free soil of their own. Again, the explicit meaning of "the people," and the center point around which republican appeals pivoted, was the poor white male.[15]

If the apotheosis of the poor white male reached its height in the 1850s, the movement originating it first tasted power in Illinois during the 1820s. But the shift to a politics of the class interests of the white folks was so complete there that after 1823 appeals to class interest were no longer a usable cleavage for organizing voters. With the big folks in retreat, leaders in Illinois were early on forced to appeal to other divisions. The result was a division at the level of culture and individual temperament. This division evolved two distinct styles of pursuing poor white male interests, the whole-hog style and the milk-and-cider style. The big folks/white folks cleavage remained hovering in the background, but afterwards, the politics of class conflict in Illinois was sublimated into a politics of cultural conflict.

To the extent that this shift occurred in the nation at large, it helps to clarify the puzzling relationship between class and culture during the Age of Jackson. Almost all scholars agree with Lee Benson that in the decades between 1820 and 1850 the country as a whole experienced an "Age of Egalitarianism." But the idea that the Jacksonians were all defenders of the poor whereas the Whigs were all defenders of the rich—a notion bequeathed by the Progressive Era historians—was too simple. Even Arthur M. Schlesinger, Jr.'s, view that the Democratic Party was built from a combination of western farmers and eastern workers can be faulted on grounds of oversimplification. This has led many scholars to argue that it was culture—not economics—that really divided Jacksonian America. As Louis Hartz had it, although party rhetoric may have emphasized class conflict, in reality American political ideology was marked by a social consensus. Richard P. McCormick strengthened this line of reasoning by arguing that the second party system was as much about the mechanics of party formation as about substantive issues.[16]

In Illinois, however, the cultural division between Democrats and Whigs grew out of a class-based dispute between the white folks and the big folks. The economic cleavage between these two groups transcended the local setting and could claim national and international roots. For if white folks' identity had been formed by oppression in the South, its history of oppression reached back, as Rowland Berthoff has argued, into the European Middle Ages. The complicated culture war fought in Illinois over the convention controversy must be understood within this larger economic context. The ethnocultural and religious conflicts that structured the controversy, although often apparently local in nature, were often merely western echoes of broader national divisions. Thus, understanding early Illinois politics requires that local issues be placed in a national context, and that cultural differences be viewed from the perspective of larger economic realities. A new generation of scholars, recognizing the intricate relations between class and culture, identity and race, nation and region in the early republic have produced narratives that stress both broader patterns *and* local diversity. In this study I hope to contribute to the trend by viewing changes in the Illinois microcosm through the prism of the American macrocosm.[17]

The changes hastening the new politics in Illinois began with the Panic of 1819. A Madisonian political order that valued sharing power might have evolved without incident had a generation of widespread economic prosperity followed statehood, but the economic disturbance upset the delicate liberal democratic balance. Banks across the country recalled their specie, and the Illinois economy, overcommitted in several sectors simultaneously, crashed spectacularly. The economic crisis considerably heightened the frustration with state government. A freshet of demands from the people poured into the new state capital at Vandalia. Several "letters of instruction" from the counties supported the creation of a state bank. The legislature responded by passing a bank law with a bare majority. The law addressed the currency shortage directly, immediately issuing $300,000 in state bills "to lighten the burdens of our indigent and embarrassed citizens." While the economy weakened, the desire to reorder state priorities grew stronger. In February 1821, when the Council of Revision sent the law back to the legislature with a list of objections, the law was again passed, while cries against "great constitutional lawyers" and high-toned Federalists rang through the halls of the capitol.[18]

After the 1822 elections, the forces for change were strengthened in the General Assembly. Ending the economic depression was the first order of business. It is ironic that the clearest analysis of the state's troubles was offered by none other than the newly elected governor, Edward Coles. In his inaugural address, he noted that it had only been "a few years since the whole produce of the country was required to supply the wants of the emigrants to it." Yet while local production had increased with every new emigrant, emigration itself had trickled to a halt on account of "the difficulty of making sales of property preparatory to removal." The consequence was that "there is no longer at home a demand at all proportionate to the amount of produce grown." Coles tacitly assumed that the state's problems were caused by its relations with national and international economic forces external to the state. Illinois's "stagnation in trade" could thus only be solved by revivifying the state's relations with the outside world, specifically, by targeting exports to "the lower Mississippi, and West India Islands."[19] The governor's mild suggestion completely missed the sense of urgency felt by those who regularly mixed with the people. His external focus was out of touch with the legislative agenda as well. There, especially among the most ambitious members, it was felt that some concrete action within the legislature's power must be taken to save the good republican farmers of the state from bankruptcy.

Emboldened by the initial popularity of their banking plan, the legislators turned to the issue of slavery. The developing conventionist faction believed that the 1818 constitution, together with the Missouri Compromise, had caused the local depression. The outlawing of future chattel rights in Illinois, combined with their legalization in Missouri, diverted the stream of southern emigration toward the new slave state.[20] Illinois, they argued, must respond. Chapter 1 outlines their response. Recommendations included the reconsideration of state slavery policy and a proposal to build a canal to connect the Illinois River with Lake Michigan. These ideas caused great confusion, for the settlers' interests were as unorganized as the state's economy. The French style of bottomland farming, taken over from the Indians and favored by the new emigrants, appeared a strong limb in a storm. This route, however, raised a host of problems. Bottomland flooded periodically, and it also was subject to an overabundance of vegetable growth thought to cause miasmatic vapors and "ague" (malaria). These problems might be mitigated, as the French and early settlers had mitigated them, with slave labor. But this assumed that slavery, or at the very least indentured servants, would again be allowed to be imported into the state. One General Assembly proposal addressed this problem by allowing the importation of slaves only temporarily to clear the land of excess vegetation and build drainage canals; after 10 years, the slaves, or their sons and daughters, would be freed and shipped down the Mississippi for embarkation to Africa. This would require removing the 1818 constitution's bar on involuntary servitude.

With the announcement of this "limited slavery" plan, the minority in the legislature erupted in protest. These followed a wide-ranging but inconclusive debate over the state's future that the legislature left unresolved when it adjourned two months later. Legislators were uncertain because the state's agricultural policy was uncertain. Chapter 2 encapsulates the debate over agricultural policy. In 1822 it was still unclear whether Illinois farmers would follow either a dominant staple-producing approach, focused perhaps on corn, hogs, or flax, along the lines of southern agriculture, or a value-added approach along the lines of northern agriculture, which mixed a diversity of products from husbandry, field, and orchard with "proto-industrial" cottage industries and outwork. Complicating the choice was the unfinished market revolution, which was just then luring the state's farmers away from their traditional subsistence agriculture. Leaders and followers alike searched diligently for the one strategy that would provide a clear direction.[21]

Chapter 3 examines the political context—the battle to unseat Illinois's territorial elite—in which the economic debate unfolded. Fiercely localist, members of the backcountry had by the dawn of the nineteenth century become as diverse as the regions of the country they inhabited.

They nonetheless retained a shared vernacular republicanism that rejected the Federalist view of government, just as their Anti-Federalist parents and grandparents had done a generation earlier. They believed they were completing the democratic revolution begun in 1776 by insisting that legislatures conform to the people's instructions. Backcountry politicians everywhere came into conflict with a set of governing institutions and elites who ruled by fragmenting community identity and checking blunt expressions of majority will. These institutions and elites were the chief legacy of the Federalist belief in virtual representation. Elected assemblies, Federalists argued, if properly insulated from local passions, would better manage the people's interests than direct democratic government. In Illinois, Ninian Edwards attempted to implement the Federalists' pluralist but passive vision of "the people." His political faction failed after statehood largely because the democratic revolution brought to the state by the backcountry envisioned a people in active pursuit of their social aspirations.

The conventionists grew from a mere faction within the Thomas party, to an independent force within the legislature, to a statewide political organization. Their grasp for control over the state climaxed when they removed a representative from office and replaced him with his county rival, two weeks before the end of the session, in order to get the Convention Resolution passed. The night after the vote, the first Vandalia mob, filled with conventionists, paraded charivari-style in celebration. Following the course of these events, Chapter 4 examines the conventionists' claim that in celebrating their own victory at Vandalia, they were celebrating the arrival of popular government in Illinois. Chapter 5 chronicles the efforts of conventionists and non-conventionists alike to drum up support among the electorate in the counties. The non-conventionists took the organizational lead and quickly demonstrated their strength by forming anti-slavery societies in the counties. The conventionists responded by organizing a Central Committee, as well as several county-based convention societies of their own. A series of attacks and counterattacks in the newspapers and on the ground kept the controversy boiling and left the state in upheaval. Sectional jealousies, racial tensions, and a large number of murders intensified the question of who would be the masters in Illinois.

Chapter 6 focuses on the religious differences that opened the controversy's central ideological cleavage: the division between Arminians and Calvinists. The Arminian view stressing salvation through works and the Calvinist view stressing salvation through grace were convenient, broadly understood vehicles for conveying different approaches to politics, and to culture generally. The conventionists expressed a Calvinistic whole-hog support for the new white folks' democracy, while the non-conventionists expressed an Arminian milk-and-cider position, one equally supportive of the people but less willing to identify with the white folks as a group. The differences between the whole-hog and milk-and-cider persuasions were substantial enough to produce fundamental political disagreement, as the controversy's violence and tumult indicate. With both sides opposed to the big folks, however, neither side was able to claim the democratic high ground permanently. Given this fact, the milk-and-cider adherents, clearly a minority in Illinois political culture, were able to play the role of loyal opposition.

Chapter 7 addresses the question of why Illinois political development was so precocious. The state produced early versions of both majoritarian and identity politics. The size of the state's yeoman class, its fragmented elite, its geographic location, the regional mix of its population, and timing—all contributed to the strength of its majoritarianism. The conventionists created an explosive mixture when they used the power of the majority to verify and validate the purity of their identity by opposing the corruption of big folks and black folks alike. In Illinois the conventionists' politics of majority identity pioneered two patterns of development that have endured: a short-term pattern, in which, during crises, majoritarianism trumps liberal protections in the public sphere, and a long-term pattern, in which the private-sphere liberalism of the market trumps egalitarian dissent within republicanism.

The story of Illinois's bottomland republic reveals that Americans in the early nineteenth century were deeply engaged in what today would be called culture wars. As distasteful and potentially illiberal as these wars over identity are, they are not an affliction unique to the contemporary era. The politics of identity have been with the republic from the beginning. Identity politics may be unavoidable under the republican form of government, but its origins and development in Illinois exhibit patterns that can be recognized and lessons that should be learned by the present generation.

CHAPTER ONE

THE WHITE FOLKS CHALLENGE THE BIG FOLKS

A colonial tradition of deference, even after the Revolutionary War, continued to keep poor and uneducated citizens from public office throughout the nation, and elites remained secure in the assumption that the educated and the socially prominent would be asked to lead. Yet a new generation of leaders emerging in Illinois was determined to turn this inherited political culture upside down. The call for a convention was the culmination of their growing challenge to elite control. Leaders such as John McFerron, Conrad Will, and Theophilus Smith, keenly aware of the settlers' social inadequacies, compensated with an equally keen belief in majority rule. By 1822, the feeling of inferiority fed a desire for political power that turned the slavery issue into a struggle for political control. The immorality of slavery was overshadowed completely by the perceived purity of the poor settlers' claims to political and social equality. For many settlers the convention became a simple matter of power, a question of who had the legitimate authority to rule. Safe in their knowledge that as the majority they would control elections, they still bristled at being called "the swinish multitude." Colonel Thomas Cox, speaker at the first conventionist meeting, summed up their impatience with their opponents by wondering aloud: "Are they ignorant of the irresistible powers of the people . . . ? Have they not seen them, moving like the terrible powers of a *tornado*, sweeping in their course all before them?"[1]

Because of the slavery taboo, the convention story has been retold mainly from the perspective of non-conventionist leaders such as Edward Coles and Morris Birkbeck. As a consequence, Coles's importance as a galvanizing force on the pro-convention side has been misunderstood. In fact his arrival on the scene coincided perfectly with the need for a clearly defined enemy on the part of the ambitious leaders looking to ignite a localist movement. It was predictable that the desire for political and social equality that the Illinois settlers brought with them would find a voice in the new state legislature. Altogether less predictable was that Coles, a newcomer and nonmember of the territorial elite, would be the legislature's first real opponent. Fortunately for them, Coles's "urbane temper and manner," his aggressive anti-slavery views, and his agricultural biases unified the opposition in a way no earlier elite could have done.[2] Unsuited to trimming his rhetoric to suit local tastes, Coles became a lightning rod for the opposition. He not only embodied, he proudly displayed everything that western republicans resented in eastern republicanism—its deference to social standing, its refined education, and its preference for rule by abstract principles.

HIS EXCELLENCY THE GOVERNOR

Edward Coles was as close to a born aristocrat as the United States produced in its second generation. He paradoxically embodied both the worst qualities of Adams's "artificial aristocracy" and the best of Jefferson's "natural aristocracy." In 1809 at the age of 23 he was appointed private secretary to the president of the United States by his cousin's husband James Madison. The position was in the family, so to speak, having been held by Coles's brother Isaac under Jefferson. Edward acquired further valuable experience in 1816 when Madison sent him on a diplomatic mission to Russia. But having cavorted with royalty was a liability in Illinois, which he first visited in 1818. According to newspaper editor Hooper Warren, with whom Coles lodged on his visit to the bustling Madison County town of Edwardsville, the trip to Russia left him with a taste for the arcana of aristocratic refinement. Coles boasted of his exploits with European "Ladies of the Courts." He proudly indicated his "F.F.V." (First Families of Virginia) status. He talked about himself late into the night. All of this produced in Warren feelings of inferiority and animosity. After this poor first impression, Warren doubted whether Coles's social preferences left him much of a future "as a leader" in Illinois politics.[3]

Yet this same man, upon inheriting 19 slaves from his father, found himself unable, as he wrote, "to screen myself . . . from the peltings and upbraidings of my own conscience." He exchanged letters on the subject with Jefferson, an Albemarle County neighbor who considered him a promising member of "the younger generation." Jefferson tried to persuade him to stay with his slaves in Virginia, "to reconcile yourself to your country and its unfortunate condition," and to "become the missionary" of gradual emancipation in the Old Dominion. But Coles's conscience was the stronger persuader. Although it meant "social ostracism at home" he decided to emigrate to Illinois and to free his slaves there.[4]

Another Virginian, James Monroe, appointed Coles Registrar of the Land Office at Edwardsville in 1819. In a public ceremony on July 4, 1819, Coles emancipated half the slaves he had inherited from his father. Then in 1822 he ran an anti-slavery campaign for governor, making his abolitionist principles well known in the legislature. His reputation as a refined member of the gentry was recorded that same year. The General Assembly *Journal* describes him as "his excellency the governor." It was a moniker not bestowed on the less distinguished first governor, Shadrach Bond, who was a farmer and *"emphatically* one of the people." Noble of both birth and heart, Coles was determined to use his exalted position to do good. But conventionists such as Conrad Will and Theophilus W. Smith resented just this use of position. They saw in his public display of nobility only an assertion of power.[5]

The Third General Assembly convened in joint session on December 5, 1822, to hear the inaugural address of the newly elected governor. He surveyed the state's economic condition. He offered advice on the management of the new State Bank and lightly touched on the economic depression and the canal project. He then proceeded to the central item on his agenda, the state's creeping slavery policy. Coles began his discussion of the issue prudently by asking the legislators to clarify the legal rights of the state's indentured servants and freedmen. But he surprised everyone by adding a request "that just and equitable provisions be made for the abrogation of slavery in the state."[6] It was, he noted, the least to expect of a state made formally "free" by the Northwest Ordinance of 1787.

In response, the House formed two ad hoc committees to address the governor's requests, one on the indenture system and a second on the "abrogation of slavery." The first was chaired by Risdon Moore of St. Clair County, the oldest and most respected slaveholder in the assembly. Moore had brought 18 slaves with him when he emigrated from Georgia in 1812. He kept control over the slaves by indenturing them under the "voluntary servitude" system—the so-called Black Code, which had been enacted during the territorial period. Known as a benevolent master, he had been brought up Episcopalian but converted to a Methodist congregation that espoused anti-slavery sentiments. Indeed, Moore had signed an anti-slavery address to the *Western Intelligencer* in the summer of 1818 and had been elected as an anti-slavery delegate to the first constitutional convention. Two weeks after the governor's address, Moore announced the committee's recommendations in a bill intended to shore up the legal status of black freedmen and clear the way for the gradual emancipation of all the state's de facto slaves.[7]

Moore's decorous report struck all the chords of humane treatment that Coles expected to hear. But the harmony between gentlemen in the two branches of government did not last. An immediate note of dissonance was sounded when "Honest Irish" John McFerron of Randolph County rose to respond to Moore's "Bill relating to Negroes and other Free persons of Color." McFerron briefly made two points. He first explained that owning slaves as property was a natural right that had been recognized by positive law in Illinois ever since Virginia passed its Act of

Cession in 1783. The Virginia cession rights were a legacy of eighteenth-century Illinois history. In 1783, the French comprised the vast majority of European inhabitants in the area. Following the 1673 expedition of Captain Louis Joliet and the Jesuit father Jacques Marquette, the French had established a string of villages along the Mississippi collectively known as "Le Pays des Illinois." By 1752 they had imported as many as 1,000 African and Native American slaves to help them farm the area's bottomland. After 1763 they all lived under British rule until Virginian George Rogers Clark claimed the area in 1778. As the inhabitants of the "Illinois Country of the Commonwealth of Virginia," their ancient "laws and customs" were recognized when Virginia ceded the Illinois Country to the United States in 1783. By 1810, the territory's population surpassed 12,000, of which three-quarters were American emigrants who believed they shared the legal endorsement for slavery secured by the French when the Virginia cession rights were ratified in the second article of the 1787 Northwest Ordinance.[8]

Under the local interpretation followed by McFerron, the Ordinance protected preexisting slavery in part by advocating the "preservation of rights and property" and "private contracts . . . previously formed." The provisions of Risdon Moore's Free Negro Bill were, the Irishman remarked, "the first time, sir, I have ever heard that right doubted—but upon the contrary, universally admitted; and admitted to be a right which no human legislature could violate or disregard." McFerron was alert to the fact that Coles and Moore were threatening the compromise over slavery that the territorial inhabitants had made with the Ordinance, namely the Black Code's "voluntary servitude." As one newspaper writer put it, the Illinois "people have the indisputable right to permit blacks voluntarily to indenture themselves." The author, signing as "The Legitimate Power of People," concluded with the note: "Indeed, so universally was this law believed to be obligatory that no member of the bar has ever yet contested its validity in a court of justice."[9]

McFerron had lived in the South before moving west. He had run with Moore as an anti-slavery candidate to the 1818 convention. Thus his second point carried weight: he assured the House members that slavery in Illinois had never and would never take on the characteristics of "the southern slave State, with all its horrible consequences." He spoke from personal experience, his Randolph County experience with the French slaves in the towns of Kaskaskia, St. Mary's, and Prairie du Rocher:

> Those people of color which are held as slaves by the French, enjoy as much happiness and the good of this world as their masters. They have no overseers to wave the lash and domineer over them, at whose nod they must bow, and at whose appearance tremble—They are treated as humble members of the family to which they belong, and are clothed and fed in the same manner—they look to their masters as

their protectors; and as well might you attempt to sever the child from the parent as those servants from their masters.

The upshot was that slavery in Illinois had been and always would be unique. It was the tack of a man who felt he needed to educate the governor, a recent emigrant from a plantation state, in the ways of the West. McFerron was speaking to the local faith that a special set of circumstances prevailed there, that all things would be remade in this land of opportunity and equality. In short, republicanism in Illinois would force even slavery to wear a new face. So believed the generation of leaders that emerged after the War of 1812. McFerron could point to those who opposed him, humane slaveholders such as Moore and Coles, to reinforce his contention.[10]

Conrad Will, one of the many second-generation Germans who had emigrated from the state of Pennsylvania, also spoke to this faith. The day after McFerron's speech, Will delivered the House report on the governor's abolition plea. In the previous session, he had led the fight for a state bank to help relieve the people of their debt burden. Now he rose in support of McFerron's argument that the legislature's power did not reach to the matter of slavery. But while he shared the Irishman's western biases, he gave them a distinctive shape. He represented Jackson County, which was populated predominantly by American emigrants from the southern and southwestern states; he made no mention of the French. Nor did he feel that the 1783 Virginia cession—or any other act of an outside government, including the Northwest Ordinance—could safeguard individual property rights against the people's countervailing interests. He was impressed instead by the power of social norms, the norms of the emigrants who had arrived between 1815 and 1818; the large numbers of these southern emigrants had given them the power to determine the course of Illinois slave policy.[11]

In Will's view the northern and southern sections of the United States had followed divergent slave policies because each had confronted different circumstances. Far from there being a difference in principles or even different degrees of commitment to principle, similarly self-interested individuals on both sides were led to opposite conclusions by practical considerations. In the North, after the revolution, slaves were by and large freed, since their population was "not numerous," did not contribute greatly to the region's economy, and posed little threat upon emancipation. In the South, the reverse of all these conditions held; hence, the principles of the Declaration of Independence "received a severe check."

In both cases, Will reminded his listeners, the people had decided. In both cases, moreover, the fundamental choice of the people proved socially stable. The recent slave uprising led by Denmark Vesey, which he noted briefly, did not undermine the claim. In fact, he pointed to

Vesey's influences—the abolitionist rhetoric articulated by some north-erners during the Missouri Compromise debate—to support his doubts that a workable regional social policy could be made at the federal level or by using abstract principles.[12] The conclusion to be drawn from all this was that unfettered democracy below the federal level had worked. There had not occurred the instability and mob infatuation with power so often predicted to be the inseparable companions of popular govern-ment in the states. The pursuit of self-interest had not degenerated into mere selfishness even in the southerners' case, for there "reasons of moral obligation, deduced from a regard to humanity itself" had been contemplated in the decision to continue the slave policy.

Will was now poised to unveil the centerpiece of his report. Like the North and the South, the West had also developed a unique slave policy. For years the western territories had welcomed slaveholders by asking only that they register their "property" with the county clerk upon ar-rival. This indenture system allowed southern emigrants with slaves to maintain control over their servants and farmhands. Will failed to men-tion, however, that there was nothing "voluntary" about the indenture contracts the former slaves signed. Many included lifetime terms for as long as 99 years. To restrict this practice and to come into compliance with article 6, which declared slavery and involuntary servitude illegal in the Northwest Territory, the authors of the 1818 constitution had limited future indentures to one year.[13] It was just this change, prompted by outside pressure, that Will opposed. It had artificially dammed up the stream of southern immigration into the state, stopped the flow of money, and precipitated economic depression. If the state's growth was to reach its full potential, he concluded, the southern slave-holder must again be courted.

The representative from Jackson County next addressed his anti-slav-ery colleagues. Whatever immigration policy was pursued, he said, it was not his intention to suggest that Illinois become a slave state. As he knew, vague insinuations in that direction had already stirred apprehen-sions of reigniting the Missouri conflagration of 1819–1820. Again and again during the following months, the specter of a national dispute such as attended the Missouri Compromise would be raised. An address soon to be published in the House predicted that a new slave constitu-tion would unhinge the federal compromise. Appended to it was the biblical warning: "a house divided against itself cannot stand." After this, the senator from Crawford County, Baptist preacher Daniel Parker, moved to begin each day with a prayer.[14]

Will, who was not "a church member," considered these insinuations of spiritual demise anti-republican.[15] No "mere principle," whether ad-herence to the Union or to states' rights, whether belief in natural or in divine rights, should limit the people's freedom to shape society. Only this would he concede: "On shaking off the yoke of a foreign master from our own necks, principles were laid down and acted upon [in the revolutionary period,] which in their fullest application" would have freed the slaves. Will was presumably referring to the equality clause of the Declaration of Independence and article 6 of the 1787 Ordinance. But he did not consider these documents an acknowledgment that slavery in every form was unacceptable to American republicans. A genuine specimen of the new western mentality, he drew another conclusion: that principles promulgated under conditions of oppression, under the "yoke of a foreign master," were not binding on a people once made free.

No one in the room would have failed to recognize the implicit comparison to the 1818 constitution and the people of the Illinois Territory. In this regard, it is important to distinguish the 1818 experience with "popular sovereignty" in Illinois from the position Douglas made famous 30 years later. In some ways, Will prefigures the Little Giant in that both rely on the special power of western republicanism to cure the nation's ills. Will came to Illinois at the age of 36, otherwise he might have said, with Douglas: "I came out here when I was a boy and found my mind liberalized and my opinions enlarged when I got on these broad prairies. . . . I have become a *Western* man." Will would also have joined Douglas's estimation of how "the West" affected his political outlook: "I have indulged an enthusiasm, which seemed to others wild and romantic, in regard to the growth, expansion, and destiny of this republic." But Douglas, in opposing Lincoln, tried to minimize the influence wielded by the federal government over local slave policy in the territories and during the transition to statehood. The previous generation knew from experience that federal influence could constrain territorial choices. In the face of southern indifference, the northeastern states were especially eager to see the Northwest develop without slavery. They read article 6 literally, and they attempted to enforce it. They made sure, for example, that the 1818 Enabling Act granting Illinois statehood stipulated that the state's new constitution be consistent with "republicanism, and not repugnant to the Ordinance of July 13, 1787."[16]

Before he was through, Will would express more concretely his intention to associate his position with the local control movement. He implored the body to read in Coles's request merely another instance of a privileged minority attempting to cow the Illinois people into submission. What Illinois needed, he countered, was more—not less—freedom of action. Illinois's localist leaders needed to hold firm their faith in the people, to simply reaffirm the modus vivendi long countenanced by the people. With the proper legislative supervision, in fact, the people's way could form the basis of a new constitutional "plan." The practical necessity of state growth might be combined felicitously with the lofty purposes of strengthening the bonds of the Union and gradual emancipation of the slaves. The generous-minded ("liberal" was the word he used) Illinois people had previously laid out the rudiments of this plan in their practice. Conrad Will had reached his peroration. In such a plan, he noted, "both . . . wisdom and policy . . . might be consulted," as well as

> an essential service rendered to the cause of humanity and justice, by admitting slaves to be brought into the state and held, on condition that either they themselves, or their children, born here, should become free at a certain age. By this qualified introduction and modification of slavery, which, as hinted above, would be the most that the advocates of slavery could hope to obtain, the country would derive all the advantages in point of wealth and improvement which it so much needs—and a system of gradual abolition established, which would be the means of restoring thousands to their liberty, to whose bondage there is now no prospect of termination. To their liberty! Perhaps to their country—for no state furnishes better faculties for their transportation to the islands, or even to the African continent, than Illinois, by means of her great outlets to the ocean.

What is to be made of his far-flung vision? Its western character reaches deeper than mere boosterism. For what northern statesman would have considered slavery a possible source of economic boon? And what southerner, even at this early date, would have so casually suggested that slavery was a national problem? The idea of colonization was not new to the nation. Gary B. Nash has traced its roots to the desire, as early as 1776 and 1790 in Virginia, "to be quit of slavery . . . [and] the simultaneous desire to be quit of blacks." The American Colonization Society had been founded in 1816; Edward Coles himself was a member. In 1824 the Ohio legislature and in 1825 the Owenites at Hew Harmony, Indiana, seconded Will's proposal by offering their own national plans for gradual emancipation, as did Thomas Jefferson in a private letter. Nor was Will's plan exceptional within the state itself; a plan contemplating "temporary" slavery was presented by "Pacificus" in the *Western Intelligencer* during the 1818 convention. The national aspect of the plan had also been broached. "Everywhere much is being written now concerning the possibility of getting rid of slavery as an acknowledged evil in the entire compass of the free states," the German visitor Ferdinand Ernst wrote in 1820 after visiting Edwardsville, "so that people in general actually entertain the hope of seeing even the southern states soon freed from this plague." Of Will's proposal, then, it may be said that both the plan and its promoter were respectable and representative products of the Illinois scene.[17]

Will's plan exposes to view some of the underlying assumptions of the convention movement. Although its "limited slavery" opened democratic participation in Illinois to white slaveholders, it obviously also excluded their African slaves. That the needs of the former were recognized and supported while those of the latter were ignored or rejected was typical of the way general terms such as "the people" were used in Illinois: the interests of the part were presented as the interests of the whole. Some recognized that the natural rights of the slaves were being violated, but defenders such as "Brissot" assuaged these concerns by noting the plan's eventual intention to "relieve the burden of suffering humanity in an eminent degree."[18] There were those, especially among the older generation, who viewed such claims as unforgivable hubris. But this view was held by a decided minority.

For all its exclusionary aspects, the vast majority considered the plan special for the opposite reason, because of its inclusive feature. It opened the state and western republicanism to southwestern slaveholders. These were not the plantation aristocrats of the coastal South, but the "yeoman farmer" slaveholders who pioneered the use of "short staple" cotton in the frontier states of Alabama, Mississippi, and Louisiana.[19] However accurately the yeoman label applies to these budding gentry, welcoming them as backcountry brethren was an unmistakable sign to many that the republicanism in Illinois was to be open and egalitarian. More important, the plan fostered a utopian vision of a society of poor whites with the power for the first time to develop organically on its own terms. The lure of this social vision, with its promise of wholeness and community, compensated for whatever troubles might sprout along the way.

A DUTIFUL CHILD OF THE UNION

McFerron's and Will's visions of an Illinois vernacular republicanism were the first to be registered in the Third General Assembly's records. It should not be assumed, however, that these two men were the first to articulate it or that they were its leading lights; certainly Senator Theophilus Washington Smith of Madison County and Senator William Kinney of St. Clair County stand ahead of them on both counts. But McFerron's and Will's remarks were written down and published in the *Illinois Intelligencer*, the capital newspaper, whereas most of the political commentary made in the Vandalia session went unrecorded. As indicative of the new view as McFerron's and Will's speeches were, however, it was given to T. W. Smith in the Senate to orchestrate the new faction's first legislative move. Although less direct, Smith also framed his report in opposition to Coles, and his rhetoric hinted at the larger political movement that conventionists would soon be taking to the streets.

Smith reported the Senate's response to the emancipation plea in Coles's inaugural address. The reaction against the governor had been much quicker in the upper branch of the legislature. Immediately after the joint session, a committee was formed on "so much of the Governor's message as relates to . . . the total abolition of slavery within this state." The committee consisted of five members, all of whom owned slaves or indentured servants, with two living in counties containing salines, and one having been responsible for the operation of the large Gallatin County saline. The salines or saltwater springs produced salt for export. Conrad Will operated the Jackson County saline. The use of slaves to capture the water and boil it down was one of Will's reasons for retaining servitude in the state. In 1823 the state auditor reported that the Illinois salines had provided nearly $11,000 in tax revenue. This covered almost one-quarter of the state's expenses for 1822. The 1818 constitution allowed slaves to be brought into the state, under one year contracts, to work the Gallatin and Jackson County facilities. However, the constitutional allowance was scheduled to end in 1825.[20]

A frank recognition of the state's dependence on saline revenues would have been expected from a committee formed of these members. One might also have expected a plan to extend the time limits on saline indentures through a constitutional amendment. In place of the expected, the committee handed its report-making duties over to their colleague T. W. Smith. The move was extraordinary not only because Smith was not a member of the committee, but also because of his reputation for intrigue. It was recognized that the report would require literary skill and political acumen. But Smith, who studied the art of politics in New York City before emigrating to Illinois, was the logical choice for crafting the Senate's response only on the assumption that the body was committed to an all-out war against the governor. Smith would soon emerge as one of Coles's most dedicated enemies. After the session, for example, when the faction wanted to injure Coles politically, Smith sprang into action as the prime mover behind the lawsuit brought against the governor for emancipating his slaves without giving bond and surety against their becoming Madison County charges.[21]

Opponents said that Smith rarely undertook a public project unless he was sure it would repay a private compensation. Another episode in Madison County politics is worth noting in this regard. In 1820 he artfully promoted the expansion of Edwardsville town into Upper Edwardsville, land owned by the wealthy Benjamin Stephenson. He faced a strong opposition and was burdened with defending the interest of the "rather exclusive, if not aristocratic" part of town, nicknamed "Buncomb," which was home to both Stephenson and former territorial governor and U.S. senator Ninian Edwards. Smith prevailed by arguing "that the inhabitants of the county are more immediately interested in [the expansion's] acceptance, than are those who are certain to be directly benefitted thereby." He would soon use a similar argument to defend the Canal Bill, which was intended to mark out the path of the canal proposed to connect the Illinois River and Lake Michigan. Smith's promotion of the canal led to his being named one of four canal commissioners.[22]

Smith's career in Illinois politics represents that great ideal type of state legislative politics, the promoter. There was a lot of economic de-velopment to promote and governmental aid to distribute in Illinois. But, as the New Yorker recognized, in the state's Anti-Federalist climate, distributive politics would have to be conducted on the non-ideological, "open and equitable" basis of pragmatism. Smith saw in the potential opposition to Coles a cover for his far from equitable intentions. To pro-mote the faction that had opposed Coles in the legislature, he founded and co-edited with William Kinney the *Illinois Republican* immediately upon adjournment. In a sense, his greatest promotion was the General Assembly itself, the power of which he continuously trumpeted; and the institution paid dividends. In 1825, the legislature appointed him to the Illinois Supreme Court. He held the position until 1842, when he was forced to resign. By then his intrigues had become an embarrassing re-minder of the "erratic" politics of an earlier era. Nevertheless, his career demonstrated how far an adroit mixture of public and private interest could take a General Assembly member.[23]

That the committee delegated its duties to so partisan a member demonstrates a high level of deterioration in executive and legislative relations only two weeks into the session. The governor's political posi-tion was weak. He had been elected by a plurality in a three-way race (see Figure 1). But Coles had assumed the mantle of authority appar-ently undeterred by these underlying realities. His style was high-toned; the preemptive emancipation plea suggested it could become overbear-ing. He was also an easy target on the wealth and status issue: besides the Edwardsville farm worked by hired men and servants, he owned over 6,000 acres of land, much of it granted as a consequence of his ap-pointed positions.[24] Detecting in Coles a potential whipping boy, Smith took full advantage of the platform granted him.

He began under the guise of a respectful devotee of eastern paternal-ism. "The people of Illinois," he wrote, "have been watched over from childhood to maturity by the Congress of the United States." At every stage of growth, Congress had acted in "obedience to the solemn obliga-tion of public faith and paternal responsibility." Anti-slavery emigrants shared Smith's motif, although they took the metaphor considerably further. Even though a territory became an "independent" state, "A Whiteman" wrote in a letter to the *Illinois Intelligencer*, "still it should be a member of the general Union, a 'child' of the general family, having Congress for its parent." It should, "A Whiteman" continued, "be regu-lated in common with the 'original states' by the parent . . . [and] be bound, as a dutiful child, to obey the voice of the parent."[25]

This parental-care metaphor contrasted sharply with the social-com-pact imagery favored by the servitude adherents. For the anti-slavery ad-vocates there was no clearer expression of the parent's voice, no more solemn instance of the child's duty to follow, than the Ordinance of 1787. "This Ordinance," intoned Benjamin Ruggles of Ohio, "has been

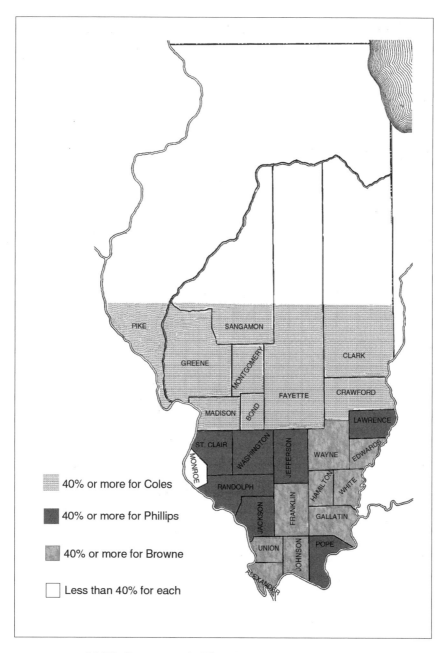

Figure 1 **1822 Governor's Election**

to the people of the Northwestern territory a rule of action—a guide to direct their course—'a cloud by day, a pillar of fire by night.'" Madison County Representative George Churchill echoed the paternal theme in opposition to Will and Smith: "The Congress of 1787, with parental solicitude . . . [has] confided to you the sacred boon of liberty." Churchill argued: "The fact that slavery does exist in this state, in some degree, notwithstanding the ordinance, and notwithstanding the courts of the United States, is sufficient to caution us against depending upon *them* for protection against an evil which it is our own duty to avoid."[26]

Such reverential praise required that anti-slavery advocates emphasize the Ordinance's article 6, which proclaimed: "There shall be neither slavery nor involuntary servitude" in the territory. To the more representative "Aristides," writing in the *Western Intelligencer,* the 1787 document was an "accursed badge of despotism" since it had laid out the territorial governing system that turned settlers into subalterns. Yet many of the first settlers did read the Ordinance in Churchill's terms, among them emigrants from the South whose religious convictions led them to an anti-slavery position. These settlers reinforced the theocratic interpretation of the Ordinance with a sacred view of American republicanism. Such were the believers in the mythic "Jefferson-Lemen Anti-Slavery Pact." According to the myth, the great father of American republicanism, Thomas Jefferson, who was thought to have authored the original version of article 6, dispatched his Virginia neighbor James Lemen to watch over the territory's freedom. Whether Lemen ever made such a pact with Jefferson, he did come to Monroe County in 1786, and he later founded several anti-slavery Friends of Humanity Baptist congregations. Lemen's very presence in the state served as a local reminder of the moral imperative of the Declaration of Independence. Edward Coles, who had previously won a place in the mythology of American republicanism by helping Jefferson reunite with Adams in 1811, alerted Illinoisans of Jefferson's disapproval of slavery by having his 1814 exchange with Jefferson reprinted locally.[27]

As Smith continued to write, however, he began to turn the paternal-care motif on its head. "When the country northwest of the Ohio was ceded to the nation," he opined, "slaves (a species of property well known to the laws of Virginia) were secured to the then citizens of Virginia inhabiting the ceded country, by language too plain to be misunderstood or evaded." He then added: "this compact between the contracting parties was solemnly made, and binding upon both, upon every principle of universal law." In other words, Jefferson was still the great father, the Ordinance of 1787 still the pillar of fire, but now it was slavery that was being protected and the slaveholders who were being guided. Smith arrived at this reading by connecting article 2, which stated that "no man shall be deprived of his liberty or property," to an earlier passage that acknowledged the rights of "the French and Canadian inhabitants, and other settlers of the Kaskaskies, St. Vincents and the neighboring villages who have heretofore professed themselves citizens of Virginia." The Ordinance guaranteed to these former Virginia citizens the continuance of "their laws and customs . . . relative to the descent and conveyance, of property." Smith read this passage as a "compact between contracting parties," rather than as a command from a superior to a subservient. With these passages in tow, the republican movement in Illinois claimed authority to extend the right of owning slaves to all white settlers wherever they lived in the state. The upshot was to limit the slavery prohibition in article 6 to the future importation of slaves alone.[28]

"Compact" readings that emphasized settlers' rights had been made before, but previous defenses had always been made on pragmatic terms. This had been the approach, for example, of Arthur St. Clair, the first territorial governor of the Illinois Country. In 1805 the Indiana Territory legislature (then including Illinois) at Vincennes used rights language when it authorized the indenture system compromise in an effort to encourage southern emigration. Smith by contrast audaciously eschewed rights language, even if he relied upon it in principle. Instead he tried to take the moral high ground, using the parental metaphor and modifying his implicit compact view with phrases such as "universal," "public faith," and "solemn obligation"—language heretofore the exclusive possession of the anti-slavery adherents. Nonetheless, the parental metaphor existed in tension with the compact premise. For if the Ordinance was a contract, then it was an agreement formed of mutual consent and its basis was the right of self-government, not parental oversight. Smith could counter with the argument that the parental founder's true gift had been to empower the children to make their own social contract. Here he matched Coles's appeal to Jefferson by echoing the Declaration. In this spirit *Illinois Gazette* editor Henry Eddy published a letter by Jefferson, dated September 24, 1823, which repeated his long-held belief "that a preceding generation cannot bind a succeeding one by its laws or contracts."[29]

Smith's devious purpose became obvious as he proceeded to declare that, however much the paternal guidance was appreciated, it had now been outgrown. The territory of Illinois had consequently become a state, and having been "admitted into the Union upon an equal footing with the original states," it presently held

> the same right to alter her constitution as the people of the state of Virginia . . . and [the people] may by an alteration of that instrument make any disposition of negro slaves they choose, without any breach of faith or violation of compact, ordinances or acts of

Congress; and if the reasoning employed by the committee be correct; there is no other course left by which to accomplish the object of the Governor's message, than to call a Convention to alter the Constitution."[30]

Smith's use of anti-slavery rhetoric to express the territorial compromise represented by McFerron and Will was effective, if diabolical. As he recognized, the image of the federal government's parental oversight glossed two competing ideas of parenthood: one whose aim was that the territory attain the freedom to govern itself, and another whose aim was that the territory attain a free government. The one focused on political means, the other on political ends. As even anti-slavery advocate George Churchill conceded, a legalistic view of the matter could cut both ways. Smith's rhetorical shift from ends to means signaled the larger shift from an ends-oriented to a means-oriented republicanism in Illinois.

Smith's audacity portended the change in political culture simmering just below the surface of the state's politics. Old assumptions of deference to political authority were being reordered. The prospect of rewriting the constitution only deepened the feeling that the time was ripe for a free and candid expression of the West's new republicanism. Colonel Thomas Cox defended the call for a new constitutional convention in precisely these terms, noting that "aristocratical features were introduced into our constitution at its formation," and that these features notoriously jarred with "that purity, which ought ever to characterize . . . those who so successfully resisted the oppression of one of the most powerful nations of Europe."[31] No longer subjects of the English or children of the East, Illinois citizens were now autonomous adults; their familial prerogatives and obligations were ripe for redefinition.

For many the need to express a suppressed identity was thought to be long overdue. Calling for it now, Smith and his colleagues could point to the emerging political prominence of the West and Southwest. Did not the growing economic prominence of Cincinnati, Louisville, and St. Louis confirm it? Did not the military victories at Tippecanoe and New Orleans confirm it as well? Abroad, too, one could read of republicanism's march, as local newspapers reprinted countless articles on the Greek struggle to gain freedom from the Ottoman Empire. Indeed, had not God confirmed it? *Illinois Gazette* editor Henry Eddy believed so, assuring his readers that the United States had been "manifestly called by the Almighty to a destiny which Greece and Rome, in the days of their pride, might have envied."[32]

The struggle against colonial tutelage throughout the world captured the imagination of young Illinois. Elias Kent Kane, the twenty-four-year-old attorney who had drafted the 1818 constitution, typified this spirit. Writing as "Timour" in the pages of Kaskaskia's *Republican Advocate*, Kane observed with satisfaction that, all over the world, the "arrogant pretensions of those who are pleased to style themselves sovereigns and kings" were falling to the true sovereign, the people. For others, the call for a new constitutional convention in Illinois, one unfettered by congressional compromise, best confirmed the pattern. "That some change is necessary for the advancement of this state," "Brissot" observed, "none I presume will pretend to deny." He predicated this claim on an assumed superiority in the state's geography. Here, he averred, was a land "situated between two great navigable rivers . . . with large navigable tributaries flowing through every section of the state, with a fertility of soil that cannot be equaled by any other state in the union, or perhaps any other country in the world; and although these advantages are crowned with a climate as agreeable as that of Italy, we make no progress either toward agricultural or political importance."[33]

Flush with a nationalism that appeared cosmopolitan, Illinois politicians eagerly boasted of their world-class bottomland and unparalleled social freedom for poor white people everywhere. Many agreed with T. W. Smith that the Illinois people had grown up; it was their turn to act in the republican revolution now playing on the world stage. Conrad Will, for his part, could "never believe the policy to be either unwise or unsafe which directly refers questions of doubtful expediency to that great and final tribunal THE PEOPLE."[34]

THE WHITE FOLKS AS BACKCOUNTRY DISSENTERS

The conventionist understanding of "the people" is best conveyed in Thomas Cox's tornado image, published in all four newspapers then in operation. In this image, power is equated with action—an organic, unified action that stems from the solidarity of a single social class. It was this unity that allowed Will to assume that the evolution of local norms would produce social peace and homogeneity. By contrast, the conventionists felt that the minority in the legislature considered themselves empowered to replace "the people." The minority had brazenly ignored the people's instructions on the Convention Resolution. Thus conventionists considered the non-conventionists a haughty elite who, once placed in the "windsor chairs of state[,] . . . forgot that they were even elected by the people."[35] The tornado image signaled a shift in political concepts, which opened the door to the identity politics of the convention movement. Legally, of course, only eligible voters counted as "the people." The 1818 constitution granted voting eligibility to white males over 21 who had resided in the state for at least six months. But for the conventionists, the people of Illinois did not match the people of the Declaration, a text in which they appear "universal rather than racial or ethnic" in nature. The conventionists' insistence effected a shift from a "universalistic" to a "particularistic" political style.[36]

Will tried to restrict the meaning of the universal "people" to the recent white emigrants who had brought their slaves to the state. Intentionally or not, his rhetoric excluded some who were included legally. Indeed, the whole tendency of the conventionist argument was to privilege the poor white claim to power. The people to whom Will referred had a particular social task to perform; they were working collectively to build a haven in the West for the excluded poor whites of the East. In order to open a commodious space for this lowly class, other social groups had to be excluded. It is doubtful, for example, that the "Old French people" were considered part of "the people" even though many conventionists attempted to appropriate certain aspects of the French lifestyle. As relatively open as the legal definition of "the people" was, local leaders tried to make it do the work of exclusion. "Foreigners," "aliens," and "men of color," wrote Senator William Kinney, were not among "the people," for technically they had not the "right to aid in the altering or amending [of] the constitution."[37]

After the legislature adjourned, the convention leaders went to work fleshing out the details of their social vision. As the conventionist portrait of the people became clearer, their ideal for the new state of Illinois also became clearer. They imagined a paradise for poor whites, a place where the soil was fertile, the rain plentiful, the sun smiling, and the government "liberal." They wanted a bottomland republic able to blend prosperity with equality. If the bottomland republic was not a complete invention of ambitious localists, neither was it a natural or authentic social vision of "the people." It was plausibly connected to reality, but it so strategically appealed to the class interests of the poor whites that it bore all the markings of a product cobbled together by politicians in search of a majority.

The connection between the Illinois white folks and the backcountry tradition helps flesh out these class interests. While analysis of the cultural and political impact of the Puritans, Anglicans, and Quakers is commonplace, the role of the backcountry people has received less attention. Only in the last few decades have scholars begun to recognize the importance of backcountry Americans in shaping the politics of the early republic. It is remarkable how the social biases of the white folks are paralleled in Fischer's portrait of a border people who "brought to America an indelible memory of oppression" from the Old World. Their experiences with political and religious oppression prepared them for the American Revolution, in which opposition to "conspiracies" among the powerful played a crucial role. Their concept of freedom was aptly expressed by Patrick Henry as a "spirit" that had "triumphed over every difficulty." This freedom to act lacked the reciprocity of the Quaker view and the elements of order and place encouraged by the Puritans. It was the very inverse of the Anglican view. If the Anglicans also emphasized the will to power, they had practiced it on backcountry subalterns. Indeed, the struggle between the Virginian cavaliers and the backcountry dissenters formed both groups, leaving the one with a view of freedom that had congealed into class prerogatives and the other with a view of freedom that stressed opposition to elite authority.[38]

Opposition to elite authority characterized backcountry politics generally. After the revolution, the backcountry continued to fight as a largely debtor class against the oppression of absentee property owners. All told, between the 1740s and the 1830s, Alan Taylor counts 10 such conflicts in the backcountry including Shays's, Ely's, Fries's, and the Whiskey Rebellions, and uprisings by the Paxton Boys in western Pennsylvania, the Regulators in North and South Carolina, the Liberty Boys in New Jersey, the Green Mountain Boys in Vermont, and the Liberty Men in Maine. Taylor's story of William Cooper's travails on the New York frontier further demonstrates the pervasive nature of class resentment during this period, as does Charles Sellers's work on the later period.[39]

The white folks who emigrated to Illinois formed a special subset of this dissenting backcountry population. They came especially from the Virginia and North Carolina backcountry, which after 1790 spilled into Kentucky, Tennessee, and Ohio, and from there after 1800 into Indiana, Illinois, and Missouri. Scholars who have studied the migration pattern in Illinois call their pre-emigration home "the upland South," because of the generations they had spent in the mountains. Solon Justus Buck sampled about one tenth of the population that entered the state between 1815 and 1818 and found that 71 percent came from the seven states of Kentucky, Tennessee, Virginia, North Carolina, South Carolina, Maryland, and Georgia. Author Clinton Boggess concluded that the polity of Illinois upon reaching statehood was composed of "a people practically southern in origin . . . being governed by officials from the south under southern laws." Ex-governor John Reynolds, who strove to portray the Illinois settler as following no guide other than "nature," often inadvertently demonstrated the pioneer's southern biases. In his description of a corn shucking, for example, he noted that "the fiddler on these occasions assumed an important bearing and ordered in true professional style, so and so to be done; as that was the way in North Carolina, where he was raised."[40]

From the social experiences of these upland southern white folks, the local politicians attempted to craft a political program. The embattled "middle-class" nature of backcountry culture was reflected in the effort. The proposal to reinstate slaveholder emigration was thought to be egalitarian economically, politically, and socially. Economically, the plan to clear the bottomland of excess vegetation would benefit the community as a whole. It would reinforce the communal "habits of mutuality" instilled by centuries of "producer" class status. Politically, the call of a convention would shift power into the hands of the majority. It would shift power to the mass, the common voter. Socially, by obviously denigrating the status of free blacks, the status of poor whites would be

raised correspondingly. This second feature of the convention movement underscores how important status fears and anxiety were in the
West, which still relied to some degree on the pecking order that made
the southern code of honor and standing possible. It is ironic that status
concerns were heightened just as they were removed. Although in their
new home, the social scene had changed radically, since the gentry and
slave classes above and below them in the South were diminished almost to non-existence, the emigrant upland southerners retained the
backcountry class biases they had formed in their homeland.[41]

The experience of Morris Birkbeck, a prominent English emigrant, re-
inforces the notion that race and class remained tightly interwoven for
the white folks. The settlers he encountered in Edwards County on the
eastern side of the state insisted that the English emigrants not attempt
to stall their "floating population," or fetter their independence. It was
not for the white folks to adjust to others, but for outsiders such as the
English to adjust to "the polity, laws, or disposition of the people," as
the writer "Americanus" put it. "Though the people are seldom intrusive, or troublesome, to those who do not seek their society," wrote
James Hall, then the editor of the *Illinois Gazette* at Shawneetown, Gallatin County, "if you commence a conversation, they expect it to be
continued on terms of equality, and are offended if you are less unre-
served than themselves." Birkbeck had the misfortune of being taught
this fact in the public columns of Hall's newspaper. His anti-slavery position raised the suspicion of one "John Rifle," who wrote: "The fact is,"
such Englishmen have "been used to having poor white folks for slaves,
and they want to keep the same rule here." When Birkbeck attempted to
defend himself as a republican, Rifle piled on the abuse: "British republicanism indeed!" he countered. "That is a good one. It seems that the
English are not satisfied with decrying our country . . . but when they
find in it a splendid monument of national virtue, which the world ad-
mires . . . they would appropriate that to their own name."[42]

Again however, within their own group, the white folks professed to
follow a strict egalitarianism. As Madison County settler Daniel M.
Parkinson noted: "When new-comer arrived in the country . . . the old
settlers . . . turned out, and built the new-comer a house, cut and split
his rails, hauled them out, put them up in a fence around the land he
wished to cultivate, and then his land was broken for him ready for the
seed." These inclusive economic and racial sentiments were the inverse
of their attempts to exclude the class above and the race below them.
The conventionists' project was aimed at including and excluding simultaneously.[43]

The conventionists' spin confronted one major complication: the
white folks were divided. The division was both generational and political. On the generational side, Ford reported in *A History of Illinois,
1818–1848*, that "the young people of that day were powerfully ad-

vanced in the way of civilization" by the new modern ways, but "the old people regretted the change." Parkinson captured in a superficial yet telling image this difference of degree between the old and young settlers: "And to conclude these friendly attentions to the new-comer, a most joyous and convivial occasion was enjoyed, when the younger portion of the company would trip the light, fantastic toe, over some rough puncheon floor."[44] The effect of these differences within the white folks' community was a political rhetoric that attempted to blur the distance between the two value systems. Most politicians spoke as if the Illinois people sought a middle course: individual competition combined with obligatory cooperation; an economy open to gain, but one that did not make the people grasping.

Luckily for the local politicians looking to make of all this a coherent political platform and social identity, the division within the white folks could be covered over by the more all-encompassing shared feeling of inferiority. According to Ford, a sense of "inferiority mingled with an envious malignity toward all excellence in others" existed in the "extreme frontiers" amid "those neighborhoods where the people habitually neglect to attend public worship on Sundays." In such places "the young people of both sexes are without self-respect and are conscious of not deserving the respect of others." This was the typical condition among the white folks until Sunday worship "regularly brought [them] together at stated times; and their meeting . . . accustomed them to admire and wish to be admired." Looking back over the period of a generation, Ford believed that local conditions had improved, even though the cause was the "desire to gratify artificial [read: eastern] wants." Ford here confessed to feelings shared by only one half of the white folks. To a full-fledged devotee of western republicanism such as Timour, the rough-mannered Illinois man presented "man in . . . his original greatness . . . without this boasted civilization and that dark mantle of hypocrisy which is its certain consequence," in the East.[45] Thus, although the white folks disagreed fundamentally over the route to social equality, they converged on the belief that their social condition was one of inequality and inferiority.

The clearest and most abundantly recorded evidence of the white folks' feelings of social inferiority comes from the writings of Daniel Parker, the Baptist preacher, "backwoods hunter," and state senator from Crawford County. Parker opposed the "missionary system" brought to the state by eastern preachers such as John Mason Peck. Poor and only semi-literate, he found religion under the pressure of an overwhelming desire to quench his envy of other people and imitate the simplicity of the "primitive saints." Earlier in life, while preaching in a multi-denominational venue, he was shunned. "Being rough and course in my language and manners," he noted, "I made but a poor appearance as a preacher." Before his conversion, he despaired of ever being saved on account of the strong envy of others he found welling up in his heart. When the conversion came, "my eye was immediately caught to some members of the church who had formerly stood very low in my esteem." Now they were "the most lovely people I had ever beheld" for he realized that "God has chosen and sent instruments, that perhaps would have been among the last choice the world would have made." The last were the white folks. The new eastern missionaries, with their Sunday schools and paying of preachers, threatened to reestablish the dominance of eastern over western culture. Parker fought them to the death, producing in its most extreme form the relational process of identity formation in Illinois.[46]

Young and old, the Illinois white folks attempted to create a society that was free from the oppression of social conformity. Ironically, the younger generation maintained this new ideal while at the same time becoming more integrated politically, religiously, and economically into mainstream society. They became more entrenched than their parents had ever been in the world of society and its "artificial wants." Whereas "each one" of the youth, Ford thought, "wanted to make as good a figure as he could" among the others, the older settlers, such as Daniel Parker, took their feelings of inferiority and turned inward. Lurking behind Ford's generational division was the question of whether backcountry emigrants ran to or from the market. As George Dangerfield put the query, were they "driven by necessity, or drawn by hope"? The localist movement had a convenient model at hand for synthesizing these two contradictory social goals: the French example. Indeed, it would be a mistake to discount the influence of the colony of French who had settled in "gay and fashionable" towns in the "American Bottom" along the Mississippi on the generation coming of age with statehood. Although the French were located mainly in Randolph, Monroe, St. Clair, and Crawford Counties, their influence, emanating from centers of trade, reached to the whole state. Their open and convivial nature was universally commended. Even the hardheaded Ford observed that "the whole [French] population lived lives of alternate toil, pleasure, innocent amusement, and gaiety." Here was an antidote to the difficult, dreary work of acquiring property and mastering middle-class occupations that Marvin Meyers found to be the dark reality lying behind the people's "equalitarian" dream.[47]

Insofar as the French model can provide a clue to this question, it suggests that the white folks hoped to get the best of both worlds. As a classic example of a "people of plenty," they hoped western abundance would deliver them forever from the struggle to survive and all the compromises the struggle entailed.[48] The lure of bottomland plenty, however, created a myopia over social conflict. It not only effaced the debate over differences within their community but also blocked the recognition of social struggle outside it. The fact that their egalitarianism was built upon a struggle over the land with the Native Americans, for example, or that it tended to exclude minorities such as the Yankees, the English, and later the Methodists simply did not figure in the conceptual universe of the backcountry's vernacular republicanism.

The white folks may have been made into an ethnicity in Illinois without the political transformation that was taking place in the conception of the people, but its crystallization sped up under the rigors of political competition. Political rivalry aided the making of identity, because it gave the local leaders an opportunity to focus on an "other." Through this relational process, the new emigrants discovered at first only that they were not, as Thomas Sloo, Jr., put it, "big folks."[49] The ideological opposition of white folks to big folks shaped the drama of politics in early Illinois. The white folks' identity may not have fit every settler, but the political construction of this identity in the legislature was not simple delusion. The local leaders, if typically neither white folks nor big folks themselves, were caught up in a web of power relations that structured the interactions of the two groups and determined their respective roles.

These relations were determined by the territorial government. Between 1809 and 1818, the most powerful patronage dispensing posts in the territory belonged to a governor and three judges. All four positions were federally appointed and immune to popular election. Two U.S. senators, added in 1818 when Illinois became a state, were also remote from the people, being elected by the General Assembly. From 1809 to 1824, these positions—territorial governor, territorial judge, and U.S. senator—were all but monopolized by Ninian Edwards and Jesse B. Thomas. The power field created by the appointment privilege kept the local politicians under their control.

Statehood altered the field of power. After 1818, widespread local support was needed to garner a majority of the General Assembly's votes for U.S. senator. Local votes would also be necessary to advance the economic interests of the two men, who had invested extensively in land and various business ventures. Both attempted to extend their spheres of influence, which had originally included only those immediate clients bestowed with tangible favors such as positions in the federal land office and the judiciary or jobs as county clerks and recorders. They did this by buying off the regional newspapers with the intention of flooding the surrounding country with print and of painting their allies (or potential allies) in colors favorable to the people.

In order for power to remain in the hands of the big folks, then, knowledge of white folks' preferences was necessary. Candidates among the local politicians who could represent the locals were eagerly sought out by the territorial elite. This further increased the pressure to produce a manageable, unified local identity. In this sense, the big folks were responsible for cultivating the very mentality that would eventually undermine their political control. Given this fact, a distinction should be made between the frivolous and personal content of a political contest and the political uses to which it is put. "Personal politics" was the vehicle of political development in Illinois.[50] Combined with the shift to statehood, personal politics provided the incentive needed to produce a new social image of the people.

Previous studies of early Illinois politics have tended to collapse factional into personal politics and have, by emphasizing their common chaos, tended to ignore any distinction that might exist between the two types. Factional disputes can—and in Illinois did—include disputes over principles. Egalitarianism, if normally felt as a sentiment, was shaped into a guiding principle. Factional politics in Illinois, influenced though it was by the force of personality, should not be explained away by personal differences. For if the white folks' social vision of equality was not universal, certainly not as universal as the concept of "the people" might be, it was as good an incarnation of it as was brought to the United States from Europe.[51]

CHAPTER TWO

BOTTOMLAND
FARMERS IN THE
MARKET
REVOLUTION

Young Illinois was a northern state filled with southerners. This left its latitudinal identity in doubt, but its longitudinal identity was never contested: leaders could safely proclaim their western allegiances. Their sectionalism divided mainly along the Appalachians, not the Mason-Dixon line. Yet the rhetoric of western egalitarianism, of opposition to eastern big folks, only partly displaced North-South sectionalism. Indeed, at moments the North-South division threatened to overwhelm state politics. As the convention debate grew in volume, so did southerners' fear of northern influence in the state. Only after a long bout of sectional rivalry did convention leaders attempt to redirect these fears and project them against the putative encroachment of Methodist preachers into political life. To the extent that they succeeded, politics in Illinois during this "era of good feelings" served to displace latitudinal sectionalism by promoting other divisions, just as it did at the national level.[1]

If the use of regionalism in Illinois presaged the national pattern, the state's politics and economics represented the nation's extremes. The state's democratic revolution was precocious, its economy underdeveloped. By 1818 its farmers were poised to reinvest the profits they had made selling grain to realize at last their dream of property ownership. But just as independence from the big folks appeared to be within reach, the state's economy went into a severe depression, caused by a dearth of outside money flowing through the state. Between 1819 and 1823 almost all trade with the outside world stopped. This hiatus underscores the importance subsistence farming still had in the Illinois economy. During this period Illinois farmers reconsidered the state's economic strategy, and a widespread debate on agricultural policy ensued.

It was unusual that economic policy became a political matter so quickly. The impact of the economy on society was usually an issue reserved for the most developed parts of the nation, where the transition to a market economy had come earlier and its impact on labor patterns was already clearly established. But the fact that the debate occurred in Illinois where the democratic revolution was uncontested meant that the state was again rehearsing a pattern later to be replayed at the national level. In the local debate, there was no doubt that economic policy would be tailored to suit the needs of the vast majority of poor whites. But once this question was conceded it was unclear, in Illinois as in the nation at large, what approach to the market was in the white folks' interests. Over time a division developed between those who used the market to mimic the big folks and those who used it to further oppose them.

The consequence of this split was that what began as an economic issue quickly became a cultural one. The centrality of class conflict, often assumed to be an inevitable element in any debate over political economy, was largely eliminated in the Illinois debate by the democratic presumption that whatever the white folks desired would prevail. As scholars of American political development have often noted, the early assimilation of poor whites into the political system set party politics in the United States on a unique path.[2] Instead of the propertyless masses struggling against the propertied few, they struggled among themselves, and elites joined both sides. Consequently, whereas the struggle for political equality involved the relatively simple matter of white folks squaring off against big folks, no similarly simple opposition characterized the struggle for social equality. Unlike the big folks, the market never presented a clear target to oppose, at least not until Andrew Jackson hit upon the notion of demonizing the "Monster Bank."

The democratic revolution brought by the white folks to Illinois promised an ideal society of independent freeholders. Scholars have called this the "Jeffersonian dream . . . of becoming independent landowning farmers." Backcountry emigrants came to Illinois to create a fee-simple republic, where every family owned the land they farmed. While many personal motives drove emigration, the underlying cause of the backcountry migration was that subsistence farming produced more children than any immediate area could handle on independent farms. Carving a farm from the wilderness required the labor of two parents, with at least two children and usually many more. But the parents' farm rarely had room for more than one child to remain permanently. The others set out to repeat the pattern with their own children. As Charles Sellers observes, "the subsistence culture could not reproduce itself over generations without a constant abundance of cheap land to provide farms for its ever more numerous offspring."[3]

Historians use the term "yeomen" to describe those engaged in such migratory family farming. Yeomen were driven by the desire for independence, whereas capitalist farmers, whether in the land or in the staple market, aimed at maximizing profit. Yeomen feared the dependency represented by wage labor; they produced goods for their use value, not their exchange value; where market exchanges were involved, the goal was family security and competency, not capital accumulation. Yeomen resisted the market revolution with a producer republicanism shaped in the crucible of the revolution. But while early Illinoisans considered independence a key part of their republican purity, they did not resist the market so much as attempt to use it to their advantage.

No hard production data exists for early Illinois agriculture, but the available evidence suggests that most Illinois farmers practiced "subsistence-surplus" agriculture; they placed a "safety-first" priority on producing food for the family. Only what was left over would be exchanged in the market. Yet, market goods were often valued additions to the subsistence-surplus lifestyle. A succession of good years and high prices in the 1810s together with a thriving local exchange market blurred the lines between production for use and production for exchange.[4]

For the most part the market revolution diffused its charms of prosperity with security so subtly in the early Illinois experience that most farmers were enmeshed in market relations before they recognized the threat to their independence. Commercial agriculture grew with the European demand for wheat and cotton, a demand that began in earnest in the 1760s and raged throughout the period of the Napoleonic Wars. The Illinoisans' political and agrarian dreams at first happily coincided with this favorable trend, as the international market economy penetrated the Mississippi River valley.[5] In this period too the economic dimensions of the debate over the market was muted, and local politicians were free to emphasize other, more easily managed cultural issues. In sum, when money was flowing freely local leaders tended to stress Illinois's longitudinal identity: Illinois agriculture, as a western agriculture, had room for all types of farmers, commercial as well as subsistence. When times were hard, they tended to get embroiled in debates about latitudinal identity.

Regionalism used to articulate cultural differences containing economic overtones: this was the unique dynamic of early Illinois politics. In negotiating among regional, cultural, and economic forces, convention leaders were often as much at the mercy of these forces as their followers. But the conventionists did try to use the local reaction to market dependency to their advantage. The market revolution caused a reordering of preferences in Illinois, while political institutions such as factions and legislatures operating on cultural norms also shaped preferences. For although economic interests do structure and often determine behavior, the political purposes that shape interests are themselves subject to cultural influence. The limits of subsistence life fostered in the Illinoisans a ghostly desire for equal status. Some used the market to prove themselves equals, others engaged in a broader effort to shape the direction of the state's economy. In a political system based on popular sovereignty, such actions can be as powerful as market forces. The political shaping of preferences had an independent impact on individuals as well as on the market itself.[6]

These underlying realities complicate any assessment of the market revolution in early Illinois. The state's political leaders were intent on fitting the economy to their republican specifications. The people believed that all things in the state, the natural landscape and slavery alike, would bow to their will. In simple terms, they wanted improved economic conditions in which to exchange and sell their surplus crops. Many wanted nothing more than to earn enough money to buy their property and retire "by the fire most of the time." But when this proved impossible for some and not enough for others, a wider debate developed about what kind of economy western republicanism required.[7]

THE ELYSIUM OF AMERICA

Why emigrate to Illinois? The briefest survey of the early settlers' memoirs reveals a perhaps forgotten answer. The vast majority chose to settle in Illinois because it was so evenly spread with good farming land. Every new family had its pick of locations. The best land lay adjacent to the innumerable small rivers and creeks that fed the three rivers bounding the state, the Wabash, Ohio, and Mississippi. These river lands, called "bottoms" or bottomland, combined what geologists have identified as three distinct soil types: bottomlands, old river bottoms, and deep loess areas. Each had been transformed by glacial melt, which flooded the land and readjusted every river bed. Their different soils resulted from a variety of wind-blown and silted deposits. All contained loess, a "rock flour that was ground in the mills of the Pleistocene ice-rivers and left behind in outwash deposits."[8] Evidence from settlement locations, squatters' reports, and the first five years of land sales indicate that those who first settled the Illinois Country (see Figure 2a) chose primarily to settle bottoms that lay within reach of a navigable river (see Figure 2b). By 1825, it was not too much an exaggeration to say that settlers were concentrated in four distinct areas along the river systems formed by the Mississippi, Ohio, Wabash, and Illinois.[9]

For the settlers the most important fact about the bottoms was their fertility. Bottomland had been made rich and fertile by flooding over the millennia. The German reporter Gottfried Duden captured the economic overtones of the phrase by calling it land that "required no fertilizer for the first century and was too rich for wheat during the first decade." The famed American Bottom alone ran some ninety miles long and four to seven miles wide at points on the eastern side of the Mississippi. This bottom, *Republican* editor William Orr boasted, "was about

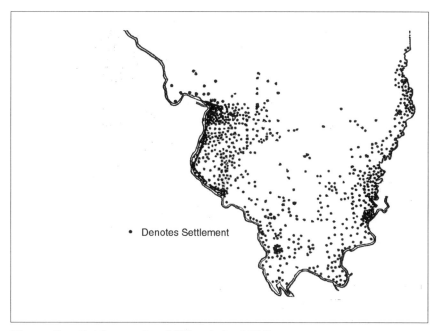

Figure 2a **Settlements of Illinois in 1818**

Source: Solon J. Buck, *Illinois in 1818*

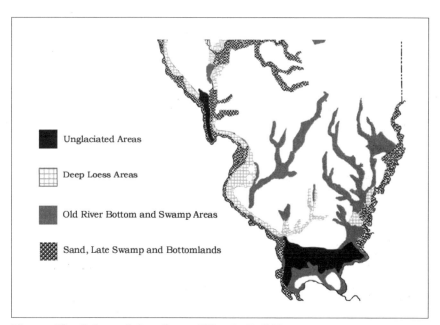

Figure 2b **Selected Southern Illinois Soil Types**

Source: Douglas C. Ridgley, *The Geography of Illinois*

five hundred square miles." Emigrant William Sewall, who bought a tract of land "in the Sangamon bottom" in 1830, included a special entry in his laconic diary for his visit to "the American bottom where it is supposed to be the richest soil in the U.S. with 20 or 30 feet of soil." In 1817, a visitor wrote in the *Western Intelligencer:* "Indian corn, wheat, rye, oats, tobacco and hemp are raised with as much facility and ease as in the neighborhood of Lexington [Kentucky], where I was raised . . . the productions in the American bottom in particular, are greater and reared with more ease than in the neighborhood of my nativity. . . . A more congenial soil for general cultivation I believe no where exists, it may be called the Elysium of America."[10]

Bottoms included a mix of alluvial and non-alluvial lands, as well as swamps. Precise boundaries between the ancient and current floodplains were often unclear, and some bottomlands were never cultivated. These included the timbered lands immediately adjacent to the rivers, which "produced burr oak, hickory, butternut, or black oak"; they were found from experience to be "generally poor and often worthless for agricultural purposes." Other stretches were avoided because of frequent flooding. One such bottom was the famed Big Bottom, south of Kaskaskia. In 1827 Pierre Menard advised the Shawnee Indians to spend the winter there, indicating that no one else was living there at the time. Other bottomland tracts, settled immediately and prized for their fertility, were nonetheless subject to unexpected flooding. The land in the vicinity of Kaskaskia had been settled by the French for over a hundred years, and for thousands of years before that by the Mound Builders. Yet this land flooded in 1844, when the Mississippi altered its course, inundated many farms, and made an island of the first state capitol.[11]

Many settlers attempted to minimize the flooding problem by settling away from the larger rivers or in the bottoms around smaller rivers and creeks. The lowered risk of flood, however, also raised the risk of other dangers, such as more difficult access to water and markets. Nonetheless, many bottomland farms were settled on smaller waterways, miles from the four larger rivers. Other rivers and creeks with significant bottoms that were rapidly settled included Wood River, Macoupin Creek, Sangamon River, Silver Creek, Shoal Creek, Kaskaskia River, Crooked Creek, Beaucoup Creek, Big Muddy River, Little Muddy Creek, Cache River, Saline River, Skillet Fork River, Little Wabash River, Bonpas Creek, and Embarras River. Almost every town was located adjacent to a river or creek (see Figure 3).

One concrete indicator of the value of bottomland to the early Illinoisans is land valuation for tax purposes. In Madison County, for example, the land tax on "first rate" land was one dollar per acre. This applied to "bottomland." The rates for other unspecified "second rate" and "third rate" land was 75 cents and 37.5 cents per acre respectively. On bottomland farms of every variety, crops could be raised and marketed,

Figure 3 **Rivers and Towns of Frontier Illinois**

hogs masted, horses and oxen fed, bees tended, fruit trees cultivated, and whiskey distilled with a fecundity rarely matched elsewhere in the entire nation. It was typical, under these circumstances, to hear writers such as "Brissot" claim that Illinoisans would very soon "enjoy that stand in the Union, to which the fertility of our soil, navigable advantages, and the agreeableness of our climate so eminently intitle us."[12]

The economic importance of bottomland fertility was noted by English visitor William Oliver: "From fifty to eighty bushels an acre is reckoned a good [corn] crop on most prairie; but on the Ohio and Mississippi bottoms, 100 and even 120 bushels are sometimes raised." This luxuriant fecundity would allow a margin of comfort during the dangerous transit to the fee simple. The venture was dangerous because, for subsistence farmers, it required at least a partial shift to commercial agriculture in order to raise the capital needed for purchase. After public land was reduced from $2.00 to $1.25 an acre in 1820, the purchase amount varied in estimates from $250.00 for a 40-acre farm to $976.00 for a quarter-section (160-acre) farm. Under these conditions, only a soil "the most fertile of any in the Union," offered the potential for both freedom and social equality, both security and prosperity. Here, indeed, was the American Elysium—the western promised land and the bucolic fulfillment on earth of what their parents only dared to dream of heaven.[13]

How plausible were these hopes of a unique Illinois dispensation from dependency? To assess them, one must consider the perimeters of entrance into the market economy for the average Illinois farmer in 1818: a family of from six to eight working members, with two years of labor in a standard quarter section of land (160 acres). The family has little capital and has not yet paid for their land. This is reasonable given that, as the editor of the *Illinois Emigrant* noted, of the approximately six thousand heads of households in 1819, only "one fourth part of this small number, may have paid for their possessions, and are able to purchase stock, tho' not to a great amount." Further assume that the family either has built its own cabin or has the $50 it will cost to have it built and to seed an adjoining garden plot.[14]

Before 1820, public land was two dollars an acre, though it could be paid off in four years. This made for a first payment of $80 on a quarter section. Purchases of private land might also be had on credit, but at a higher price per acre. If the family's first two years were spent squatting and clearing approximately 30 acres for planting, using the government's credit, the family will owe $80 in the fall for each of the next four years. In addition, the family is raising corn, with 13 bushels subtracted for each member's yearly consumption. If prices stayed high, as they did between 1812 and 1818, with corn going from 33 to 75 cents a bushel, then 30 to 50 bushels good yield per acre could bring a gross profit ranging between $254 and $1,028. In the price depression that lasted from

1820 to 1828, when corn brought only 15 to 20 cents a bushel, gross profit was lowered to between $116 and $274. Even in the worst case, then, the family could possibly raise the gross profit needed to pay the land office bill in the fall. The yields could improve to over 100 bushels per acre when stumps and brush were removed. These yields are remarkable, especially when contrasted with reports of yields between four and sixteen bushels of grain per acre in states such as Massachusetts and Maryland, and from five to fifteen bushels of corn per acre in the South. Illinoisans by contrast gushed over yields as high as 150 bushels per fully cleared acre. Here was the lure of the bottomland.[15]

For the lone family farm, there needs to be subtracted from these amounts the start-up costs incident to running a farm, at minimum an outlay of between $200 and $400 for oxen, yoke, plows, and a wagon. If the market was in New Orleans, there must be added the costs of packaging and shipping, which could run from $200 to $1,000 or half a year's labor. Evidence indicates, however, that farmers from the same settlement shared tools and shipping costs. Many farmers lowered transportation costs by cooperating on making flatboats, as a group of Lamotte Prairie farmers in Crawford County did every year. Together or separately, Illinois farmers regularly made the trip to New Orleans. Each spring flatboats could be seen floating down the Wabash, the Ohio, and the Mississippi. The *Western Sun* at Vincennes reported as many as 152 passing the city in the spring of 1826.[16]

Settlement life was a life of barter and exchange, and these calculations have assumed that the average family was able to trade for corn grinding, supplemental foods, clothing, and accessories. Nonetheless, if disease, an unstable or nonexistent currency, and the lack of resources to clear a full 30 acres are added to the equation, the margins of bottomland farming become less munificent. If prairie farming, as opposed to the usual bottomland variety, were involved, the margins are further reduced by additional time and labor for more extensive plowing and fencing, costs not always offset by fertile prairie soil.[17]

After 1820 the credit system at the land office was abolished but the price was lowered to $1.25. This raised the onetime cost of a quarter section to $200.00. Sales figures indicate that land in the military bounty tract sold for as cheap as 20 cents an acre, but the average was 63 cents an acre or approximately $100.00 for a quarter section (160 acres). Yet the depression and currency crisis made raising capital nearly impossible. As one Madison County farmer put it, the incentive to raise a surplus was vitiated by the fact that it might only be "sold on credit." Political office was one of the rare ways to raise capital once the depression began; preacher Daniel Parker was able to purchase 80 acres of federal land for $100.00 in 1822 on the basis of his successful election as Crawford County senator.[18]

Taking all factors into account, it is fair to say that the journey to fee-simple ownership was still a risky venture, even in Illinois's fertile bottomland. How many made it through to safety? There are no ownership statistics for the state as a whole during this period. John Mack Faragher found that, by 1830, in the Sangamon County community of Sugar Creek "squatters made up over half of the one hundred and thirteen farm households." A round 50 percent figure accords with property ownership percentages from later in the century. If this held for the rest of the state, it can be surmised that approximately one-half of emigrant families secured a fee simple; most of the other half either rented or moved on; only a small number could find gainful employment in the small towns.[19]

If many failed outright in the emerging commercial society, most of those who succeeded were not able to make much headway in property accumulation between 1819 and 1823. For when the flood of emigration stopped, property owners encountered a weak or nonexistent wage labor pool. Yet producing for the market often required hired help—either domestic or in the field. Many ambitious householders declaimed the difficulty of obtaining and keeping "Dutch girls," "plowboys," and other indentured servants. As visitor Duden reported, "As long as the population is scarce, servants are very expensive." Elias Fordham, George Flower's cousin, argued that a farm laborer paid $13 a month in 1817 could expect in two years' time to save enough money to put down the first payment on a quarter section, as well as "buy a horse, a plow, and tools." Given this, it is not surprising that laborers were scarce. Faced with the dearth of domestic servants, the Yankee Tillsons of Montgomery County, despite moral misgivings, succumbed to the local conditions—they purchased two slaves.[20]

The high demand and low supply of laborers provided a reason for the well-off to become pro-slavery conventionists. There is, however, little evidence that the commercial class led the drive to make slavery legal in the state. Indeed, narrow economic concerns such as the sorry condition of the state's books, which could have been used to argue in favor of the slavery extension, were rarely used. In 1823 the auditor reported that were it not for the income received on taxes of nonresident land, the state would be running a $8,775 deficit; even with these monies, the state would have been in the red but for the $10,563 paid by the Gallatin County saltworks. In the same year the state's top financial officer expressed concern at the rapidly approaching constitutional deadline (1825) for importing slaves to the salines. Yet, neither the interest in keeping the saltworks' revenue nor an improved labor market was emphasized by the conventionists in the counties. The reason may have been that they were embarrassed to do so. Very few Illinois farmers could afford to purchase a laborer's time, let alone a slave. Families that were "too poor to buy a quarter section of land, or who require an eight year credit" to do so, could not afford the amount (from $300 to $550) required for a slave. The conventionists preferred instead to emphasize the benefits to be had from a new wave of wealthy southern immigrants, who would again flood the land with money. Their mouths would need food, which local farmers could supply, and their surplus labor would help clear the land of excess vegetation thought to be the source of disease.[21]

In the counties, renewed immigration was the main economic justification for a new convention allowing slavery, but advocates for slavery using these grounds had to walk a fine line. The money and slaves from the South that could save their bottomland state and its republicanism could also crush them under the force of too much money. "A Mechanic" wrote:

> At this time, there is perhaps no part of the civilized world where the people are more upon an equality than they are in Illinois. A man who is foolish enough to be proud, is sure to be despised. This equality is the essence of republicanism. We have now no purse-proud nabobs to turn up their noses at their poorer neighbors—no haughty masters of a hundred slaves, to display their superiority. If one citizen is a little more wealthy than his neighbors, he assumes no additional importance on that account. But introduce slavery and the case will be altered.[22]

The local Illinoisans were intent on opening a space for egalitarian republicanism. As long as the bottomland would support them, they strove to keep the economy in motion and the forces of concentration of wealth at bay long enough to establish their own equality. Insofar as slavery could be seen as aiding this end, they favored it.

DISEASE AND DEPRESSION

If the story of the convention controversy were told not from the perspective of the emerging political class but from that of the county locus alone, its theme would be the steady disintegration of prosperity since the first days of statehood. From the Wabash Counties to the gateway for emigrants in Shawneetown, from the saline districts across to the American Bottom and from there up to the new Sangamon county (then spelled Sangamo), one question was beginning to form in every mind: was the garden stillborn? Beginning in the fall of 1819 and continuing through 1822, everything stopped. The money stopped, and immigration stopped. In the summer of 1821 the rain stopped.

The Panic of 1819 was followed by three consecutive "sickly seasons." "Our old men tell us," wrote "An Observer" in the fall of 1822, that "Illinois might be estimated as healthy as any of her neighboring sisters," even though "beginning [with] the year 1819 . . . sickness has been prevalent to an extraordinary degree." Indeed, "whole families . . . panic struck . . . by the three years prior to the present . . . are preparing to emigrate they know not wither."[23]

On the east side of the state it was called "the Wabash chills," in the south it was "the bilious fever," in the north the "Illinois shakes," in the west "the ague," and in the town of Edwardsville "the yellow fever." Everywhere people were laid low with the bottomland sickness. Daniel Brush told of the onslaught in Greene County:

> As the fall season of 1821 approached, sickness incident to the new country attacked all, great and small. The "fever'n ager" was in every house. No one in the settlement, I think, escaped. Some had it every day, others each alternate day. Many had the real "shakes" and when the fit was fully on shook so violently that they could not hold a glass of water with which to check the consuming thirst that constantly beset them while the rigor lasted, nearly freezing the victim. Then came the fever, the blood seemingly at boiling heat and the flesh roasting.

It was common for the disease to visit the settlements and last for two or three months. Although Brush reports that no one died in his group, many did die from it. In the same year, at Atlas in Pike County, it was said that "over one-half the entire population were numbered with the dead." Thomas Lippincott's first two wives at Alton died from it or from complications caused by it.[24]

The hope of ridding the land of disease was certainly the most immediate motive for contemplating limited slavery. "If the change in policy which is contemplated takes place, in this state," William Orr anticipated, "a few years will produce a very important change in the appearance of the American Bottom." Instead of "the deleterious particles that rise from stagnant water," there will be vast tracts under cultivation, producing for export "those articles which command the specie of other countries."[25] Connected to the problem of disease was the problem of economic depression. Even if farmers were healthy, many told that they were still short the money needed to pay off the land office. One such convention supporter, a Shoal Creek farmer in Bond County, summed up the squatters' dilemma by putting the question of slavery into local focus:

> The distresses of the country are increasing; the means of alleviating them are unheaded; and if ever slavery is admitted into this state, it will be owing to the improvidence of the people. What is the only strong inducement held out to the voters for slavery? Inquire of every candid advocate for the measure, and he will tell you, it is pecuniary interest—a relief from his distresses, his embarrassments. He admits all the evils attending a black population; but he tells you, his land is not

yet cleared out of the office; that his money is expended; that sickness is a frequent attendant of his family; that when able to labor, his produce brings him nothing but a trifle in state paper, which he cannot exchange for specie enough to meet his ordinary necessities.

This view was echoed by "One of the People" in the *Illinois Intelligencer.* "Two hundred dollars," he declared, was "a sum out of the power of nine-tenths of our population to raise." It was not a mere coincidence that he chose the amount needed to purchase a quarter section fee simple after 1820.[26]

Part of the problem was the shortage of exchangeable currency. The state bank's money, which was intended to alleviate shortages, compounded the problem because of its severe depreciation. "Upon [the state money's] first appearance" in 1821, William H. Brown wrote, "it was at a discount of thirty-three percent; it soon fell in value to fifty cents on the dollar, then forty, thirty, and even as low as twenty-five cents." By 1825 its value had stabilized at 30 cents to the dollar. But, Brown continued, when "the Legislature, by a severe statute, had prevented the issuing of shin plasters, the people would have experienced no little inconvenience for change, had not the plan of tearing these bills been adopted. . . . To pay fifty-cents, you divided a $3 bill, giving your creditor one-half, right hand or left, and putting the other half in your pocket."[27]

Beyond the failure of the local currency, the collapse of larger markets spread the woes of the Illinois farmer. As Thomas Senior Berry concluded: "If we are to judge by Cincinnati quotations, the grain situation in the West was anything but propitious between 1820 and 1828." In 1818, at the height of the postwar expansion, corn sold for between 33 and 75 cents a bushel at New Orleans; by 1822, in deepest depression, it brought only 20 or even 15 cents a bushel. Flour could sell for as low as one dollar a barrel in Pittsburgh, and there were stories of farmers getting even less at New Orleans in 1820. Although flour generally brought from three dollars to four dollars a barrel throughout the early 1820s at the southern market, editor William Orr noted, "our farmers think they cannot afford to raise it for less than five dollars per barrel." The average price in the five years between 1815 and 1819 had been nine dollars a barrel. These prices undoubtedly encouraged many settlers to try their hand at market farming. In the decade between 1821 and 1831, however, the price of flour per barrel at New Orleans averaged $4.95 a barrel.[28]

Not only had regional and national markets stalled, but the price of commodities sold in town also plunged. This was because of the sudden dearth of emigrants. Wheat, which in 1817 had sold at 75 cents a bushel locally, was eight years later hardly worth 25 cents a bushel in Illinois, although the larger market had recovered. The town market—typified by a Jefferson County farmer who traveled to Carmi, his packhorses loaded with cornmeal, to sell at a high price to the "movers"—had been a prime source of income for the small farmer. Even the trip to town could be precarious, however, given the undeveloped condition of Illinois roads and bridges. Brown observed that "swimming creeks was so much a matter of course and necessary that horses were selected with a view to this object—and an animal that took water fearlessly and swam so high as not to immerse his rider, was held in great esteem."[29]

All the outlets for their surpluses on which the Illinoisans had depended had failed. In this failure lay the roots of the budding alliance that Illinoisans as westerners generally made with the South. The problem of market dependency was faced elsewhere in the nation most starkly by the South, dependent on the British for its exports and the North for its imports. The ways of getting around this dependency were through either a tariff or free trade. The new anti-imperialist ideas of Adam Smith prompted southern leaders to embrace free trade, and this opened up the New Orleans market, Illinois's main trade outlet. Abraham Lincoln's encounter with the New Salem milldam in the spring of 1831, while taking goods down the Sangamon River en route to New Orleans, perfectly captures the thrills and chills of commercial agriculture experienced by many Illinois farmers. Beginning after 1814 when public lands first began to be sold in the Territory, many settlers turned to the market of New Orleans.[30]

By attempting to purchase land, were Illinois farmers yeomen aiming at familial independence or were they budding commercial capitalists hoping to invest their profits and build capital? For all its clarity, this question is easier to ask than to answer from any analysis of behavior, partially because the difference between family independence and capital accumulation may not be very great in practice.[31] A certain amount of accumulation is necessary for independence and stability, especially with an extended kin network. The distinction between yeomen and capitalists is most useful in situations where the yeomanry make the family farm an explicit end in itself, and where capitalists farm with the express purpose of reinvesting profits in other businesses. When the contrast between the groups is drawn this sharply, the distinction provides a clear means of identifying both groups. But the local record rarely offers so clear a line of differentiation.

Thomas Ford thought that "the money" streaming into the territory after the war "turned the heads of the people and gave them new ideas and aspirations." As John Reynolds remembered it, "the same energies that defended the country in times of war were now turned to commerce . . . [in one settlement] several flatboats were constructed; laden with corn, hogs, cattle, etc., and started to New Orleans." Yet Reynolds also recalled a wide variety of behaviors among the early farmers. William Kinney, his competitor as a boy in frolics and as an adult in politics, was so wild in his youth, "he had neither time nor disposition to accumulate property." But becoming "the head of a family" changed him. A French merchant convinced him to take on some merchandise in 1809; from that point on "he traded in merchandise, lands, horses, and almost everything that had any value attached to it and always made on the business he embarked in." Reynolds contrasted Kinney's capitalist proclivities with Thomas Ford who "never cared for wealth more than a support, and scarcely that much." Ford's "notions of probity and integrity were refined and well defined. With these notions, speculation, talented financiering was foreign from him."[32] In fact most households combined both extremes. Visitors often remarked on the uneven work rhythms of the bottomland farmer. John Woods, an Englishman who lived in Edwards County, an area settled primarily by immigrants from "Virginia and Kentucky," found his neighbors "sometimes truly industrious, and at other times excessively idle." He pointed to the similarities among Illinois, Virginia, and Kentucky in a more telling way—they all shared the same exchange rate for shillings and dollars, a rate different from the ones found in New York or Pennsylvania.[33]

Such impressions recorded for posterity by visitors were usually of the inhabitants living in towns along the rivers and roads. Merchants, by trade an optimistic breed, were especially maladroit at handling the new tight conditions. Reports indicate that Ninian Edwards's stores did well, and John Reynolds's "two dry good stores" (bought with speculation profits) also succeeded, whereas William Kinney's venture may have broken even; but by 1820 these were the exceptions. Thomas Lippincott's venture at Alton, started with St. Louis capital, folded in one year, for "it was soon found that twelve thousand dollars worth of goods was too much to hold in a place where there was nobody to buy." The towns in the eastern half of the state were particularly hard hit. In 1822, industrialist Thomas Hulme was struck by the inability of the Americans at Princeton, Indiana (just across the Wabash River from Mt. Carmel in Edwards County), to make the necessary adjustments to the busted market: "They cannot *all* keep stores and taverns!" "One of the storekeepers," he wrote, "told me he does not sell more than ten thousand dollars value per annum; he ought, then, to manufacture something and not spend nine-tenths of his time in lolling with a segar in his mouth."[34]

Yet if John Reynolds fondly recalled the times when foot and horse races filled the days, and games of "Loo" played under the shelter of the French "galleries" filled the nights, he also related other times when "the whole neighborhood assembled and split rails, cleared lands, plowed up whole fields and the like." At harvest time a corn-husking contest would be held, during which, Oliver noted, "the yells of defiance, mingled with Whoops and shrieks in Indian style, arose in one continued medley . . . whilst an unceasing shower of corn streamed through the air towards the roofless crib. . . . No match at football or shinty was ever engaged in with more uproarious animation."[35]

A similar cycle of energy and dissipation was played out when the economy boomed in the years between 1815 and 1819 and then went bust for the ensuing five years. When Thomas Lippincott first visited Edwardsville in 1818, he saw there a hive of "prospecting" activity that reached to the lowest levels of the community. He found the recently opened land office a

> centre from which they were accustomed to go out *prospecting* . . . and, as if to excite speculation still more, a person might by depositing sixteen dollars on a tract (eighty acres) i.e. one-tenth of the purchase money, secure a pre-emption for a certain length of time, and then . . . transfer it to another tract, (if he preferred it). Such was the state of things at that time, and consequently there were many . . . whose object and business it was to enter many or large tracts of land to be kept until the price of land should rise.

This "land market" was the first market many Americans "played." Ninian Edwards had made his fortune in Kentucky by playing this market, back in 1807. But by 1819 the typical Illinois speculator could be found back on the farm, rapidly liquidating assets, and reengaged in the familiar cycle of clearing, planting, harvesting, and collecting. Robert Patterson, arriving at Bond County in 1821, noted that "a considerable proportion of the more stable population . . . devoted themselves, a great part of the time, to the hunting of wild game, bee-hunting, trapping, and fishing."[36]

Alexis de Tocqueville is famous for stressing the liberal, proto-capitalist restlessness of the Americans. His observations have lent support to the "liberal consensus" interpretation of American politics, under which Americans were "born equal" and capitalist at the same time. But Tocqueville also thought that the Americans' essentially commercial nature created a general "distaste for agriculture." In effect, he ignored the yeomanry, perhaps in an eagerness to foretell emerging trends. Historians have since divided over the issue of how Americans developed their commercial values and consumer culture. Some have documented many "traditionalists" hiding in the corn crib and "small producers" in the artisan's shop. Against this, others have argued that "[c]apitalism emerged as much within as outside the American countryside." Daniel Vickers has offered a nuanced position in support of the latter view by arguing that even the traditional goal of family "competency" was "a socially divisive force" leading to competition and accumulation. The mixture of competency with competition best captures the Illinois pattern. Communitarian traditions, like many traditions from the East, were weakly developed. If linguistic usage is any test, the term "yeomanry" was applied mainly to New England producers; in Illinois, the word "farmer" was used almost ubiquitously.[37]

Individual examples of both strict yeomen and strict commercial capitalists can of course be found in the record. John Messinger of St. Clair County, for example, was a classic yeoman. He was not interested in expanding his landholdings beyond his first and only purchase of 160 acres in 1817. Yet, according to John Reynolds, such behavior made him remarkable. Though Messenger purchased a mill in 1804 and published a surveying manual in 1821, his only ambition was "to appear plain and unassuming." "He never acquired any great amount of wealth, although he had great opportunities to acquire property . . . he seemed to be proud of his want of pride." At the other extreme was land agent John Tillson. He and his wife, Christiana, scared their neighbors with their preoccupation with work. In compiling land lists, they reported many a "season of hurry" lasting late into the evening and even "the morning hours."[38]

Richard J. Ellis has developed a modernization topology that accurately fits the changes wrought by the market revolution in Illinois. Dissatisfied with the starkness of the "transition from classical republicanism to liberal capitalism" assumed by many scholars, Ellis has proposed an alternative model that draws upon Mary Douglas's "grid/group" analysis. The grid axis tracks the level of societal regulation of individual behavior; it runs from the rigidly hierarchical at the high end to the informally individualistic at the low end. The group axis tracks the amount of meaningful interaction among a given society's members. High group societies are organized extensively at both the family and community level; individuals in low group societies have relatively weak family and community ties. The intersection of the two axes creates four "ideal types" of society: hierarchal traditionalism (high grid, high group), such as most European feudal societies; fatalism (high grid, low group), which describes the slave subculture in the American South; competitive individualism (low grid, low group), which characterizes most highly developed liberal capitalist societies; and egalitarian individualism (low grid, high group), which delineates the forces shaping early Illinois society.[39] The Illinoisans' rebellion against the big folks establishes their anti-hierarchy, low-grid credentials. Similarly, their demand for rights validates their individualism, but the demand was predicated on the group need for recognition—an egalitarian impulse—more than on a commitment to the freedom of individuals.

Ellis's model thus posits two alternative paths to modernization and individualism, one competitive and one egalitarian. It is a helpful model for the Illinois case because, on the whole, the evidence does not fit a simple transition from a traditional to a modern capitalist society, as the yeomanry/commercial farmer distinction implies. On the one hand, the people populating the state were driven by a "rolling agrarian crisis" fostered by traditional agricultural practices. But the crisis was also partially driven by the market for grain created by the successful development of commercial, production-for-exchange, wage-labor capitalism in the East.

The impact of these national and international trends was too strong in Illinois for it to be called a pre-capitalist society. It is more accurately described as an economy in transition. On the other hand, there was a real lack of clarity in class aspirations prior to 1815, when attacks by Native Americans and the war kept market farming in check and accentuated the advantages of neighborhood cooperation. In such a climate, the pull of group solidarity could well tip the balance in favor of the egalitarian variety of individualism.

Although the postwar boom brought competitive individualist impulses to the fore, their triumph was again stymied by the depression following the Panic of 1819. As Steven J. Ross has shown in the case of Cincinnati and the Panic of 1837, economic depression quickly exposed the tensions between the competitive and egalitarian world views. An additional factor confusing values was North-South sectionalism, which colored the expression of values in early Illinois. Support for cooperative values was often voiced in southern accents, while support for commercial values indicated a northern dialect. Many Illinoisans hoped not to have to make the choice between northern and southern models of development; this, they reiterated, was the great privilege of the West. It was an ambiguity that erased conflict and fed the broad support for western republicanism.[40]

THE AMES LETTERS AND NORTHERN MEDDLING

Illinois land was so fecund, it was said, that it needed to be cleared of "surplus vegetable matter" in order to rid it of disease. The "bottoms of the Mississippi," land office clerk Nicholas Biddle Van Zandt noted, were "from two to six miles wide" across from St. Louis down to Kaskaskia. "[n]o lands can exceed these bottoms in fertility." But, he added, "they are considered unfavorable to health, owing to luxuriant vegetation." An initial clearing of the land was essential to bottomland farming. Its importance to the conventionist case was underscored by a series of letters in the *Republican,* printed under the pseudonym "Ames" during June and July 1824. Internal evidence suggests they were authored by the young Sidney Breese, an apprentice in Elias Kent Kane's law office in Kaskaskia.[41]

Ames showed how the convention controversy could be put into the larger perspective of state politics and at the same time could be tied to the agrarian economics faced by the local farmers. He shrewdly compared the non-conventionists with the big folks, a comparison made easier by the presence of Edward Coles. He set the conventionists in opposition to all things eastern, including abolitionism. Furthermore, he made the crucial step of tying the conventionists to the love of the land. The fertile land of Illinois held the key to prosperity, which would unlock the chains of social inequality and free the white folks from their subservient social status. To produce these results, however, the land must be cleared, even by slaves if need be. Ames tied the extension of slavery to the redemption of the bottomland's promise of prosperity. It was a promise whose viability had been sorely tested in the aftermath of the Panic of 1819.

Ames's letters are cultural propaganda equal to T. W. Smith's earlier effort. It will be helpful to dwell briefly on them for, although they were much noted throughout the state, there were factual errors in his formulation.[42] His was not the only, nor was it the most accurate attempt to capture local sentiment with a rhetorical distinction. But the inaccuracies in Ames's claims are significant because he himself recognized them and because he attempted to correct them in ways that indicate some of the hidden attitudes of bottomland republicanism.

He began by frankly pointing to the populist rhetoric that drove the state bank measure. "Did not the legislature pass the Bank law, by a *triumphant* majority, though disapproved and returned to them by the Council? And thus will it *ever* be, with any favorite measure of a popular body—they *will* carry them sometimes perhaps from the mere *opposition*." A similar spirit of opposition was driving the conventionists, but, he conceded, more than high-toned resistance would be needed to persuade the people to allow limited slavery. Unlike the bank law, which was justified as a matter of temporary relief, the calling of a convention would "affect *vitally*, the general interests . . . [and] the destinies of thousands unborn yet."[43]

Ames supplied the extra justification needed by slightly altering the conventionists' image of the people. The shift came at a crucial time in the controversy, the summer of 1824. By this time it was clear the vote would be close. The conventionist leadership had earlier decided to mount a two-pronged attack, tactical and rhetorical, against the surprisingly strong non-conventionists. In December 1823 a Central Committee was formed, which began planning to nominate candidates for the legislature. If the convention vote really was going against them, then a move to consolidate their votes by nominating candidates for the legislature was a matter of political survival. This tactic was especially important in light of all the appointments the General Assembly would control—including a reorganization of the state's judiciary as per the 1818 constitution—at its next session.

The second prong of the new attack was a rhetorical shift that had been signaled by the Central Committee's report. Issued after the public meeting of December 6, 1823, at Vandalia, the report denied that the convention movement was about the single issue of slavery. It resurrected the banner of political equality under which the conventionists knew they could mobilize a majority. The muffling of the slavery issue was later replicated in the Monroe, Wayne, Pope, and Randolph County conventionist meetings. At the Randolph event, Breese wrote under his own name. He issued a brief for the convention solely in terms of the disproportional representation of the 1818 constitutional convention. He "cheerfully admitted" the Madisonian principle that a people's constitution "formed by their own voluntary consent, ascertained and expressed upon the principles of equal representation, ought not to be disturbed for trivial reasons." But the Illinois constitution of 1818 had not been thus formed; it "was formed by a far less number than a majority of the people then inhabiting the country."[44]

From this opening salvo until the election, conventionists at the *Republican* filled column after column on the question of representation. The Central Committee had an explanation of the opposition's sudden popularity; it was the hypnotic hold of slavery—"this old hobby"—on the voters. "Massachusetts may have her convention," "Respublica" complained, "New York has had her new convention, all the states have had, or may have, their new conventions—but poor degraded Illinois, must be denied the dearest privilege of a sovereign independent state." The conventionists also blamed the stymied political atmosphere created by the Edwards faction. "Illinois has been long enough governed by a political dynasty, formed for the purpose of self-aggrandizement," "Vivele Convention" wrote. "It is time she should exert that redeeming spirit, which I know she possesses, and save herself from the grasp of faction." He would return politics to the people, literally, and to the common good, figuratively: "Let there be no party but 'we the people' and let every consideration but *the good of the whole* be sacrificed upon the great convention question."[45]

The reemphasis on political equality did not exhaust the purpose of the rhetorical change. As Breese soon showed, an additional goal of the new rhetoric was to create a bond between those who had been misrepresented under the 1818 constitution and those who, arriving after 1818, were completely unrepresented by that document. Ames was attempting no less a feat than the complicated task of putting the overt opposition to the big folks and the covert support of slavery together in one coherent narrative. He did this by connecting the anti-slavery sentiment of the non-conventionists with the superior ways of the big folks.

It was well known that the strongest opposition to the convention movement in the western part of the state was from the oldest American settlers—the Lemens, the Ogles, the Moores, the Mathenys, the Gilhams—who had come to the territory at or before the turn of the century. They had seen a "pillar of fire" in the 1787 Ordinance. But they never amounted to a majority, even among the French. By 1806, 4,311 people lived in the Illinois half of the Indiana Territory. The later emigrants, arriving between 1806 and 1818, increased the population tenfold. Ames's strategy was to cast the earlier settlers as a privileged minority. "No one class of men in *this* state," he wrote, "is entitled to greater privileges than another—the 'settlers' under the Ordinance of '87 have *no* rights *superior* to those who have migrated to this country" after them. "What!" he incredulously demanded: "Are we told that a comparatively *small* number of people, shall control and direct, and forever fix the destinies, of a *far greater* number!" By associating the anti-slavery non-conventionists with the territorial elite, Ames was pitting this group against those who had arrived, or come of age, with statehood.[46]

Ames's division of Illinois immigration into two simple parts—anti-slavery and pro-slavery—was partially flawed. On one hand, as he conceded, many of the people who came to Illinois in the later period were strongly anti-slavery, including Madison County Representative Curtiss Blakeman and English farmer Morris Birkbeck of Edwards County. On the other hand, many who came in the earlier period were pro-slavery. Indeed, having fought through the War of 1812, they exemplified precisely the kind of people whose need for social recognition would incline them to demand the rights to equal representation the *Republican*'s writers were defending. Ames courted this group, on the wrong side of his distinction as it were, by trying to awaken their southwestern biases. Before 1818, he explained, Illinois had been populated mainly by immigrants from southern and western states. These had brought with them "the patriotic valor of the yeomanry of Kentucky, Tennessee, and Louisiana . . . where slavery was tolerated." On the surface Ames was saying that since slavery did not dampen patriotism in the Southwest, it would not do so in Illinois. He also had a covert message, however: local social solidarity ought to be extended to the veterans of the southwestern states who had recently emigrated but not to veteran neighbors who had lost the spirit to fight for the people's rights.[47]

New emigrants from the North were especially vulnerable to this attack. The point was not lost on Vandalia editor David Blackwell. He responded by arguing that "in the west, the war, was a *war of the people;* and in the northeast the war was against the sentiments of the people." Yet the response was ineffectual in Illinois where almost every family could count one member or extended kin a casualty to some frontier skirmish with the Indians. One thing that Blackwell and his generation did not need to be told was that spilling blood in an effort to obtain a piece of land endears the land to the survivors in a lasting way. Ames and others further developed and appealed to this sentiment for the land in their quest to define bottomland republicanism.[48]

Concerning those who had arrived in Illinois after 1818 and tended toward anti-slavery, Ames suggested that only those emigrants committed to social equality were worthy of solidarity. These could be determined by their appreciation for the fecundity of the land. The litmus test would segregate the desirable newcomers from the undesirable ones. Pursuing his idea, Ames listed the clearing of excess vegetation as one of the purposes of a new constitution. The unfortunate policy choices of the 1818 constitution had caused the "pestilential vapors" and the concomitant disease. "Our soil is uncommonly fertile," he wrote, "and its productions luxuriate in all the wildness and richness of nature. From a decomposition of this vegetable matter, at certain seasons of the year, arises almost all our diseases." Yet, instead of encouraging southern slaveholders who would bring money, and slaves to clear the land of its excess vegetation, Illinois pursued a quixotic policy of admitting only "small" farmers. It could not be denied that "no constitution except that of the negro can bear exposure to our summer," and that "negroes are seldom, if ever afflicted with the diseases of the country"; nor could anyone "name fifty whites in the state, whose business leads them to much exposure who have escaped disease." Only those who had a true appreciation of the land's fertility would understand this; only those committed to the white folks' social condition would care.[49]

Why should Ames and those who were attracted to the bottomland set out to attack an anti-slavery minority and a few northern newcomers who accounted for so small a proportion of the population? With respect to the newcomers, there were two underlying conditions familiar to all Illinois residents that politicized the northerners' arrival and their sectional affiliation. The first was the presence of a surprisingly large proportion of northern-born officeholders and leaders. Approximately 70 percent of the population was southern-born, whereas only 20 percent were northern-born. But this 3.5 to 1 ratio did not hold up in the legislature. In the Third General Assembly, it was lowered to 2 to 1. The prominence of northern-born men in leadership positions reached to the conventionist camp as well. As David Blackwell noted, "the leaders of the Slave party in this part of the state, Messrs. Kane, Smith, and West, are Yankees."[50]

The sudden rise of northerners might have passed unnoticed if it had not been framed in the minds of the locals with the memory of another, more oppressive experience with outsiders: the federal government's supervision of Illinois's "policy" with respect to slavery. Although the Illinoisans did their best to ignore federal prescriptions, Congress was empowered to act with great discretion in the dimly lit arena of territorial management. This de facto power was given de jure support by the federal constitution's use of the conditional tense; article 6, section 3, states that Congress "may" admit new states into the Union, not that it "shall" or "must." The framers also, in article 4, section 3, granted Congress full "power to dispose of and make all needful rules and regulations respecting the territor[ies]" of the United States before they became states.

Resentment of Congress was also based on the fact that, before Illinois could walk in the open sun of political autonomy and legal equality with the other states, it had first to pass through the dark labyrinth of congressional approval. Every future state faced this maneuver, but the position of Illinois was more precarious. It had become customary to require a territory to have at least 35,000 inhabitants, the number of citizens then apportioned to each U.S. representative, to qualify for admission. Some in Congress, like Representative John Randolph of Virginia, held out for 60,000 inhabitants, the number suggested (but not required) by the Ordinance of 1787.[51]

Illinois in 1818 did not contain 35,000 people. The first census taken for statehood tallied only 34,610.[52] A supplement was ordered on the argument that immigrants had been streaming into the territory all summer long. The constitutional convention had already convened when it had to stop to receive the results of the supplement! So much for the ideal, articulated by Stephen Douglas throughout the 1850s, of state conventions as open venues free of all influences but popular sovereignty. Holding its first session in early August 1818, the convention finished its work, elections were held, and the first legislature had been convened and adjourned, all before Congress met on November 16, 1818. The legislature had unfinished business, but the majority questioned their authority to pass laws.

The leaders of the convention were simply not sure the state would be accepted, even with the August census tally of 40,258 inhabitants. Uncertain about the numbers, the convention bent over backward to make the document as uncontroversial and acceptable to Congress as was palatable. The result was a constitutional potpourri less striking for its elements of "western democracy" than for its rushed construction. The framers wanted old French resident Pierre Menard to serve as lieutenant governor but limited the office to thirty-year U.S. citizens. When it was discovered that Menard had become a citizen only two years earlier, a final emendation changing the citizenship requirement to two years was added to the final "schedule" section of the document, "any thing in the thirteenth section of the third article of this constitution contained to the contrary notwithstanding."[53]

What is the connection to the northern men in the state? Consider that when the convention of 1818 gathered at Kaskaskia, its immediate political situation was one of obeisance, however much the advocates of statehood desired the independence assumed by Douglas. Although the general right of federal control over matters such as public lands and slavery in the new states was being strongly urged at the time by "certain leading newspapers in the Atlantic cities," that is, northern *and southern* cities in the East, the assertion of Congress's power to limit the extension of slavery was articulated by *northern* members. The battle over the Missouri Compromise only increased this perception. Moreover, since the North as a whole was associated with anti-slavery attitudes, this whole chapter of eastern meddling came to be thought of as distinctly northern meddling. Elias Kent Kane as "Timour" put local sentiment into words when he regretfully admitted that Illinois had, since 1818, "remained in a kind of torpid state, under the contaminating influence of what might justly be called a foreign or Northern policy." Experience reinforced rhetoric as men of northern birth sprouted into positions of prominence throughout the young state.[54]

It should not be surprising, then, that the resentment felt toward northern paternalism in 1818 reappeared four years later in the form of resentment toward northerner emigrants suspected of attempting to continue their region's influence. "The Yankees," David Blackwell wrote in the most accurate assessment of the conventionists' problem with northerners, "are accused of wishing to overturn the established institutions of this state and introduce their own." Settlers in the newly designated Military Bounty lands illustrated the problem of the northern stiff neck. Illinoisans welcomed to their new country those settlers who shared their reverence for the unprecedented opportunity it offered to acquire fertile land on western republican terms. But those who came with these aspirations contrasted sharply, in the minds of local observers, with those who arrived to claim their Military Bounties on a vast tract of Illinois land (situated between the Mississippi and Illinois Rivers) offered by the federal government to entice northeastern volunteers during the War of 1812.[55]

The Military Bounty lands were not intended by the federal government to upset the sectional makeup of any state. But, in 1816, there occurred one of those accidents which repeatedly forced early Illinoisans to confront, in editor Blackwell's terms, the problem of "sectional jealousies." The U.S. government had deliberately chosen three *regionally* located tracts, in which the War of 1812 veterans might patent land in return for military service. There was a northern tract in Michigan Territory, a southern tract in Louisiana Territory, and a central tract in Illinois Territory. In the process of surveying the land and marking out townships, however, it was discovered that the Michigan tract, of easiest access to the northerners, was, on the report of a deputy surveyor, "either useless swamps, or poor and barren." Learning of this, and on the advice of the Surveyor General, President Madison decided to abandon the Michigan tract and to increase the Illinois plot by almost half. Those who came to settle their grants in Illinois—estimated in one county to be only about 10 percent of those receiving patents—by this turn of events came from the North in disproportionate numbers. Many, like Leonard Ross and John Tillson, traveled ahead of their families; in the years between 1818 and 1821 others like them swelled the adult male population in the towns of Edwardsville, Belleville, and Greenville, all just below the tract.[56]

How did the newcomers find the "Illinois Country," a district thought to be "the very throne of the vegetable kingdom of the United States"? To suggest that this wondrous land was somehow inadequate or that the traditional ways of farming it ought to change would be an insult to local pride, though not that alone. It displayed a complete ig-

norance of the significance of the bottomland as a path to independence for the white folks. Yet this is exactly what certain newcomers—
many Bounty land speculators, all outsiders from the East impatient
with local ways—did unwittingly suggest. A disproportionate number
of these newcomers viewed their new landholdings as a capital investment. They often had the means to ship lumber to the prairies and
their crops to distant rivers. They talked endlessly and glowingly about
the potential beneath the prairies; they did not flinch at the large sums
needed to transform the prairies into farms. This was undoubtedly the
case when German visitor Ferdinand Ernst wrote to his countrymen
with high praise for Illinois's fertile prairies but made no mention of its
bottomland. It was this new commercial sentiment that Ames targeted
in his articles.[57]

It is true that far from all the newcomers were northerners, but, in all,
a larger number of Yankees and "Yorkers" arrived at this time than previously.[58] The salient fact about the Bounty newcomers for the current residents was that they were getting their land after it had been wrenched
from the Native Americans, after roads had been blazed, after in many
cases improvements had been made; after, in short, the locals had done
the hardest part of securing it. When it was discovered that these newcomers, who had gotten their land on the cheap so to speak, were not
overly appreciative of this fact and that they brought with them practices and attitudes which threatened to overwhelm the locals, many followed Ames's lead and treated them with suspicion. When it was found
that this new group was anxious to make an impression on the government and future policy of the state, convention leaders began circling
the wagons. No more efficient means could have been found to harden
their love for the bottomland ethos. The result was a stiffening of positions and an exaggeration of differences that kept the convention controversy bubbling for months.

AMATEUR PROFESSORS OF AGRICULTURE

The brief life and times of the State Agricultural Society indicates how
poisonous the sectional rivalry could be. Lasting only from 1818 to
1826, the life of this organization was bitter and short. Originating, according to visiting Englishman William Faux, in the practical desire "to
rid the state of stagnant waters," it soon began advocating a radical
transformation in local farming methods. To most corn and hog farmers, the society in its brief existence never amounted to more than a collection of "amateur professors of agriculture." The members thought
otherwise. They imagined themselves involved in a deadly serious crusade, "to repair the errors of former days; to abolish injurious practices;
and to recover the fertility of soils exhausted by a ruinous succession of
crops." They further recoiled from the overall local system of farming,

"that system, which if it replenishes the purse at first, and gives a temporary show of prosperity, impoverishes the land, and leaves a barren inheritance for our children." Above all, there came from the organization a steady stream of suggested crops, which could be used in manufacturing and could be turned into durable, value-added export products. Premiums were offered in 1824 to the manufacturers of "best suit of homespun clothes," "the best sample of wine," "the greatest number of gallons of cold pressed Castor Oil," and "the best piece of cloth, manufactured in this state, either of wool, cotton, cotton and wool, hemp, flax, cotton and flax, or wool and flax."[59]

From the start the Agricultural Society was dedicated to a program mixed of equal parts reproach and inducement to change. Its first president was Morris Birkbeck. Both he and Edward Coles were great advocates of farming prairie land. Although they had little actual experience in the field, they regularly repudiated the bottomland farming clearly favored by earlier residents. Not surprisingly, the Englishman's theories, when published with the Agricultural Society's minutes, were received with the contempt that experience holds for abstract conjecture. Observers at first ignored his exhortation to dig "clay suitable for pottery" or "iron ore" for sod-busting plows. But silence turned into a derisive chorus when it was learned that the English Settlement at Wanborough, Edwards County, was faltering. At least one observer recorded the outsider's comeuppance: "Mr. Birkbeck felt sure of constructing a[n iron] plough . . . and ploughing up the tough prairie turf, with a very small horse power, but he broke his plough at the beginning, and instead of 100 acres of corn, had half an acre of potatoes!" Birkbeck proposed several solutions to the problem of fencing-in prairie land; he worked assiduously at them during his first year on the ground. But his efforts in this area were equally unappreciated. The otherwise sympathetic Thomas Hulme wrote: "I have heard it observed that *any* American settler, even without a dollar in his pocket, would have *had something growing by this time.*" Disappointed by the reception, Birkbeck resigned from the presidency in 1822 after his fourth consecutive term.[60]

In 1823, Marine Settlement (Madison County) Captain Curtiss Blakeman became president, and soon after, Edward Coles and George Churchill surfaced in prominent positions. Leonard Ross, a native of Massachusetts, and Gershom Flagg, who settled at "Yankee All-town" (Alton), became enthusiastic supporters. None of these men had resided in the state before 1817. Yet, in 1821, Coles wrote with great zeal to the society's secretary to voice his "mortification and chagrin" at local farming practices and to inform the society of an "experiment" in prairie farming he had recently conducted. In 1823, Blakeman published the results of Coles's experiment with "less than 10 acres . . . [of] newly turned up prairie," which produced "the prodigious quantity of 1350 bushels of shelled corn." Under their leadership the Agricultural Society never saw its seventh year of life.[61]

The economic hard times that swept the country after the western Panic of 1819 only confirmed to the newcomers the righteousness of their cause. "Jonathan Freeman" (Morris Birkbeck) proclaimed: "No country ever acquired lasting wealth and prosperity by exporting raw produce." The depression, he continued, "will be a fortunate event which we are now deploring as a calamity, should it put us in the way of working up our own produce." Such commercial sentiments hardened the beliefs of the locals. Timour, for example, construed the prolonged scarcity of specie as an opportunity for community leaders to re-dedicate themselves to the territorial order he claimed had been abandoned by the compromised constitution of 1818. "I am persuaded," he wrote, "that the policy hitherto pursued by this state has been destructive of its prosperity—that it has, not withstanding our invaluable soil, and manifold resources, been productive of the most serious and alarming injury." It was imperative that the new emigrant "adopt a policy compatible with a citizen of a young state—a citizen of the west. . . . The fact that our state is the most valuable of any in point of soil and yet derives but little advantage from emigration, should speak volumes to those in whose hands its destiny is at present placed."[62]

Ames, Timour, and Brissot had hit upon a way to speak to a select group of Illinoisans, the poor whites, in language that appeared to speak to all. This was through the common subsistence approach to farming that characterized the backcountry's shared past. Birkbeck, who had founded his own town and was labeled a "Federalist," would miss its significance. It would also be lost on his companion George Flower, who originally hoped to settle in Virginia where there was "just enough of aristocracy left, to let an old country man down easy among republicans." The commercial farming biases of Federalists and upper-class moral reformers have been noted by scholars. Such class differences were not missed by the status-conscious Illinoisans. The anti-aristocracy summation of one "John Rifle" voiced the fears of many: "If they expect to introduce Nobility, Taxes, and white Slavery among us, they will be mistaken—they tried that before the revolution, and much they got by it!"[63]

A social experience combining a settlement life with its norms of mutuality and an opening economic system stressing a new competitiveness is not easily captured in a simple phrase. Ames and the conventionists used regional biases to cover whatever contradictions they uncovered. For the rest, they relied on the weather and the land, for farming technique was more influenced by climate and soil conditions than ideas, whether homemade or imported. In his analysis of early "Corn Belt" farming, Allan G. Bogue found little evidence to suggest that "members of ethnocultural groups farmed in ways that were significantly different from the practices followed by others with different backgrounds in the same neighborhoods." This was true even in the face of stubborn adherence to old ways. Governor Coles ironically showed his own stubbornness when he accused the early settlers in 1821 of improperly adjusting to Illinois conditions. "A great portion of our citizens," he argued, "have been accustomed to make their farms, by felling and clearing off the timber." They have, "from long habit, become so familiar to this kind of labor," that when they encounter the mixture of timber and prairie in Illinois "they seem to be loath to avail themselves of the advantages of their situation." Instead "from the force of habit, in many cases," they prefer "the laborious task of clearing lands, and cultivating crops in the midst of stumps and roots, to cultivating [prairie] lands already cleared, in which there is nothing to obstruct or impede the plough."[64]

Yet, one agricultural historian has concluded that in Wisconsin in the 1830s and 1840s, where the "Yankee and German settlers" were the first to arrive, they "cleared land in the woods for crops and used the adjacent prairie only for hay and pasture." The reason was that in both Illinois and Wisconsin short-term survival and long-term prosperity for those without means depended on the water, wood, game, and the quick start to harvest offered by forested bottomland. Such considerations were not necessary for Coles, who by 1820 owned 6,000 acres, much of it in the Military Bounty tract. For the average settler, the optimal site contained a high ridge to protect the cabin from winds and fire; timber nearby to supply wood for buildings and heat and mast for the pigs; a stream for water, fish, and transportation; and from 10 to 15 acres of land, hopefully flood-free bottom, on which the trees could be girdled and partially cleared during the winter for a crop to be sown the next spring.[65]

Those who had not achieved the optimum were likely supporters of the convention movement. Some poor settlers, "fixed . . . on the edge of a creek, or in a stinking flat," believed that "the slaveholders, if they were allowed to come, would give them two to three dollars an acre" for their bottomland because their slaves would be able to clear the land. Then the settler without slaves might "buy land in healthier situations." This might make buying it easier for some, but it also clearly encouraged speculation and overall instability in the land market. Very few had the capital to purchase a slave. But even if this had been plausible, what effect would an increase in slaves and slaveholders have on the status of the white folks? "A Mechanic" felt that "by the introduction of slaves, labor will become a badge of servility—a token of disgrace." Would the state have to tax citizens to pay for the emancipations proposed in ten years' time? What about the state bank? Was it in the citizens' interests to have the legislature, in effect, run the bank? And the tariff? What impact would a national tariff have on a far western state like Illinois? Here the most widespread view was probably not unlike that of the Indiana farmer who said of tariffs "that he had never seen one but he believed it was hard on sheep." Simply to ask these questions indicates the scope of

the social dilemma facing the Illinois egalitarian. In spite of all these un-
certainties, and precisely because of them, the conventionists were
never in doubt about their political strategy. They forged a position
aimed at winning the support of the majority of the white folks. The genius of the bottomland republican vision was that its promise of plenty
in a subsistence pattern appealed to the majority while it avoided the
uncertain and unsolvable questions.[66]

The pioneers of Illinois, not unlike farmers similarly situated elsewhere, adapted themselves to the land, working together when work
could be done without fatigue or the threat of disease or when the land
was pliable. Throughout the raw western lands at a time when concentrated capital was almost nonexistent, whether one came from Vermont
or Georgia, the pace of the seasons all but dictated economic behavior.
Speculation on land was also cyclical. When money was flowing, many
Illinoisans quickly adapted, adding a season for "prospecting" to their
cyclical patterns. It was a game for the shrewd and they came to it with
all the energy and competitiveness of a corn-shucking competition.
When the game ended suddenly with the depression, the taste for it lin-
gered. Many were restless and ready to exercise their wits in the only
other high stakes game in the state, the game of politics. It was this
game that drove the factional competition in the legislature. The convention faction decided early on that the game's purpose was to revivify
the state's economy. The conventionists gambled on the bottomland republic, on making Illinois a slave state if need be, in order to preserve
their equality and extend it to their neighbors. In the republican game,
the people ruled.

CHAPTER THREE

NINIAN EDWARDS
IN THE DEMOCRATIC
REVOLUTION

Making common cause with the white folks enabled the new generation of leaders to seize the initiative for political change. But some had grown accustomed to the territorial system. Government in the Illinois Territory had by 1818 developed into an elaborate set of patron-client networks. Federal appointees ruled pluralistically by distributing positions and honors to recognized leaders in the state's settlements and towns. The charms of pluralism, along with the rise of the market, conspired to complicate the majority rule promised by the democratic revolution. Individuals competed in land deals, farming contests, and town trade. Towns battled for designation as county seat, settlements vied for drainage projects, newspapers campaigned for roads and mail routes. The simple image of the people grew less and less plausible as the symbolic need for majority authority grew more and more urgent. The class interest of the white folks was losing coherency just as the new generation of leaders began to use it.

Denigrating the big folks did enhance the white folks' status but, used alone, turned politics into a blunt instrument. Once an issue moved away from the question of means to the question of ends, new cleavages divided the people, as the convention issue demonstrates. What began as a struggle for recognition and legitimacy led inexorably to a debate over slavery and religion. The moment non-conventionists granted the argument about local control, the conventionists lost their advantage. As a March 2, 1824, editorial in the *Republican Advocate* conceded: "there can be no doubt that a very considerable majority of our citizens are in favor of a convention; but [very few favor] . . . the unqualified admission of negro slavery."

Nevertheless, one can hardly overestimate the role of anti–big folks sentiment in reorganizing early Illinois politics. It has sometimes been forgotten, just as a foundation is forgotten once it is built upon, because the rapid development following it forced it into the background. One person, Ninian Edwards, was never allowed to forget it, however. "Father of Illinois" and archetypal big folk, Edwards encountered difficulties in leading a popular party in the state that are inexplicable without reference to the class biases he labored against. But Edwards is the slipperiest of subjects because, although it is true he was quite wealthy, it was not his economic status itself that made for tough going in Illinois. It was rather his disdain for the democratic revolution that had taken place in the people's minds.

Edwards subscribed to the moderate Madisonian version of republicanism: government for the people, but not by or of them. Power, to be legitimate, was not to be held by "one, a few, or many," but in constitutional structures sponsored by popular sovereignty. The failure of the "Edwards party" to unite on candidates and issues was the failure of a group of Madisonian republicans to adjust to "a plebiscitarian view of democracy" in which popular sovereignty authorized the majority to rule.[1] By 1823 the party's patron-client system lay in ruins, a casualty of the state's new conceptual universe.

WE ARE ALL POLITICIANS, WE ARE ALL CANDIDATES

It is a "commonplace in the study of political development," observes Amy Bridges, that community in complex societies does not come naturally; it is instead "a product of politics." But it is often unclear which community values and practices are newly manufactured and which are inherited. Community in Illinois drew on both sources. Its politics was molded in the folkways of the national backcountry tradition and fired in the kiln of state politics. Backcountry politics was an egalitarian offshoot of the politics formed before and during the Revolutionary War. The republicanism of the revolution was the one national political tradition that the white folks embraced. They not only routinely referred to themselves as republicans; many loudly claimed to have the purest strain of republicanism in the country. As Ames put it, "the principles which avowedly govern the Conventionists as a *party,* are of the purest and most republican kind." Furthermore, national republicanism figured prominently in the conduct of Indian affairs and the disposition of public lands, policies that affected daily life in the new West.[2]

In the game of national party politics, Illinoisans were eager to play the role of "pure" republicans. By 1826, when Ninian Edwards was a former U.S. senator and a candidate for the governor's office, his surprising strength throughout the southernmost counties of the state was believed to have been caused by the voters' support for his side in the battle against the "caucus" candidate for president, William H. Crawford. "They believe that a great injustice has been done to you by Mr. Adams in offering to reappoint Crawford," a local resident wrote to Edwards, "and they are determined that you shall be their Candidate let what may happen." The voters assessed Edwards against the resentment they held for Washington insiders—"caucus" republicans—who exerted control over the Republican Party.[3]

Illinoisans were "the *first* republicans of the nation," according to newspaper writer "Rattlebrain," who believed that western republicanism increased equality precisely because it avoided the mass society of the eastern city. "In the midst of a dense population he who is of the common mass, whatever may be his worth, is of no more account than a drone in a bee hive—he is just as undistinguished as an ordinary stock of grass in the midst of a large meadow: he falls indiscriminately with his fellows, and it is scarcely known that he ever existed." Equality also magnified the importance of the average citizen: "Here there is everything to keep away *ennui*—we are all politicians, we are all candidates—and the policy of the nation is the peculiar study of every wight, whether of the plebeian or patrician order." John Woods, an early emigrant to the English Settlement in Edwards County, confirmed Rattlebrain's thesis. Woods found Illinoisans to be "a most determined set of republicans, well versed in politics, and thoroughly independent. A man who has only half a shirt, and without shoes and stockings, is as independent as the first man in the States."[4]

Other local aspects of Illinois republicanism were created on the run. The mob scenes at Vandalia were its rites of passage, public displays of its new meaning. Their leaders chose a mixture of old and new forms to express themselves: they marched in a charivari—an old French custom at once a symbol of old "laws and customs" and of the white folks' taste for rough republicanism. At the same time, however, Saturday county meetings, ferocious newspaper wars, and Fourth of July festivities carried on backcountry traditions first initiated back East. In the cathartic excitement and madness of forging a new identity, the people of Illinois ritually freed themselves from the bonds of territorial tutelage.[5]

The Illinois republican community thus consisted of a unique combination of local and national patterns. As a logical matter, there are three potential sources of community in emigrant societies: the society left behind, the experience of migration, and conditions in the new society. In Illinois, the challenge facing politicians was to supply a migratory people with a meaningful political culture built to the larger society's perimeters but fitting the new society's specifications. Social theorist Thomas Bender argues that early nineteenth-century politicians throughout the United States confronted this "task of cultural leadership." The maneuver required uniting what might be called the liberal constitutionalist ideals and institutions of the eastern elite with the egalitarian aspirations and practices of the dissenting republicanism that spread rapidly wherever the backcountry moved. In his survey of communities in the early republic, Bender detected "a marked dissonance between local *social patterns* and translocal *ideology*." He discovered, in effect, the dissonance between the white folks' and the big folks' cultures. "One was a localistic oral culture based upon intimate, face-to-face relations, while the other was abstract, general, and based on the written word. One pattern of solidarity was popular, the other was based on a formal tradition in the custody of the elite."[6]

The cultural task of Illinois politicians, as Bender might argue, was to integrate the egalitarian practices on the ground in the state with the translocal principles and institutions inherited along with the Ordinance of 1787 and the Constitution of 1818. Here the largest barrier was conceptual. "The people" imagined by translocals like Ninian Edwards were virtuous precisely because they were passive; they wished only to be let alone or to have the public interest rule. In actual practice and self-conception, however, the people of the American backcountry were active and interested. They were committed to carrying on the revolutionary ideal of independence, which they interpreted as self-government by the people.[7]

The Illinoisans were determined to assert their conception of the people and the political culture it implied. Part of their determination was motivated by their migratory status. Migratory societies fiercely defend their cultures wherever they go. But a more important social imperative was also involved. The white folks also defended their culture in order to distinguish themselves both from the gentry above them on the ladder of social standing and from the slaves below them. In Illinois, they set about the task of building an entire culture out of one social class. Their task was analogous to the American colonists who, drawn mainly from the middle and working classes of Europe, left the cultures of the aristocracy and the peasantry behind. Whereas in some ways this simplified things, in others, as Louis Hartz demonstrated for the colonists, it produced complications. Although aristocrats and agrarians in their classic European forms were not prevalent in America, the colonists, having learned their politics by opposing these groups above and below them in Europe, re-created them in a "phantom world" of rhetoric in America. Just as the rhetoric of "monarchists" and "mobs" does not quite fit American politics in its first half century, so too the white folks' rhetoric of opposition to big folks, on one hand, and disdain for black folks, on the other, often strikes the reader as overwrought. Surely such rhetoric was an overreaction if simple numbers are any guide: using slave ownership as a surrogate for big folk status, the numbers amounted to only 333 in the 1820 census; the numbers of slaves, servants, and "free people of color" came to only 1,367 out of a total population of 51,160. Nevertheless, by these exercises in rhetorical opposition, republican political culture in Illinois was manufactured.[8]

In their redefining of republicanism, the conventionists saw an opportunity for members of the young generation coming of age in Illinois to make their contribution to the nation. The conventionists took the lead by shaping an ideology legitimated by the revolution in their own image. All the evidence suggests that the Illinois people validated this part of the conventionists' effort. After the convention legislature adjourned sine die, a spate of newspaper articles immediately appeared defending the right of the people to change the government through a constitutional convention. Colonel Cox opened the controversy in Vandalia by attacking the 1818 constitution for its "aristocratic features." Newspapers from around the country responded with incredulity. They found it preposterous for the conventionists to attack aristocracy when one of their avowed goals was to establish slavery in the state. But the conventionists in the counties were keen to follow the lead of the legislative faction.[9]

No group whose goal was the exclusive promotion of the social equality of poor whites had controlled a state government before, North or South. The precocious Illinoisans benefited from their state's unique regional mixture and its largely monolithic class structure. Their reconstruction of republicanism was the first to be effected by leaders who hoped to forge the ruling ideology of a state from the class interests of the white folks. Although the state bank and convention movement both ultimately failed, they succeeded in laying down a rhetorical precedent, which Illinois set for the nation as a whole. A majority in a state legislature could reject the federal government's attempt to dictate a state's fundamental social choices from the outside. This precedent in favor of "popular sovereignty" in Stephen Douglas's sense, the only precedent to be recognized by the rest of the Union, would within a generation reappear at the national level with all the contradictions it held in Illinois.

The Illinois pattern can in no simple way be said to have caused the later national pattern, but it prefigured it faithfully. The dilemmas that the white folks were attempting to resolve with their republicanism were endemic to the nation. Indeed, the dilemmas had surfaced in the debates of the previous generation between the Federalists and the Anti-Federalists. The necessary first step facing the state's young leaders in their attempt to connect Illinois to translocal currents was the recovery of the Anti-Federalist definition of republicanism. This definition, born of the same rhetorical division between great and common men, consisted of at least five related points covering instability in republics, representation, the public interest, legitimate authority, and public opinion.

LIBERAL CONSTITUTIONALISTS AND DISSENTING REPUBLICANS

Americans generally agreed that republics formed inherently unstable governments. Federalists such as Alexander Hamilton, however, believed that the problems of republican instability had been greatly diminished by "principles . . . now well understood, which were either not known at all, or imperfectly known to the ancients." The science of politics,

Hamilton continued, "like most other sciences, ha[d] received great improvement." The improving principles included: "The regular distribution of power into distinct departments; the introduction of legislative balances and checks; the institution of courts composed of judges holding their offices during good behavior; [and] the representation of the people in the legislature by deputies of their own election." In such institutional mechanisms, Hamilton and John Adams rested what faith they had in a solution to the republican problem of faction.[10]

By contrast, Melancton Smith, Hamilton's principle Anti-Federalist opponent in the New York debate over the Constitution, believed that the most effectual checks on government were not institutional but social in nature. He thought the most important check was the tenacious spirit of a people determined not to let government "fall into the hands of the few and great." Thus, his ideal representative was "a substantial yeoman of sense and discernment." Such yeomen brought an important social bias in favor of "the poor and middling class" into the government. "The knowledge necessary for the representatives of a free people," Smith argued, "not only comprehends extensive political and commercial information, such as is acquired by men of refined education, who have leisure to attain to high degrees of improvement." It also includes "that kind of acquaintance with the common concerns and occupations of the people, which men of the middling class of life are in general much better competent to, than those of a superior class." Besides this bias in favor of the poor and middle classes, the yeoman representative, by crowding out some of the "natural aristocrats," helped the government avoid the corruption that came with political ambition, since "that ambition was more particularly the passion of the rich and great."[11]

Smith proudly called himself a "republican," but he had a much more egalitarian notion of republicanism than Hamilton's. Indeed in *Federalist,* No. 8, Hamilton laid out a geopolitical vision for the future of the United States that confirmed every Anti-Federalist fear. Hamilton's republic was to be a commercial "empire" reaching as far into the world as the empire created by the islands of Great Britain. "If we are wise enough to preserve the Union," Hamilton wrote, "we may for ages enjoy an advantage similar to that insulated situation." This is what he had in mind when he referred, in the opening paragraph of *Federalist,* No. 1, to "the fate of an empire in many respects the most interesting in the world." In such a far-flung society, educated and refined leadership would be essential.[12]

Smith had a different view of the ideal representative because he had a different view of the ideal republican society. When Smith talked about representatives who "resemble those they represent" and form "a true picture of the people," he had a definite social type—the yeoman farmer—in mind. Like the Illinoisans, Smith's "people" were not all the people, but a particular subset of the middle and lower classes. Yet his yeomen were not anti-capitalist traditionalists. Indeed, he explicitly countered Hamilton's macroeconomic vision, with a bottom-up, localist version of commerce: "To understand the true commercial interests of a country, not only requires just ideas of the general commerce of the world, but also, and principally, a knowledge of the productions of your country and their value, what your soil is capable of producing[,] the nature of your manufactures, and the capacity of the country to increase both." Smith, too, was a capitalist. The great difference with Hamilton arose from his explicit bias in favor of "the common people."[13]

Furthermore, where Hamilton thought that commercial prosperity and effective administration would create "confidence in and obedience to a government," Smith feared that too much luxury would undermine the republican spirit. Indeed, he feared the people's virtue had already been greatly undermined by the Federalist bargain premised on a growing economy. In 1788 he put it this way: "A recollection of the change that has taken place in the minds of many in this country in the course of a few years, ought to put us upon our guard. Many who are ardent advocates for the new system, reprobate republican principles as chimerical and such as ought to be expelled from society." Indeed, "Who would have thought ten years ago," he added darkly, "that the very men who risqued their lives and fortunes in support of republican principles, would now treat them as fictions of fancy?"[14]

Here Smith expresses in classic form the siege mentality that characterizes the egalitarian variety of the republican discourse. The "spirit" of equality was under attack. Since "the great consider themselves above the common people, . . . it has been the principle care of free governments to guard against the encroachments of the great." Because the "ambitions" of the wealthy are ever-present, the power of this class continues to grow unless beaten back. Failure to do this leads to the corruption of the people; they become less attached to their own self-government. The class bias generated by "great men" is always on the verge of corrupting society. For this reason, the Anti-Federalists took their stand as dissenters, and their republicanism was a dissenting doctrine.[15]

The hierarchical-egalitarian cleavage within republicanism also figured in competing concepts of the public interest. During the revolution, bottom-up "artisan republicanism" defined the public good in terms of the good of the majority—the lower and middle or producer classes. Melancton Smith continued this thought by arguing that members of the middle class made the best representatives because, "when the interests of this part of the community are pursued, the public good is pursued." Being a virtuous republican for Smith's yeomen thus actually required that they pursue their own interests. This view of how republican representatives attained the public good contrasted sharply with the hierarchical view implied in the Federalist approach. Typical of all eighteenth-century liberals, they conceived the public as a sphere that stood outside and above private concerns. The public good, in other words, required the sacrifice of personal interest, including class interest. Such sacrifice was rare according to the Federalists; for just this reason, government had to be constructed so as to synthesize the public interest artificially. This synthesis took place not among the people but in the legislature. After voting in an election, the people were passive, their "instructions" at an end. It is precisely this quality of passiveness that distinguishes Federalist "popular sovereignty" from the Jeffersonian "people." In the Jeffersonian view, democracy needs instructive representation and the central state is weak, whereas popular sovereignty is consistent with virtual representation and a strong central government. The distance between the government and the people under the Federalist view opens the door for all the schemes and techniques whereby power is managed via decision rules and institutions under liberal constitutionalism.[16]

The Federalists had the luxury of presenting their thinking as abstract deductions, unattached to any social "interest." They were philosophers who produced ahistorical reflections; their deductions were put in practice by disinterested statesmen. The disinterested quality of Federalist thought is also imparted by its focus on the "big picture." By appearing not to take sides in the struggles for power *within* the people (that is, between classes), the Federalists acquired the appearance of impartiality. They focused instead on the larger justificatory principles that sovereigns, whether popular or not, had to face.

Although the purely Federalist view was never voiced in Illinois, the moderate wing among the Jeffersonians, which was present, often did a good job of approximating it. The moderate pose was taken up by big folks such as Ninian Edwards, Jessie B. Thomas, and Edward Coles—the last two eventually becoming Whigs, while Edwards became a Calhoun-oriented Jacksonian. The difference between Calhoun and Jackson neatly parallels the difference between Edwards and the Illinois white folks. Calhoun's *Disquisition on Government* reads as a set of logical deductions from Madison's doubts about majorities; against this Andrew Jackson maintained: "Never for a moment believe that the great body of the citizens of any state or states can deliberately intend to do wrong."[17]

The Federalists often doubted the people. Their version of leadership was directed by the "public good," which could take precedence over the good of the majority. For them, the majority meant the short-term political interests of the people, and the public good meant the reasonable suppositions of the learned about the long-term interests of the people. They surveyed the state legislative battles of the 1780s and uprisings such as Shays's Rebellion and concluded that rule by the lower classes could be as tyrannous as rule by kings. Although this position could simply mask class interests, it had its romantic element as well.

The virtue of opposing tyranny could potentially swallow selfish motives, as it did for Hamilton himself, who called himself a *"public fool"* for never having profited from public office.[18]

The Federalists might have said to the Illinoisans, as they said to the Anti-Federalists: "your class is but a part of the whole people, your drama is a temporary drama." Of course, as Madison conceded, all attempts to obtain the disinterestedness necessary for justice by creating an "external will . . . independent of the majority—that is, society itself" had failed. His statist alternative was at best a middle ground. In response, the white folks might have noted that impartiality was a luxury afforded only to those whose story of oppression had already run its course. Such folk could abstract themselves from the story of the people because their social standing was secure. They could see "the people" in real time and not in the sacred time of the white folks' narrative, but only because their inherited wealth allowed such a perspective. This was in effect how the early Illinoisans reacted to Ninian Edwards. Edwards's disinterestedness, even when void of ulterior motives, increased the state's—not the people's—authority. Thus, if the Madisonian case against direct democracy could not simply be reduced to a rationalization of class interest, it was at least vulnerable to the charge of statism.[19]

Constitutions had been invented, in the Federalist view, in order to provide social balance between classes, to prevent any one class from monopolizing the power of the state. "The great desideratum in Government," Madison wrote Jefferson, "is so to modify the sovereignty as that it may be sufficiently neutral between different parts of Society to controul one part from invading the rights of another."[20] But with only one predominant class in Illinois, this idea was a decidedly minority view. It was not thought that one could promote two or more opposed class interests through government and still be a republican. Of course, national Federalists who held this belief, such as John Adams, insisted they were good republicans. But for Adams republicanism was a commitment to the Constitution above any one class interest in society. The Constitution, not the people, ruled Adams's ideal republic; thus he conceived of the Senate in terms of the word's literal meaning: as a place where elder statesmen might find the leverage to check the impetuous majority.

This view of constitutions rests on the assumption that public opinion is hard to determine. Today anyone who wants to learn the people's preferences simply hires a polling firm. But as Garry Wills points out, the process was far from so straightforward in the late eighteenth and early nineteenth centuries. Popular elections were just beginning to have an effect on the collective consciousness. Political theorists employed the vague term "taste" rather than the precise language of preferences. Jefferson, for example, while calculating his agrarian ideal for America, conceded that the people had shown a "decided taste" for navigation and commerce. Tocqueville argued that "the people's tastes" would forever remain vague, because "the greater or less ease with which people can live without working sets inevitable limits to their intellectual progress." The realities of making a living placed a limit on public opinion. "That limit is further off in some countries and closer in others," he conceded, "but for it not to exist at all, the people would have to have no more trouble with the material cares of life and so would no longer be 'the people.'"[21]

The Federalist notion of public opinion was even more static. This was the idea that the people's values had evolved over time. It focused on the historical struggles against kings and nobles on the European continent and the British Isles between 1160 and 1689. In the story of "the Anglo-Saxon People" as William Blackstone told it, in the rebellions and revolutions of these years, the people's "positive constitutions" were developed. These constitutions contained cultural preferences that modified the natural law of property in favor of certainty in land tenures. The sure, and therefore coveted, "copyhold" and "socage" tenures of the yeomanry were the two most famous cases in point.[22]

Blackstone's positive constitutions were, in effect, constitution-level social preferences expressed opaquely by the people and developed by the positive law systems of particular societies. As the first "arbitrary" elements grafted onto the universal natural law, positive constitutions were the jurisprudential equivalent of popular opinion. American lawyers in particular learned from Blackstone that "the law of England (which is a law of liberty)" greatly favored the Saxon yeomanry who groaned under the Norman yoke. The common law "hath always shewn to this species of tenants . . . [a] favorable disposition . . . by removing, as far as possible, every badge of slavery from them . . . by declaring, that the will of the lord was to be interpreted by the custom of the manor." Anglo-American law was thus a customary law, and its customs, based on the yeomanry's preferences for liberty, conveyed the people's will in their very interstices. This "Whig history" was popular enough to find expression, if at times an irreverent one, among political radicals such as Paine.[23]

The politicalized story of Saxon freedom and Norman slavery, the moral of the common law story as told by Blackstone, was itself based on earlier ideas of the goodly but immobile people. For many centuries beginning with the Middle Ages, the idea of the virtuous people had hovered in the background of political thought. But in this tradition, in order for the people to be virtuous, they had to be passive. As Wills argues, once the Enlightenment idea began to spread, that "Virtue was no longer given from above, a grace of God . . . [but that it] was induced, here below," there developed a problem. Passivity ensured purity of motive and hence virtue, but no active, power-laden source of virtue was believable or extant. Natural law theorists from Grotius to Locke solved the problem by borrowing a pastoral landscape from the ancient poets in order to create an otherworldly image of the people in action. They posited a more or less static state of natural bucolic plenty where greed was originally unknown. Here in the people's first appearance as actors on the stage of modern history, they were scripted as beyond the pull of power. The Roman historian Livy, who pioneered many classical republican themes, labored under similar constraints; in the story of the rape of Lucretia, her ultimate act of selflessness was necessary in order to unleash the miraculous transformation of Brutus from Roman dullard to republican freedman.[24]

This tradition continued to influence the Americans. Whenever republican government was seen as a result of the active efforts of the common people (as it must in Illinois), there was a tendency to supply extraordinary or otherworldly motives to their actions. For Puritan thinkers, only those who had accepted God and rejected the self were capable of entering the social contract constituting secular government. Early nineteenth-century American writers also followed the genre. William Wirt (an orphan adopted by the father of Ninian Edwards and Ninian's lifelong friend) represents the trend with *Sketches of the Life and Character of Patrick Henry,* his popular biography of the Virginian published in 1817. Wirt's effort harked back to the oldest version of the story, Livy's. Wirt's Henry is portrayed as one of the common folk, who is miraculously transformed from a clown into a genius during the course of his first speech in support of the people. Here was a Federalized version of a backcountry rebel. Wirt "solved" the contradiction between virtue and rebelliousness by assuming a lack of self-consciousness on Henry's part.[25]

The tradition of the passive people also strongly affected Jefferson, whom Tocqueville nevertheless called "the most powerful apostle of democracy there has ever been." Confronted with the absence of a peasantry, Jefferson invented a New World pastoralism and located the source of the people's virtue in the soil. Scholars often quote his remarks on "those who labor in the earth" from his *Notes on the State of Virginia,* but they as frequently gloss over the peculiar geological metaphor he used at the same time. The full quotation is as follows: "Those who labor in the earth are the chosen people of God, if ever he had a chosen people, whose breasts he has made his peculiar deposit for the substantial and genuine virtue. It is the focus in which he keeps alive that sacred fire, which otherwise might escape from the face of the earth." Although the rise of commercial society had long forced those who developed this discourse to modify the poet's image of the staid farmer, Jefferson locates Virginian virtue in a "peculiar deposit" of the human terrain as if he were observing a Mesozoic layer of rock.[26]

Already by the 1780s, the idea that democratic politics involved the active pursuit of interest was common enough to make a strictly disinterested devotion to the public good difficult to maintain for leaders such as George Washington. "Few decisions in Washington's career called for such handwringing," reports Gordon Wood, as his decision to accept the state of Virginia's gift of 150 shares of stock in a canal company. The adjustment of republican ideology to commercial society put great stress on the classical republican concept of disinterestedness and the citizenry's concept of independence. As Drew McCoy argues, by the 1790s republicanism "was an ideology in flux, caught precariously between traditional concerns anchored in classical antiquity and the new and unstable conditions of an expansive commercial society."[27]

Nonetheless, as many have demonstrated, the ancient ideal of civic virtue did not die so much as adjust. In Illinois, it was adjusted in two distinct directions, a liberal constitutionalist direction attractive to the elite and a dissenting republican direction popular among the middle and lower classes. The crucial move of the dissenters lay in sublimating all interested behavior into the class interests of the middle and lower classes. Self-interested promotion among politicians or merchants was consistent with virtue as long as the interests of the "artisans" and the "yeomanry," the producers in society, were also promoted. From this idea it was not a long step to the Jeffersonian Republicans' acceptance of representation based on "instruction" from the people. Political virtue was thereby tied directly not to a "ghostly body politic" but to the particular interests of a particular people. "The people" were no longer an inert, passive mass. They had specific social and class interests that it was the purpose of republican government to pursue.

Federalists, by contrast, did not assume that any one class should be favored; avoiding any class bias was what it meant to be disinterested. In this view, self-interest could be sublimated successfully only into the pursuit of fame. Great men received acclaim in republican society by putting the public interest ahead of their self-interest. They did this not by grasping for power or by ingratiating themselves doing the people favors, but by artfully crafting just policies while the people looked on in silent approval.[28] Great men act on the public stage, seeking to impress the people who act as the audience. Under this image, the people forfeit the role of actor.

In short, the new commercial value of acquisitiveness posed two conceptual problems, one for the republican citizen and one for the republican leader. Classical republican leadership required the disinterested and hence independent pursuit of the public good. The personal agony that leaders faced in negotiating the Scylla of dependence and the Charybdis of self-interest is revealed in Washington's tormented decision concerning the State of Virginia gift. Ninian Edwards underwent a similar torment in early Illinois. The problem facing the republican citizen was even more profound. Once money was introduced and gave the people, as Thomas Ford put it, "new ideas and aspirations," there was a threat that the new goal of prosperity would destroy communities based on the old aspiration of social equality. One sign that this was happening is the changing stories of how travelers and strangers were treated. In the 1820s, Christiana Holmes Tillson, having had her family's wagon stuck in the mud, reported that the norm against leaving "a stranger in a fix" was strongly reinforced. By the 1830s, emigrant Eliza W. Farnham's report was less unequivocal.[29]

Republican "society" had thus arrived at a paradox. In the inherited script, the poor played the pure and simple people; the leader played the disinterested doctor. There were no third parties or institutions of "civil society" to provide an independent set of public standards. Either a critique from the outside or a division within the white folks themselves would be needed to change or reform public life. Wealth and social refinement allowed for disinterestedness but were also marked by money and power, those telltale signs of corruption.

How did Illinois's leaders and people respond to this changing conceptual landscape? Some among the people held on to the ideal of disinterested virtue, but for many others, disinterestedness had come to mean devotion to the interests of the white folks. The symbols contained in myths die hard, however, and although the new view meant that the people themselves were no longer a mythic entity but instead a particular people with particular interests, the old story of the people lived on in a new form. Illinois's vernacular republicans developed their own version of double vision: they were realists when they thought of the contemporary people who were actively battling the wealthy big folks, but romantics when they thought of the people generally and in the past.

The double vision was most prominent in the egalitarian social vision of the conventionists. Like other dissenting republicans, they valued the simple, the pure, the basic, all of which they located in the past, the people's past, when they had struggled endlessly with the forces of oppression. Further back in the past, in the prehistory of the people's struggle, was an even simpler and plainer state of nature, when social equality and the sentiment of equality prevailed. This sort of romancing the past appears antimodern, as it did in Rousseau. But understood as a rhetorical move in a political context, its real motive is not traditionalism but egalitarianism. Egalitarians, as Richard J. Ellis points out, should not be confused with traditionalists.[30] Producer republicans articulated a quite modern dissent from the standards of social standing that dominated all previous hierarchical societies.

While the rejection of hierarchy separated Illinois's dissenting republicans from moderates such as Ninian Edwards, republicans of every stripe in the state should be distinguished from traditionalists for the additional reason that they all lacked the corporate view of society entailed in traditionalism. Perhaps in response to the market revolution they were experiencing, they viewed society not in terms of orders, castes, and classes as was traditional, but atomistically, in terms of individuals and families. To this extent they had embraced modern liberalism.[31] This meant that for all their romance of the people's corporate past, they thought of the future in individualistic terms. The result was an at times confusing mixture of modern and traditional elements in their thought.

Here again the Illinoisans reproduced in their own way a pattern pioneered in the East. The distinction between a corporate view of society and an atomistic one often lay behind the political disagreements between Federalists and Republicans in the early republic. A prominent illustration is contained in John Adams and Thomas Jefferson's debate over aristocracy, which they carried on by correspondence after retirement. John Adams was a traditionalist with a "modern" controlling idea. He thought hierarchical standards were inevitable in all societies; his emphasis on the "natural aristocracy" stemmed from his belief that what Robert Michels later called the "iron law of oligarchy" was natural. The fixed social status of "the ruling" and "the ruled" is responsible for the bleakness in Adams's view. Yet it was a "liberal bleakness," as Louis Hartz noted, because Adams believed that the natural rulers, the aristocracy, could be cabined and controlled by modern institutions and rules, by the liberal constitutional structures he so often championed. Whereas, for Adams, society caused all the problems that clever governance might partially amend, for Jefferson, the new atomistic society would solve all social problems given time and a virtuous (i.e., noninterfering) government. Jefferson was a modernist who retained the people's ancient hope; he hoped an atomistic society that had dissolved all "artificial" distinctions would replace them only with "natural" ones morally acceptable to egalitarians, such as talent.[32]

Transformed in these ways, republicanism in Illinois became an ironic combination of elements, both forward and backward looking, ancient and modern, realist and idealist. Illinoisans participated in this new understanding of republicanism but as a new generation creates change, more through a new set of implicit feelings or assumptions than through a new set of arguments. At its most basic level, the new version of republicanism emphasized its egalitarian dimensions. It was most effective as a rhetorical tool for dissenting from the hierarchical assumptions of many eastern social, economic, political, and religious beliefs. Opposition to hierarchy culminated during the convention controversy, which figured as the great climax of the antieastern sentiment that had been building under the "despotic" territorial system. The embrace of egalitarianism sent a ripple through everything political, including the notion of political representation. This more than any other ideal was transformed in the press of political protest; and nowhere was its influence more telling than in the state's fitful acceptance and rejection of Ninian Edwards.

NINIAN EDWARDS: REPUBLICAN AS LEGAL PATERNALIST

Ninian Edwards was the most famous and flamboyant national-level politician produced by Illinois in its first 30 years. The eldest son born to a farm family in Montgomery County, Maryland, in 1775, Edwards traveled to Kentucky and cleared a new farm for his father before he was 20. He read Blackstone and soon became interested in politics. In 1795 he was elected to the first of two consecutive terms representing Nelson County in the lower house of the Kentucky legislature. Success as an attorney led to appointments as presiding judge, circuit judge, and finally chief justice of the state of Kentucky; he was serving in the last office, and only 32 years old, when he induced Henry Clay to recommend him for the office of governor of Illinois Territory. In 1809 he received James Madison's appointment and held the governor's post until Illinois achieved statehood, whereupon he was elected by the legislature to be the state's first U.S. senator.

As territorial governor, Edwards held the appointing power, a tool he used to dominate Illinois politics between 1809 and 1823. But the position was also the source of his greatest weakness. When he first came to the territory, he confessed he was "a total stranger to everyone." By 1824 he had accumulated 15 years of public service, yet he had never been elected to any position by the people. These simple facts shed light on an otherwise puzzling career. Here was a man who led the Illinois people through some of the darkest moments of the War of 1812; who was memorialized as the "Old Ranger" for his decisive leadership; who in 1821 delivered what many thought was the most eloquent speech to be made during the Sixteenth Congress; who was appointed minister to Mexico; and who died in 1833 providing medical assistance to his St. Clair County neighbors during a cholera epidemic. Yet here too was a man whom few voters ever loved; whom opponents loved to hate; who turned almost every friendship into a rivalry; who in 1824 allowed a minor squabble with Secretary of Treasury William Crawford to destroy a carefully planned national career; and who threw away his governorship when he pitched a political "hobby" that the people neither cared about nor understood.[33]

In Edwards's career one finds short flashes of brilliance and long stretches of mediocrity. His erratic behavior has sent scholars searching for a personal flaw. "The quality of mental balance," wrote Theodore Calvin Pease, "was almost completely lacking in Edwards." The white folks thought him merely self-absorbed. Memoirs and newspaper accounts describe him as an "aristocrat," the "Chief Ruler of the Realm of Illinois," and head of the state's "reigning family." The clever William Kinney found a way to ridicule the self-importance he took to be the governor's greatest offense, saying he only "employed the little 'i' as a personal pronoun" in his writing since "Governor Edwards has used up all the big I's." The frequent letters in the state's papers make clear that many considered him the sinister embodiment of a politics they had left behind. In the long view, Edwards ungratefully refused to acknowledge his reliance on the people. "A Republican" vented in the Kaskaskia sheet: "Oh ingratitude! Thou haggard monster, with greenish, sickly eyes, poisonous teeth, a skin spotted with loathsome leprosy; thy breath is pollution; thy touch is death. Thy canst with equal ease infuse thy poison into Judas Iscariot, and—a Minister to Mexico."[34]

His friends also found him difficult; not least because of his idea that political alliance was a function of friendship. He viewed a party as a collection of friends who had become prominent through their talents, education, and public service. That they would cooperate to further their own interests and the interests of the state simply followed from "the imperious calls of public duty." Yet the act of cooperation was one of friendship, conducted by individuals without commitments (friendship aside) beyond each transaction. In 1823 he wrote from Washington: "If then a party has existed, I can not believe that its object has been so exclusively personal to myself, as to forbid my withdrawing from my present station whenever my interest requires it." By then Edwards had hardly a political friend in the state besides his paid editor. In spite of this alienation, and partially because of it, Edwards pulled off an unexpected comeback in 1826 when he was elected governor—albeit by the slim margin of 447 votes out of 12,113 cast. But the people's approval was momentary, and he quickly lost their confidence. His last year in elected office was 1830. He was 55.[35]

Thus the paradox surrounding Ninian Edwards: a leader dedicated to service but scorned as selfish; a politician embraced but rapidly dropped by friends and voters. The first step in unraveling the paradox lies in carefully distinguishing the connection between ends and means in his politics. On the one hand, he was so ostentatious about his wealth and education that these traits alone impacted his reception. His style, anti-egalitarian down to his boots, was enough to alienate most voters. He wore the finest broadcloth, raised thoroughbred horses, purchased thousands of acres of federal land, financed a string of grocery stores, sent his son to a private school in St. Louis. The twenty-two slaves he held in Missouri would have been the fourth-highest number listed in the 1820 Illinois Census. He was a man of intellectual passions. After attending Dickinson College in Pennsylvania, he devoured medical texts as voraciously as those on law.[36]

On the other hand, each of these facts might have been overlooked had they not also been woven into his otherwise democratic beliefs on political ends. Despite the rhetoric of his opponents, it must be understood that his values were not literally aristocratic. Almost every citizen of the United States by this time, Edwards included, believed in political democracy, the view that the authority behind government comes ultimately from the people. But if Edwards was not an aristocrat, he was an elitist. Although he always included the people in his proposals, voted for Jefferson, and became a Jacksonian, his refined, frequently pedantic style was exclusionary; it spoke privilege more clearly than it spoke equality. He insisted that the people's authority needed mediation; it was made fully legitimate only upon being expressed reasonably. He further believed that the people could not generally produce their own reasoned expression. They needed leaders, political experts like himself, who had specialized in mastering the fundamental principles of constitutional government found in Blackstone's *Commentaries on the Laws of England*. Reasoned political expression acquired a quasi-scientific status in Edwards's formulation that is reminiscent of Hamilton.[37] Discoverable laws of realism underlie all politics; those who ignore them, such as inexperienced democrats, are destined to illustrate them.

Edwards's view of leadership also followed the moderate republican currents of his day. The good leader was like a good doctor.[38] Politics, like medicine, combined science and art. The science was the abstruse science of the law, and Edwards reveled in its abstruseness. The art came in applying legal principle to matters of practical politics. In this he was a master, but the people rarely appreciated such work, for it required putting devotion to principle above devotion to their immediate interests. In the face of unpopularity he sought comfort in the labyrinth of legal rules, an intrinsic reward to compensate for an elusive fame.

The love of legal intricacies was costly to the political doctor. It alienated his patients. Even when they recovered, his services were resented. Under such conditions, he did more damage to his reputation in victory than in defeat. This situation created a pathetic trap. To receive the recognition and fame he craved, he needed to call attention to himself as he acted virtuously on the political stage; but by insisting on impartiality and a commitment to abstract principle and by refusing to embrace the white folks' drama, he cultivated a fatal distance between himself and the voters. In a sense he did too good an acting job, for his detached style persuaded many that he could only be an aristocrat at heart. His interest was to display his disinterested service and to make his role appear effortless; the voters were only willing to appreciate actors who repeatedly and obsequiously referred to their role.

Edwards was enough of a devotee of classical republican beliefs to find the assertion of self-interest completely inconsistent with "the purity of election." In arguing against treating with whiskey at elections, he asked, "Can you suppose that a man is not influenced by motives other than the public good, when he endeavors to succeed in his election by purchasing it—in other words, by bribery and corruption." And corruption, he warned sententiously, was the downfall of all republics: "He who has paid the least attention to the current of events, or histories of other countries, may be satisfied that unless this most formidable enemy to freedom, corruption, is successfully repelled by the virtue and wisdom of the people, in his first attempt to invade us, he will rise in his strength, like a mighty torrent, and tear down everything before him."[39]

Nonetheless, the call for integrity was a cry in the dark. Indeed, Edwards realized that his appeal to an ethic of disinterest in public office was ridiculously out of touch with social reality. During the boom of speculation that followed the War of 1812, the burn of self-interest was brought to a white heat. "*Self-Interest* . . . [scorches] . . . all the unruly feelings of friendship, pride, independence, dignity, and self-respect," wrote one contemporary: "The creed of the Persian is becoming universal; my friends and acquaintances all worship the *rising Sun*." In the five years between 1815 and 1819, a new wonder came streaming into the state—"money." As Ford perceived, it "turned the heads of all the people." The hot rays of self-interest evaporated much community goodwill among the white folks, but the heat was felt by the big folks as well. "I wish to hold my dish while the porridge is falling," Daniel P. Cook wrote to Edwards in an 1817 letter. He was informing his future father-in-law of his attempts to purchase "land in the neighborhood . . . where the seat of government will probably be fixed." In 1818 two of Edwards's peers, Nathaniel Pope and Benjamin Stephenson, attempted to move the state capital from Kaskaskia to land they owned at Pope's Bluff. Thomas and company considered this effort, which failed, a gross example of using influence over public power for private gain.[40] This suggests that the modernizing market revolution also contributed to Edwards's woes. It introduced just enough self-interested behavior to weaken him by undermining the deference he assumed and by making his non-ideological approach to political organization untenable. At the same time, the economic interests introduced by market capitalism among the white folks—by the 1830s enough to give the Whig party respectable poll returns—were not yet sufficiently developed in the early period to make Edwards's paternalism appealing over an extended period.

The way that Edwards's paternalistic means could infect his moderate republican ends is seen most clearly in the public lands question. He put forward the potentially popular idea that the states, not the federal government, ought to control the public lands within their boundaries. He arrived at this position after canvassing Illinois's territorial history. He devoted special attention to the "conditions" Virginia included in the 1783 Deed of Cession. Preeminent among these was that the French and others living in the territory ought to "have all their possessions and titles confirmed to them, and be protected in the enjoyment of their rights and liberties."[41] But, for Edwards, as for most of the Illinois public, the U.S. purchase of the Northwest Territory from Virginia was more than a land deal; it created an independent state. Here was the real social contract, not the Ordinance of 1787 that followed. The ex-Virginians northwest of the Ohio River gave over their allegiance and their unclaimed land to the federal government, but they reconstituted themselves as a people with a government of limited powers that recognized their customary rights.

By this contract theory, Edwards acknowledged that for years American settlers in Illinois had been an autonomous community; and having been an independent polity "cut off from Virginia, and owing no other allegiance to the United States than they had previously owed as citizens of Virginia, they had a right to govern themselves." As an independent state, they were "in the meantime entitled, by the terms of the cession, to the same protection from the United States as Virginia herself." Neither the Articles of Confederation, the Constitution, nor the Ordinance gave the United States the power, as sovereign, to withhold any rights or change any community rules; to assume otherwise was to postulate a "monstrous power of degrading any portion of the citizens of a free, sovereign and independent State to colonial thraldom." Here is the local sentiment of popular sovereignty, packaged in the liberal language of rights against the state. Substantively, Edwards's positions often coincided with popular opinion. Formally, however, his positions were always cast as theoretical propositions; he presented his solution to the public lands problem as a matter of deduction from natural law principles. Thus, he hoped to determine "what form of government [was] best calculated to secure the welfare and promote the happiness of a nation." Or, again, he cautiously pointed out that there was "enough similitude between the ancient republics and our own to induce us to take a warning from their experience." It is not hard to imagine how these views played among the white folks. If the written word was foreign to local culture, we can expect that so too was the big folks' attempt to govern on the basis of "book larn'in."[42]

The issue of public lands highlights the contrast between the two perspectives. The local view on public lands was that they belonged first and foremost to those who settled them. In early 1819, when fears of overheated speculation caused Congress to scrap the system of purchasing land on credit, Edwards attempted to amend the bill by adding preemption rights, lowering the price, and reinstating the credit system. This was nothing more than a plea to protect the settlers' rights. He was defending his constituents' rights as he perceived them. Although he found himself in the minority, his defense was eloquent and valiant, even to the point of his fainting on the floor of the Senate. Later Edwards's larger philosophy on public lands surfaced in Congress during his successful opposition to an 1821 Maryland land bill that would have founded eastern schools with western land sales. His success came as a result of his mastery of the language of natural law and federalism. Yet there are no signs that his efforts in this vein ever impressed the local voters. For they were concerned not with Edwards's problem of "respect and obedience to the law of nature" but primarily with the problem of earning the respect of social equality from their eastern counterparts.[43]

Ironically, he captured perfectly the local distinction between those who lived in the West and had rights on their side, and those who wrongly tried to control the area from the outside. As early as 1808, Illinois petitioners had asked for preemption privileges because they had "acted in the double capacity of cultivators of the soil and defenders of the frontiers."[44] Even the view of Union County pioneer John Grammer, an illiterate but popular local leader, confirmed the basic thrust of Edwards's view. Grammer's view has most likely been preserved because of its crude language, but it is also one of the few recorded expressions of the predominant view of slavery among the white folks. When the Deed of Cession's slavery rights were questioned during a session of the territorial legislature, Grammer rose in their defense. "Fittener men," he announced, "mout hev been found to defend the masters agin the sneakin' ways of the infernal abolitioneers; but havin' rights on my side, I don't fear." The view that the right to own slaves violated the Northwest Ordinance misunderstood the sovereign nature of the people who were living in Illinois at the time. Grammer proceeded to demonstrate why the abolitionist view was thus "unconstitutional, inlegal, and fornenst the compact. . . . Don't everyone know, or leastwise had ought to know, that the Congress that sot at Post Vinsan [Vincennes, 1805], garnished to the old French inhabitants the rights to their niggers, and hain't I got as much rights as any Frenchman? . . . answer me that Sir."[45]

Since Edwards's view was substantially the same, why didn't it win support? There are two key reasons. The first is that Edwards refused to clothe his position in terms of the white folks' group interests vis-à-vis the French or the African Americans. Such a view not only violated the norm of disinterestedness, it was clearly motivated by social standing in a way Edwards would have found unseemly. Judith Shklar has argued that "citizenship as standing" preoccupied a broad class of Americans in the early nineteenth century. Although Edwards was similarly preoccupied with status, it was not as mere participant but as a leading figure that he sought acclaim. For this reason, he could hardly join Grammer's chorus.[46]

The other reason Edwards's position failed goes beyond both his manner of expression and his lack of attention to the matter of social standing. While both his and Grammer's views stress the independent status of the Illinois people, the results in the two cases differ. The localist version of independence joins the Illinois people firmly to the national movement for republican independence whereas Edwards's version has a separatist result. He grounded his analysis of the right to own land in the ability to cultivate it. Here he cited the natural law thinker Emmerich de Vattel. The United States took rightful possession of North American land against the Native Americans because the latter were a people who "thinly scattered over its surface, who neither would nor could cultivate it, and who consequently could not lawfully claim the whole of it." The European settlers cultivated the land, and by this action established the right of ownership. In the decades-long debate over occupancy rights in Kentucky this view was finally championed by the Supreme Court in 1831: "No class of laws is more universally sanctioned by the practice of nations, and the consent of mankind, than laws which give peace and confidence to the actual possessor of the soil."[47]

Edwards began with the cultivation principle in every public presentation of his public lands position, in his inaugural as a governor in 1826, and again in a string of speeches in 1828. He hoped to unite the state around a reproach of the federal land policy, which "contrary to Divine intention and will" refused to allow its citizens freely to occupy and cultivate the lands under its control. All these attempts to shape public opinion failed. The doctrine of state autarchy simply did not serve the political interests of the youth of the state. For, as they made known to all, they wished to emphasize just the opposite: that is, their continuity with the revolutionary tradition represented by Jefferson and Paine, and their opposition to the repression represented by the territorial elite. Edwards may have seen the position as contradictory. If the Illinoisans left the East to do better in the West, he may have argued, they knew what better meant because they had learned it back East. As Earl Pomeroy wryly observed of the incessant cries against territorial tyranny: "Citizens resented the territorial status not only because they were Westerners, but also because recently they had been Easterners." But the fact that Edwards did not miss this contradiction underscores the distance his natural law theory placed between him and the people.[48]

Unlike Edwards, for whom the Ordinance was practically irrelevant, the new breed in the legislature needed the Ordinance to oppose in order to define and legitimate themselves. It is instructive to examine the response Edwards's position elicited from his fellow Illinoisans. "While the feudal systems of Europe are upheld by the writings of Vattel, Pufendorf and others," "Clio" wrote in the Gazette, "it is hoped we may be allowed to quote our Jefferson as authority." There followed Jefferson's 1823 letter to Thomas Earle arguing that "a preceding generation cannot bind a succeeding generation." For many, the need for the cover of the revolution was all the greater because they had grown up in the margins and backwoods of American society. They recognized in the republican ideal of self-regulation a doctrine suitable to their condition, if it was not pushed to the extreme position taken by Edwards.[49]

As in the public lands issue, Edwards's view of partisanship was also at odds with the needs of the local politicians. He maintained that those who wished to run without a record did not deserve public office. But one needed already to hold office for this strategy to work. The requirement of service was fine for Edwards personally; between 1803 and 1830, he was out of public office only 29 months. Such an approach offered little, however, to the minions in his party who often had no public record on which to run. Yet, for such, Edwards had little sympathy. Thomas Ford articulated the flaw in Edwards's logic, partially out of sympathy with the local perspective and partly out of cynicism for being old and misused: "Up to the year 1840," he wrote in *A History of Illinois,* "the capacity to be grateful for public services, short of fighting the battles of the country, existed to but a limited extent."[50]

Ford, himself once an Edwards client, eventually subscribed to the ideal of disinterested public service. But as he bitterly acknowledged, it brought him little popularity. The voters did not associate public service with public office. More influential were "considerations of mere party, men's condescensions, agreeable carriage, and professions of friendship." Ford here exposes the chauvinistic tribalism of the new egalitarian politics. But he was writing late in life; he conveniently disremembered that he too had been a member of the tribe of the people. He too had thought it necessary to condescend to the people's taste for sycophants, for example, when in 1824 he wrote, in announcing a new newspaper: "Most papers grow up under the fostering hand of some powerful patron, whose interest it is bound to advocate. The editors of this paper solicit the patronage of none but the sovereign people."[51]

"Powerful patron" Edwards struggled his whole career to overcome the attitudes that fueled Ford's cynicism. Ford remembered Edwards as "a large, well-made man, with a noble, princely appearance." Thus, when he ran in the 1826 governor's race, he had at least one of Ford's factors in his favor, although under "agreeable carriage" Ford certainly would not have included Edwards's broadcloth, top hat, and slave-driven coach. But Edwards canvassed the state denouncing "almost every man that had been in the Legislature since 1821 and all the Bank and Circuit Court interest." After surveying the sorry condition of the state's finances, Edwards intimated that "the people" once again needed his services, that they needed his tutoring and ought to sit back and listen. His lengthy speeches certainly made them sit back, and with them in this position, the doctor would administer cures for their economic fever and political ague.[52]

When he ran for governor of the state in 1826 and won, his victory amazed the new generation for whom he had become "worn out." They had discounted him because, they said, he was too big a man and too old. But he turned the tables on them. He first attacked the "log-rolling caucuses of the big men at Vandalia." Then, taking a cue from the political science of David Hume, and of James Madison in *Federalist,* No. 49, he accepted the mantle of "Old Ninian," making old age and veneration his great trump card. He ended every stump speech with the same incantation:

> Old Whiskey, old wine, old bacon, old servants, old acquaintances and old friends are quite agreeable to us all, and I should not be surprised if you should even like some of the good old ways by which we contrived to get along somehow or other while I had the honor of being your Governor. Everything, therefore, is not to be rejected merely because it is old; and among those good old things which you may not consider the less worthy of your regard on account of their age, I hope you will not forget to include the Old Ranger.[53]

Both speech and campaign were successful because Edwards had subtly reminded the voters of his past services.

If this suggests that traditionally deferential political approaches still had some cache among Illinoisans, Edwards's appeal as the "Old Ranger" must be put into context. At various points in his career, Edwards had succeeded in impressing his constituents by leading their efforts to displace the native Indians. During these episodes, local sentiment did defer to the territorial executive; but "fighting Indians in a swamp," as underwhelming a civic ideal as it seemed to Perry Miller's Puritans, was a decidedly western method of attaining deference.[54] Edwards's victory in the 1826 election also needs to be understood in context. By then, the people were reeling from five years of economic depression that the state bank had not only not ameliorated but had actually prolonged and magnified. The reassertion of paternalism was perfectly timed.

He had discovered what the Jacksonians would later exploit with even more subtlety. The people often feared the new liberal order that was developing; traditional appeals to paternal authority could be attractive if they were presented in the humble garb of the first settlers. It was his scolding diffidence, one might surmise, not his cultivation principles that appealed to the voters. Some among the young and active voters may have been reminded of their stern parents. But if they were capable of veneration, they would not kneel at the altar of liberal abstractions. They needed a picture. The image of a stubborn old patriarch would do in a pinch.

THE EDWARDS PARTY: FAMILY AND FRIENDS

Ninian Edwards was a transitional figure whose peculiar combination of moderate political opinions and elitist social assumptions were unsuited to an era of republican purity. Born in an era of virtual representation and disinterested leadership, he died in an era of instructional representation and partisan leadership. Straddling the two, he failed to satisfy the norms of either, while the transition from one to the other caused him much anguish. He had been, it could be said, too well educated at an early age. A precocious pre-revolution baby, he soaked up too fully the norms of the eighteenth century, norms of social standing and deference, which were a hindrance to a politician operating amid the democratic revolution of the early nineteenth century.

Edwards's commitment to eighteenth-century notions of standing show up most clearly in the criteria by which he determined who was worthy for appointment or election to public office. Office for Edwards was the reward for virtuous public service. Leaders, he believed, should be acknowledged for the actions they performed, not the identities they assumed. Those who would lead should be recognized for the record of public services they had accumulated. Although Edwards was uncomfortable touting a purely disinterested position, he nonetheless insisted on his own independence in representing the people's will. This unlikely combination left him open to charges of hypocrisy even among his own supporters.

In fact, what has for the sake of convenience been ubiquitously called "the Edwards party" was perpetually divided and, when united, exhibited a strange form of cooperation between patron and client in which neither side fully appreciated the other. His clients could claim he would have been nothing without them, but he could reply that, with them, he felt less honorable and worthy. He proved utterly incapable of keeping his clients united under a common cause. In Edwards's case, his technique for engineering an electable coalition—not to mention a party platform—was usually a failure.

Edwards always found it awkward to make appointments and select candidates; doing so in conjunction with others placed him in a state of paralysis. Here too his eighteenth-century personal style got in the way of nineteenth-century realities. When Edwards wrote about "the party" he headed, he had in mind the network made up of his "personal and political friends," who had come to the West to win fortune and fame. They considered themselves the first families of the Illinois territory; together they constituted a notorious "family of rulers."[55] After 1818, Edwards faced the problem of converting a clique built of family ties, past public services, and friendship into an effective vote-gathering organization. Individuals who had become "allies through marriage" would need to recruit new members from outside family circles.

During the territorial period, he had relied extensively on the advice of his "political Godfather," Kentucky cousin John Pope. Under Pope's tuition Edwards developed a preference for "ties of blood" in his political alliances, which Illinoisans found threatening. "Partyism has its limits; a man should never sacrifice a great principle at the shrine of party," Pope reminded him, "but he must not be too nice or squeamish upon subordinate questions." In the future, rule by reason and the public interest would surely be established, but until that time, parties would be necessary for reaching "the public good." For the sake of "political preservation and usefulness," the immediate goal must be to "strengthen our own party." Pope concluded: "we must, therefore, in the present state of things, identify ourselves with those allied to us by ties of blood and such others as we can rally around us by honorable means." The Pope family sent a lot of blood to the territory, including Nathaniel Pope, Daniel Pope Cook, and Alexander Pope Field, each of whom played important roles in the Edwards faction. Benjamin Stephenson, also from Kentucky, who became the state's first congressional delegate, was Edwards's closest friend after whom he named his son.[56]

When this intimate governing circle was threatened by statehood status, Edwards did try to respond. He was most successful when he was able to make disinterestedness and political advantage overlap. He made William Whiteside, the great "patriarch and leader" of the Whiteside clan from Kentucky, a Ranger captain during the War of 1812. The appointment recognized, he claimed, Whiteside's accomplishments, not his Kentucky roots. "I really recommend him," he wrote John Pope, "for the good of the country and from no other motive." Whiteside's case had hit a sore point, for earlier in his term as governor, he was criticized for carrying his preference for his Kentucky friends to the level of militia appointments. At that time, in 1809, he had diffused the controversy by allowing an election to determine an important militia post. He took the opportunity to make a speech emphasizing this democratic aspect of his "political creed" and reiterated his belief that "good republicans ought to submit to the majority." But as he elaborated the point, it was clear he had a rather attenuated notion of submission: he observed that the people "may be wrong sometimes" and that voters appreciate "a firm and independent course, even if they should not entirely concur; for there is a native magnanimity in the soul of freemen, which leads them to admire a man who is nobly wrong much more than one who is meanly right." Noble wrongness and mean rightness hit the perfect notes, but the scale was off; Edwards's ideas of nobility and meanness were the exact social opposite to those of his listeners.[57]

Edwards thought, along with Blackstone, that the law, while ultimately deriving from the people, remained above to check them. In discussing public drunkenness, he expressed the belief that "mankind is generally more disposed to embrace error than truth, to adopt vice than virtue, and knowing the fascinating influence of example, the law will not permit these persons to transfuse their poison into the breasts of others." He thought along with Hamilton that the "fantastic light of reason" could lead the best minds to a science of politics. He believed along with Madison that the masses needed laws and institutions as "necessary checks" on their passions. Edwards's struggle for the people only made sense if their advocate was assumed, Lycurgus-like, to be outside the body politic.[58]

It cannot be said that Edwards never tried to build a party organization. He brought his considerable economic might to bear on the task of cultivating local leaders with broad influence among the settlers. He set up Hooper Warren at Edwardsville to publish the *Spectator*. In the fall of 1822 he lent Henry Eddy $350 to buy co-editor James Hall's share of the *Illinois Gazette* at Shawneetown.[59] With Hall out, Edwards's rival Thomas was left for a while without a printer in the state; this alone is an indication of the reach of Edwards's economic power and a crucial political fact, since editorials, printed ballots (in 1818 and from 1824 on), and handbills were essential to the political organization of the time.

The economic power of government positions was also put to use. During the territorial period Edwards was the federal agent for the state's salines. Through his leasing prerogative, he made favorable connections with Leonard White and Willis Hargrave, political leaders from the eastern side of the state. As U.S. senator, he obtained federal depositor status for the Bank of Illinois at Shawneetown, also on the eastern border. By this action he secured the loyalty of bank president John Marshall and director John Cadwell. Edwards used as well his extensive store-keeping operations to cement relations with influential Yankee merchants such as Thomas Mather and George Cadwell in the western region of the state. Finally, federal jobs—including receiver of public land moneys and Indian agent—were found for Thomas Cox, Joseph Street, Pascal Enos, and Samuel Lockwood, all from the northern counties. Nonetheless, despite these statewide efforts, it was not long before the Edwards party fell apart.[60]

Party cohesion was weakened by the fact that statewide elections would be held for governor and U.S. representative while the General Assembly would be appointing U.S. senators. Control over the far-flung and unwieldy county elections thus became a key source of political power. By contrast, the territorial government had been easy to manipulate. The distance of Washington, D.C., from Illinois also added to the party's coordination problems. Its two strongest candidates, Edwards and Cook (elected U.S. representative in 1819), spent most of the first five years of statehood in Washington. This left Nathaniel Pope in charge of day-to-day political maneuvers. If Pope realized the profound change that would be caused by the shift from appointed to elected government, he gave little indication of it. Instead, he appeared content to continue to support the ring of friends and relations that controlled offices under the territorial system. The only changes necessary, he seems to have thought, were that the arena of politics would now be the whole state, and that he would become the faction's patriarch.

Pope soon discovered otherwise, however. As a circuit court judge in the territorial nerve center at Kaskaskia, he failed to detect the youth movement that had developed in Thomas's faction. As it spread to his own side, he watched the factional developments in the legislature with alarm. This body had given Edwards only twenty-three of forty-two votes in the 1819 U.S. Senate contest whereas, a mere five months earlier, it had given him thirty-two.[61] Edwards considered a six-year term his due, but he would not condescend to lobby for it. "Your hinting and not openly avowing your wish has left you almost defenseless," wrote an ally from the field. Possibly, he would have been content to retire into private business; nevertheless, his friends had plans for the patronage he would control as senator. They joined in alarm at his inattention to the matter; at the same time, they reported warily on the strength of the enemy. Any opposition must be evil to deny his personal achievement—to this they readily assented. But, in a pattern that frequently repeated itself, they made sure he was aware of their work for him in the trenches. He would have lost, Edwards was informed, "were it not that your friends are ever on the alert . . . in suppressing those feelings which wickedness has been attempting to excite in the minds of many."[62]

In 1821 David Blackwell, promising young attorney, anti-slavery advocate, and strong Edwards supporter, suddenly broke rank while the legislature was in session. To protest both Thomas's and Edwards's votes in Congress granting Missouri statehood with slavery, Blackwell adopted a resolution asking for their resignations. More threatening to Pope than Blackwell's anti-slavery principles was his principle of republican government. The resolution proscribed "any representative of the people or of state who will disregard the known wishes of the people." The senators should resign, Blackwell concluded, "to make room for those who will respect the opinions of the people, the legitimate source of all political power."[63] Pope was confronted with a changing political landscape. New measures would have to be adopted and new men brought onboard to court more aggressively the emerging youth. Most urgent, choices had to be made about whom to support for governor in 1822 and for senator in 1823.

Given these circumstances one can imagine Pope's indignation when, early in 1822, Edwards in Washington refused to support his— and by implication, the faction's—candidate for governor. Edwards was taken aback by his friend's anger; he later wrote, "I understood you were dissatisfied with me."[64] The question of sorting out potential candidates plagued Edwards. It was as if he was unable to reconcile his political motives with his classical republican principle of disinterestedness. In the 1823 senatorial election, with a wellspring of federal patronage on the line and with a chance to unseat his rival Thomas, Edwards was unable to find anyone to support. He remained uncommitted to the end of the election.

Pope finally threw his support behind John Reynolds, the most popular young man among the faction's unelected members. Edwards, chafed at the decision, made no response; from Pope all that came was a reproach, and "in pretty strong terms."[65] When election day arrived, the faction was badly divided among John Reynolds and two old-guard members, Leonard White and Samuel Lockwood. On the day before the election, in the legislature, the faction had been able to win places for their men as attorney general and state treasurer; but split among three candidates, they were unable to stop Thomas's reelection.

The year 1823 saw the death of the Edwards party. One sign of morbidity came from the town of Springfield. In early 1823, its name had been changed to Calhoun in honor of Edwards's friend, the secretary of war and presidential hopeful. The change had apparently been made with the approval of the townspeople, but by early 1824, after Edwards had become embroiled in a controversy with presidential hopeful William Crawford, the county quietly reinstated the town's original name.[66] There were other portents: the Pope-Edwards rift, having begun, was further rent by the death of their mutual Kentucky tie, Benjamin Stephenson. Most important of all, slavery, an issue on which the faction had no public stand, had resurfaced in a new incarnation, the convention question, which was already the preeminent political issue of the day.

The resulting lack of direction within the faction was especially glaring on the slavery issue. The faction's young members were divided: John Reynolds, William Kinney, and Alex Field, all for some form of servitude; Cook, George Forquer, and Thomas Ford ultimately against continuing the old territorial compromises. In Cook's run for reelection during the summer of 1822, his opponent attacked his landholdings and speculation efforts, which had the effect of keeping the Kentucky-born representative on the defensive and his campaign limited to the public lands issue. Pope was probably anti-slavery, but additional confusion was caused on the ideological front because Edwards, while privately arguing against the continuance of slavery in Illinois, voted to allow Missouri into the Union with slavery and, indeed, owned 22 slaves there.[67]

Pope was at first undecided on who to run for governor in 1822; then, without consulting Edwards, he moved toward Reynolds. After being checked by Edwards, he finally settled on Thomas Browne, a mildly pro-slavery candidate already in the race. It is indicative of his network's disarray that at a crucial point in the race Pope traveled from Kaskaskia to the office of the *Edwardsville Spectator* to urge Hooper Warren to pull back from his criticism of the anti-slavery candidate Edward Coles. He "remarked with great earnestness" to Warren: "If you do not want Phillips elected, you must let Coles alone."[68] Acting thus, not from an anti-slavery interest or at the behest of Coles but as the only means available of blocking the victory of an old Thomas supporter, Joseph Phillips, Pope was demonstrating that revenge was the sole positive action remaining within the power of the disintegrating faction.

It is impossible to know whether the party would have survived even if its leadership had been able to reach a consensus on nominations. Viewed as a whole, perhaps its truest resemblance in maturity was to the territorial governing system that spawned it. Federal control in the territory involved a loose collection of powerful enclaves—governor, judges, land officers, military officers—whose cooperation toward the public interest was implied on paper but rarely actualized in practice. Similarly, the "Edwards party" brought the wealthy and influential men of the community together without binding them to an overarching public purpose or goal. The results were not unlike those of colonial rule. At best, it encouraged public service among those who were already predisposed to offer it; at worst, it cultivated in a closely knit circle of notables the inability to distinguish public service from self-service.

CHAPTER FOUR

THE POLITICS
OF SLAVERY IN A
NORTHERN STATE

"A tyrant never yet attempted the subversion of the liberties of his country by cold deliberate reasoning." So wrote "Aristides" in the *Illinois Intelligencer* in the spring of 1823, attempting to explain the political upheaval besetting the state. "It is always by letting loose the whirlwinds of passion, and becoming the demon of the storm," he continued, "that an aspiring monster lays in the dust everything that opposes his march to power and empire." Taking Aristides' figure literally one might ask: what let loose "the whirlwinds of passion"? The non-conventionists pointed to slavery as the demon of the storm. "Slavery is so poisonous," Coles observed, "as to produce a kind of delirium in those minds who are excited by it." Morris Birkbeck concurred; he perceived in the people's interest in slavery a kind of "infatuation." "Slavery is the *alpha and omega* of this mighty bustle," Aristides added. "The veil has become so thin," that it was blasphemous for the conventionists to claim to be "pristine republicans": "this crusade against the rights of man is not waged for these, but for . . . the political *heresy*, that . . . *republicans have an undoubted right to enslave a portion of their fellow men.*"[1]

Yet it was not the delirious, infatuating force of slavery that started the legislature down the road to mobocracy. If it was any passion, it was a passion for freedom. It was democracy—not slavery—that the majority sought so insistently and, in the end, so violently. Slavery was a taboo they violated partially because it was a taboo. It became a mere obstacle thrown up to block their march to self-government, and they were determined to clear all obstacles. Indeed they considered it a solemn duty.

Nor was it the venal democracy of distributive politics that opened the door to slavery. Impassioned calls for the Convention Resolution did not begin until the end of the legislative session, well after the feeding frenzy of county favors and benefits had ceased. It was the community as a whole—or rather, the whole that the legislators as a body represented—that remained unsatiated. Indeed the voters had not called for slavery. In the elections preceding the 1822–1823 session, only two counties indicated a pro-slavery sentiment. The relatively small number of slaves in the state (917 in 1820, compared with over 12,000 in Missouri) was of concern only to an equally small number of humanitarian crusaders. If the number of free blacks was a concern, it could not have been because of their increasing numbers; between 1810 and 1820, the numbers of free blacks decreased in Illinois from some 600 to 450 while increasing in Indiana from 400 to over 1,200.[2] In January 1823 the deadline for amending the constitutional limit on indentured servants working at the salines was still three years, two elections, and two legislative sessions away. There is simply no evidence that large numbers of voters called for slavery as a solution to the depression. Bad as economic conditions were, some intermediary catalyst was needed.

This catalyst was the new structure of political incentives created by statehood. The rewards of power and money now awaited those politicians who could organize and control the legislature. These incentives hastened the maturation of the division between the big folks and the white folks. The cleavage enlarged the "scope of conflict" beyond the narrow limits of territorial politics and left a fresh set of strategic boundaries and political meanings. Into this new setting walked Governor Coles. His inaugural was the bolt of lightning that recharged a neutralized system. More experienced anti-slavery citizens, seeing the terminus for the right to hold indentured servants quietly approaching, had favored the status quo. The issue had become dormant ever since the Thomas party had tried, and failed, to organize a pro-slavery coalition in 1820. Hooper Warren, who had met that earlier challenge, considered Coles's inaugural address a blunder. For all his Granite State stubbornness, Warren cautioned against reducing anti-slavery to an exhortation that the people give up their right to own slaves. As the conventionists realized, if republicanism meant anything in Illinois, it meant that a people who had fought to secure their rights would not surrender them easily. In Christiana Holmes Tillson's acerbic words: "The desire of an ignorant westerner to stand up for his 'rights,' was the predominant feeling of his nature."[3]

Coles, oblivious to local dynamics, hoped his address would energize anti-slavery sentiment in the legislature. Instead of gaining converts, however, Coles's bluntness only put off the anti-slavery men and infuriated the rest. He later wrote that "this part of my speech created a considerable excitement with those who were openly or secretly in favor of making Illinois a slave-holding . . . State." After the conventionists had mobilized against him, Coles complained bitterly in a private letter to Madison: "Never did I see or hear in America of party spirit going to such lengths, as well officially as privately, as it did here on this question." The irony of Coles's statement is that, previous to his arrival, the line dividing Illinois's political parties had cut across the slavery issue. Had the established parties continued to rule, the issue might very well

have remained stalemated. Coles's anti-slavery rhetoric was truly urbane, but this urbanity was precisely what allowed the conventionists to
correlate anti-slavery with the big folks.[4]

Important as Coles's role was as counterpoint to the legislature, other
background conditions must be kept in mind. If the anti-slavery inaugural provoked the legislature, it cannot be said to have broken the old
stalemate alone. Anti-slavery was able to break that barrier only because
a series of more powerful forces had already weakened the established
lines of territorial politics. The slavery issue tore the Thomas party apart
even as it brought together the conventionists in the legislature. But
without the transition to statehood, the conventionists would have
lacked legitimacy. Moreover, without the Panic of 1819 and the depression that followed, conventionists would have lacked the impetus to
act. The chain of causes can be traced farther back, for had the class anxieties among the white folks not been provoked by a decade of big folks'
control, the resentment driving the anti-Coles movement may have remained personal. Then, too, without the white folks' sectional fear of
Yankees and their racial fear of African Americans, the mixture of motives needed to sustain politicalization would not have been present.
Nor would violence have likely broken out had the new political culture
created by the white folks not developed an internal division. In Illinois
the politics of slavery were explosive as much because of who people
were as because of what they said.

JESSE B. THOMAS AND THE DILEMMAS OF A PLURALIST PATRON

Like Ninian Edwards, Jesse Burgess Thomas also felt he needed political distance, but unlike Edwards, his thought ran in practical grooves,
along tracks that visited tangible groups such as farmers and townspeople. Politics for Thomas operated on the quid pro quo: his supporters
recognized him as their leader, and he used his position to further their
interests. Thomas understood this much about instructional representation. But the quid pro quo required freedom to compromise. Thomas, a
master of the political compromise, demanded to be free and independent of his supporters. Like Edwards, he showed a talent for pursuing
self-interest and community interest in tandem. In 1817, he had a wool-
carding machine shipped from Pittsburgh to Cahokia, where he practiced law. Carding wool by hand, a necessary preliminary to spinning
thread, was a tedious process. An investment beneficial to the community and profitable to himself, "the machine," John Francis Snyder reported, "was well patronized from the day it was set in motion." Previously Thomas had orchestrated the controversial deal to divide the
Indiana Territory. After he signed a secret "written bond" tying himself
to the settlers in the Illinois half of the territory, they elected him congressional delegate from Indiana in 1808. He pledged that upon election

he would seek to split the territory. The deal was unpopular in Vincennes where Thomas and the majority of voters lived. By "keeping dark" he succeeded, and soon obtained from President Madison an appointment as one of the new Illinois territory's three judges.[5]

The Americans who settled around the judge in the French town of Cahokia respected the French for their congenial way of life. Many married French women, as did Elias Kent Kane, who became secretary of state under Governor Bond in 1818. Thomas too participated in the French life of the town. "They all spoke the Creole dialect and conformed to Creole customs," John Snyder wrote of the American Cahokians. Yet, Thomas never hid that he thought himself distinguished; he moved about in "the mode of a refined gentleman of the last [eighteenth] century." Thomas's strategy was to contrast his friends, the lawyers and farmers of the early frontier community in Illinois, with Edwards's friends, who, Thomas claimed, acted on behalf of speculating interests in the East and emigrants not yet a part of the state. In 1820 Congress passed a law lowering from $2.00 to $1.25 the price per acre of public land but abolishing the credit system. For Thomas, Washington's change in its land prices was an unmistakable and unfortunate signal that existing settlers were being forced to pay higher prices than prospective buyers.[6]

Thomas's traditionalism, moored to local vested interests in which he figured prominently, did not however disagree in principle with the paternalistic style Edwards manifested at every turn in the political game. Politically, Thomas insisted on articulating the principles behind the sentiments and interests of those he represented. Socially, he was recognized as "a man of gentlemanly and pleasant manners." Nonetheless, he was often seen "in the streets joking and laughing at the public table which was public literally." Common social manners came naturally to him given his childhood on a poor farm in Maryland. After clerking in his brother's law office, he pursued a successful career as a county clerk in Kentucky and later as both attorney and legislator in Indiana. If, in the Illinois Territory, Judge Thomas demanded and received the deference elicited by his wealth and experience, he never forgot what George Flower called the cardinal rule of politics in the "new western country . . . [a] man to be popular . . . with the country people around, should be acquainted with everybody, shake hands with everybody, and wear an old coat, with at least one good hole in it." To the less critical Snyder, the judge "was one of the people—plain in dress, in language and manners, exceedingly social and affable, and consequently popular with all classes." In fact, a backwoods style was hardly an affectation in a man who had been schooled in a Kentucky cabin and who never attended college.[7]

He soon discovered that his most enthusiastic supporters were the young generation of leaders who came of age with the War of 1812.

They were "the young, ardent, and energetic men," recalled John Reynolds (a premiere representative of the class), those who were "mixing everyday with the people." These supporters became essential to Thomas's success; they were his "shield of popularity," a necessary weapon for "any man of standing in [the territory]." They ingratiated him with "the boys," who, while "rather illiterate," could run "horses, drink whiskey, and play cards" with the best. This "different class" of men, as Thomas Lippincott referred to them, came to town on Saturdays to meet at the grogshop and carry out "the practices of rowdyism." On Sunday mornings they might compete in a foot race or a shooting match, or gather to hear the paper read. From this generation of 1812, Thomas drew his greatest support.[8]

It is in his interest in and support for "the boys" that Thomas contrasts most starkly with Ninian Edwards. Edwards wanted to be famous, Thomas wanted to be influential. Edwards used natural law abstractions, Thomas emphasized his common touch. Edwards insisted upon his distance from the people; Thomas embraced, or made sure he appeared to embrace, social equality. Edwards considered "the people" an abstract and undifferentiated whole; for Thomas, popular will was inherently fungible: the leader's job was to aggregate interests in order to craft a majority. If Edwards thought in terms of citizens and governments, Thomas promoted the interests of local groups like the French or the farmers whose deeds had "not yet cleared out of the [land] office."[9] Thomas's pluralism, the source of his flexibility as a politician, enabled him to advocate many disparate interests. Here was his secret competitive advantage against Edwards in courting the white folks, but here too was the explanation of his ultimate demise at their hands. For the more interests he championed, the more he must sacrifice when the time for compromise arrived.

Thomas's greatest moment as the white folks' advocate came with his attack on the Public Lands Bill of 1820. This measure abolished public credit for purchasing land while also lowering land prices. The majority in Congress felt that the credit system had created "the spirit of speculation" by which the settler had been "deluded" into "prospecting."[10] Thomas argued, with the minority, that the change would produce inequity. It would give incentives to wealthy speculators to renege on their old contracts with the government; at a later date, they could repurchase the same land at the reduced price. The common farmers, who had purchased smaller tracts of land, would then be paying a higher price for their land than the wealthy, for the former could not act with the same freedom as the speculators. First, their land was more likely to be improved, and therefore more costly if placed on the open market; second, they were less free to gamble—if they lost their lands, they lost their livelihoods. Thomas raised this point in his address to the Senate: "If saved from this necessity [losing their farms], it will be by compliance with terms from which they see their wealthy neighbors exempt." He continued with a detailed assessment of the plight of the poor farm family:

> But it has been shown to be their interest to suffer their lands to revert, and run the risk of re-purchasing, when the land shall be again offered for sale. It certainly never can be a sound policy in any Government to act in such a manner as to make it the interest of its citizens voluntarily, and from a regard to their pecuniary interests, to incur forfeitures, and to fail in the fulfillment of engagements which, though not legally, ought always to be considered morally binding. Such an example could not fail to have a baleful influence upon the public morality.[11]

This view partakes of the Randolph County "Le Pays des Illinois" world from which it emerged. Government is a tool for policing morality. At the same time, the medium of this morality is the fulfillment of obligations and contracts that have the effect of regulating inequality in the community. Precisely because these rules reflect the class structure of community life, Thomas suggested, they ought to be protected from the countervailing interests of individuals, rich or poor, who wish to bilk the established order. But by stepping back and taking in the entire social system, Thomas betrayed his lack of solidarity with any one element within it.

Thomas's mixture of paternalism and pluralism reflected the unique history of the French towns. As Winstanley Briggs has argued, the French country in Illinois had declined greatly since 1763 when the British took over and separated the colony from the rest of New France. By 1818, the French merely lived off the surpluses that had made them wealthy 50 years before. It was a model of community life that intrigued the Americans. The French lived and farmed in and around the bottomland: the very design of their houses reflected the ebb and flow of the alluvial bottoms (see Figure 4). They engaged in continent-wide trade with the cities of Montreal and New Orleans and employed slave labor. Yet the rich and poor among the French interacted as equals. It was not unlike the social contract backcountry settlers received in the South, where they were admitted to "the only true aristocracy, the race of white men." But this was an egalitarian, western variety of the model that mixed market prosperity with community mutuality. The fertility of the bottoms, cleared and cultivated by slaves together with their masters, provided a social buffer for every French family in the leap from subsistence to market farming.[12]

If Judge Thomas shared this vision with the conventionists, he viewed it, not from the inside as they did, but from outside the social structure altogether. This freed him from any one class or ethnic identity, and provided the distance he needed to negotiate nearly any deal.

Figure 4 French bottomland habitation. Courtesy of Illinois State Historical Library.

His most famous contribution came with the pivotal Thomas Amendment during the Missouri Compromise debate. Compromise as a route to influence had its drawbacks, however. It lowered his standing and made him less estimable as a person than Edwards. According to Thomas Lippincott, he was thought to be "without any remarkable powers of mind (of which he was sensible)." Yet, it might be considered a fair deal, for he "could and did exert a great influence over the people." As Snyder's portrait concluded: "There were few citizens in the Territory so implicitly trusted as was Judge Thomas, and none whose opinions were more respected."[13]

Thomas's attempt to block the wealthy from taking advantage of the 1820 land law failed, but it confirmed a pattern in his leadership. In 1818, for example, he took the lead in the defense of the community's moral sense when he stopped several of Edwards's partisans from cashing in on the state capitol property.[14] His battles for the poor farmer demonstrated that pluralism could rise to a defense of community morality without the offensive paternalism of the deferential political culture. Battling Edwards also solidified his reputation with the white folks. They trusted him because he looked and acted like one of them; in return for trust, he took the lead whenever local ways—whether French, American, or the new creolized hybrid—came under attack.

Although he tried hard, Thomas was ultimately unable to overcome the challenges he faced in representing the white folks' interests. They were mainly an illiterate people with a distinct set of social norms. Settler Daniel M. Parkinson, who came to Madison County in 1817 from Tennessee, found the local culture remarkable precisely on account of its oral form. "Among the settlers," he wrote, "the utmost confidence was reposed in the honor and integrity of each other; consequently all business was done upon the confidence principle." Trade in goods, labor exchanges, even land deals were sealed with a handshake. "Afterwards, when the Yankees, as we called them, came among us," Parkinson continued, their "system of accounts, written notes and obligations" was looked upon "with great suspicion and distrust"; the white folks regarded "their mode of doing business as a great and unwarranted innovation upon . . . established usages." The Yankees' use of the written word intimidated the white folks. Mrs. Tillson's Tennessee neighbor unwittingly articulated this fear when she confessed that her people suspected the Tillsons of using "a heap of words to Yankees that you don't use when you talk to us."[15]

When the election season arrived, Thomas moved with the sure step of a man who had lived with backcountry people all his life. He had learned how to use, if he did not accept, local resentment of federal power and eastern ways. He went along with the anti–big folks rhetoric of his supporters such as Thomas Sloo, Jr., and James Hall. In 1819, he even contributed to that rhetoric by resurrecting old fears about disputed land-office cases settled in 1812, claiming that Edwards intended to reopen the cases. The cases were never reopened but the threat of opening them played on the voters' suspicion that Edwards might place loyalty to his wealthy friends above the people's interests. No doubt Edwards and company were big folks; Thomas's accomplishment lay in associating his circle, which also included wealthy speculators such as John McLean, William and Robert Morrison, and Michael Jones of Shawneetown, with the young generation of leaders. This was possible only because the new men were offended more by social pretensions than by wealth.[16]

Thomas was also a skillful party builder. He persuaded James Hall, then co-editor of the influential *Illinois Gazette* at Shawneetown, to denounce his opponent's first family orientation. In a series of articles during the summer of 1821, Hall conjured up the image of a landed "nepocracy" fostering within its domains "a nursery of political eminence." The implied Federalist arrogance and the intimated comparison with the Adams family were too damaging for Edwards to ignore; by the fall, he offered his old ally Henry Eddy the financing to purchase Hall's share in the paper.[17] But Thomas's political skills shone their brightest at the dinner table. He would travel long distances to dine with the leading men in each county. These encounters always netted a good number of recruits, sometimes including former opponents. Recalling Thomas's political acu-men, Thomas Ford wrote: "It was a maxim with him, that no man could be talked down with loud and bold words, 'but anyone might be whis-pered to death.'" Daniel P. Cook frequently complained of the supporters who had been winnowed to the Thomas party by its leader's promises and "exertions." Thomas exerted himself mightily in the months before the Third General Assembly convened in December of 1822. He was busy lining up votes for the impending U.S. Senate election.[18]

His success in the 1823 U.S. Senate race marked Thomas's personal apogee in Illinois politics. He received the vote of anti-slavery newcomers such as Yorker Nicholas Hansen, who settled in Pike County, the north-ernmost settled county at the time, and Yankee Curtiss Blakeman, the re-spected former ship captain and recognized leader of the Marine Settle-ment in Madison County.[19] Dissatisfaction with the anti-democratic territorial system, Thomas's positive identification with the interests of the local community, and the negative rhetoric against the Edwards's "family of rulers" made this success possible. That Thomas was able to se-cure his reelection in the face of opposition, however muddled, from the powerful Edwards group is evidence of the strong discontinuity between the image of a territorial aristocracy and the political realities in the newly emerging Illinois political community.

Of course, playing fast and loose with rhetoric can backfire on a plu-ralist. And backfire it did. In the summer of 1822, at the peak of the U.S. representative election, Thomas accused Cook of blocking a bill provid-ing for a new land office in Sangamon County. In a newspaper article, Cook responded to charges that he "wished to drag the people of that county to Edwardsville to purchase their lands, and of speculating my-self upon them." It was true that Cook had invested in property at Springfield; the land office was another matter. Actually, he argued, he had voted for the new land office, whereas "Judge Thomas . . . had [the bill] so amended as to keep the appointment of officers back at least un-til the next session of Congress and the lands from market, therefore, for six months thereafter." Thomas, who at this time was employed by Treasury Secretary Crawford to inspect the Ohio, Indiana, Illinois, and Mississippi land offices, was calculating that by the next session he would have a stronger position vis-à-vis Edwards in the competition for appointments. His interest in supplying jobs to his followers was thus exposed to open conflict with the interests of the poor farmers he sup-ported rhetorically.[20]

The biggest threat posed by rhetoric, however, came from the issue of slavery. Sectional tensions dogged Illinois politics from the moment the first territorial legislature adopted its first "black code." Tensions arose in the last territorial legislature, which debated a bill censuring indentured servitude. They arose most subtly of all in the letter Nathaniel Pope sent to Congress as territorial delegate to recommend statehood for Illinois.

He asked that the new state's boundaries be altered from those proposed in the Northwest Ordinance. He suggested that the northern border be extended to give the state a port on Lake Michigan. This northern visage might counteract the state's then southern visage and "afford additional security to the perpetuity of the Union."[21]

A brief review of the Thomas party's political strategy between 1818 and 1823 with respect to slavery indicates how the issue changed from a tool for reinforcing the politics of pluralism to a rhetorical device that the younger generation exploited to take control of the state government. Thomas was elected president of the 1818 convention, and his young friend Elias Kent Kane became its directing spirit. Both men owned five slaves and both worked on the provision authorizing the saltwork indentures. It was probably because of Thomas's pragmatic leadership that roll-call analysis does not show factional disagreement over slavery during the first convention. Both sides favored a continuance of the territorial status quo. Although his support for slavery was never in question, he treated it with the flexibility he treated everything else. John Snyder reported that "he firmly believed it to be right in principle and practice." He also supported it in Illinois as a legitimate part of the saline operators' interests, since the saltworks were thought to be profitable on account of their slave labor alone. But he saw in it above all a way to cement a new coalition of constituents in the state's rapidly changing population.[22]

A keen observer of people and trends, Thomas recognized the impact being made by the wave of immigrants beginning in 1815 who streamed down the Ohio to enter Illinois via Shawneetown. He had targeted these newcomers in his earlier positioning against Edwards. After 1818, they came in increasing proportions (though still far from a majority) from the free states. Thomas surmised that party member John McLean lost the U.S. representative election in 1819 on account of some anti-Yankee remarks he made, which "some of the more recent immigrants from the Eastern States" found insulting. The Thomas party agreed to rethink its strategy.[23]

The electoral results from the contest between Daniel P. Cook and John McLean in 1819 showed a state divided between eastern and western counties (see Figure 5). That year the Thomas party tried to fortify the division by proposing a jurisdictional dissection of the state for the upcoming U.S. Senate race. The subsequent halves, divided by the nineteenth meridian, would each send a senator to Washington. The meridian dividing line reflected the state's settlement pattern; very few settlers had chosen to live in the hilly central counties of Franklin and Jefferson. The meridian had recently been used to define zones for the "practice of Physic and Surgery." But the real goal of the scheme was to remove the mighty Edwards from the contest, since Thomas would already represent the state's western half. Yet, the pattern of election results suggested

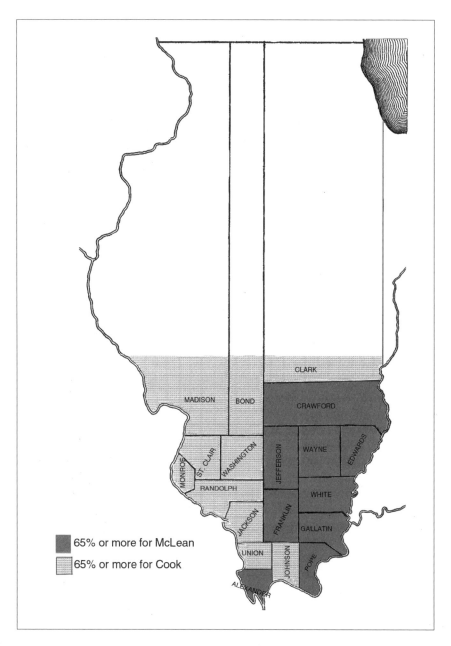

Figure 5 **1819 Election for U.S. Representative**

by the 1819 map was wholly artificial and might be continued only with a huge influx of patronage jobs. It was already being said that Thomas used a single federal judgeship to lure 20 men to his side. Such extreme tactics had still not succeeded against the popular "little Cook." Nor would the newcomers, who were entering a state in the Union, be as politically powerless as the territorial wards had been.[24]

In place of the east-west alignment, Thomas set out early in 1820 to press the flesh in support of a new strategy. He hoped to entice the opposition members in the older counties of the western side to join the eastern block over a new issue: reintroduction of the territorial right of converting slaves into indentured servants. From a factional point of view this right had three political benefits in its favor. It could be defended easily, because servants were not considered unusual anywhere in the state. It was endangered by the 1825 constitutional deadline for indentured servant contracts at the salines and so would continue to be a pertinent issue. Finally, promotion of the right had the potential of paralyzing the Edwards group by dividing group members among themselves.

Word of this ploy reached the Edwards camp by the summer of 1820, in the middle of Elias Kent Kane's campaign for Cook's congressional seat. Kane, a Yale graduate from New York, received the unified support of the Thomas party. James Hall was sent to Shawneetown to edit the *Gazette,* and Joseph Street to Edwardsville where he was to establish a pro-slavery paper. But Hooper Warren "exposed the whole plot in an editorial on July 11, 1820, laying special emphasis on the significant fact that a determined effort to force a slave constitution upon the people of Illinois would be made within the next two or three years."[25] This had the effect of quieting down the rhetoric on slavery, particularly as Kane made a surprisingly poor showing in 1820. But the Thomas group had to have been alarmed when the loss was repeated in 1822, this time by John McLean of Shawneetown. The trend indicated by the latter election map shows the northern counties voting in a block against the faction, while the southern counties were still partially split along the old east-west line (see Figure 6).

Just at this point, when he needed to rally his troops, Thomas paused, reassessed, and spent the fall campaigning for himself. After the 1822 election loss, Thomas concentrated on getting reelected himself to the U.S. Senate, which transpired on January 9, 1823.[26] But the day before, the legislature had given two important positions in state government—attorney general and treasurer—to two stalwart Edwards men. The next year, when a new supreme court was chosen, in accordance with the 1818 constitution, every selection came from those who had followed Edwards. This signaled Thomas's inability to translate his personal success to the faction as a whole. Once again the call of self-interest had sabotaged the legitimacy of an incipient politics of deference. For all his

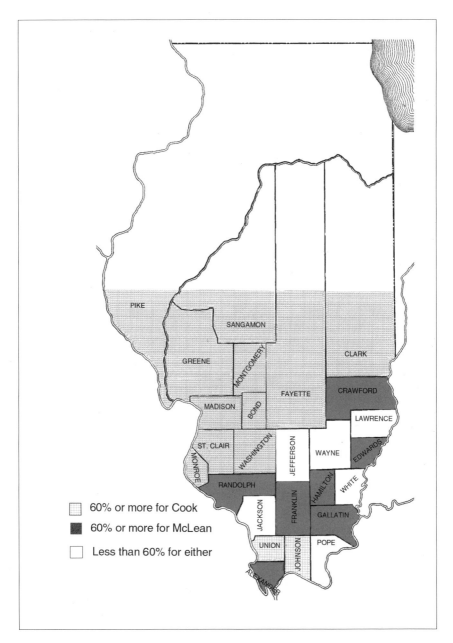

Figure 6   **1822 Election for U.S. Representative**

positioning as the moral champion of the traditional order and as the people's patron, Thomas was, of necessity, also committed to his own political and economic advancement.

A final piece of evidence of failure can be found in the complaints of Thomas's foremost young supporter, Elias Kent Kane. As Governor Bond's secretary of state, Kane acted as the clearing board for the faction's distribution of state offices between 1818 and 1822. After the party lost the governorship, Kane found himself out of a job. In 1824 he ran successfully for state representative and from the General Assembly was chosen for the U.S. Senate. But in 1823, writing as Timour, he expressed dissatisfaction with what had become of the Thomas party: "Every person is courted and flattered," he vented, "in proportion as he has the power of disposing benefits." A change of fortune, however, brought a complete abandonment: "let it be known that he requires assistance himself, and those whose professions of friendship before were unceasing, and who had shared most liberally of his bounty, are the first to treat him with neglect, and even to indulge in strictures on his weakness and misconduct."[27]

If at one point Jesse B. Thomas could look upon slavery or at least "limited" slavery as a potential solution to the host of problems facing his party, the rigid anti-slavery position Coles brought to the issue made it difficult to control through compromise. After January 1823, Thomas did lose control of the issue and of his party. It is noteworthy that Thomas's name does not appear on the report published a few weeks later to defend the intentions of the majority in passing the Convention Resolution. The report had seven authors, four former Thomas men and three former Edwards men.[28] They formed the nucleus of the developing "Convention Party," which had come to life in the legislature and soon spread to the people. When the sonorous bells of slavery began ringing, the state's "new men" held their ropes firmly. The bells tolled on the patrons' republic.

THE DISSOLUTION OF THE PATRONS' REPUBLIC

In the "deep game" over party alignment that was played out during the Missouri crisis at Washington, Thomas was a loser. He could not have anticipated that "Old Republican" William Crawford, to whom he tied his fortunes, would exit the political game, from a stroke in 1824. Yet, in truth, the loss of his influential friend was not the sole cause of his fall from the national scene. His great negotiating skill, his ability to find a compromise among conflicting groups, ironically contributed to his sunken hopes in Washington. Unlike Edwards, who approached the Missouri question with characteristic concern for states' rights, Thomas thought the uproar could be quieted with a compromise. On February 17, and again on March 2, 1820, he introduced an amendment to prohibit the expansion of slavery into the Louisiana Purchase, north of thirty-six degrees thirty minutes of latitude. The South viewed this part of Henry Clay's Missouri Compromise an extorted concession to federal authority. Ever after, the western politician who authored it was discounted from southerners' political plans. Thomas's treatment at their hands only confirmed that, however loudly Illinoisans proclaimed their western or southern loyalty, the South treated them as northerners. In the end, Thomas's loyalty to Crawford—rewarded with appointment to the land office examiner post—only brought him before a House subcommittee on the charge of accepting a public contract while an active senator and brought down upon him charges of electioneering.[29]

Furthermore, Thomas still faced the same democratic revolution, try as he might to sidestep it, that brought low the mighty Edwards. Attempting to convert deferential into electoral authority, he confronted a collapse in political distance that was accelerating across the country. In Massachusetts the younger generation deferred to older leaders to the point that the elders could use oral voting to their advantage; though it sometimes backfired, Ronald Formisano cites this as an example of the persistence of deference in that state. In Illinois, however, oral voting benefited the grogshop boys, who plied group pressure in order to override the opinion of the local notables. With the democratic revolution in full swing, the situation of leaders in Illinois was even more precarious than that of leaders in New York City during the 1820s and 1830s. Paul A. Gilje singles out the "hogcart riots" of this period as heralding an era in which the city patricians "began to see themselves not so much as the guardians of a clearly perceived single-community interest as, instead, referees striving to ensure that all the rights of each individual were secured." But as Thomas attempted to step into even this reduced role, he confronted the white folks' class- and race-bound vision of community.[30]

By 1823 Thomas's and Edwards's claims to independent status had made their leadership untenable. The favors they received from friends and followers after statehood were no longer mere favors, adding to the ease and enjoyment of their lives, but had become vitally necessary to the continuation of their status and power. Yet they both perceived the new set of rules for gaining and holding power as vulgarly self-interested. The public assertion of self-interest was taboo in their world, even if the taboo itself partially served upper-class interests. Their very identity as leaders depended on the appearance of having no personal interests at all. As Max Weber argued, status involves the "prestige" associated with "a specifically regulated style of life." Those of "highly privileged" status "base their sense of their own worth or dignity on their awareness of the 'perfection' of their mode of life as an expression of their qualitative 'being.'" In other words, high-status actors believe that the prestige they have is self-generated. Weber also implies that self-sufficient actors

nonetheless expect their prestige to be recognized, desired, and ultimately purchased in the form of favors and benefits by others. Yet it was
just this dependence on recognition, and the old leaders' refusal to acknowledge it, that motivated resentment among the locals and their democratic revolution in the first place.[31]

High status in territorial Illinois was limited to those whose economic worth or political office allowed them to participate in a self-
generated lifestyle that was both widely recognized yet not dependent
on the resources of others in the community. Membership in the club
of such high status was, it seems fair to say, limited to men who received an income from the federal government or who were independ-
ently wealthy; for all the rest, reliance on others was directly connected to survival. Taking slaveholding as a rough surrogate for big folk
status, in 1820 only one in one hundred fifty men and their families
were eligible as members.[32]

High-status actors, precisely because of their limited numbers and
self-sufficiency, need agents to facilitate their relations with the larger
world. Agents are culled necessarily from those of low status. Their
self-worth also has a cultural dimension, though one diametrically opposed to that of high-status actors. Weber defines "low-status actors"
as those whose "own worth is bound up with some 'promise'" and
who rely on this promise to complete their being.[33] Ambitious low-
status actors desire to mix with the world, and especially with those of
higher status, for their sense of being will be determined by what in
the world they can become. In Illinois, such actors were the younger
associates of Edwards and Thomas. They were the successful farmers,
the shrewd merchants, the popular preachers, above all, the young
lawyers who were prepared to trade their influence with the people for
contact with the big folks and their favors—loans, legal aid, militia and
county office appointments, and introductions to powerful or wealthy
national figures. After the territorial system fell, the local politicians—
having been trained in the ways of brokerage—continued to think of
politics in terms of personal exchange; the only difference was that
now "the people" were their new patrons. Edwards strained to ignore
his clients' brokerage altogether; Thomas insisted on mastering all
deals. But the politics the clients made tied all deals back to the interest of the white folks.

The federally appointed territorial governor and judges exercised
complete political discretion over the territory's citizens. The result
was a pent-up political agenda that had to await the change that came
with statehood, a change that brought, in Stephen Skowronek's terms,
the "alteration of the strategic universe of political and institutional
action." In the new setting, the patronal system quickly disintegrated
when its leaders failed to develop a fair and coordinated method of
sorting out and supporting candidates for office. What was autocrati-

cally controlled by one man, under the old system, now had to be managed by the entire party.[34]

As formerly self-contained entities, neither Thomas nor Edwards wished to move beyond themselves or their individual accomplishments. Yet the emphasis on the individual, on each person's actions and initiatives, did precisely that: it focused the faction's attention on the person at its head. Tocqueville commented that the prevalent equality in democracies created a great "envy" to be directed against the few who achieved distinction.[35] In early Illinois politics, envy burned greatest among the new men. Followers were jealous of their leaders' knack of organizing issues to serve their own interests along with the state's. In the new political market created by the rush of democracy and self-interest, one could no longer act this way and expect political cooperation from associates. The French observer lauded self-interest rightly understood; what he did not count on was that right understanding would become a commodity, that its supply would be limited, and that its price would be raised precipitously by ambitious politicians demanding insatiable quantities.

In this new world there was little use for patrons. The democratic revolution in Illinois meant that citizens not only determined political goals (as they reputedly did indirectly under the territorial system), but they also determined the manner by which those goals would be identified and carried out. Granted, the voters' message was not immediately clear. If they had elected a Cook and a Bond, they also elected a Coles. But the local politicians in the legislature sent a clearer message. The state bank was passed over the objections of the Council of Revision and in direct rebellion against "great men." And, if Edwards and Thomas could still locate goals on which they and the voters could agree, their style remained disagreeable. Although Illinois's great men and most of its white folks agreed that slavery might be allowed in Missouri, for example, neither Thomas's latitudinal compromise nor Edwards's natural right of cultivation captured the local imagination like the claim that Missouri had a republican right to determine its own course.

Once "the people" themselves are seen as interested, the public interest can no longer be a matter of disinterest, and disinterestedness can no longer serve as a tool to legitimate authority. Washington's disinterestedness, like all self-sacrifice, has held scholars in its thrall. But its importance in terms of political development was that it provided a widely recognized, publicly acknowledged, and potentially imitable standard for others to follow. It provided limits on the meaning of republican leadership so that leaders knew what they were doing when they led as republicans. Such limits are essential for political stability. The white folks' identification with the people provided a similar limitation. But in their new world (cleared, as it were, of all disinterest), political leadership no longer involved the "doctoring" of political means by which the patrons justified their authority.

The democratic revolution ushered in by the dissenting republicans of the backcountry undermined the classical republican idea that the political realm existed independent of private interests. The young clients' dissent was to this extent consistent with modern liberalism, for their view made the state wholly subservient to society. They jettisoned the static view of society based on a virtuous self-control and replaced it with a view based on the constant pursuit of interests. The current social vision of those interests pursued by society gives the state an immediate purpose. Even the new-modeled commercial republicanism pursued by Madison in the 1780s did not go this far; it countenanced a society dedicated to an industrial purpose, but only under strict state control.[36]

As soon as ambitious local politicians began to gravitate to the legislature, Illinois reached the Tocquevillean moment when state becomes subordinate to society. Thenceforth, the key to popularity and elected office lay in finding a "nice" issue with which to shape society's vision of "self-interest rightly understood." The politician who most clearly seized the moment was Daniel P. Cook. From his birthplace in eastern Kentucky, he found his way to a clerkship in the Kaskaskia law office of his uncle Nathaniel Pope, who served as Edwards's territorial secretary. In 1816 he wrote to Edwards about his interest in associating himself with "a subject of such acknowledged importance that a man who is able to develop its niceties may well expect to acquire some fame for so doing." In the same year he was appointed to the visible and well-paid public auditor's office. But neither this office nor an opportunity to work for John Quincy Adams in the state department was suitable to the twenty-year-old Cook; "it would not satisfy my ambition," he told Edwards, "to be buried in an office—merely a servant as it were—where the world, perhaps, would never hear of such a being." Consequently, he continued, he had decided to "return to the West, and remain there until an opportunity presents itself for my advancement."[37]

Such an opportunity as did arise, Cook himself created. This was the drive for statehood, begun by the *Western Intelligencer* in 1817. Cook, then editor of the Kaskaskia-based paper, began the debate for statehood with only "effusions of visionary hopes." But he had found his "nice" cause; the whole territory responded to his charge that the federally appointed government was "a species of despotism." Between 1818 and 1826, he received the backing of the Edwards faction for the state's lone U.S. representative seat. After winning a second term in 1820, Cook wrote to Edwards, asking for his daughter's hand in marriage, a woman whom he had known "almost from her infancy." "Whether she entertains correspondent feelings or not I have yet to ascertain, and in doing it I wish to tread on peaceful ground," he concluded. "I wish to know that no parental sensibility will be wounded." The cautious, if unromantic, client was awarded the highest token of patronage: marriage into the family.[38]

John Reynolds also seized the moment. Although less favored and less talented, he was more popular than Cook. Reynolds brought to the political table strong support from the populous Goshen settlement in Madison County; and he acted with an audacity that only popularity could have nurtured. After distinguishing himself as a Ranger in the War of 1812, Reynolds tapped Edwards for a different kind of patronage: legal aid. He had some lands tied up in the courts, their status uncertain under the law. In 1818 he wrote to the most powerful man in the territory, Governor Edwards, perfunctorily asking him to present his claims before "the proper tribunal for justice. I want no more." He added, "I fear by this time you are much tired with me and my claims but treat them and me as your feelings and judgement may dictate and I shall be satisfied."[39]

Reynolds did not fare as well as Cook in the game of obtaining favors, a consequence related partially to his rough manners. A more pointed reason may have involved the mechanics of factional politics. It was not a mere coincidence that the central political coordinators in each faction were lawyers, Nathaniel Pope for the Edwards group and Elias Kent Kane for the Thomas group. Nor was the increasingly cool treatment Reynolds received from the territory's leading politicos a coincidence. Leaving as a young man for Transylvania University in Kentucky, he came back in 1815 a lawyer. Suddenly the boy who had won all the foot races was advocating preemption rights for squatters. This had the effect of short-circuiting the authority of the territorial patrons by making obsolete their powers over land claims. It is not too far-fetched to suppose that Reynolds's early predilection for the white folks (when he first hung out his lawyer's shingle, he took on the cases of the poorest members of the community) was one of the reasons barring his access to the inner circle of either party. Edwards refused to back him for the U.S. Senate in 1823 and generally regarded him with suspicion; Thomas considered him "a presumptuous ignoramus." By this remark Thomas let slip a telltale sign of class jealousy, but his was from the top down.[40]

THE CONVENTION RESOLUTION AND ORDINARY POLITICS

In the legislature, the spark from Coles's speech was half-heartedly fanned into a flame by Madison County representative George Churchill. Churchill, a reclusive bachelor-farmer from Vermont, was one of the House's most diligent members. He had been preparing an election bill he would soon present when the excitement caused by Coles's bill began. Four days later, it must have been with only the most casual intentions that he requested and—surely, to his surprise—was granted leave to introduce "a petition from certain free persons of color in this state praying the right of suffrage." This was a remarkable grant because the petition amounted to a plea to amend the constitutional proviso on "free white male" suffrage.[41]

Churchill, who knew the 1818 constitution well, realized what he was asking; it was later written that he "presented" but did not "support" the petition. The petition was in fact a political hot potato since it had been drawn up by a political opponent on behalf of a community of free blacks who had previously been threatened by kidnappers. A defender explained his predicament. For "if Mr. Churchill had refused to present the memorial, the cry would have been raised that he was the friend of kidnappers, or that he was so illiberal and vindictive that he would not present a memorial written by a gentleman who opposed his election." Churchill was strongly anti-slavery and a public defender of Negro rights. If anyone should have been motivated by Coles's action, he should have been. Yet he was not encouraged enough to "support" the petition. When Jacob Ogle, a longtime settler from St. Clair County, tried to introduce a similar petition the next day on December 10, leave was denied.[42] Thus ended the House's anti-slavery response to Coles's brave inaugural. On December 20 and 21, 1822, Risdon Moore and Conrad Will gave their reports on kidnapping and manumission. After December 21, the House would not hear another word on the subject of slavery until the convention leaders tested the strength of their resolution on January 27, 1823.

If one could visit the Third General Assembly while in session, enter its "wooden building . . . two stories high . . . not very high though," according to Thomas Lippincott, one would find most of the members attending to a full agenda of their own business. Nicholas Hansen, for example, had three purposes upon coming to Vandalia from Pike County. He wanted to keep the Military Bounty lands under the control of local recorders, so that the present recorder (a close friend) could continue— and the Fulton County recorder (a business associate) could begin—to do a good business in deed-recording fees. He wanted to keep Atlas (a town founded by yet another ally) at the center of the new boundaries being drawn for Pike County so it would be the logical choice for county seat. And he planned to get as much as he could of the money the state had set aside from its non-resident tax monies for county improvements. Hansen considered the completion of these tasks a duty; they were to be fulfilled or left undone at the cost of his friends' destruction. He later wrote, "Upon my conduct depended their present and future welfare . . . and the relief and amelioration which their condition demanded were expected at my hands."[43]

Hansen's agenda must be regarded as typical. Although throughout the 1820s the Illinois legislature dealt with statewide issues, each of its members was anchored by county life in bays of local political reality. Hamilton County senator Thomas Sloo, Jr., had, by January 12, already called the Third General Assembly "a very tedious and unpleasant session" since there had "been nothing but a continued scene of intrigue and electioneering."[44] As this comment implies, a productive session was considered one in which legislators were unfettered by wider ambitions or factions. Except for the most malleable of politicians (Hansen was one) "intrigue" was not conducive to the steady pursuit of county interests. There is abundant evidence that most members attempted to treat the meetings at Vandalia as mere extensions of county business. These tended to vote for their county's regional interests, to support the governor's proposals, and to respect the powers of the executive; above all, they avoided controversial committees and turned down invitations to grogshop meetings and nocturnal card games where informal vote trading occurred and statewide deals hatched.

When legislators drank and played cards, their veins flowed hot with whiskey and mercenary instincts surfaced. Lippincott, who was elected secretary of the Senate for the 1822–1823 session, remembered meeting Thomas Reynolds in T. W. Smith's "somewhat public room" and finding him playing cards. Reynolds had just been elected chief justice of the state supreme court by the General Assembly. In the weeks preceding the election, he had made it a point to be seen attending the weekly Sunday afternoon sermons given by the reverend members William Kinney, Daniel Parker, William Kinkade, and others. All the "respectable" members, Lippincott reported, attended. Prominently displayed among them, Thomas Reynolds could be seen, "facing the preacher, looking earnestly and listening devotedly." Then Lippincott recounted what happened when he encountered him gambling in Smith's room: "Laying my hand upon his shoulder, I said, 'What's this?' He looked up over his shoulder at me and replied, 'I don't tain a _____. The election's over.'"[45]

One man who avoided such scenes was the senator from Randolph County, Samuel Crozier. Situated in the most developed section of the state, the county not only contained the state's two oldest cities, Kaskaskia and Cahokia, but also a small portion of the American Bottom. Crozier's committee appointments reflect the county's economic importance in the state. He sat on the state bank committee where he advocated an anti-speculation, hard money policy and he joined the internal improvements committee where he supported various road-building projects. But he also remained loyal to local concerns by continuing to serve on the county commissioners' court in 1822, two years after being elected state senator. Randolph County had the largest number of "free people of color servants and slaves" among the counties listed in the 1820 state census, with 342 among a total of 3,533 inhabitants. Crozier voted against Daniel Parker's bill to strengthen the executive branch's role in supervising indentures and protecting free blacks. This was in effect a vote for local control; county records indicate that the registering of indentures, conducted under the auspices of the county clerk to the advantage of the masters, often violated the spirit of the 1787 Ordinance and the letter of the territorial laws. Crozier also voted for the Convention Resolution, though not the first time it was offered.[46]

Other votes by Crozier mark him as decidedly non-partisan. He voted, for example, for preacher Parker's proposal to begin each day's business with a prayer. William Kinney, Joseph Beaird of Monroe County, Milton Ladd of Johnson and Franklin Counties, and Michael Jones of Gallatin County, all voted against Parker's servitude reform; they all also voted to table the prayer idea. Parker's rigid, puritanical manner contrasted with the "liberal" demeanor of these other gentlemen. In terms of his anti-slavery views, Parker was the Senate's equivalent to George Churchill. Crozier's support for Parker on the prayer issue suggests that he sought to dissociate the slavery issue from any irreligious intentions. The view of Parker's opponents surfaced in the Kaskaskia (Randolph County) newspaper, the *Republican*. Parker's prayer "proposition," "Honestus" wrote, would have encumbered "that branch, with two or three hours of prayer." "Had it succeeded, [it] would only have been at the expense of two or three hundred dollars a day—and who would have paid for it? why only the people—it would only cause the increase of taxes, and that's but a trifle."[47]

Crozier apparently refused to make the connection between prayer and politics, however. It was characteristic of the man not to notice the special interests that local leaders brought to the body as politicians. Precisely for this reason, he seemed out of place in the partisan atmosphere of the legislature. Thomas Ford observed in Crozier's character "a remarkable example of the most pure, kind, and single-hearted honesty," but Ford had not made the observation as a compliment. He used it to make a point with his readers. He observed that Crozier, after "serving the two sessions in the Senate [1820–1821, 1822–1823], at the close of the second, and after he had been bought and sold a hundred times without knowing it . . . said he 'really did believe that some intrigue had been going on.'" Here Ford concluded incredulously: "So little as this are honest men aware of the necessity of keeping their eyes open." Even when Ford's need to settle old scores is discounted, Samuel Crozier's story suggests the limitations of the argument that devilish passions lay behind support for the Convention Resolution.[48]

Who, then, made the convention the central political issue in the 1822–1823 legislature? Two contemporaries, George Flower and William H. Brown have recorded their opinions. The prime movers were, in the words of Brown, "a few designing men . . . from the northern counties . . . who hesitated not to betray their constituents." These men cooperated with the representatives from the southern counties who were "always ready to vote for the introduction of Slavery." Flower was even more explicit, arguing that the northern county representatives traded their votes on the Convention Resolution for others' votes on the Canal Bill. "My impression," he wrote, "is that the treachery came from the south [of the state] and the traitors from the north [of the state]." Between these two entities a deal was struck: "the Southerners offered to the Northerners their support and votes in these terms: 'If you vote for our convention, we will vote for your canal.'" The idea for the canal was first suggested to the General Assembly by Governor Bond; Coles again brought it up in his inaugural. The canal, to connect Lake Michigan with the Illinois River, would provide the Illinois farmer with access to the New York market through the Great Lakes and the soon-to-be-completed Erie Canal.[49]

At the intrastate regional level, Brown's analysis is solid. A map of the 1824 convention vote in the counties indicates a clear north/south division (see Figure 7). Nor is there any doubt that the convention was supported by representatives from the southern counties. It was well known that representatives Henry Eddy of Gallatin County in 1820 and A. J. Field of Union County in 1822 campaigned and were elected on the promise of proposing a new constitution. It is also true that, as Brown suggested, the leaders of the convention fight were Kinney in the Senate and Emanuel West in the House, from St. Clair and Madison Counties respectively. Both were located in the most northwestern part of the state then inhabited by whites; both counties appeared in a list titled "northern counties" by Brown.[50]

But there is a fundamental problem with the quid pro quo part of this analysis. In order to make a deal, two sides must need to trade, and whereas the convention supporters needed votes, the canal supporters did not. The canal bill only authorized commissioners to hire an engineer and surveyors to inspect the area between the Chicago and Illinois Rivers. In the House, the only debate connected with the canal bill was over how high to set the per diem for the overseers, and even this question was resolved by a vote (twenty-seven to six) on William Alexander of Monroe County's motion to set it at five dollars. It is hardly probable that this lopsided vote, the only one recorded on the canal bill in the House, could have been involved in a trade for the tight Convention Resolution vote one month and ten days later.

To suppose that a quid pro quo was involved is to impute altogether too much control on the part of the convention leadership over the other members, even those in their own coalition. This is not to say that no offers of vote trading existed; but, rather, that neither the party control necessary to tally trades nor the power to enforce them was present. Indeed, the very notion of enforceability trampled on the tender region of each member's responsibility to "the people" in the county. According to "Americanus" (who claimed to have been present), the session was not ruled by a "junto or caucus formed by the majority, nor was there an offer by them to buy or sell a vote." He acknowledged, "there were many jocular proposals, to wit—if you will support the resolution for calling a convention, I will support the law for cutting a canal, vice

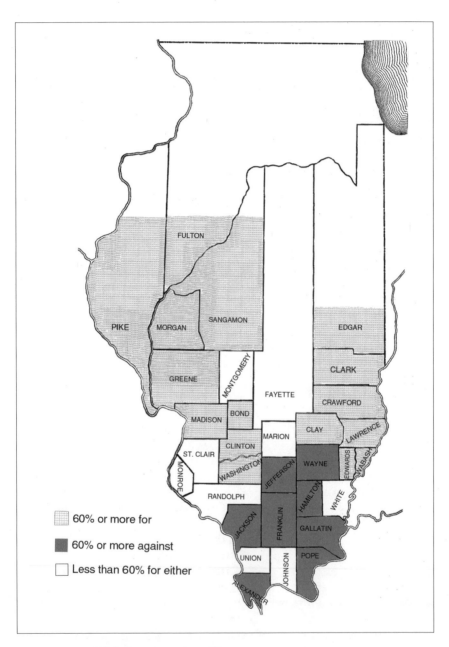

Figure 7 **1824 Convention Vote**

versa," but, he added, "that will not prove the least inclination to buy or sell a vote."[51] Americanus's comment suggests that the legislators were often uncertain in their vote counting. The most prominent example is the convention vote itself. The outcome of this all-important issue, on which all votes traded and log-rolled, bought and sold, should have been known with precision, was unknown to Emanuel West, the "prudent general" of the conventionists in the House. Not only did West have to test the waters on the vote as late as January 27, 1823, but on February 11, when he thought he had the votes, his miscalculation on Nicholas Hansen's vote caused the uproar that eventually led to Hansen's ejection and the testing of politics "out of doors" at Vandalia.[52]

If then one is to understand the cause of the "excitement" at Vandalia, one must look beyond sectional biases. "History," J. Mills Thornton has observed, "is the story of the collision of perceptions." A more accurate explanation, one never taken seriously because of its source, is the conventionists' own justification of their behavior. The extraordinary politics in the legislature occurred, they argued, when they reacted to the governor and the minority's attempt to usurp the authority of the people. In their view a simple republican exercise—of returning the power of government back to the people—had been imperiously derailed by a superior-minded minority, who in their "windsor chairs of state forgot that they were even elected by the people."[53]

When asked to name the culprit, the conventionists pointed to Nicholas Hansen. By the end of the session, Hansen had secured his three items of local business, but two personal interests remained elusive; he hoped to get appointed recorder of deeds in a Bounty Tract county and to receive the Thomas party's nod to run for U.S. representative in 1824. By then he knew that he had gotten all he could from the conventionists. He had voted with them on January 27, 1823; in return, on February 1, he received the crucial votes of West, Logan, Phillips, Ford, Whiteside, and Field on his proposal for the Pike County share of non-resident taxes. The amount of his proposal was higher than these men would have agreed to if it had not been for his crucial vote; and he was not likely to win acceptance for another plum in the recorder post, let alone win support for the House. At this point and for this reason (so the conventionists argue, for here the evidence is inconclusive), he turned to the non-conventionist side.[54]

Hansen well understood the importance of his vote, the twenty-fourth, for the passage of the Convention Resolution. This was the exact number needed to have a two-thirds majority in the House; it also could be the thirteenth vote needed on the other side to stop the resolution. Sometime after February 1, it was believed, he visited Coles. He agreed to be the thirteenth vote in return for both plums: his (or a close friend's) appointment to recorder in Fulton County or Morgan County, and pledges from the minority to support him for Congress. "And in this very contract between the minority and Mr. Hansen," one of the legislators later wrote anonymously, "is to be found, in great measure the excitement produced by the convention question"; he added, "If [Hansen] had acted consistently, the measure would have been quietly submitted and quietly settled."[55]

One can imagine the effect such a plan, or even a rumor of it, would have on the convention leadership. They were determined to pass, above and beyond county concerns, significant measures to help the state break loose from its current torpor. Last session, they had created the state bank. The circumstances of this action are illuminating: "the Bank Law," Ames recalled, had been passed "by a *triumphant* majority." The young Edwards's client David Blackwell had led the fight. When the council of revision rejected the bill for exceeding the constitutional authority of the state, Blackwell reacted as if personally insulted. The state's constitutional provision for a bank had "passed the ordeal of congressional criticism. . . . Is it not strange that no *great constitutional lawyers* were found there to discover that these provisions contravened the Federal Constitution? *Where slept the Federalist the while?*" Having passed this test, the people of Illinois had hoped they would be left in peace to exercise their rights. Yet now the council "by great constitutional lawyers contended, that there exists no right in the state to bank." After Blackwell repeated the phrase *"great constitutional lawyers"* a few more times and finished his speech, the legislature proceeded to repass the bill. Now these same men, and it was acknowledged on all sides that bank and convention were popular with the same people, had again been challenged by the governor. The conclusion was obvious: Coles and and his "Immaculate Fourteen" in the Senate and House were deviously attempting to direct the future policy of the state.[56]

Suspicion about Hansen had been aroused in the first days of the session. John Shaw came to Vandalia from his home at Coles Grove in Pike County to contest Hansen's election early in December 1822. Shaw told anyone who would listen about his rival's exploits back in Pike. The county had been quiet and agreeable, he said, filled with men like him—"a peaceable citizen and a laboring farmer"—until Hansen and the Ross clan of New York "Dutch" arrived, and began to nurture in Atlas a competitor to Coles Grove for the county seat. In Atlas they set up "a company of Yankee pedlars" engaged in the business of recording deeds. Hansen, who "enter[ed] the county as a [probate] Judge," was first seen by Shaw among this group; it was through Hansen's lobbying at Vandalia the winter before that they had obtained control of the recorder's office in the first place. That office recorded the deeds to 338,000 acres of Military Bounty land in 1821 alone.[57]

Their next goal was to funnel the "750.00 dollars in non-resident taxes allotted to Pike" to their group by sending Hansen to the legislature. But Hansen's ambitions did not stop there: "it was expected that by

Mr. Hansen's being elected representative from Pike, it would serve him as an introduction to public business; where his brilliant talents might attract universal applause." Shaw's portrait continued, dripping with sarcasm: "and from being a representative from a county, he might become secretary of a state, and from this he might get on the floor of Congress, and that the balance of his precious days might be passed in the capacity of a public character." Shaw succeeded in casting doubt on Hansen. Sometime around February 2, 1823, Hansen's communications with the minority were detected and John Shaw was brought into the conventionist nightlife at Vandalia. The meetings began in earnest on January 27, 1823, when West and Field discovered that they needed two more votes in the House to pass their resolution. That night, at William Kinney's Vandalia home, the convention leaders plotted a strategy for obtaining those two votes. They consulted with John Shaw and realized they had three votes to secure. After January 27, 1823, the atmosphere in Vandalia changed permanently. The next night, the state bank and land office buildings were burned, even though Col. James Kelly, the bank's well-respected attending cashier, had secured the fireplace, which had not been used since the morning before. Strangely, while the buildings were saved, the records both of the bank's loans and of the land office deeds were destroyed.[58]

To sway the minds of certain targeted members, the conventionists decided to play their trump card: their connection to the people. They would send out "couriers" to Madison, St. Clair, Johnson, Washington, White, Randolph, and Greene Counties to obtain signed petitions of "instructions" from a majority of voters in those counties, instructing their wavering representatives to vote for a convention. In this task, John Shaw was engaged, traveling to Greene County. However, "after the most indefatigable efforts . . . [he] could only get about 130 or 140 persons to sign." Yet, this petition, directed to Thomas Rattan, the representative from Greene and Morgan Counties, contained enough names to provide the uncertain Rattan with the incentive he needed to change his vote. Shaw had proved his dedication to the cause.[59]

The three weeks that followed, from the January 27 meeting at Kinney's house to the "break up" or adjournment of the legislature on February 18, were a time of heady giddiness in that body.[60] If Thomas Sloo, Jr., thought the scenes before January 12 had been filled with "intrigue," he must have considered these last three weeks outright rebellion. The feeling that the will of the people was being subverted by a willful minority filled the members with a new sense of purpose. The truth of the white folks' struggle against oppression never seemed fresher. For William Kinney, the truth came early. He had focused his hopes on the day when senator John Grammer of Union County would arrive. For some unrecorded reason, Grammer had not attended the session to which he had been "anominated" by his friends.[61] But by early January, it was clear to the convention supporters that the Senate, as presently constituted, would be one and possibly more votes short of the constitutional majority needed for passing the resolution. Thus, Grammer, over 100 miles away, was sent a message, probably from A. P. Field also of Union, to come posthaste to the capital.

In the meantime, the Senate's remaining work had become unimportant to Kinney. By January 21, he was already getting tired of all the talk. On that day, his friend Theophilus W. Smith was laboring to get the canal bill through the Senate's committee of the whole. The question on the floor was, should the House or Senate version of the bill be taken up? On Kinney's prompting they took up the House bill. But after a short discussion in which nothing had been resolved, Kinney moved to rise and vote against the bill. Smith was shocked, or so William H. Brown reported. Smith had written the Senate bill in part himself. He had only taken up the House bill because Kinney had favored it. In an earnest tone, he remarked that he "wished to act with perfect liberality and good faith . . . but when he saw the course which some gentlemen were taking. . . . Suddenly, the gentleman from St. Clair wanted the second bill so much he seemed to have fallen in love with it."[62] At this point, Brown's report indicates that Kinney rose to speak. "He never said he had fallen in love with either of the bills . . . [in fact] he hated both bills, but he hated the last worse than the first. It put him in mind of the old woman who had three husbands—she hated them all bad enough, but she hated the last much worse than the first two."

In the course of Smith's earlier defense of the canal, it was clear what had awakened Kinney's sense of humor. Smith made two basic arguments in favor of the canal. First, present inhabitants would be obliged to invest the money advanced in property taxes by non-residents; second, the canal would attract emigrants who could help the state out of its languishing condition. This last point, he recognized, was a "delicate subject," for he knew it might be urged that "this is not the description of population which we require." He ended with emotion: "I, sir, feel no prejudice against any portion of the population of the United States—I feel myself to be a Western man."

Kinney responded by saying he was sorry that "so much earnestness was exhibited on this occasion." Although he recognized that the bill had almost unanimous support, he personally could not go along. What, he asked, did the locals owe the non-resident landowners? Had not the latter been given their land as an "incentive" to fight? What good, then, would they be when they came? "He believed some of them were not forward to go into warfare, even on the defensive." At this point, the Senate speaker stepped forward to end the debate and restore the "harmony" that had heretofore characterized the Senate room. Nonetheless, a threshold had been breached. Joseph Beaird of Monroe County remarked that "in the course of the discussion, different reflections had passed through his mind," such that he no longer thought he would support the measure. When the canal bill came up for a vote in the Senate two weeks later, only Kinney, Beaird, and newly arrived Grammer were found on the negative side.

On February 4, 1823, Joseph Beaird, now more firmly than ever under Kinney's sway, moved that the General Assembly establish a special recorder's office at Vandalia to service the Military Bounty lands, since the recorders in the Bounty Tract counties had become tainted with political favoritism. This bill passed only with the aid of the speaker's tie-breaking vote. Here was a foreshadowing of the attacks to come on Hansen and the deed business in Pike and Fulton Counties. The disruption of regular business proceeded along these lines, with William Kinney periodically inserting humorous riders and amendments and with the conventionists biding their time, until Grammer arrived on February 6. Kinney had, for example, proposed an "internal" improvements bill as an alternative to Smith's "external" improvement canal bill. On February 5, Kinney realized that his bill would not pass, as it had been encumbered with too many additions. Not to be bested, even in a humourous contest, Kinney added a rider to the effect that, as "almost every swamp and slough in the American Bottom was to be drained, Lake Michigan too ought to be drained."[63]

Finally, on February 6, John Grammer arrived in Vandalia, and next day, the atmosphere in the chamber quickly regained a somber air. Kinney took up the resolution from the House, introduced by A. P. Field, which argued that the 1818 constitution's requirement of a two-thirds majority vote for the passage of a convention resolution referred to the total number of votes cast, that is, of both houses of the legislature, not each separately. Field's resolution was put forth in the early confidence of the House "instructions," under the belief that an expected avalanche of votes in the House could make up for whatever number of votes might be lacking in the Senate. It passed the Senate by the vote of eleven to six, with Martin Jones of Bond, Fayette, and Montgomery Counties abstaining. Andrew Bankson, William Kinkade, Daniel Parker, Stephen Stillman, George Cadwell, and Samuel Crozier voted against it. With the exception of Crozier, these men, along with Robert Frazier, would vote against the Convention Resolution when it passed the Senate by a twelve-to-six margin on February 10.[64]

On the morning of February 10, 1823, William Kinkade presented the Senate with a "protest," in which he, along with Stillman, Parker, and Cadwell, declaimed the Field Resolution. It was, Kinkade read aloud, "very injurious to the people and in open violation of the constitution."[65] The two branches were intended to be "mutual checks on each other," but these checks are destroyed since under it "a Convention may be recommended to the people though a majority of the Senate be opposed to it." Was it not "evident," he asked, that the constitution of 1818 "intends that it shall take more members to recommend" a new constitution than to pass a bill? Although ten members of the Senate could stop a bill from becoming a law, he continued, under this resolution, "eighteen members in the Senate might not be able to prevent a law from being passed in favor of a Convention" since it could receive the votes of all 36 House members. When Kinkade sat down, however, the Senate immediately turned to the Convention Resolution vote. He rose again and protested; he asked to be recognized by the speaker but was called to order. Then he began to yell that the secret purpose of the resolution was to legalize slavery in the state, that there ought to be discussion on that issue before voting. When he could no longer be ignored, he was "gagged . . . and made to take his seat."[66]

After the Senate voted, it was found that the Convention Resolution had been passed by the same votes as Field's earlier resolution, except that the "no" vote cast by Robert Frazier of Edwards County was made up by the "yes" vote of Samuel Crozier, and Martin Jones, no longer abstaining, voted yes. The vote being twelve to six there was no question of constitutionality: it had passed the Senate by the required two-thirds majority. They immediately passed the canal bill by a margin of fifteen to three and sent Thomas Lippincott, the Senate secretary, downstairs to the House chamber just below to announce the vote to the House.

HUZZA FOR THE CONVENTION: EXTRAORDINARY POLITICS AT VANDALIA

In the House, the same quickening pace characterized the conventionist effort. However, in this body of 36 members, when the end came, it was more swift and sure. While Field and West awaited the results of the "instructions" during the first week in February 1823, House members were content to address familiar topics. Indeed, that week was dominated by the perennial problem of finding an appropriate per diem pay rate. But there was no escaping the deep division that simmered just below the surface. Between February 1 and 7, there were 13 roll calls on the question of members' pay. The pay issue, which had been settled in the past with a minimum of debate, had been infected by the convention issue. The minority in the House, originally split on the issue, became suspicious that a higher pay rate was being used to allure reluctant members to the convention side. As the instructions came in, it was realized that the results were inconclusive in William McFatridge's Johnson County and Thomas Rattan's Greene County. When changes in their county seats were added as an incentive and also failed, the pay issue was taken up. Whatever amount would be settled upon, the minority wanted the vote recorded.

By February 11, 1823, Field was sufficiently satisfied with his arrangements to move that the Convention Resolution be put to a vote. The vote found McFatridge and Rattan on the conventionists' side—but the suspicions about Hansen had proved correct. After voting with the convention majority on at least two previous occasions, Hansen showed his true colors in a last-minute switch. The vote stood at 23 to 13. This put the majority in a tight spot. Their resolution had passed the House, but it was one vote shy of the constitutional two-thirds majority. However, since it had passed by a majority it could not be reconsidered, except on the motion of a member who had voted in the minority. When no minority member agreed to reconsider, J. G. Daimwood moved reconsideration. The speaker of the House, Dr. William M. Alexander of Alexander County and a resolution supporter, declared Daimwood's motion out of order. Field jumped up and moved that the House vote. He dared the body to let the speaker's motion stand. The resulting vote showed the weakness of Field's coalition, and the weakness of the slavery demon in the House. Field was voted down 19 to 16, with the speaker abstaining and Zadock Casey, James Turney, John McFerron, Raphael Widen, William McFatridge, and William Alexander of Monroe switching to uphold the integrity of legislative procedures.

Fast-thinking James Turney saved the day for the conventionists by moving to send the resolution back to the Senate. He asked that the senators take another vote, this time including the numbers for and against the measure before sending it back to the House. The speaker considered this motion legitimate, and it passed 21 to 15, everyone back with the original 23 to 13 majority except McFatridge and Widen. At this point, "business for the remaining part of the afternoon was suspended." Amid thunderclaps of noise and contention, with "the countenances of the conventionists . . . beyond the reach of a yard-stick," both houses adjourned for the day.[67]

The convention leaders gathered at Kinney's house. It was decided that Hansen's vote had been bought—rumors to this effect immediately spread through the town—and it was agreed that the issue should be addressed at a rally that night in the capitol square. To this place "a little after dark, as by instinct, the citizens, legislators, strangers, and almost all denominations, flocked." There speakers gave "by far the best speeches upon the liberties of the people and the rights of a majority when obtained without fraud or deception." Among the crowd, "a bond was passed . . . [and] sixteen or eighteen members signed," pledging to right the wrong of executive usurpation by unseating Hansen.[68] The meeting then dispersed, but it formed again two hours later; this time, an eyewitness reported, they were carrying Hansen in effigy, with "the strong shrill cry O Yes, O Yes, O Yes, and instantly the cry of Hansen's effigy, Hansen's effigy, Hansen's effigy, and fire, fire, fire." They marched the burning strawman about the square with "musical instruments, such as the drum, the fife, the horns, (God knows how many) triangles, tin-pans, etc." until the dummy exploded from a ball of gunpowder placed in its center. Finally, "the company, about two hundred of them" proceeded "to pay a visit to a Mr. Churchill" giving "three groans for Churchill . . . and three cheers for a Convention." "I have before seen mobs," an eyewitness remarked, "but never before witnessed [one] so respectable." "Judges and negroes, legislators and wire-dancers, Congressmen and trumpeters," he observed, "were so united and blended that it would have puzzled a man of common capacity to have distinguished 'the hopes of the nation.'"[69]

Remarkably, the excited members who returned to the House on the morning of February 12, 1823, attempted to return to their accustomed paces. R. C. Ford, an obscure but "zealous" conventionist, opened the debate. A doctor from northeastern Crawford County, Ford moved that "the House re-consider their vote on the contested election in Pike county." George Churchill rose to object. He "recollected perfectly well" that Ford—a member of the committee on elections that in early December 1822 had decided in favor of Hansen—told him "it was the clearest case he had ever witnessed." Had Ford, he wondered, uncovered some new evidence to change his mind? There was new evidence, Ford replied, which had altered his former clarity of mind. This was the testimony of one Levi Roberts who maintained in an affidavit (dated January 28, 1823) that Shaw was the choice of a majority of Pike voters. The affidavit, a product of the strategy meetings at Kinney's house, proved how important organization could be to the conventionist cause.[70]

At the beginning of the session, when the original challenge to Hansen's seat arose, there were many who voted for Hansen simply because he was believed to be a yes vote for Judge Thomas in the Senate election. Hooper Warren, ever on the lookout for the political operations of the Thomas faction, remarked that "the majority [of the House] have acted perfectly consistent with themselves. . . . There was no more impropriety in turning Mr. Hansen out of the House to accomplish a particular purpose, than there was, in the first instance, in permitting him to retain his seat for the purpose of accomplishing another." Shaw, never oblivious to the politics of his situation, had tried to bargain on the matter. In one version of the story, he had "insinuated" to William Alexander of Monroe County "in terms so plain as not to be misunderstood" that if the representative would vote for his seating, then, in his own words, "he, said Shaw, would vote any way I would direct him at the approaching election for Senator to the Congress."[71]

William Lowrey, the representative of Clark and Edgar Counties, rose to give his testimony. He agreed with Churchill and was able to tie Dr. Ford's original position to the Senate contest. He remembered asking the neighboring representative about the case, and "he perfectly remembered that the gentleman from Crawford had told him that Mr. Hansen was clearly entitled to his seat, and besides, that 'if Hansen was turned out, Thomas would lose a vote.'"[72] If Lowrey was correct, it explains how Dr. Ford, though a member of the committee that examined the ambiguous case, could have been so certain about his previous position at the beginning of the session. Everyone knew he was a staunch Thomas man.[73] Editor Henry Eddy, who was present for his own contested election hearing, remembered that he had remarked at the time (December 1822) that the principle of "the decision [for Hansen] . . . would not be of authority as a precedent in future cases." From the calm of his office at the *Illinois Gazette,* he explained his position:

> By every principle of reason and justice, the person having the highest number of votes [Shaw] is the representative of the county, notwithstanding any slight informality in conducting the election . . . [and] if the formalities of an election have been disregarded or dispensed with by the voters present, and this should be thought a matter of moment, the very utmost that could be done with propriety would be, it should seem, to declare the election void, and order a special election *pro hac vice.*[74]

Eddy's reasonableness did not prevail, not only because of the factional interest but because of a fact that even the most impartial observer had to concede: no fair election could take place in Pike. Between August 1822 and December 1825, Pike County would have no less than four disputed elections. The trouble in 1822 was not only the disputed county seat, but a redistricting change that cut through the heart of John Shaw's base of support. Before 1822 there had only been two voting places, Coles Grove and the Ross settlement. But as Pike County included at that time all of the state north of the Illinois River, including Galena, Peoria, and Chicago, only those who lived around the Ross settlement voted in their town; everyone else voted at Shaw's Coles Grove, the county seat. John Shaw, who had been a supplier in the War of 1812 and who spoke French and several Indian languages, was the acknowledged American leader of the voyageurs and Indians who still lived on the Pike frontier.

In 1822, after a disputed election for the county commissioners' court, that body, now controlled by Hansen, divided the county into three election precincts and appointed pro-Hansen election judges. Shaw's supporters should have voted in the northernmost precinct, at another Ross family settlement in what became Fulton County. But Shaw, fearing that he would lose control over the "Kingdom of Pike," had them vote, as before, at his county seat. There, after the nationality of the first of his voters had been questioned, he moved the precinct to another poll, finally receiving eighty-three votes to Hansen's zero. However, Hansen ally and county clerk James "Lord Coke" Whitney discounted these votes on account of the changed polling place. When this decision was contested on September 4, 1822, circuit court judge and conventionist John Reynolds agreed with Whitney. Thus Shaw had a majority of votes, by 29, but only if the disputed election precinct was included. The reputedly "illegal" precinct that Shaw had removed to in protest had been, prior to that election, the only voting place; it had been changed only in a sly move by the Hansen forces who controlled the election judges.

Now this convoluted history was rehearsed before the whole House. The sole trouble with Shaw's poll, A. P. Field of Union County rose to argue, was that it was not certified by the election judges "according to the provisions of our statute." "And," he resumed, "the only question now to be decided by this House is, whether it was proper—whether it was equitable—whether it be doing the people justice, to reject the votes given for Mr. Shaw at the poll opened and conducted by judges elected by the qualified voters there." Field was in favor of dropping the excessive concern with formality, for it undermined the freedom of the people; "when a man approaches the polls to exercise his dearest right," he noted, "he never stops to make the inquiry, will my vote be rejected if I exercise it there?"[75]

The response to this came from House non-conventionist leader Thomas Mather, a wealthy merchant from Kaskaskia. Unlike George Churchill, who continued to appeal to the reasonableness of Hansen's case and to the consistency of the committee's decision with the new, improved election law (that is, his own law, which had passed the House on December 23, 1822), Mather argued his case on the grounds of the integrity of the legislature itself. From the start, he said, he had "felt disposed to be liberal towards the parties and not confine them to a rigid construction of the [previous election] statute." Although he felt that a new election ought to have been held (given the incomplete evidence of the case) and although he voted against accepting the committee's report, when a majority of the House voted to accept it, he "acquiesced" in the decision, since "so respectable a tribunal would not have made such a decision" without additional evidence he did not have. Now the only evidence brought against Mr. Hansen was the bare statement of a citizen of the county. "If a member of this House is to be deprived of his seat upon such testimony," Mather ended, "whose seat, let me ask, would be secure?"[76] Mather appealed to the local politicians' common interest in preserving the order of the body they controlled. But this common interest had now dissolved; it had been replaced with a stronger one, the war against Governor Coles and his pawn Hansen.

Soon enough the vote was taken. Hansen was put out, Shaw in, and the Convention Resolution passed. The conventionists swarmed the streets in celebration. Again that night they gathered in rough music style for a charivari. They "illuminated the town, collected forces, had the drums, fiddles, bugles, tin horns, cowbells, and old daddy Will's hounds" and converged on Kinney's house. A non-conventionist poem describes their behavior:

> With this the meeting then broke up,
> and sallied forth to take a cup
> of good, hot, new convention whiskey,
> in order to feel fine and frisky.
> Soon was each good convention fellow,
> If not quite drunk—at least right mellow,
> And most internally intent
> On having fun and devilment . . .
> "Huzza for the convention!" bawl'd
> The men—dogs howl'd, and women squall'd.
> "Huzza for the convention—boys
> Bring out what'er will make a noise
> Let's march through all the streets in town,
> And turn Vandalia upside down."

They marched directly "to the residence of the Governor . . . [and crying out] 'Convention or death!' . . . [attempted] to subject the Governor to the control of mobocracy."[77]

The debate in the House over the nature of Pike County elections foreshadowed a division among the locals that would soon develop in the counties. Field was quick to point to the thinly veiled disdain expressed by the Mather contingent for the informal, vocal nature of the Shaw vote. Nor did he fail to hint at the battles over ballot and viva voce style voting that had previously split the Edwards and Thomas members. The Thomas group felt they benefited from the open public setting of viva voce elections. The convention leaders, Kinney, Field, and West, had in the past directed this element of the elections, considered distasteful but necessary by their respective sponsors. Having become experts in its operation, they were interested in continuing and extending its reach.

Churchill's election law was aimed at eradicating exactly this element in the election proceedings. His speech to the House in December 1822 identified the open viva voce balloting process as responsible for the fact that many "men possessed of fine feeling" in Illinois were voting "contrary to their real sentiments." In the effort to remain on friendly terms with a candidate, they avowed support in his presence even if they did "not think so highly of his qualifications as himself." This subtle influence, operating on the republican consciences of those with "fine feeling," was exacerbated when combined with the pressure of a town or settlement sentiment that was often controlled on election weekends by "unthinking and intoxicated mobs," who "overawe the peaceable and orderly voter" and sweep before them "the passions of a large number of unreflecting men."[78]

What Churchill did not recognize was that the mob spirit captured perfectly the contradictory essence of western republicanism. Vandalia's mobs were spontaneous public demonstrations for "the people," but at the same time, they allowed the younger generation of leaders the opportunity to enforce an internal consensus through face-to-face interaction and physical intimidation. This subtle dynamic was nowhere more apparent than in the county election. Nothing could succeed or fail in early Illinois that did not succeed or fail there. The legislative leaders now took their case to the country arena, and to the state's poor farmers who dominated it.

CHAPTER FIVE

ORGANIZING
THE PEOPLE

VIOLENCE, SECTIONALISM, AND
RACISM IN THE COUNTIES

Between the legislature's adjournment on February 18, 1823, and the convention vote on August 4, 1824, over 45 county meetings were called throughout the state.[1] Mixing words and deeds, the county meetings tested the meaning of politics in Illinois as never before. An intangible uneasiness, caused by the worsening depression, became tangible on the public stage. As it became clear that the state was more or less evenly divided between conventionists and non-conventionists, the state's citizens wondered and worried about the contest's outcome. The state's farmers, while sharing this public concern, confronted disparate dilemmas in private: some faced starvation; others deferred payments at the land office; others watched overdue taxes grow on sinking investments. To be successful in their bid to become the masters of Illinois, the conventionists would have to master the fears of squatters, yeomen, and speculators alike.

Over the next 18 months, these anxieties colored every point and clouded every motion. People asked questions and talked in public about how candidates for public office should be nominated, the ability of the legislature to represent the people, and whether the Bible sanctioned slavery. They engaged in heated grogshop discussions, found spiritual meanings in worldly messages, and felt the fabric of society fray. As conventionist battled non-conventionist, mobs, murders, and effigy burnings became common occurrences and the sense of foreboding spread. Under these crisis conditions, the state's new politics struggled to get organized.

The meetings represented an unprecedented mobilization of political activism among the citizenry. They embodied Illinois's surging participatory democracy, even if the grass roots never took full control over the political agenda. Scholars have puzzled over "the popular roots of Democratic Party organization" in the early 1820s.[2] Some have described political participation in the Jacksonian era as a "golden age" in

American citizenship. Undoubtedly, the Illinois people were more involved politically after statehood than they had been during the territorial era. For one thing, they now voted more often and in greater numbers than they had previously. Turnouts in the statewide elections held between 1820 and 1824 ranged from 65 percent to 87 percent of the eligible voters, with percentages generally in the high seventies.[3]

Public engagement was meaningful in itself. Thomas Ford noted that "the rank and file of the people were no less excited than their political leaders" during the controversy. "The whole people," he added, "for the space of eighteen months did scarcely anything but read newspapers, hand-bills and pamphlets, quarrel, argue, and wrangle with each other whenever they met together to hear the violent harangues of their orators." Greenville (Bond County) doctor Horatio Newhall wrote in an 1822 letter that "when party politics were at the highest point in Massachusetts, there was, probably, never an election more warmly contested, than our election will be for *all* our state and national officers. Everywhere you go, you hear of nothing else." Madison County resident Nathaniel Buckmaster wrote his brother: "The whole state is overwhelmed by a sea of politics."[4]

Citizenship was primarily a matter of status for the white folks. Citizens had to be active if they were to confirm their standing in public. Participation in politics demonstrated their victory in what Judith Shklar has called "the primordial struggle for recognition." In Illinois as throughout colonial America, "radical claims for freedom and political equality were played out in counterpoint to chattel slavery . . . [such that] political equality . . . was proclaimed in the accepted presence of its absolute denial." The conventionists are a case in point; the status anxieties they mined contained veins of envy directed toward the big folks as well as views of spite directed toward the black folks. Such illiberal motives inflated the convention vote's "golden age" turnout.[5]

The people's heightened political activity should not, however, be separated from the heightened role of "management" by leaders who guided involvement and molded meaning. The democratic revolution in the people's minds had doomed the territorial parties. The idea of "government of the people by the people themselves," to use Henry Eddy's phrase, introduced a rough and vulgar political style, but the new style still had to be organized to have an impact. The organizational efforts of the leaders on both sides during the convention controversy indicate that, as Martin Schefter has argued, style alone does not create electoral organization. Organizing the people into conventionist and non-conventionist voting blocks did not take place automatically; indeed, the process was at times made more complicated by spontaneous and decentralized participation. The convention controversy thus confirms Ronald Formisano's observation that management and participation "are interdependent."[6]

The leaders of both sides of the controversy engaged in an almost endless round of action and counteraction. The non-conventionists organized early. They established county groups and newspapers, and they wrote letters and published pamphlets. Ten months into the controversy, the conventionists found their cause rapidly losing ground. They moved quickly to reassert the legitimacy of the people's right to change the constitution in an effort to reorient the debate along a winning cleavage. Ames and his cohorts initiated a rhetorical war over the nature of representation, which unleashed sectional and racist sentiments.

These organizational and rhetorical tactics took time and effort, and those leading the battles expected to be rewarded with office. Recognizing this, the conventionists initiated a decidedly centralized and planned approach. By December 1823 they had organized a Central Committee at Vandalia, whose purpose was to send emissaries to every corner of the state carrying the message that slavery was not the primary object of the convention. Instead, the problem was the constitution of 1818 and its inadequate representation of the current population. In addition, all future efforts would focus on electing a conventionist legislature. Public dinners were to be replaced with the tactically more controllable county meeting, where speeches could be scripted and candidates slated.

The goal of both sides was to frame the issue of slavery so as to give their side a majority. Finding the right rhetoric took time, during which the white folks' core beliefs were creatively manipulated. Charges and countercharges were rapid and rancorous. Throughout the competition, only one guiding principle remained sacrosanct: the people were opposed to the ways of the big folks. The new political style would be limited only by what it could not be; it could not defer to wealth, social refinement, or education. The leaders and cultural figures thus engaged in a curious dismantling and rebuilding process. They became forces of order and disorder. They wrought disorder by publicly demeaning the big folks; they then rebuilt the political order by fabricating a usable political culture from the white folks' beliefs.

In the tearing down of the big folks' authority, spontaneous, decentralized participation was welcome and effective, but it also unleashed a rash of murders and an assault on private property. Since opposition to the big folks emphasized what the Illinois people generally lacked, it also generated needs and desires that could not easily be satisfied; the result was a redirection of status striving in new areas of competition. Local settings such as the county seat, normally a haven for deference and order, became charged venues for public displays of discontent and arenas for new competitions in displaying solidarity and cronyism. In all these ways the door to social disruption and violence was opened. In fact, almost all the violent episodes that took place between February 1823 and August 1824 were cued by the convention movement or associated with actions taken by leaders in the dispute.

Political leaders are motivated by a desire to influence events, even if their reasons for wanting influence vary. For some it might be simple love of power, as was the case with Jesse B. Thomas; for others it might be desire to do good or to expiate past sins, as was the case with Edward Coles; it might even involve the love of fame, as was the case with Ninian Edwards. The people's new leaders were also subject to the pull of influence; they too wished to control events. For all their purity, as Karl Marx realized, even "pure republicans" seek influence. "When you play the fiddle at the top of the state," he quipped, "what else is to be expected but that those down below dance?" To influence events, Illinois republican leaders needed to impose order. Just as the legislature's institutional incentives gave a new generation of leaders their own reasons for tearing down the territorial system, those same incentives now supplied reasons to organize the people around achievable goals. The interests motivating these leaders thus interposed a distinct force for change in early Illinois, a force partially independent of the democratic and market revolutions.[7]

Yet the new political elite was far from truly independent. It was not free to choose the social tools used to build the new order. In fact, with traditional deference and standing, social refinement, and wealth ruled out by the people's opposition to the big folks, the new elite's choices were limited. Leaders turned first to local experience as a rhetorical tool for organizing opinion. Experience was the one thing they had, the one thing people have when they have nothing else.

THE CENTRAL COMMITTEE AND ANOTHER VANDALIA MOB

To organize "the people," the conventionists developed the most prominent mass communication instrument in use at the time: the Saturday "go-to meetin'." Local politicians learned the political power of the county meeting during the passage of the state bank bill in 1821, their first great victory over the big folks. Meetings were held in Bond, Crawford, Gallatin, Randolph, and Madison Counties. Although the first four were against the bank, the Madison meeting, led by Kinney and Smith, generated considerable attention and excitement. There they discovered that David Blackwell's attack on the "great constitutional lawyers" of the council of revision played well to the crowd. The meeting had little to say about why a bank was desirable; it simply resolved to support it on grounds of "policy" (that is, expediency). This was politically astute, for although "hard money" sentiment was strong among the poor farmers of the Old Northwest, it never developed into an orthodoxy when the banks involved were state banks. Ridiculing great men in public had been exhilarating, however, and Smith and Kinney grew confident of their ability to sway opinion in the new era.[8]

The use of the county meeting as a technique of political organization, only inchoately developed in 1821, entered a new phase with the convention controversy when it became broadly accepted throughout the state. The county meeting had one feature that made it especially susceptible to popular affection: it was, or could be made to appear, relatively spontaneous and open. They excluded only those seeking privileged arenas, such as Nathaniel Pope, who thought such meetings produced mere "senseless noise."⁹ Such meetings could be controlled by men whose only access to power was their popularity or their ability to articulate the undigested sentiments of an open-air meeting. For these same reasons, they had the potential of putting rowdy spirits in motion.

The use of public meetings had been radicalized during the tumultuous passing of the Convention Resolution. Now the ferment that had bubbled up in Vandalia threatened to spill over into every town and to infect everything. The removal of Hansen and his replacement with Shaw was extraordinary, John Reynolds reflected: "a movement that has no parallel in the history of legislative proceedings."¹⁰ It required little imagination to see the connection between the "revolutionary" actions taken by the legislators at Vandalia and the increase in violence and disorder in the counties. Before order was imposed, a period of general disorder ensued. Anything seemed possible under the white folks' rough and rowdy rule.

"The state of morals is truly deplorable in this State," Baptist preacher John Mason Peck wrote in his diary on December 4, 1823. "No less than six murders, or homicides in affrays, have been perpetuated in nine months, and as yet not one is convicted."¹¹ Between July 22, 1822, and June 12, 1824, the state's newspapers reported 11 murders—an alarming number, if placed alongside the state's population of approximately 55,000 inhabitants. James Davis found that a population of 317,000 in northern Illinois experienced only one murder between June 1849 and 1850. Added to this number also were the murders of Daniel Smith and Richard Flower. Smith was called "Rarified" to distinguish him from T. W. "Tammany" Smith. He was knifed in "a crowded barroom of a public house in Edwardsville" on January 29, 1825. Smith was known for his outspoken stance against slavery. At an Edwardsville Fourth of July dinner in 1819, he toasted:

> A comet appeared last night in the sky,
> to give us a toast for the Fourth of July:
> May she sail up Missouri, and—slavery—end it,
> and scorch with her tail all who wish to defend it.

At an Alton (Madison County) Fourth of July dinner in 1823, he offered another witty toast:

> The Legislature and rag currency of Illinois
> Both a disgrace to the state
> and both sixty six and two thirds percent below par
> may the former be purified and the latter burnt.

Hooper Warren speculated that his murder was politically motivated. Richard Flower, English emigrant George Flower's son, was murdered on July 12, 1825. His father believed the motive was tied to his stance against the convention, which was bitterly contested in his town of Albion in Edwards County. This raises the number of murders to thirteen in little over two years.[12]

Other indications of widespread social dislocation exist. Senate secretary Thomas Lippincott noted that "there were more than forty couples divorced that winter by act of the Legislature." Calls for an imposition of order were common. "Something must be done," one "Citizen of Madison County" wrote, about the general lawlessness that had erupted "within a very short time" in the surrounding area. A short review of disturbances by the "citizens" included horse stealing in Madison, St. Clair, and Bond Counties, the kidnapping of "free negroes" in St. Clair and Madison Counties, house break-ins and robberies at Carrolltown (Greene County), Vandalia, and Edwardsville, and counterfeiting in instances "so numerous, common and well known" they went unspecified. The Edwardsville break-in occurred at the home of Jesse B. Thomas, where two drunk and armed men had to be talked out of murdering the senator in his bed.[13]

Circumstantial evidence links the growing disregard for authority with the populist sentiment stirred up by the convention movement. Three days after the Convention Resolution had passed on February 12, 1823, the conventionists held "a very large and respectable meeting of citizens in the Hall of the House" on a Friday night. A committee was elected to write an address and offer resolutions in favor of the convention. This committee proclaimed its work at a public meeting three days later on February 18. After this the conventionists did not assemble publicly again until March 6, when they held an informal "convention dinner" at Edwardsville. This dinner was a response to a dinner held the night before by "a number of citizens of Edwardsville and its vicinity, desirous of showing their respect for, and approbation of the conduct of the Governor of Illinois." Both dinners followed the Fourth of July tradition, in which toasts were a prominent after-dinner entertainment. Many toasts for and against the convention were offered. For example, Coles gave his assessment of the convention proposal in a toast, "The Crisis: it is big with the fate of Illinois, and requires every friend of freedom to rally under the banners of the constitution"; and at the following dinner William Kinney offered a rebuttal, "The Crisis: it is big with the fate of Illinois, and requires every friend of freedom to rally around its constitution and amend it so as to promote their prosperity, safety, and political happiness."[14]

One Russel Botsford had also given a conventionist toast: "The freemen of Illinois—May the majority always rule." Two days after this dinner, the state bank robbery at Vandalia occurred while the cashier James Kelly was away on business. Kelly, who had been almost unanimously elected to his office by the legislature (he had 50 of 53 votes), attempted to find the thief in the months that followed. He eventually accused Moss Botsford of complicity in the case, and the accusation brought him athwart Moss's brother Russel. When Kelly pursued Russel with "a Pistol in one hand and horse whip in the other," Botsford pulled a "Spanish knife" and killed him on the spot. Kelly was evidently less popular with the people of Vandalia than with the legislature. At the trial, a prolonged prosecution of Botsford left the jury unimpressed; he was acquitted after two minutes of deliberation.[15]

On March 6 another dinner was given at Greenville (Bond County) in support of Representative Jonathan H. Pugh's "vote against the convention question." At this dinner, it was resolved that only non-conventionists would be supported for "offices of public trust." The non-conventionists next organized a "St. Clair Anti-Slavery Society" at Belleville, and held two meetings on March 8 and 22, 1823. In response, the conventionists offered another dinner on March 24 at Vandalia. But the non-conventionists again countered with two elaborate "nominating" meetings in Madison and White Counties. At these, non-conventionist voters were formerly pledged to slates of candidates for the General Assembly. Throughout the summer of 1823 non-conventionists continued to organize, meeting and nominating slates at Alton (Madison County), Waterloo (Monroe County), Edwardsville (Madison County), Edgar County, Greene County, Belleville (St. Clair County), Lawrenceville (Lawrence County), and Morgan County. In the organization war, the conventionists were losing.[16]

By the fall of 1823, the conventionists had reason to rethink their approach. Once the strength of the people's support for the non-conventionists was recognized, it was impossible to continue to condemn them as a legislative minority. "If there is not a majority opposed to the [convention] measure," wrote "A Voter," "there is at least a very large minority. . . . [For this reason] the abuse formerly thrown upon the 'select' few . . . in the General Assembly" had ceased. Before December 3, 1823, there is evidence of only two conventionist "societies" forming, the original one at Vandalia and an impromptu group that formed during a county commissioners' court election in White County. All other conventionist gatherings had taken the form of dinners. This practice conformed to the "liberal" republicanism that conventionists felt defined their movement. Whatever scruples the non-conventionists may have felt against "management," they had already formed eight "Anti-

Convention Societies" during the first year of the contest.[17]

The conventionists regrouped in December 1823 "during the sales of Public Lands, and the sitting of the Supreme and Federal Courts" at Vandalia.[18] Leaders from every part of the state converged on the capital to attend the courts and the sales. An informal poll on the convention question indicated that the tide of opinion had turned against the conventionists. Edward Coles rejoiced in private, writing from Vandalia to Robert Vaux of Philadelphia: "for the last four weeks there has been a great crowd of persons here . . . [and] I am more confirmed in my belief that a majority of the people will be opposed" to the convention.[19] General Willis Hargrave and Samuel McRoberts, two members of the "Convention or Death" uprising in the spring, responded by calling a meeting on December 3, 1823, in which they proposed forming the Central Committee, to consist of eighteen representatives from around the state who were to receive reports from five-man subcommittees in each county. Each of these men would be responsible in turn for three-man "security . . . guards and pickets, corps of advance and reserve," in each election precinct.[20]

These changes brought renewed energy and focus to the conventionist cause, but predictably, the governor became a lightning rod for those wishing to display their republican standing in acts of solidarity to the cause. Indeed, beginning with the reappearance of the conventionists at Vandalia, Coles was under attack. On December 9, 1823, six days after the Central Committee was formed, the state house burned down. Again land office papers were destroyed. The following is an account by an eyewitness who observed the mob that harassed Coles:

> In attending the sales of non-resident's land, I have been so fortunate, or unfortunate, as you please, to witness the proceedings of a Vandalia Mob . . . [after the Governor had failed to subscribe to their rebuilding effort] in the course of the evening a number of persons collected together, and as the night advanced, grew more noisy. . . . About two in the morning I was again awakened by the appalling cry of fire! and from the light that was thrown into the window of my chamber, I concluded that there was serious danger. Instead of a building on fire, I saw a man of straw, which the mob called the Governor!—and which was burnt, amid the groans of the mob, and the cry of State House or Death!

The head of the mob was reported to be one C. B. Berry, who had toasted at the second convention dinner: "The Representatives of the People—Obey the instructions of your constituents." At the same dinner, Thomas Coates, the maker of Churchill's effigy, toasted: "The executive of the state, let him remember that he is the servant of the people, and not the political chief of any party." At the first convention dinner, General Samuel Whiteside had celebrated: "Executive influence, neutralized by the sovereignty of the people."[21]

Two weeks later, the governor's farm outside Edwardsville, some buildings, and over 400 fruit trees were destroyed in a fire. The attack continued in the form of a lawsuit taken out against Coles on January 7, 1824, in Madison County court. A party of conventionists claimed that he should be forced to pay $200 bond for each of his freed slaves brought into the county, even though the law requiring such payment was published after he entered the state. A dejected Coles wrote to Morris Birkbeck: "The Friends of a Convention appear to become more and more bitter and virulent in their enmity to me, and seem determined not only to injure my standing with the people, but to break down my pecuniary resources."[22]

Clearly, then, the establishment of the Central Committee signaled the end to the conventionists' "liberal" style. Soon to follow were meetings and societies complete with slates of nominations to the legislature. The conventionists later claimed that their own "caucus candidates" were elevated to counteract a prior non-conventionist "plan." The *Republican* offered its view of the subject in a supposed "Dialogue between two non-conventionists":

> You are opposed to a convention, ain't you?
>
> Certainly; but what has that to do with the election of members? I thought that depended on our vote and not upon the members that are elected.
>
> Ah! I see you don't properly understand *matters*. You haven't seen our *head men* lately.
>
> Our *head men?* I thought every man had a head.
>
> Oh! don't be impatient; I'll tell you what plan we have fallen on and then I think you will be better satisfied with our non-convention members. Our constitution says, if a majority of the people shall vote for a convention, the next legislature shall pass a law for the election of members to the convention, and the convention shall meet in three months after such election. But the constitution does not say when the election for members to the convention shall take place, and our object is (and we will carry it into effect too) to elect non-convention members to the legislature, and then if there should be a majority of the people in favor of a convention, we shall put the question off for four or five years.[23]

The non-conventionists responded that they were only taking precautions against conventionist tricks. And such tricks did exist, as evidenced in the January 1824 attempt to elect Baptist preacher William Jones to the Madison County Commissioners' Court without mentioning his pro-slavery sentiments. The plan, Hooper Warren announced, was to trumpet his victory after the election as a sign of conventionist strength in populous Madison County. When this tactic was "found out," it put the non-conventionists on guard against conventionist management. In fact, the first non-conventionist meeting to take notice of the Central Committee's change in tactics, at Belleville on February 5, 1824, was also that side's first "caucus," that is, nomination meeting. Amid objections that the system was "anti-republican," a township nomination system was accepted. The meeting resolved:

> Let all them who are opposed to the call of a convention, cordially unite in the plan this day proposed for harmonizing the jarring interests of the country, and determine to vote for those who shall be nominated in pursuance of such a plan. . . . Let us shake off this alarming apathy that puts everything to hazard, and take these matters into our own hands. The convention party are making every effort to effect their views; and if we sleep on our posts, they will carry their measures.[24]

The Central Committee had signaled its shift in tactics by resolving that "the people have a right to alter and amend their social compact whenever they shall find the same oppressive or inefficient"; that the Illinois constitution ought to be changed to promote "the happiness of the people"; and that the right of the people "of expressing their sentiments through their representatives" in the coming elections ought to be upheld. Previously the question of voting for or against the convention at the upcoming election had been kept distinct from the election of General Assembly members at the same election. Before January 1824, only three county meetings resolved to restrict their voting for members to the legislature on the basis of the convention issue. These were typified by the Lawrence County "Society to Oppose the Introduction of Slavery in Illinois" where the resolution was tied to disapproval of the *previous* legislature's behavior. "We will not support any man for any office," they declared, "who walked in that nocturnal procession at Vandalia, the night that Hansen's effigy was burnt." Thus, here, proscription was retrospective. The first reference to prospective proscription as a general rule began with the conventionists at Vandalia who emphasized that voters should express "their sentiments through their representatives."[25]

Along with this new emphasis on representatives came an attempt to regain the rhetorical momentum of the previous winter by denying that slavery was the sole intention of the conventionists. A week after the Vandalia dinner, another was held at Lebanon in St. Clair County. The Lebanon toasts indicated the pro-slavery cast of the conventionist cause at the high tide of its confidence:

> Mr. Seth Crocker. *The enemies of a Convention*—may they ride a porcupine saddle, or a hard trotting horse, a long journey, without money or friends.

Mr. Thomas F. Burgess. *The State of Illinois*—The ground is good— prairies in abundance—give us plenty of negroes and a little industry, and she will distribute her treasures.

Mr. Abraham Kinney.—May those individuals who are opposed to our cause, before the next election abandon the state of Illinois, and then we will have a free silver circulation, combined with a numerous black population.

But by the second meeting of the Central Committee on February 2, 1824, the conventionists had resolved that "the question of slavery" was not their "moving consideration." Instead they insisted that the "council of revision," the county commissioners' court, and biannual elections (all mandated by the constitution of 1818) be abolished. There was also a new explanation of non-conventionist motives. The real controversy, they argued, revolved around "a mere struggle for power," which the non-conventionists had attempted to cover up "by raising the hue and cry of slavery! slavery! slavery!" The real conflict of interest was between "these gentry (we mean the anti-convention party)" and the people: "The warmest opposers to the convention agree that the constitution is defective and needs amendment. Yet, they are not willing that the people should, in the plenitude of their power, take upon themselves the exercise of this inherent right, at this time." The committee concluded that these gentry were elitists unable "to trust the people."[26]

A GOODLY PORTION OF MEANNESS: THE USES OF SECTIONALISM

Once the leadership on both sides had begun nominating candidates for the legislature, the rhetorical war began in earnest. Just as the organizational moves had been made only after a series of escalating actions and reactions, so too the minds of the local leaders were radicalized only after a series of rhetorical escalations. The first involved the old party struggle. The process of nominating candidates for General Assembly offices threatened to submerge the convention issue in the Edwards-Thomas party cleavage. Nomination may have been resisted by the conventionists precisely because they hoped to avoid the influence of the old ties. But, as has been noted, the old parties were in no condition to respond to the convention issue. Even so, the old world took time to dissolve.

The gradual dissolution of the old party politics is demonstrated in the personal transformation of Hooper Warren from chief mouthpiece for the Edwards party to paid editor of the non-conventionists. Between December 7, 1822, and February 15, 1823, Warren was engaged in a paper war with the *Star of the West*, a pro-Thomas paper that had recently begun printing at Edwardsville. In this period, Warren was engaged in typical party duties: he was busy digging dirt on Thomas, who was facing reelection for the U.S. Senate in the upcoming legislative session at

Vandalia. He filled his columns with whatever cast the senator in a dubious light. Warren accused Thomas of setting "his traveling distance so as to receive 130 dollars more than . . . the other members of Congress residing at Kaskaskia, St. Genevieve, St. Louis, and in this town." He pointed out that the Thomas family had left the state to go live in St. Louis, and that they did not intend to return. He brought out the old story of Thomas's betrayal of the Indiana party in 1809, when the Illinois Territory was carved from the old Indiana Territory. Warren placed special emphasis on Thomas's broken "bond," and the subsequent burning of his effigy at Vincennes. He also reported that when Emanuel J. West arrived at Washington looking for the new "Sangamon Land Office" job, Thomas had suggested a way to make himself useful: election to the Illinois legislature. West did get elected, from Madison County, and even voted for Thomas in that body, but Warren warned him against getting his hopes up for the land office job, as Thomas had promised the job to "fifteen or twenty candidates."[27]

All this, the *Star of the West* editors responded, was to be expected from the foremost tool of the Edwards group. The most significant response they made in this regard was through the contributions of none other than Nicholas Hansen. He took up the case of Edward Coles against Warren's repeated bashing. Warren responded that Hansen was merely acting on Thomas's behalf, and that his support for Coles stemmed from the fact that he was now "a candidate for the office of secretary of state." Warren's feud with Coles originated in 1820 when he claimed the Virginian ordered a "personal attack" on him. Coles had lent legal and financial aid to a political associate who physically attacked the editor; Warren responded by ridiculing Coles's slavelike tenure as James Madison's manservant.[28] In addition, Warren argued that far from having "been made to persist," he was being encouraged to stop the abuse: "the very persons or 'party' who are insinuated as making us 'persist' are those who have remonstrated, in the strongest terms, against it."[29]

February 15, 1823, found Warren summarizing the convention vote and the Shaw-Hansen debacle while complaining that Hansen's majority in the election had been accepted only because "Executive influence was used in favor of Judge Thomas" and on his behalf. He claimed that "the Executive . . . bought off [Hansen] with a promise to give him a lucrative appointment of Recorder of Fulton County." Thus for the first two months of the convention movement's life, the leading newspaper that would attack it during the eighteen months of its growth and maturity was mired in party conflict. Warren published excerpts of the Will Plan on December 28, 1822, with no comment. On January 11, 1823, when Thomas Coates was combing Edwardsville for petitions to instruct Warren's friend George Churchill, the *Spectator*'s editorial included only a comment on Thomas's election and a letter praising Edwards's speeches in the Senate. The February 8, 1823, editorial, aimed at the *Star of the West* crowd, was entitled "Who's the Dupe?" It told how, the week after Thomas was elected, his family moved back to St. Louis.

Between February 15 and March 8, 1823, while making a deal for financial support with the minority in the legislature, Warren did not publish a paper. From that point on he committed his "labors" to the non-conventionist cause. Nonetheless, his lack of an immediate commitment to the non-conventionists in January and February laid the ground for T. W. Smith's later claim that Warren was bought out. Smith argued in the columns of the *Illinois Republican:* "Let our readers remember that during the whole session, a period of 76 days, while the contest is going on with unexampled opposition; while it is notorious that instructions are for weeks in circulation . . . the *Spectator,* never breathed even a lisp on the question."[30] Thomas Lippincott, who represented the minority in its dealings with the *Spectator,* responded to these charges. He admitted that there had been doubts among the non-conventionists, but these, he said, were either from those who were unfamiliar with Warren and his paper or from preachers such as Daniel Parker who feared the power of money and wanted no mercenary support.

After their first meeting as the legislative session was winding down, the minority decided to get together a "subscription paper." At these meetings "it was frequently expressed, and unanimously recognized, as the wish of the meeting, that no intimation should be given to Mr. Warren, that money had been, or could be raised, until he had declared himself unequivocally in favor of an active opposition to the Convention."[31] No longer the tool of Edwards, Warren was not yet perceived as an independent man. But by the summer of 1823, the transformation was complete. On June 7, he could be found giving a "hint" to Ninian Edwards to keep out of his way; he stated publicly that he no longer felt himself to be "*in the power* of a certain gentleman in Edwardsville."[32]

We can observe a similar release from factional allegiance and rebirth as local political operative in John Reynolds. In the *Edwardsville Spectator,* "L" reported remembering that this "judicial character . . . declared a few years since that a government which tolerates slavery is not a republican government." But in a letter to Edwards on February 6, 1823, Reynolds stated: "The legislature will in my opinion give us a Convention and a Canal Law—the first I do not care for: yet the people can vote on it to their satisfaction—if they be pleased I will be." By 1824, however, "L" indicated that Reynolds had "become a strong advocate for the introduction of slavery into this state . . . and the only reason he offers for this change is this, if slavery is not introduced, the Yankees will rule the state." Reynolds's transformation from anti-slavery to anti-Yankee was indicative of the shift taking place in many conventionist leaders.[33]

Once the local leaders' minds had changed, they turned to converting their followers. To shape public opinion, they relied on a new form of deference, which might be called crony solidarity. The *Republican* printed the story of a conventionist wife who was in distress over her husband's political activity. She worried that "Mr. office-hunter, who visited him before the election . . . was too successful in unhinging [his] placid mind." She wondered why her husband spent "more than half his time in political cabals." "Why neglect his ordinary business," she queried, "break his rest, sour his temper, impoverish his family, and break his wife's heart by unkind words and ill looks, in his zeal for politics?" Her puzzlement deepened as she reflected that "even *he* admits, a decision of the question either way, would not affect materially *our* interest." Yet political meetings were great tools for rallying conventionist sentiment; they helped solidify deference to local leaders. The writer "Julius," for example, argued that he became a conventionist on the example of "Judge Reynolds" and other leading local men. "I should think," he wrote, "the fact [of] these gentlemen wishing slavery, was at least pretty good evidence that it would be for the interest of the country." Remarks like these succeeded in stirring up the emotions of many county voters, creating the conditions under which Churchill's feared "unthinking and intoxicated mobs" could carry a wavering polling ground.[34]

The non-conventionists thought that "every species of address and management [had been] resorted to" in order to ensure compliance at "the GROG-SHOPS," to extract consent from the "clan," and to obtain "condolence from the BOYS." The Central Committee's organization, reaching to every "election precinct," was particularly ominous to them. "A Voter" asked: "Can the public good be the primary object of that party, whose measures are born in silence and concealed in darkness? Which finds it necessary for its support to establish and sustain an internal police, more vigilant and vigorous, than was ever established by the emperor of France?" In spreading their views, the conventionists attempted to portray themselves as the authentic representatives of a spontaneous local will. They typically attacked the non-conventionists' nominating meetings for featuring "Caucus—Usurpation—Dictation." Such methods violated local mores. The *Illinois Republican* printed a letter in which "A Conventionist" reported his "mixed feeling of pity and contempt" at the non-conventionist nominating meeting:

> It appears to me, that nothing can be more illiberal, intolerant, and reprehensible, than to denounce indiscriminately all, who are in favor of a convention. This, the constant practice of non-conventionists, is in direct opposition to the principles for which the whole party professes to contend, namely, liberty; but where, I ask, is the freedom or liberty which every man ought to enjoy of expressing his sentiments on any public question, if, when he ventures to speak in favor of a convention, he is to be branded with the epithets of corrupt, oppressive, dishonest, inhuman, and unjust?[35]

The non-conventionists responded that the conventionists represented only the sick and demented part of the local scene. Henry Eddy dryly described the Vandalia mob as a "proceeding . . . of a very interesting character, [that] produced a considerable degree of excitement, as well within as out of doors." But for the non-conventionists, the excitement was a telltale symptom of a new type of "disease" known as "convention fever." It raged throughout the country but was "most prevalent about the little towns and villages, and in that section of the state bordering on the Ohio River." In his first pamphlet, "An Appeal on the Question of a Convention," Birkbeck wrote: "The disease in the legislature demands our immediate attention." The disease could not be cured; it must be isolated and destroyed. This tract, previously referred to by Americanus, was circulated in the fall of 1823 and signaled the beginning of a new non-conventionist tack. They now began to be less cautious of exposing the true proportions of their outrage. The legislature, Birkbeck began, was intended to be a gathering of representatives for the public interest; it had become a den of self-serving intrigue, where "the interests of the public have been bought and sold in the face of day; the law of elections, and the established rules of legislative proceedings, have been set at nought, in order to thrust the question upon us." He concluded, "Such a scene of base intrigue was never before exhibited under a representative government, as prevailed at Vandalia through the last session."[36]

It was the non-conventionists who, following up on the implications of Birkbeck's argument, first broached the sectionalism issue. The true motor behind the convention movement, they reasoned, could only be the notorious greed of slaveholders. The leading men in the conventionist camp were slaveholders who used manipulation for their own ends. The prime movers were these "wealthy men who have been raised in the slave states," who "have never done much labor, and have no disposition to do any themselves, [having] been taught from childhood that greatness consists in having slaves under their control." It was this "slave gentry," whose members had "a few hundred dollars due them in the slave states, and [could] not get [the debt paid] in anything but slaves." For this greedy class the state's fertile soil was actually more of a curse than a blessing, for these "were tempted by the rich virgin soil of Illinois" to bring in slavery.[37]

The conventionists responded by arguing that they hoped to skew emigration toward "agriculturalists," not "merchants and manufacturers." The latter came from the North, but the state's "present condition" suggested that "future prosperity" lay in farming. This meant looking for immigration from the South: "our neighbors in Kentucky are already complaining of want of room." Many conventionists hoped to follow Alabama and Mississippi in the short staple cotton revolution following Eli Whitney's invention. Benjamin Harding traveling in the area of

Shawneetown noted that, although "cotton is a plant which, in late seasons, will not grow further north than the thirty-seventh degree north latitude," still it "is here cultivated, and grows exuberantly . . . between forty and forty two degrees north latitude." This was because "the climate is milder in the same latitude west, than it is in the same east."[38]

The view found in an unsigned non-conventionist letter, however, claimed that the slave gentry were motivated by a "short-sighted covetousness," which went "all lengths" to bring the slave "pollution" down upon the state. Here—not among the people—was to be found the root cause of the movement's excitement. It is important to note that the non-conventionist use of sectionalism was subordinated to their own attack against big folk usurpation. The attack was most evident in their reviews of the Central Committee and of the "caucus nomination" of John Reynolds for the legislature in St. Clair County. These were, in the view of Aristides, the actions of a domineering junto:

> This is a practical illustration of *convention Republicanism*. The *"swinish multitude"* must have no hand in making the nomination: that power belongs to the *nobles*—the *patricians*—the *lords*—the *big men*—of the party. But the people will be *graciously permitted* to vote for the men who have been nominated by the junto! Yes, and if they are loth to exercise this *glorious privilege,* the junto and understrappers will pull them along to the polls and *make them exercise it.* What a happy thing it will be for the people, if a convention is called, and the members of these county juntos are employed to make a new constitution!!

Thus the conventionists, in usurping the power of the people, had become big folks themselves. It could no longer be assumed that the legislature represented the people. "The voice of the Legislature then," Aristides concluded his erudite analysis, "is not the voice of the people."[39]

But some non-conventionists went further. They proceeded to question, as did Birkbeck's Jonathan Freeman, the very legitimacy of untrammeled majority power. Could the majority establish monarchy or feudal tenures? he asked. Others concluded that "in this state every individual is free by *right.*" Unlike Ninian Edwards, however, when they looked to larger "principles," they did not use the language of natural law, but that of individual rights and freedom: "If there be principles in our constitution too sacred to be infringed, even by a majority, on a plea of interest, this is such a principle . . . freedom is the basis of our social compact, a majority can regulate the institutions founded on this basis, but the basis itself is impregnable." These rights were inviolable not because they were natural but because granting rights was a mutual proposition. "What security remains to you or me," non-conventionists asked, "if a majority have the power of fixing the brand of slavery on a portion of the community?" Looking at the matter from this larger perspective allowed the non-conventionists to highlight the reality of social power, a power well understood by the white folks. As "Plain Truth" argued, the slave gentry had settled on black slavery because the Africans were a powerless class in society. "They are prepared to avail themselves of their power over the wretched African, *because* he is wretched and weak."[40]

Yet non-conventionists had to be careful not to appear to push their rhetoric too hard lest it be tarred with resemblance to "Yankee" thinking, a form of thought universally scorned by the white folks. Bond County resident Robert Patterson argued that anti-Yankee sentiment was tied to the aggressive sales techniques of Yankee "clock-peddlers," who would leave the clock and have someone else come back for the money. This subtle form of intimidation made them "extremely unpopular . . . [which] contributed largely to the prejudice of the people against the Yankees." Anti-Yankee prejudices, whipped up by localist rhetoric, motivated violent displays of anti–big folks solidarity. The conventionists actively fostered suspicion of the different ways of newcomers and northerners. A lingering suspicion was created, for example, by Vermonter John York Sawyer, who chaired a Madison County meeting of non-conventionists, which "proscribed those in favor of a convention." His name had been withheld from the report of the proceedings sent to the newspaper, but the strategy of secrecy backfired when his involvement was discovered. Sawyer held three lucrative offices in Madison County (justice of the peace, judge of probate, and recorder of deeds); now, by appearing to grasp for control over the others, he displayed, to wary conventionists, the telltale signs of Yankee greed.[41]

The rhetorical battles over sectional prejudices increased after the non-conventionists began nominating only non-conventionist or openly anti-slavery candidates. When William Orr at Kaskaskia singled out the St. Clair Society for "resolving to tyrannize over the opinions of men" through nominations, it was probably not a coincidence that the society's president was the Yankee John Messinger. House member William Berry published a prolonged attack on Randolph County Representative Thomas Mather of Connecticut. Mather, a short, corpulent man christened "Lumpy Doodle," was accused of disregarding his constituents' instructions and voting against them on the Convention Resolution.[42]

Disregard for instruction, an institution so near and dear to the people's jealous love for their rights, stirred up suspicion as no other issue. And again a Yankee was made the bugaboo. After the Convention Resolution failed to pass the first time, the conventionists targeted eight members whose counties they believed could be combed for signers of a petition to instruct their representatives. The list of those who would not alter their vote in spite of petitions included well-known southern-born members such as Risdon Moore of Delaware and Georgia, Andrew

Bankson of Tennessee, and Jacob Ogle of Virginia. Those who held fast to their original positions had a ready justification since many of the petitions contained forgeries, or signatures obtained through deception.[43]

Yet, of all the non-conventionists who disregarded the instructions, obloquy descended alone on Vermonter George Churchill. William Berry, editor of Vandalia's *Illinois Intelligencer*, began the tirade. On February 22, 1823, he directed the attention of his readers to the "small minority" that had attempted to "disarm the people of their sovereignty" by denying "the right and refus[ing] to obey the instruction of the people." Berry kept the attack up for several months until he lost control of his paper; thereafter the *Illinois Republican* at Edwardsville continued the assault by focusing attention on the Madison County representative. For almost a year Churchill was the reviled all-purpose Yankee. It was claimed he called the convention petitioners "Jack-asses," though he had earlier submitted the free negro petition. This disclosed a perverse preference for individuals "guilty of a skin not colored like his own." It was further contended that Churchill arrogantly held his beliefs "above the people," for he continued in them after losing a Madison County commissioners' race in 1819 and the race for representative in 1820, both times running on an anti-slavery platform.[44]

Early in the 1822–1823 legislative session, Churchill's election bill was passed; it replaced the viva voce voting system with the ballot system—a change he considered a victory for his New England ways, for he privately called the ballot system "elections conducted in the Yankee fashion." The conventionists, however, painted his motivation as self-promotion. They had found, Editor William Orr announced, one of "those in whose composition nature has thrown a goodly portion of *meanness.*" "Convention" added that the plan simply allowed Churchill to "vote for himself" without having to acknowledge it. Churchill's effigy was twice burnt at Troy, a town in eastern Madison County, suggesting that the conventionist perspective often prevailed. The perpetrator in each case was probably Thomas Coates, the courier sent out by the conventionists to secure Churchill's instructions. At the March 24, 1823, Vandalia convention dinner these acts were memorialized in a toast to "the member of the last legislature who declared that 364 of his constituents were Jackasses—May they keep kicking him, until (like Lucifer) he falls to rise no more."[45]

The subtle use of sectional prejudice to appeal to the egalitarian sentiments of the white folks could be quite effective, and its use occurred generally on both sides throughout the contest. The conventionists, following Conrad Will, had argued that the unique Illinois experience with regard to indentured servants was good policy for the whole community. As a policy, it had withstood the test of time. The non-conventionists in response attempted to expose what they thought was the inefficiency, the social intrusiveness, and the physical danger that would result when

Will's plan inevitably ballooned into "southern slavery." The more that "limited slavery" could be made to appear a temporary pattern inevitably yoked to the southern plan of slavery, the less convincing would the conventionist case appear to be.

OPENING THE DOOR TO SLAVERY AND RACISM

The uses of sectionalism as well as its catholic appeal are well illustrated in two meetings, one conventionist and one non-conventionist, held in Monroe County. George Forquer, Thomas Ford's half brother, carried the non-conventionist banner in Monroe County. A "mechanic" turned lawyer and cofounder with Daniel Cook of the town of Waterloo, Forquer gave a long speech before the Monroe Antislavery Society. He addressed that part of the conventionist plan which suggested the state take an active role in the African colonization of freed slaves. He began by chiding "some worthy citizens" whose opposition to the convention savored "too much of the dawning of political or religious fanaticism." Instead of an attack motivated by "a factious and unsteady spirit," Forquer asked whether it "would be politic to introduce slavery." Taking "the future prosperity of the state" as his guide, he reviewed the plan proposed by Conrad Will. How, he asked, would the costs be borne? Could any reasonable guarantee of carrying out the plan be given? How would the state's authority be triggered? He did not expect to be persuaded by a response to these questions, but he conceded that, if "the many good men . . . who differ honestly with us in opinion" could answer these objections, "then a limited slavery might find more advocates."[46] In all these moderate opinions, Forquer hoped to shape local sentiment in his image of it as favoring liberality and opposing absolutism of all varieties. But by not opposing slavery outright, he also demonstrated that his sectional loyalty was first and foremost western.

A year later, on April 3, 1824, Col. William Alexander addressed the Monroe Convention Society in the town of Harrisonville. Alexander had been active in local politics during the territorial period, serving as a Randolph County justice of the peace in 1809 and as recorder of deeds, county clerk, and on the county commissioner court when Monroe County broke away from Randolph County in 1816. As Monroe's representative in the General Assembly, he voted for the Convention Resolution. While Alexander's speech was one of the last to be given at a county meeting, its theme returned to the question of political means that had first been broached fifteen months earlier. "The present," he said, "is a momentous crisis in the history of the world with regard to representative government." To explain why, he chose a very simple metaphor. It was because a door had been closed. The door to the "house or temple" of government had been closed to the people. Simple as this "figurative expression" was, it was still necessary "to examine a little into the history of past times, to see how this door came to be shut."[47]

Fortunately for his listeners, the colonel did not find it necessary to review the lengthy history of oppression under which the door of representative government remained closed to the people. He did, however, have reason "for this purpose, [to] go as far back as the year A.D. 1818." That was when "the people of Illinois thought it necessary to employ a certain number of workmen" to build a constitution for the "temple" of state. They built well. But, "instead of giving the keys to the people, they consigned them over to their agents to be thereafter appointed." The workmen had affixed to the structure a provision that "two-thirds of those agents must agree before the keys could be surrendered."

As time passed, the agents became used to holding the keys of state. The first occasion the people had need of the keys, a full one-third of the agents rebuffed them. But the people refused to be denied; their voice "came like thunder," and the keys were given up. "Immediately after the keys were surrendered," Alexander continued, "those agents who were opposed to the people getting them, climb[ed] up and wr[o]te in large letters over the door, 'Beware how you enter, Slavery dwells here.'" This was done "to frighten" the people. But the subterfuge went further. The agents' justification was that "the people [were] afraid to trust themselves." This again, he said, indicated their desire "to forestall public opinion." Such "objections that are now being made to the call of a convention, . . . that, for example, the existing government was good enough, and that a worse one might result from the change," he likened to "the language of those who were opposed to the Revolutionary War."

Alexander ended with "an old story," which evoked his sentiment concerning the condition of the state, and covertly, the new governor. It was the story of a farm family that had taken their corn to mill on horseback in a sack balanced, ever since anyone could remember, by a large rock. For fear of change, they continued carrying the rock to market long after the need for balance was gone; after, in fact, the grandfather who started the practice had passed away. When the boy of the family proposed getting rid of the rock, he was chastised by the father. "Shall we not then, Mr. Chairman, profit by experience?" Alexander asked. "Experience, says one, keeps a dear school, but fools will learn in no other—Shall we, like the mill boy's father, still keep the old stone that has been so serviceable to the family, or shall we profit by experience? For heaven's sake let the trial come to issue, and I have no doubt gentlemen will have full scope to display their philanthropy."

Several morals can be drawn from the story, any one of which Alexander would probably have embraced. The rock of anti-slavery, perhaps at one time needed to balance the constitution and ensure its acceptance by Congress, was no longer needed; the local form of slavery had proven profitable in the experience of the state's farmers; the young sons of Illinois, eyes opened by experience, should lead the state; their older fathers, blinded by tradition and the past, should step aside. But what is the meaning of the last sentence?

Anti-slavery sentiments were considered noble, but why "philanthropy"? Slave emancipation was infrequent. When it did occur it was almost invariably connected to religious, not social or philanthropic, sentiments. In one recorded case, for example, two brothers emigrated from Kentucky each owning several slaves. Henry West kept his slaves upon entering the state, registering them as indentured servants with the St. Clair County recorder. Tilghman West, brother of Henry, emancipated his slaves in 1816 on the advice of Methodist preacher Jessie Walker. Governor Coles's emancipations, perhaps precisely because he was not affiliated with any religion, were correspondingly remarkable and remarked upon. When he ran for governor three years later, the emancipations took on a new light. Hooper Warren speculated that Coles used the event for self-promotion, observing that it was "a mark of his shrewdness, to make all the capital he could out of the performance of a praiseworthy act." Others resented Coles's inherited wealth and his social standing, which supplied the opportunity for the display; further, they feared that a proliferation of freedmen would reduce their own standing.[48]

In contrast to Coles's inheritance, the conventionists liked to emphasize their hard-earned experience. The lesson of this experience pointed, as in William Alexander's case, to a continuation of the western policy of "voluntary servitude." There is evidence that war veterans especially played the trump card of Illinois experience. New emigrant Isaac Newton Piggott complained in his address to the "Morganian Society" on July 4, 1823, that "large parties [have] formed," which claim "precedence in every political project they undertake, whether right or wrong, because say they, we have lived in the West in the time of, and since the late war, and [who] conclude no late emigrant has a right equal to theirs."[49] For these, having "lived in the West" was equated with approving "limited slavery" and all other western experiments. Because of the connection between local experience and slavery, the authority of local experience was often made the fulcrum in the conventionist rhetorical lever. From this perspective, the depression had been caused by closing a door to the people's freedom to reach their own conclusions. Who could argue against opening the door to self-government?

Of course, opening the door to self-government also meant opening the door to the desperate feelings of people trapped by a sudden economic decline. The frenzy this decline could create is most clearly indicated by the racist sentiments articulated by participants on both sides of the controversy. Open displays of racism were a commonplace occurrence. On January 1, 1824, for example, William Orr wrote an editorial indicating the bellicose attitude of the southern rim of the state: "The

question, or rather the *phantom* of slavery has been long the presiding
genius of Illinois politics, and it now appears to us that those *knightly*
displays of hostility to negroes which have made their appearance from
Wansborough to Edwardsville would show more of the courage of political chivalry, if reserved for a proper occasion."[50]

Racist statements, if read in context, are almost always found in connection with the locals' fear of losing control over the state to outsiders,
their social status, or personal security. One letter writer, "Spartacus,"
discussed the "too much infatuated" opinion of his "very poor . . .
neighbor," whom he encountered in "a grog-shop . . . [amid] a large
company of men engaged in conversation on the convention question."
The neighbor was "very zealous, in advocating the convention and slavery. He swore we had as good a right to have slaves as the people of Missouri or any other state; that a white man could not stand it to work
here—that negroes were made for slaves; that white people ought not to
be obliged to work &c." All the while he made "many furious gestures
with the glass which he held in his hand." Spartacus reflected publicly
on what lay behind his neighbor's position, concluding that he "could
not think of a single advantage which slavery could bring to my neighbor." But there was one argument he left unanswered: that without slavery "our state will be overwhelmed with eastern population."[51]

Spartacus had rejected the idea that slavery would benefit his neighbor by raising his social status, since "a poor man in a slave state is not
as much respected as in a free one." Among the non-conventionists,
this theme was squeezed for every drop of anti–big folks sentiment it
might deliver. "A Laborer" saw slavery not only as a threat to social
equality, but to political equality as well. Listing the train of abuses
that followed to "the laboring class, and especially those in *low* circum-
stance," he urged his readers "to put in . . . [n]o convention . . . tickets"
if "we wish to keep our liberties and not put it into the power of great
men, to fix it so that we shall not in future be allowed to vote, unless
we have a freehold of several hundred dollars value, and will vote as
they wish; if we wish to have ourselves and children reckoned among
white folks." As was typical in this sort of rhetoric, the writer, not content to allude to the fear of losing status from above, looked also at the
threat from below, by considering "the trouble of having every night to
lock up what we can, and stand sentry over the rest of our moveable
property [and of having] our children to contract bad habits by the
vulgar pronunciation or vicious habits of the *negroes.*" Morris Birkbeck,
writing as Jonathan Freeman, responded to "John Rifle" along the same
lines: "Mr. Rifle says something about white slaves. . . . Where, Sir, in
the Union would you look for white men in a state of the lowest civil
degradation? . . . Let the question be referred to any emigrant of common sense who has removed from a slave state. Ask him why he removed, and he will tell you it was because it was impossible for

freemen to thrive by honest labor among slave holders and slaves."[52]

The conventionists also used racism, both to indicate local autonomy sentiments and to suggest, in direct opposition to "A Laborer" and Birkbeck, that free blacks, not slavery, posed the greatest threat to the white folks.[53] "Vindex" adroitly put racism at the service of the conventionists' perception that a group of calculating "politicians" were conspiring to usurp the people's power:

> Is it strange that when we see such men as Mr. Churchill and Mr. Ogle, of the last legislature, presenting petitions from free negroes, endeavoring to extend to them all the privileges which pertain to our white population, giving them the right of voting, of electing and being elected, to office—and when we hear such men as Jonathan Freeman, alias the gentleman who resides at Wansboro, declaring at the seat of government that he would be perfectly willing to dandle a black grand child upon his knee . . . and more particularly when we find so many among us ready and willing to aid in secreting ours, to lend their legal talents even in freeing runaway slaves—I say, after all this, is it unnatural, is it unreasonable, nay, is it not certain that it has excited a confidence among the free blacks of other states to migrate to this, where they are promised such a warm reception? nay, where the idea is held out distinctly both by word and deed that they will not only be permitted to marry with the whites, but actually made eligible to office. If these are not sufficient inducements to free negroes, I know not what is. If this is your boasted freedom, this the glorious result of your free institutions, and this the free population you wish to receive, in the name of heaven receive it. I for one shall protest against it . . . for free negroes sooner or later you will have, unless you stop the mouths of some of your politicians.[54]

Racism motivated both sides in the controversy. James Hall, writing as "Brutus" for the non-conventionists, attacked Will's plan because he thought it would work too well. He imagined the mass immigration of slaves and the eventual presence of large numbers of "free men of color" in terms of an indelible "black" plague. They would bring "a moral pestilence which no human power could afterwards exterminate." "A Voter" ridiculed the conventionists, he probably thought very effectively, when he called them "admirers of curley-heads and flat noses." Even the most humane non-conventionist, writing as "A Hater of Slavery and Man-Stealing," when discussing the emigration of free blacks could see no benefit "from bringing them here at all."[55]

Jonathan Freeman was ceaseless in trying to convert prejudice against the African slaves to the non-conventionists' benefit. In his first letter, where Birkbeck attempted clumsily to adopt the folksy language of the average farmer, he argued against allowing even limited slavery on the grounds that negroes were "light fingered." In his tenth letter, he used race to implicate class. He cited the flowery prose of "a negro fellow, called Du Vasty, in St. Domingo" and sarcastically suggested that, if slavery were allowed, the legislature would need to prohibit blacks from reading and writing—since otherwise "it is to be feared they might soon prove an over-match for us at those exercises." George Flower felt that antiblack prejudice was expressed by "some Eastern men as well as Southern men." Henry Eddy, Hall's replacement at the *Illinois Gazette,* was originally from New England. He feared having "so many free blacks in our state that our wives and daughters would be continually insulted by" their presence. In the letter addressed "for the *Intelligencer,*" a non-conventionist writer asked what was to become of the state after the plan of limited slavery and gradual manumission "have been in operation for forty years . . . what then will be the nature of the population in Illinois?" The answer supplied: "Dark, indeed in complexion, but infinitely darker in moral Character!" And when "the inordinate increase of free blacks would afford matter of complaint . . . an easy and palatable remedy for this evil would soon be discovered; a convention! To prohibit the further manumission of slaves!"[56]

Racist and sectional prejudices evidently worked wonders in organizing opinion. A brief examination of the 1824 vote indicates the high levels reached by politicalization in the counties. In Monroe County, for example, the vote went 196 to 141 against a convention, and 192 to 144 for George Forquer against William Alexander in the House race. In Lawrence County, it went 239 for Rev. William Kinkade to 161 for James Bird for the Senate position; the convention vote was 261 to 158 against. In Wayne County, Bird, the leader of the Wayne Convention Society, beat Kinkade, 183 to 103, for the Senate vote; the convention vote followed at 189 to 111. Lawrence County shared its Senate seat with Wayne County that year. Consequently Bird beat Kinkade overall by two votes, 344 to 342.[57]

The larger counties show an equally impressive degree of voting discipline. In Madison County, the successful non-conventionist slate for the House, Curtiss Blakeman, George Churchill, and William Otwell, garnered between 542 and 480 votes; the vote against a convention numbered 563. In the same county, the losing conventionist slate of Emanuel J. West, John Todd, and Benaiah Robinson took 369, 369, and 366 votes respectively; the convention vote stood at 351. In St. Clair County a similar scenario unfolded: the non-conventionist slate of Risdon Moore, Sr., Abraham Eyman, and David Blackwell received 534, 525, and 519 votes respectively in the House race; the vote against a convention came in at 506. The conventionist slate of Risdon Moore, Jr., John Reynolds, and John Scott tallied 447, 438, and 430; the convention received a total of 408. The same pattern is repeated for many of the other counties, though no such pattern is evident in earlier races. In

1820, for example, the three winners in the St. Clair representative race, Risdon Moore, Sr., Charles Matheny, and David Blackwell totaled 497, 375, and 269 votes respectively. In 1822, that county gave the top three candidates for the same race between 429 and 233 votes, while seven other candidates received between 196 and 101 votes each.

In the end, the local vote, like local political culture, was divided. The process of developing a usable community identity through the practice of politics led to a division in style and attitude. But if the local identity ended up as a split personality, it was not thought an unsatisfactory creation by either of its parts. The non-conventionists felt vindicated by the vote that took place on August 2, 1824. They won by 1,668 votes out of a total of 11,612 cast. The conventionists, however, were by no means completely lost. A majority of their candidates won in the General Assembly elections and they gained control of the next legislature with its lucrative appointment powers. With time William Kinney was elected lieutenant governor, and John Reynolds was made both governor and U.S. representative. In fact, the conventionists could claim victory on a higher level, for they chose to view the convention vote as an example of the temporary error that was necessarily sometimes entailed by their trial-and-error beliefs. This understanding of the power of learning from past mistakes is worth examining in detail, for it was perhaps the most significant cultural product of the convention controversy.

THE POLITICS OF LOCAL EXPERIENCE

The idea of local experience touched a raw nerve in the backcountry psyche and was especially strong in the western mind. The power of experience to shape character was often claimed to reach beyond the slavery lesson; it extended to all local knowledge acquired through the method of trial and error in the lives of the settlers. When one of Morris Birkbeck's pamphlets attacked the legislature for its mobs and the treatment of Churchill and Hansen, the war experience of many of the legislators was enough, in some eyes, to acquit them of any sinister motives. "Americanus" assured Birkbeck: "The people of Illinois, like their laws, are equally just and liberal." They were not likely to doubt those "men whose fidelity has stood the test in times when the souls of men were to be tried, and who fought and bled for the rights and liberties of their country." It was even more unlikely that they would believe such men "guilty of the most base and infamous crimes, on the mere assertions of a foreign incendiary."[58]

Individual experimentation was celebrated as a local virtue. What explains this celebration? Why was localism suddenly so important? If one peers just beneath the surface, it is clear that a feeling of inferiority and an assertion of superiority are involved. Local ways are not only necessary, they are better. When eastern ways change in the press of local experience, they are altered for the better. If imported ways were unsuited to the local scene, they could be tailored to suit local needs. Here was a justice of the peace insisting to circuit court judge John Reynolds that, as he had the power to marry a couple, he had as well—contrary to the law—the power to divorce. Here a meeting of non-conventionists in White County noted that "the inhabitants of this state have no legal right . . . to admit slavery therein," since the change would violate "the constitution of the United States, which declares all men to be born free and equal." Here John Grammer stood firm against those who presumed to threaten his slaveholding rights, an ignorant presumption that ran "fernent the compack." These expressions suggest that the development of a unique local sentiment was tied to the willful belief that all outside influences must be subservient to Illinois experience.[59]

For many settlers, the common adjustments necessary for survival soon became familiar; over time, familiarity grew to preference. The reception of Fourth of July toasts during the convention controversy betrays this budding localist sentiment. At the Sangamon County celebration in 1823, John Moore received "9 cheers" for this toast: "The Sangamo Senator—The free choice of the people—a man of too sound integrity to be influenced by sectional prejudices or individual interest." This was more than what was received by toasts to "the Heroes of '76," "John Quincy Adams," "Gallant Greece," "the Hon. Daniel P. Cook," "The Heroes of our country," "The Constitution of the United States," and "the day we celebrate."[60]

Local experience had become politicized. Consider the following excerpt from the only published man of letters frontier Illinois produced: "We may wander long in error, the perverted mind may grope for years in guilt or in mistake, but there is a time when that faithful monitor within, which is ever true, will speak." This line appears in the story "The Pioneer," published by James Hall at Cincinnati in 1835. Previously Hall had been a consummate new man in Illinois politics: militia colonel, attorney, editor, and public official. He lived in Shawneetown from 1820 to 1826, where part of the time he co-edited the *Illinois Gazette*. Before moving to the Queen City in 1833, Hall lived in Vandalia for seven years, serving as the state treasurer. Within this public life lay the private life of a writer. During his stay in Illinois, Hall managed to write innumerable poems, short stories, essays, and travelogues.[61]

"The Pioneer" certainly reflects Hall's localist sensibilities. The defense of trial and error, just cited, occurs at a crucial juncture in the story. The main character is explaining his conversion to the ministry. He has spent over a decade repeatedly avenging his parents' murder in an Indian raid. He recalls the last time he stalked an unsuspecting, isolated American Indian family in the midst of domestic bliss. At first he felt a "malignant delight" at the equivalence of his vengeance in this case. Although he notes the differences between the "Indian father" and his own, between this "hunting-lodge" and his family's cabin, he yet finds his mind "calmed by an agreeable train of association." Before attacking, however, he recognizes the mother as his long-lost sister. Something inside stirs. He is forced to reflect upon the contradiction of his vengeance: in order to avenge his family he would destroy another. The ever-true inner monitor speaks. The line encapsulates the idealistic belief in the power of the individual conscience. Morality is achieved not by the rules of society but by the individual through a process of trial and error. The individual conscience may fail at first or become clouded by emotion, but eventually it reaches beyond passion, beyond even cultural norms of right and wrong, to the truth. Truth in this case is the realization that one's ways are not the only ways, and that, abstractly considered, other ways may enjoy an equivalent status. That the avenger reaches this point is remarkable, for he was "raised on the frontier . . . , had been accustomed from infancy to hear the Indian spoken of as an enemy."[62]

The politicized aspect hidden here is the belief in the ability of the untutored individual to develop morally and intellectually, independent of education and refined society. The pioneer turned preacher is without the aid of social refinement or "book larnin." His conversion takes place in the wild. Opposed to society is nature. "Society" on the frontier meant eastern culture, which placed the poor and uneducated at the bottom of the social hierarchy. Western culture would demonstrate, as Hall's story demonstrates, that social development can occur naturally, as it were, and that local experience is not barren of moral standards. Indeed, mere coincidence is enough to spur the local conscience to awaken. The missionary credits "a Frenchman" and "nature" for his lessons; he notes that the student of the earth "always reaps instruction in gazing upon her scenes of native luxuriance." "The wisdom of Providence is so infinite," he continues, "the ingenuity displayed in all the arena of the animal and vegetable creation is so diversified, that every day thus spent discloses new facts, and suggests a novel train of reflection." The experience of "ingenuity" taught by the "native" teacher is immediately digestible and useful. It leads to a conversion to a conventionally recognized (Baptist) religion.[63]

In some local thought, the apotheosis of experience goes so far that it is claimed to remove the need for socially inculcated standards of justice, including moral and religious standards. Trial and error teaches its own brand of moderation. Even a cosmopolitan young Illinoisan such as Daniel Cook can be found remarking glibly that "the spirit of speculation, like most other evils in this life, has corrected itself." John Reynolds took this train of thought as far as any of the locals. For him, the trial-and-error method of experience was a cherished source of self-expression "in the voyage of life." His favorite personal model of the potential of natural experience was none other than his opponent in the

1830 governor's race, William Kinney. This child of the Illinois Country tapped his "natural strong talents" to invent "a system of book-keeping" for maintaining his grocery, though "he could barely write and . . . [was] without any previous knowledge of the science." Reynolds noted: "By this course of life," Kinney developed an acute insight into "much of the human heart and various movements of human nature." At the same time, "he displayed a kindness and hospitality rarely equaled in any country or in any age."[64]

Of his own education at Transylvania University in Kentucky, Reynolds regretted only that students were forced through the mill of Latin instruction, instead of pursuing those subjects suited to their talents and inclinations. He judged self-education an inner experience of the most sacred kind, one not to be polluted by society's expectations or the pressures of external conformity. The romance of anti-social individualism extended to Morris Birkbeck, whose *Letters from Illinois* defended the settlers' tendency to assert violently "their right of defense against every aggression, even to the laws which they themselves have constituted." The lure of experience coaxed a few non-conventionists into preaching against imported manners. The anti-slavery Methodist preacher Thomas Hinde of Edwards County lamented those newcomers, "puffed up with self importance, . . . [who] endeavor to press everything into their own *mould*." He counseled instead that the "emigrant should come forth as an inquirer, and set himself down to learn at the threshold of experience." Only if the inner-directed life took the individual too far astray from community norms could society rightfully retaliate. Upon viewing the foundations of the Madison County jail being laid, Reynolds told Thomas Lippincott: "Ah, these are what will keep society in order, rather than your Sunday Schools." Those few unable to adapt were not to be "saved" by society but separated from it. It was as simple a matter, as Baptist Daniel Parker would have it, as separating the good seed from the bad.[65]

Reynolds's glorification of local experience was magnified by old age. His memoirs are larded with romanticized descriptions of the pioneers. His stories must thus be used with caution as sources of fact, but as instances of the western apotheosis of experience as a source of culture they are ideal. They indicate how far the western sense of social inferiority could drive the politicalization of the idea of "society." A typical example is his description of a corn shucking. During these "husking frolics," liquor was shared "out of the bottle . . . without using any glass or cup whatever." Neither this practice, nor the "plain homespun" dress nor the "natural earth" dance floors was "considered rude." True rudeness arises only in "this refined and civilized day" and is caused by competition and envy, "the green eyed monster." For "excessive refinement and accomplishments may polish the outside; but it is doubtful if the inside is made better by the operation." By contrast "these honest, unsophisticated children of nature love with more sincerity and honesty than the excessively refined and educated do."[66]

Of course not everyone was seduced by the romantic lure of nature and simple ways. There is evidence of the opposite impulse in the local consciousness. Shadrach Bond, known to regret his reckless youth, argued for a "duty of legislation" in regard to education. He may even have felt a responsibility to dissuade youths such as Reynolds who tried to follow in his footsteps. His 1820 address to the legislature included a request to pass a law "for the suppression of vice and immorality." He worried in public about the "youth of the state" who, under the influence of "allurements" the likes of "gaming houses and disorderly taverns," were learning "vicious and indolent habits." This strain in Bond's public posture was especially prominent in his farewell address, delivered the day before Coles's inaugural. "The dictates of pure morality," he stated, "will never influence the conduct of men, whose youthful days have been spent in the unrestrained lasciviousness of unrestrained nature." Bond reflected on the ways of "erring man" and worried about "a people incapable of reading the sacred volume." Of his own errors, he asked for "the exercise of a liberality which springs from a knowledge of the frailty and weakness attendant upon every son of Adam." Notice, however, that here was an indulgence one learned from the failure side of the trial-and-error ledger.[67]

For a good number of people in early Illinois, Bond's later position was the correct one: moderation in life was not learned directly from experience or even through the aid of a friend's experience. Daniel Cook, looking at the example of outlawing the slave trade, argued that experience was progressive only when disciplined by reason. "It is to the march of intelligence," he held, "which like the rays of the sun that illuminate our path, and stimulate to growth and perfection the means of sustaining our animal natures, that we are indebted for the convictions of the propriety of national as well as individual morality." Aristides thought that "the exercise of our reason" alone allowed the detection of "error" and only "by the exercise of this noble faculty" could the human species "continue in a state of progressive improvements." Those with this view, however, often came under attack as aspiring big folks. According to the *Republican,* "fine reason" was an attribute only of "certain *great men,*" who feared an "obscurity admidst the multitude" should slaveholding emigrants again be allowed in the state.[68]

The indomitable John Reynolds, who knew Bond well, drew another conclusion from the governor's life. Age and experience brought Bond wisdom. As a young man Reynolds himself and "the whole community" had profited much "by [Bond's] example and precept." For "his convivial parties were not based on gluttonness or intemperance; but they were sustained by the noble and generous hearts of the higher order of warm and congenial spirits." The inner-directed local was not above mimicking the successful experience of his "generous" neighbors. Colonel Alexander of Monroe County agreed. He conceded that one lost in the "thousand crooked and deviating paths . . . of Error" often required "the voice of a friend" to reach "a place that he knows." But for advocates of religious and cultural inculcation, such as Missionary Baptist John Mason Peck, Bond's farewell view was more appropriate. Peck extended Bond's logic so that it no longer required experience. Peck argued that "the mind must be trained to habits of thinking." Peck's eastern missionary and James Hall's pioneer cum preacher both arrive at Bond's conclusion, one by experience, the other by deduction. Bond's youthful position favored Hall; his view in old age favored Peck.[69]

George Forquer's Monroe County address implicitly acknowledged the conventionist picture of Peck's sentiment as a form of religious fanaticism. His response indicates, however, that non-conventionists also tried to take over the mantle of experience; they too expressed a fervent faith in local experience. The message of James Hall's story was that western culture stresses inner experience over external sign, and trial and error over standing. Those agreeing with Rattlebrain pushed the idea further: inner experience is opposed to "society," with society defined as the tyranny of eastern hierarchy and refinement. This "quest for the primitive" was prominent in western religion and in western culture generally. The lure of primitivism is behind the "innocence" that is often associated with the frontier. One of the strongest religious movements on the frontier—the antimission movement, whose ranks were filled out mainly by Baptists but also by some Methodists—gave full expression to the opposition to eastern refinement driven by this primitive impulse. Western republicans hoped to install, in place of eastern society, what they variously described as purity, sincerity, simplicity, or the spirit. The lowly, plain people could access the spirit of being because they were free of the convoluted perception that clouded the souls of the superior-minded.[70]

This understanding of the proper development of human personality put great pressure on individuals. The freedom to make socially irrevocable errors made many cautious. Depending on how integrated one was in a supportive group, the psychic energy produced by risk could lead either to egalitarianism or to fatalism. The more the stress is on individual self-help, the more the stress of failure falls squarely on the shoulders of individual and family. This psychic pressure is only exacerbated by modernization. As many political theorists have argued, liberalism privatizes social problems such as those associated with property. Here the generational division noted by Ford marked different responses: the old-timers, tied to small settlement groups, turned inward. They tended to view failure as a settlement failure and resigned themselves to move on, or redoubled their efforts to tough it out. The younger generation by contrast became more socially active. They expanded their group identity by reshaping the state's identity in their own image.[71]

The political uses of experience were exploited by conventionists who scrutinized non-conventionist reasoning for its imported, covertly self-important assumptions. By these means Americanus discovered "foreign" ideas in the arguments of Birkbeck's Jonathan Freeman. The Englishman had argued that the introduction of slavery would undermine the status of white laborers. William Orr could not impute to the slaveholders of Tennessee and Kentucky the goal of trying to new-model the social policy of the state. He elaborated the "meanness" argument:

> To suppose that the first act of a stranger coming to settle amongst us, would be an act of such direct hostility to an early settler, as to deprive him, if possible, of his land and improvements, is to suppose him not only capable of the greatest baseness but also the most consummate folly and imprudence. This argument against a convention could only have been *invented* by those in whose composition nature has thrown a goodly portion of *meanness.*

Meanness was a sign of those who lacked the "liberality of spirit" of a true western republican. It was easy to move from the fear of a loss of control, to prejudice against a "mean" and "foreign" mind, to support for the opposite position. Jonathan Freeman made the mistake of praising "British republicans" in the same breath as he pronounced American southerners traitors to the revolution. John Rifle offered this nationalistic response: "Shame! Shame! If Jonathan Freeman is an American he should blush—if an Englishman he should be silent. We cannot bear to have the laurels of our fathers torn from our brows." Slavery, if under attack by outsiders, must be defended as a right, so William McCoy of Gallatin County concluded: "As our Fathers have gained our freedom by the sword, we ought always to maintain our rights . . . the people of the slave states fought for their rights, and justice says they ought to enjoy them." Only a "foreigner," and a "mean" one at that, could misunderstand this fact.[72]

The characters celebrated in Hall's tales and the electoral success of politicians such as William Kinney and John Reynolds suggest that the image of a particular but pristine, universal but simple republican society was attractive to the average Illinoisan. This indicates that, however imbued with southern culture, early Illinoisans attempted to separate themselves from it. Bertram Wyatt-Brown has argued that the individual conscience was radically dependant on community norms in southern culture, as it had been in traditional cultures generally. He points out that the individualism commonplace in modern societies was traditionally an exception to a ubiquitous tribal rule. In traditional cultures, uncontrollable and unpredictable Nature was so threatening that individual members welcomed the succor of a hierarchically ordered community. Honor and position in the communal pecking order—based on the ancient prejudice favoring of the strong—were steady and predictable, albeit cruel, protectors. Unlike the rapidly industrializing and rationalizing North, the South remained a culture of honor throughout the antebellum period, and after. In such a culture, "the internal man and the external realities of his existence are united in such a way that he knows no other good or evil except that which the collective group designates." "Honor, not conscience, shame, not guilt," Wyatt-Brown concludes, "were the psychological and social underpinnings of southern culture."[73]

James Hall's frontier Illinois fiction rebelled against this culture; it asserted the right to an independent internal life. It exuberantly broadcast to the world a backcountry freedom from traditional shame-based culture. The bias in favor of individualism, especially of the younger generation, meant that economic failure—whether defined in terms of squatters, yeomen, or capitalists—marked the individual with a stigma. The depth of the aspiration for independence through landownership in the West can be traced to this factor. James Hall's hero spoke especially to the young; they believed, along with the egalitarian pioneers, that an individual's lessons are added to the communal store. When the individual is allowed the proper amount of freedom, Hall implies, the relation between individual and society is not adversarial.

This cooperation between individual and society was further developed in another way. If after testing their fate individuals found their personal success lacking, communal influence could be applied in nonpunitive ways, depending on the severity of the individual error. If the individual was willing and the community accepting, sanctions such as teasing or ostracism were available to guide the "lost" individual back to safety. This softer side of the reliance on experience rested on the assumption that local communal ways could be relied upon to shelter the individual in a dangerous world. Whatever innovations in social practice an individual might uncover in testing fate, the traditions of the local community remained as a reservoir of grace to which the individual might retreat in times of uncertainty. Given these assumptions, the triumph of society over the state and the use of local society as the prime regulator of order could be seen as a great advance in both political and social freedom.

Thus the relation between the individual and society was expected to be smooth and amicable in the new western version of society. It is true that some provision was made for an imperfect translation of individual into social standards; trial and error might become permanently derailed, then the only solutions were governmental. If the individual was recalcitrant, severe sanctions—imprisonment, relocation, death—were imposed. In general however, except in extraordinary circumstances, individual experience was not at first to be confined by status or by traditional rules; true freedom, true enlightenment, comes when people actualize on their own; self-actualization, recognition of the inner spirit, was the only moral guide for pure republicans. The fact that the transmission of individual discoveries into social standards would be natural, or frictionless, or in any case easy, allowed the social question to disappear. Under this understanding of society, the recognition of larger social forces such as class conflict or the social construction of race is lost. The fact that the white folks formed themselves in a social struggle with big and black folks recedes from view. The actual adjustments necessary to shape social standards go unrecognized. Indeed, the conventionists mainly ignored the violence caused by sectionalism and racism that characterized the 18 months of the convention controversy.

Furthermore, the belief that individual standards become social standards naturally means that the collection of these standards into local experience obtains the magic patina of universality. The story of the white folks is elevated to the story of the people. This assumption of universalism in what are in actuality particular norms was one of the key "illusions of innocence" that has characterized western and American political thought generally. As Richard T. Hughes and C. Leonard Allen argue, those acting under this impulse often "particularized the universal, though they imagined that they had recovered the universal in their particular perspectives and institutions."[74]

CHAPTER SIX

WHOLE-HOG
CALVINISTS AND
MILK-AND-CIDER
ARMINIANS

Illinois experienced the cultural pluralism associated today with liberal democracy the moment its citizens began to recognize the legitimacy of a "loyal opposition" *within* the people. The concept of the loyal opposition in the United States emerged first in the minds of the Jeffersonians during the 1790s and then in the actions of the Federalist Party after the election of 1800. The concept was institutionalized in the opposition between the Federalist and Republican Parties, which competed regularly only in the East, and mainly in the economically booming states of the Northeast. By majority opinion in the South and by unanimous opinion in the West, Federalists were never considered legitimate republicans.[1] In Illinois, opposition to the big folks had never been organized by two-party government; that stage was skipped altogether, and along with it the lesson of loyal opposition. The lesson had to be learned under new conditions because opposition came from an unexpected and seemingly apolitical division within the masses, the difference between Arminian and Calvinist approaches to salvation.

Both sides in the convention controversy assumed the image of poor, oppressed social underdogs. An ideal oppressor image was found in the specter of eastern society. For some members of the persuasion called "whole hog"—a name given them because of the fullness with which they identified with the group—opposition to the eastern elite was all consuming. Whole hoggers treated increases in the liberty or status of the white folks' group as equivalent to an increase in their personal liberty or status. Their celebration of local experience mixed a belief in the untutored individual with a strong commitment to the progress of the white folks' community. Combining the individual and communal was possible because the two merged in the whole-hog mind, producing cronyism in social relations. Thomas Ford emphasized the "kind of idolatrous devotion to General Jackson," for example, that whole-hog followers displayed. But Crony idolatry did not contradict white folks' independence, it confirmed it. Tocqueville noticed the same pattern when he observed that American individualists were greater "courtiers" than the medieval knights: "It is true that American courtiers never say 'Sire' or 'your majesty' as if the difference mattered; but they are constantly talking of their master's natural brilliance."[2]

The other persuasion was called "milk-and-cider" to highlight its lukewarm support of any particular script of the people's story. More individualistic and less group identified, it focused on society-wide rules for prescribing individual behavior. Milk-and-cider adherents identified with western society as a whole, not a specific subgroup. Consequently, this approach was more equivocal about the bottomland and less attached to the story of the white folks. Those of the milk-and-cider persuasion were less attached to local experience, precisely because they tended to eschew the solidarity that came from group identity. They nonetheless remained opposed to the big folks and celebrated western pragmatism. They still lived out the drama of the people's oppression but thought of the people in terms of humanity in general. This persuasion was manifest by localist non-conventionists such as Thomas Ford, David Blackwell, Thomas Lippincott, George Forquer, and James Lemon, Jr.[3]

Whole-hog attributes were most clearly displayed by activists such as T. W. Smith, William Kinney, William Alexander, William Jones, and Daniel Parker, who nevertheless opposed the convention and slavery. They took the bottomland vision whole-hog because they had so fully internalized opposition to the big folks. They wholly identified with the social traits of the white folks as they appeared in this struggle. They had wandered into Illinois with their poor parents in search of security and independence. From this identity as wanderers, as a people not quite comfortable within the American republic, they drew their moral code. The non-conventionists took the milk-and-cider tack: they were less committed to any one moral picture of the white folks. They too opposed the big folks but opposed their privilege more than their principles. When they pictured themselves as white folks, they pictured a people in need of resources and education. The romance of the white folks' story lay for them more in what they might become than in what they had been.

The convention controversy was made possible in the first place because of the struggle against the big folks, but as the controversy evolved, some of its most rancorous moments involved battles among the white folks. In this part of its development, too, the controversy exhibited in miniature some of the starkest contradictions of the American liberal democratic tradition. Intolerance of minority views and a near blindness to the human rights of those considered outsiders appeared alongside a movement genuinely committed to social equality (among whites) and communitarian goals. It is as if the fates had decreed that the best and the worst of the American political tradition would be tied together, with egalitarianism and intolerance, solidarity and myopia, developing alongside one another. Nonetheless, because the division between the whole-hog and the milk-and-cider persuasions split the community, local politicians were forced to take their first grudging steps toward acknowledging the legitimacy of minority political views. This recognition was one of the unintended consequences of organized political competition in the state.

Scholars have engaged in a long, fruitful debate over what divided the Jacksonian Democrats and Whigs during the second American party system. Some have questioned whether the cleavage was organized around economic or ethnocultural issues. Others argue that neither sort of issue formed its core: political rhetoric was used simply, albeit mercilessly, to elect party members to office. "Shrewd men in politics," Edward Pessen argued, "paid lip service to the common man" but kept an eagle eye on the all-important patronage that kept the party machinery going. Researchers focusing on the voting records of state and congressional delegations have been particularly insistent on the pragmatic aspect of party behavior under the second party system.[4]

This rejection of substantive issues, whether economic or cultural, as the driving force behind the Jacksonian and Whig parties often rests, however, on the assumption that the policy outputs of a party must directly reflect its ideology. But this assumption is false. "The key to understanding American political development and American party politics," Theodore J. Lowi has written, is recognizing that political parties serve two basic functions: one is to make policy, but the other, more basic function is to constitute or legitimate a polity. "Responsible" parties both constitute a segment of the polity and translate its interests into policy. But American parties have rarely been responsible parties. This has been, in part, because the constitutive function of parties has included more than just organizing to reap spoils. It has also included the equally important task of registering the presence—and thus legitimating the recognition—of various socially excluded parts of the polity.[5]

The legitimacy of minority opposition was the unexpected outcome of a party system forced to debate religious and cultural issues. Underlying class divisions had been temporarily displaced by the success of the democratic revolution. The Illinois pattern of the displacement of class by religion, culture, and ethnicity prefigured the larger antebellum pattern. Indeed, the pattern has been played out so often in American history, an examination of its immediate causes in Illinois has a larger significance. As has been noted, a charged rhetoric of opposition to the big folks encouraged an equally charged identification with the white folks. Once the people became the white folks, however, the logic of opposition was derailed, for one cannot keep on killing something that is already dead. When political equality and formal social equality with the big folks was attained, there was no longer a tangible class image against which champions of democracy could register the social striving of their followers. In this altered context, the job of political rhetoric changed. Leaders in the legislature, in the newspapers, and in the pulpits competed to produce an image of the people that would motivate voters among the white folks to divide among themselves. Here was the new key to obtaining political power. Given this incentive, it is not remarkable that politics during the 1820s in Illinois revolved around the creation and contestation of a usable white-folks-based identity.[6]

The story of the people in a democratic culture is roughly equivalent to a traditional culture's creation myth. For this reason the battle to define "the people" in a democracy inevitably reaches some of the deepest questions of communal life.[7] The story of the white folks assumed a moral code for interpreting life as well as politics. Understanding why some went whole-hog and some milk-and-cider thus requires an inquiry into their psyche; it requires asking questions about what life as a whole meant to them. The best way to access answers to these questions in the early Illinois setting is through a study of organized religion. From the first days of the convention controversy partisans battled over the meaning of the people; now they took the battle to the pulpits and politicized the religious debate over the nature of salvation.

"MEN OF MEANEST NAME" DEBATE THE NATURE OF SALVATION

Nathan O. Hatch has described the "Second Great Awakening" between 1790 to 1840 as a mass "revolt against Calvinism." During the revolt, great numbers of American Christians recoiled from the strict Calvinist idea of limited election and its associated idea of salvation by grace. These ideas—articulated in the terms of "scholastic metaphysics" by an "educated elite" the likes of Timothy Dwight at Yale and Samuel Hopkins at Princeton—left backcountry Protestants unmoved. Methodists, Free Will Baptists, Presbyterians, and Christians embraced instead the Arminian position, which stressed a type of salvation open to all who sincerely embraced Christ. Their hearts awakened, these believers spread their new doctrinal consensus across the country. Protestants everywhere breathed a national sigh of relief as the new view released a worried population from, as Hatch put it, the "internalized guilt and unworthiness, prompted by predestinarian preaching." Along with the shift in doctrine came a shift in style from the intellectual to the emotional. The change was manifest in the rise of "camp meetings" where great numbers of conversions took place and believers roiled with the spirit. Followers demanded from their leaders a more democratic doctrine and a more democratic preaching style. Manifest throughout was a "deep-seated class hostility" and reaction against the elite that controlled the leadership of "Reformed orthodoxy."[8]

This Arminian side of the Second Great Awakening was not fully felt in Illinois until the 1830s when the Methodists, Free Will Baptists, and Cumberland Presbyterians established a dominance among the state's Protestant sects. Before this, the antimission countermovement prevailed. This movement also dissented from an eastern elite, but it targeted the Anglican and Episcopalian traditions by denouncing their "Money and Power." While some anti-missionaries were Methodist, most were Regular Baptists. The Regular Baptists under Daniel Parker's leadership in Illinois took the predestinarian doctrine in a non-evangelical direction. They attacked eastern congregations not because they were too strictly Calvinist, but because they were too Arminian. Their critique was a throwback to the "puritanical" religion of their grandparents who had been some of the strongest dissenters to the Anglican Church in Virginia during the 1760s. Thus, part of the Second Great Awakening featured western Arminians attacking eastern Calvinists, and part featured western Calvinists attacking eastern Arminians. While both refused to defer to an eastern hierarchy, they expressed two competing paradigms of dissent, two distinct ways of expressing "deep-seated class hostility" in a religious mode. Where western Arminians dissented by loosening the accepted terms of salvation, western Calvinists dissented by making salvation standards more rigid.[9]

That both groups resented the secular advantages of big folk Christians is clear. The old hymnbooks reveal many of the cultural norms that have been associated with the white folks generally. Though neither the music nor the tunes were written locally, *The Missouri Harmony* was, according to John Mack Faragher, "the most popular and widely available Illinois songbook." The song texts were printed with "no acknowledgment . . . [of] authorship," perhaps because, as George Pullen Jackson has suggested, "the texts were, by and large a fixed and generally taken-for-granted corpus, founded on the changeless psalms, and therefore looked upon as non-individual in source." Allen D. Carden, the St. Louis editor of the hymnal, apparently felt that the collection was non-denominational because he made no claims of affiliation. A later version was generic enough to serve "Methodist, Baptist, Presbyterian, and all other Christian churches in the Western country," with tunes from "the Celtic background of early American settlers." The collection's avowed intent was to make available "the old melodies . . . identified with our most hallowed emotions." This suggests they were edited with an eye toward sales and with the lowest common denominators of backcountry culture in mind.[10]

The hymn "Melinda," for example, reads as a litany of resentment against the big folk:

> In vain, the wealthy mortals toil,
> and heap their shining dust in vain;
> Look down and scorn the humble poor,

and boast their lofty hills of gain,
Their golden cordials cannot ease,
Their pained hearts or aching heads,
Nor fright nor bribe approaching death
From glittering roofs and downy beds.

Another psalm, "Election Excludes Boasting," articulates perfectly the operating assumption of the white folks' moral code:

But few among the carnal wise,
But few of noble race,
Obtain the favor of thine eyes,
Almighty king of Grace!
He takes the men of meanest name
For sons and heirs of God;
And thus he pours abundant shame
on honorable blood.

Not only do the hymns reveal God's scorn for the big folks, they signal God's special interest in the poor white folks. The verses praise God's "strengthening hands," which "uphold the weak, and raise the poor that fall." In the promised land "of pure delight" the lands of the poor would become "sweet fields beyond the swelling flood."[11]

While Methodists and Free Will Baptists still retained the mental categories implicit in these verses, they pursued their dissent differently. In order to see how they differed, consider the white folks as a social category. Common as the psychic attachment to the white folks was, it was complicated by the low status of the category. Those having this status could reassure themselves by remembering they were also part of "the people," whom political leaders putatively held in high esteem. But for those mindful of the larger society's pecking order, internalizing a low-status identity still required swallowing a certain amount of self-hate. The more the larger society's norms were acknowledged, the more one felt the "guilt and unworthiness" uncovered by Hatch.

Given this status problem, Arminian doctrine was especially attractive. For those who had internalized their low status, the doctrine held the promise of overcoming it. In practice this meant they had to adopt, even if covertly, many of the social values of the big folks. In order to avoid the unbearable pressure of self-revulsion, however, they focused on those lower-class stigmas that could be removed, such as the lack of education. Such stigmas they hoped to change, and they openly scrutinized them from a worldly perspective. Yet they did not want to become big folks themselves so much as to become an improved version of the worthy but lowly white folks. Those stigmas that were incapable of removal they reviled; the fixed aspects of the white folks' story, such as their original standing in the pecking order, were anathema to them. For this reason they found predestinarian doctrines loathsome, which only made the foreordained more permanent. What good could come from that quarter but reinforcement of their low status?

Those attracted to the predestinarian view took a different tack, one exemplified by the Regular Baptists. They played with the notion of their meridional opposition to the big folks, whom they described with splenetic spite. Every social defect in the elite implied a social virtue of their own. In essence, they overcame their stigma by inverting the values of the larger society, which had the white folks all wrong. They were not low and mean but pure and simple. Into this romance of purity flowed all the psychic energy of the Calvinists. But finding a special meaning in their poverty led these Illinoisans straight into a contradiction: either they had to remain poor in order to remain chosen, or if they did have worldly success, it could not be cashed out in worldly meaning. Theirs was a nineteenth-century version of the seventeenth-century "Puritan dilemma" so compellingly described by Edmund S. Morgan—they struggled with being in the world but not of it.[12]

Doctrinal disputes over salvation became more prominent in Illinois after the War of 1812. In 1819, for example, Regular Baptist preachers David Badgley and William Jones announced in their association's circular at "Looking Glass Prairie Meeting House St. Clair County" that they would preach to "the very Elect" alone. In the presence of visiting Free Will Baptist missionary John Mason Peck, they railed against "false Prophets" such as Peck who believed that "mankind are born into this world pure." This view violated their understanding of human nature as being so sinful "the Lord imputeth righteousness without works." The Arminian view, according to Parker, tended "to make people believe that the *power* and *will* to repent, be converted, and worship God in spirit and truth, is *innate* in man." This led to the even more blasphemous idea that all souls were potentially saved by Christ. This was the position used by missionaries such as Peck and Isaac McCoy to open the Gospels to slaves and Native Americans. They argued that it was every Christian's duty to work to improve the condition of humanity in the world through missionary education and Sunday schools.[13]

The Regular Baptists argued that they opposed neither "translating the bible, nor educating the heathen" but insisted that these activities be separated from the church, lest it become contaminated with "filthy lucre." They clearly disdained the Arminian's quantitative view of soul-saving. It violated their understanding of the relation between God's election and preaching, since it was thought ministers could guide the saints but did not convert them. In Calvinist doctrine, only God did the converting. "Some tell us that the Lord has done his part," Badgley and Jones wrote, leaving "us to do our part, thus placing the whole of our salvation in our hands, forgetting that all we have, has been received from the Lord, and that he worketh in us to will and to do of his own good pleasure."[14]

A preoccupation with salvation runs through many hymns in *The Missouri Harmony*.[15] But whether salvation was "in our hands" and could be known by worldly signs or was wholly a matter of God's "own good pleasure" was an issue causing much disagreement. On this matter, the Regular Baptists split violently from their Missionary Baptist and Methodist neighbors. The idea that God helps those who help themselves was attractive to many in the latter group, especially as the severe frontier conditions were lifted and staple agriculture hit high gear in the 1830s. Whereas the latter groups rode the crest of a modernizing Arminian movement, the antimission Baptists and groups such as the Christians (followers of Barton W. Stone and Alexander Campbell) and the Dunkards sought the future by embracing the simple lives of the early saints.

One of the tunes known to have been popular with early Bond County residents bears on the division between the two persuasions. This tune, unassumingly entitled "Ninety-Fifth," was heard by Christiana Holmes Tillson from the mouths of her neighbors:

> When I can read my title clear
> To mansions in the skies,
> I'll bid farewell to ev'ry fear
> And wipe my weeping eyes.[16]

The conception of salvation in this hymn emphasizes the emotional relief achieved when title to land or salvation is finally secured. As with the fee simple, once individual "title" could be received from God, fear was dispersed. Like the independence obtained through the fee simple, title to this sort of salvation was certain; it could not be revoked. But herein was the rub, for not all salvation was understood in solid, fee-simple terms. Indeed, Arminian salvation, based on earthly effort, could be lost when earthly means failed. How was one to get a fee simple in salvation?

For the Regular Baptists, since title was to an otherworldly "mansion," a certain knowledge of it was equally otherworldly. They disagreed with their neighbors not only on "the subject of Baptism" but also "on the most essential doctrines of Salvation." Badgley and Jones registered their disagreement with those who "maintain that after a person becomes righteous . . . he may finally fall away and be lost." For "the Lord says, my sheep hear my voice and I know them and they follow me, and I gave unto them Eternal life, and they shall never perish neither shall any pluck them out of my hand."[17] This raised the age-old question of antinomian "latitude," since God's unequivocal selection might tempt the saints with the belief that the moral standards of the world no longer applied to them.

Regular Baptists attempted to deal with this problem by arguing that the spirit of "saving grace" was qualitatively different from the "spirit of delusion": "He must be a very queer sort of Devil," wrote Daniel Parker, "to make people feel so *happy, joyful,* lightsome, glorious and comfortable, at peace with all men!" This experience was easily distinguished from that deception when the devil made "the wicked think that they are very happy in their wickedness." The difference was that those inspired by the devil were driven by hubris; "some of them will jump about almost as bad as a parcel of hens with their heads off: and he really seems to make his children sometimes seem very happy in his religion, rejoicing in the works of their own hands, and even to dance and shout round a golden *calf.* . . . But to make people so humble, love God so well, and feel so happy in it . . . is certainly very strange work for a Devil." The humble true believers were untouched by worldly temptations, because "The Lord has communicated light to his children. It has reached their hearts . . . and converted them to hate sin and love holiness." It was the Arminian who was in danger of succumbing to the devil's temptation, the Arminian who reveled in the physical at revival meetings. This weakness was a direct consequence of the Arminian's "fears that grace is not quite sufficient to save him without his cooperating with it, by his own good works and obedience."[18]

Thus, the essential difference between Calvinists and Arminians was that the "one is converted by grace, and the other is not . . . one works because he loves, and the other to buy love. The one works because he has life, the other to get it." Regular Baptists experienced God's love so purely they were unturned by ulterior motives. Their inner-directed focus worked like a collective placebo against all fears and weaknesses. Parker's view of salvation typifies the basic predestinarian position on the matter. The purpose of salvation, he argued, was to show that God's promise to "the dear children of the spiritual kingdom" was so secure that they were "beyond the reach of corruption" and "secured in his book" forever. This view, which was indicative of the Calvinist approach generally, was as close to fee-simple salvation as Parker's Wabash Valley followers were likely to get.[19]

Parker was the leading Regular Baptist preacher on the eastern side of the state. Thomas Lippincott, who heard Parker preach regularly, noted that "he had followers and churches on his side of the state of whom he was the recognized leader." William Kinney had a similar prominence on the western side, but there is not as much firsthand information on him. Lippincott, who also knew Kinney and observed his preaching, believed that "illiterate, as he avowedly was, he possessed talents of a commanding order." He was raised in poverty, and yet having "very limited education, and opportunities for self-improvement equally limited, he had acquired and held among educated and able lawyers, by no means unambitious, the position of a leader." Like

Parker, Kinney's style was crude and his intellect penetrating: "It will not do to call it simply shrewdness or cunning. The man who is unable to write a correct sentence in plain English; who writes the personal pronoun i, and yet can stand beside the highest, the ablest, the most learned and the most practical politicians of the State, as their peer; and maintains his standing there for years, must have higher qualifications than usually come under the denomination of shrewdness." Of his religious creed, Lippincott noted, "he acknowledged a Supreme Being, who was the efficient cause of all things, each individual sin included, and who it would seem, had no rule or reason for his judgements, but his own unchangeable will. It was the doctrine of Fate, in its most absolute form. And he gloried in it."[20]

If Kinney's support for slavery was diametrically opposed to Parker's position, his salvation doctrine was almost identical. Kinney was also interested in securing salvation. His "Fate" was, as with the local identity, driven by larger forces but realized through experience. Just as the Illinoisans had used their natural talents and hard-earned experience to develop a successful culture, so Kinney had invented a persona in an assertion of will. His charismatic personality was a personal embodiment of the white folks' success as a culture. Like Parker, Kinney rejected the larger society's values, but for him the success of the white folks in the local setting had already proved the larger society wrong. Kinney believed God's chosen people were predestined, but they were not forever predestined to poverty, insecurity, and dependence. They just needed the right time and place—for Kinney, the 1820s, in Illinois.

As proof of this special status and worldly success, Kinney pointed to the elevated status enjoyed by the white folks by virtue of their whiteness. This was a sure sign of God's foreordained favor toward them. In a newspaper letter, he argued that "the Israelites were permitted to make slaves" of the heathen and strangers. "It was very evident," he thought, citing a passage in Leviticus, "that the African negroes are to be considered as 'strangers' and 'heathen' to us christians, who stand in the place and footsteps of the ancient Jews, God's chosen people; and whatever was lawful for them to do is lawful for us also." This view is echoed in a story quoted by Eugene D. Genovese in his discussion of slave culture. Two slaves are conversing with a white stranger in Mississippi. One slave asks the stranger: "Massa . . . Can you 'splain how it happened in the first place, that the white folks got the start of the black folks, so as to make dem slaves and do all de work?" At that point the other slave "fearing the white man's wrath, broke in: 'Uncle Pete, it's no use talking. It's fo'ordained. The Bible tells you that. The Lord fo'ordained the Nigger to work, and the white man to boss.'"[21]

Of course, the elevated worldly position of the white folks over the black folks violates the prevailing story line of God's chosen on earth in which the white folks' low social standing indicates the world's corruption. But in the view of Regular Baptists such as Kinney, great changes were on the horizon. Illinois was a chosen place where God's will with regard to both the white folks and the black folks was being played out. "The Crisis," he toasted, "it is big with the fate of Illinois." Kinney's Calvinism had this difference from that of Daniel Parker; it lacked the puritanical inhibitions that would have quashed such optimism. Ford recalled that Kinney's religion was "not of that pinched up kind which prevented him from using all the common arts of a candidate for office." Kinney's experience and his popularity were the morals of the story Reynolds fashioned of his youth. Yet Lippincott, who conceded that within "his own denomination he was all powerful," finished his portrait with facts that pointed to another moral: "It is sad to remember that in the last years of his life, his religious character, his standing, his hopes were wrecked by intemperance, and his course characterized by the most awful profanity." Here the Arminian delivered the comeuppance to the Calvinist turned antinomian.[22]

The Arminians did not believe that God's love caused qualitative changes in the saved. In the right quantities, however, it could tip the balance in a doubtful believer's mind. God did love the white folks more than the big folks, but the love was generally too dissipated in the world to have the proper effect. Nevertheless, under the right circumstances, such as when believers gathered in large public meetings at campgrounds, a crucial threshold was broached. More than any Arminian group, the Methodists discovered that people were especially open to salvation when in the midst of a critical mass of saints. The notion of a salvation threshold is expressed in an untitled hymn by Caleb J. Taylor published in 1810:

> Sinners through the camp are falling,
> Deep distress their souls pervade,
> Wondering why they are not rolling
> In the dark infernal shade.
> Grace and mercy, long neglected,
> Now they ardently implore;
> In an hour when least expected
> Jesus bids them weep no more.
>
> Hear them then their God extolling,
> Tell the wonders he has done;
> While they rise, see others falling!
> Light into their hearts hath shone.
> Prayer and praise, and exhortation,
> Blend in one perpetual sound;
> Music sweet beyond expression,
> To rejoicing saints around.

Implied in this view was the idea that salvation was a public matter, which occurred on terms not of a particular group but of the larger society.[23]

TWO TWICE-BORN TYPES: VOLITIONAL AND SELF-SURRENDER

In *The Varieties of Religious Experience,* William James explicitly addressed these differences in Arminian and Calvinist conversion experience. He observed that many spiritual autobiographies described moments of personal crisis during which the natural self is suddenly reviled for being connected to all the evil in the world. Conversion was the process by which this "sick self" was abandoned and the saved self inhabited. Those undergoing this religious experience James referred to as the "twice-born." James found that the Christian experience exhibited two different types of conversion rebirth: the *"volitional type* and the *type by self-surrender."* The latter type believed that no human effort could help on the path to salvation. They wanted to be saved, but they discovered so much sin in their souls that they realized they could not save themselves. Their will, as their very selves, was utterly sinful. Consequently, nothing good could come from the self, certainly not a rational estimation of one's own salvation. Nor could the sentiments of so sick a human soul be of any use. The only way out was through a complete rejection of the self, a conversion "by self-surrender," and a rebirth in a life dedicated to Jesus Christ, a process by which God's will replaced the sinful, sick, human will.[24]

The other "twice-born" conversion took a different approach to the problem of the sinful will. Those of this volitional type, while making full acknowledgment of their inherent sinfulness, nonetheless retained some faith in the goodness of their selves. After all, it was reasoned, this same self had led them partially in the right direction, however imperfectly. Some good parts of the will remained. Unfortunately, these parts were only about half of the self, the other half was rotten to the core. People of this temperament were forever at war with their weak wills. This type of psyche James termed the "divided self." It was this internal war of wills that he thought explained the sudden explosions of emotion at camp meetings. These "automatisms" occurred when the quantity of goodwill and love finally tipped the balance in the battle of will taking place inside the believer.[25]

James's analysis is ripe with implications for the cultural division in early Illinois culture. The divided-self type believed there was some goodness in human nature and the world. God had given certain human talents, basic faculties such as rationality and sentiment, to the human race as special gifts.[26] This did not make human nature "pure" as the Calvinists accused them of claiming, but it did mean that these faculties, if controlled and put to use by God's will, could help the religious individual discover the way to salvation. Here arose the first great point of disagreement between the whole and the divided selves: the potential uses of human faculties in improving the world's condition. The Calvinists remained suspicious of the guidance that "natural" faculties offered; they tended instead to trust the incremental truth of inner-directed experience accumulated in gatherings of "the very elect." The Arminians always had half a will in the natural world, which allowed some reliance on larger societal indicators or on abstracted faculties such as reason and sentiment.

Since the Methodists and Free Will Baptists (Arminians) were associated with the non-conventionists, and the anti-mission Regular Baptists (Calvinists) were associated with the conventionists, James's types suggest a reason for the conventionists' localism and the non-conventionists' relative openness to broader moral guides. Furthermore, the Calvinist self-surrender type of conversion operates by leaping into a new self. This is remarkably like the creative leap necessary in the whole-hog adoption of a new communal identity for the people. The Arminian fifty-fifty temperament worked incrementally; not adopting anything in wholes was the hallmark of the milk-and-cider position. James's portrait of the two psyches—the Calvinist converting in one gust, the Arminian converting in pieces, subliminally—also rings true in the case of the controversy. Many conventionists fit the uninhibited "liberal" type, while many non-conventionists acted the reserved bachelor-farmer type.

These types were reflected in the disagreement between Arminians and Calvinists over the proper role of the pulpit during the convention controversy. For the Calvinists, religion, like all self-development, was radically private; its use to sway the minds of men on the public issues of the day was an unacceptable political tool. Like religious decisions, political decisions were properly made by individuals, and though they should be publicly expressed, their impetus should never come from outside the individual. When Calvinist preachers did attack slavery, it was usually not because it was considered immoral in the larger society (whose values they had denied) but because it violated republican values. The Arminian preachers saw no reason not to point out what other states thought about slavery, in order to help their congregations understand the larger social stigma it carried. They stood against what they saw as a covert tendency of the Calvinists to sacralize individual experiences reflecting mere local preference. Unlike the Calvinists, they retained a part of the old self, which inhibited and checked the swelling visions of their converted self.

Some scholars have doubted the appeal of strict Calvinism among the lowly. Keith Thomas argues that the "doctrine of providence" appeals less "to those at the bottom end of the social scale" because it "jeopardiz[es] his self-esteem." But Daniel Parker was able to make it appear attractive. In one passage, he comments on the "lively figure of the man and his wife, which St. Paul has taken to illustrate Christ and his Church." Parker is keen to point out the psychologically unhealthy approach to republican family relations encouraged by good-works theology. Paul's metaphor, Parker argues, shows "the difference between the true Church, or married wife, and the false societies, or the pretended wife." "Very much engaged to buy [her] husband's love or good will . . . [the latter] has but little confidence in her husband's love, only that which she can secure by her good performances, and that but doubtful." Thus, she is "always unhappy at the approach of danger, let her husband be present or absent." The true wife, on the other hand, "has full confidence in her husband in every respect, has no doubts, dreads nor fears, at the approach of the enemy, when she knows that her husband is at hand." For Parker, as for other plain republicans out on the wild prairies of frontier Illinois, the advantage of living in a Calvinist household was sufficiently clear. This emphasis on inner-directed spirit was the whole-hog approach to reducing fear and anxiety.[27]

Of all the political views that are underpinned by doctrine, Kinney's is the hardest to square logically. If he is Calvinist and rejects the world and natural man's corruption, how can he be pro-slavery and justify it as a sign of worldly progress? One additional doctrinal dimension suggests an answer. The typical Calvinist rejection of the world is found in Parker's writings: the world that indicates the specialness of the chosen is by opposition thoroughly corrupted; believers never see in their earthly lives any benefits from their special calling. They remain God's "poor earthen instruments . . . among the last choice that the world would have made." The idea that salvation is utterly disconnected to the world is tied to a belief known in doctrinal terms as premillennialism. This is the idea that the saints will rule after Christ's second coming, which will destroy the wicked world. Kinney's understanding of salvation, however, may have assumed that God's chosen people were preparing the world for Christ's second coming. This is known in doctrinal terms as postmillennialism.[28]

There is some evidence of a confusion of the worldly and other-worldly in the hymns in *The Missouri Harmony*. In "Whitestown," the story of the white folks is told verbatim:

> Where nothing dwelt but beasts of prey,
> Or men as fierce and wild as they,
> He bids to oppress'd and poor repair,
> And build them towns and cities there.
> They sow the fields and trees they plant,
> Whose yearly fruit supplies their want;
> Their race grows up from fruitful stocks,
> Their wealth increases with their flocks.[29]

Here God's chosen people, those marked out for sure salvation, have a special destiny on earth. They have been sent to the wilderness to grow and prosper. What is interesting about this hymn is that it suggests salvation will have tangible worldly consequences for the white folks. The hymn thus contains, at least partially, a postmillennialist view.

Kinney's identification with the white folks should logically have made him a premillenarian. After all, how could anyone who so strongly believed the profane world was utterly corrupt, believe at the same time that God's saints were making headway in preparing for the second coming? This sort of claim made more sense in the hands of the Arminians, who were generally more open to the currents of cosmopolitan reformism in American national culture. Kinney's combination of predestinarian and postmillenarian views suggests that the antinomianism feared by the Arminians did play a role in early Illinois religion. Its impact on the convention controversy depended on how many voters might be convinced that the millennium had indeed arrived.

Calvinistic Baptists engaged in a radical rejection of the world's values. They believed in individual independence and praised the "power of self-determination." In this they were following in their grandparents' footsteps, for the generation that had fought the revolution engaged in a similar ideological transformation, as indicated in the pamphlets documented by Bernard Bailyn.[30] With William Kinney, however, one begins to see a different strain emerge: an extreme faith in the saved individual's ability to handle power and self-control successfully. This strain was absent in Daniel Parker's writings. He remained doubtful of the world to the end; real salvation in his formulation arrived only in the next world. Doctrinally, he remained premillennialist. But for the uninhibited Kinney, God's turning the world upside down began immediately; the lowly people were empowered to act now. Those looking for the best of both worlds in terms of security may have been attracted to Kinney's formulation, for he combined the solid otherworldly salvation of the Calvinists with the optimism of the postmillennialists.

THE ATTACK ON THE METHODISTS

Between the spring of 1823 and the winter of 1824, the two religious persuasions colored several key political battles. The cultural cleavage of the second party system appeared formally in several contests and began to harden. T. W. Smith's attack on preachers and especially the Methodists; the race between William Kinney and James Lemen in St. Clair County; and the race between Thomas Lippincott and William Jones in Madison County: all these left the state changed. These events demonstrated that pluralism within the people was fundamental and permanent.

The opening shot in the wars of religion was a preemptive strike by

Smith in the *Illinois Republican*. It involved Edward Coles's conferring with Rev. John Mason Peck in Edwardsville about candidates to fill the office of secretary of state from which Samuel Lockwood had just resigned. Coles was looking for more than a secretary; he needed "an anti-convention man . . . [and] he must be able on a certain contingency to conduct the editorial department of a newspaper." Peck, perhaps not familiar with the old factional lines, immediately suggested David Blackwell of Belleville. Blackwell, the leader of the pro-bank, anti–big folks coalition in the Second General Assembly, was also one of the most ardent opponents of slavery within the old Edwards faction. The response was sudden and unqualified. Peck remembered that "the Governor sprang to his feet, and exclaimed 'He is the very man; why did I not think of him.'"[31]

Coles recognized the shrewdness of the suggestion. Blackwell's brother, Robert, had taken over William Brown's half of the *Illinois Intelligencer* when the legislature, miffed at what William Brown had written about its conduct, had in its last days passed a resolution authorizing the firm of "Berry and Blackwell" to print the state laws. No such firm existed at the time. Robert Blackwell had been William Berry's partner, but Brown replaced him in 1820 when the Kaskaskia paper moved with the capital to Vandalia. By putting the state contract into Berry and *Blackwell*'s hands, the legislature forced Brown out—amid "threats of the destruction of the office"—and the conventionists gained complete control over the paper.[32] Peck and Coles correctly foresaw that the job offer would allow David Blackwell, a young lawyer with stymied political aspirations, the opportunity to enmesh his talents in the tangle of a "nice" controversy. By shifting the *Intelligencer* from one brother to the other, and by buying out Berry's half, the non-conventionists were able to obtain another paper—though not until May 7, 1824.

The plan was secret. David Blackwell's appointment was announced and Peck soon after left Edwardsville to establish the "St. Clair Society for the prevention of slavery in the State of Illinois" with John Messinger and Methodist Rev. Samuel Mitchell. But Smith quickly detected the scent of collusion. "We are told," he wrote on April 19, that the governor "is actively engaged in combining into a phalanx, the teachers of our holy religion to oppose the Convention, and that the pulpit is to be converted into a political forum." Nor was he far from the truth; at this meeting, Peck reported, 30 ministers gathered.[33]

The attack on the pulpit continued through the summer and the fall, lasting until December 1823. Beginning with the first issue of the *Illinois Republican* on April 12, 1823, Smith raised the possibility of Illinois banning preachers from public office, a practice followed in states such as North Carolina, Tennessee, and New York. He looked forward to a time, not far distant, when preachers would cease being "political gladiators." Preachers, he admonished, ought to stick to "the pure, exalted, and benign precepts of Him" and avoid "the boisterous ocean of politics." Yet quite the opposite was occurring. For he could "of late, scarcely step into a church-yard, on the Sabbath day, before the usual hour for public worship, without beholding a newspaper or hand bill spread before the eyes of the congregation; and those who are not employed in this way, stand in little groups, discussing with great warmth the question of the Convention."[34]

The conventionists attacked any preachers who put worldly politics above the otherworldly saving of souls, but they decried Methodist reverends above all. The Methodists radiated a general urgency about politics and an impatience with trial and error that alarmed the conventionists. One Methodist preacher was said to have "openly declared that he wished all those who were in favor of a convention, had been in the State-House at the time the vote was taken, the doors locked and the State-House set on fire." By contrast those Baptists who were anti-slavery tended to agree with James Lemen, Jr., that "the poor oppressors" needed God's pity as much as the slaves; Lemen consequently could not "pray . . . as some have done, for fire to come down from Heaven to consume them." "A Friend to Religion" was aghast, so he wrote in Smith's paper, to find a "Methodist preacher" who equated slaveholders to "cut throats; and said that, such a man as that would not be too good to cut his throat for a thousand dollars—at least, he said, he should be afraid of it."[35]

By May 1823 vituperative comments on both sides had been publicly exchanged. Josias Randle, a Methodist elder and longtime Madison County circuit court clerk, "wished to know . . . who this methodist preacher is, who has expressed himself so much like the mobbers and burners at Vandalia and Troy." On the other side, Smith carried "on a warfare against the ministers of the Gospel." All this culminated in two "attacks"—both by the *Illinois Republican* editors. In the first, Smith entered Warren's office unannounced, "with a dirk and whip," intending to discipline Warren for publishing repeated claims that he was conducting a "crusade against the preachers." Before any harm could come to Warren, Smith's "second" Emanuel J. West restrained him. The second attack occurred when Oliver Kelly, coeditor with Smith, writing in his capacity as justice of the peace in St. Clair County, accused Joshua Barnes, "a minister of the gospel, and a member of the methodist church," of escaping from custody without securing bond for a 92 dollar judgment awarded the plaintiff in his case.[36]

Yet the attack on the Methodists was more than a personal affair of one newspaper. The Methodists were also attacked because, as Rev. Josias Randle remarked, it was "a well-known fact, that the Methodist ministers are almost unanimous in their opposition to the practice of slavery." In August of 1823 Methodist Rev. Jessie Walker was quoted by "a friend to consistency" as stating "that no man could hold slaves and be a moral man." The non-conventionist meetings at Greenville (Bond

County), Belleville (St. Clair County), Carmi (White County), Mt. Carmel (Wabash County), Alton (Madison County), Lawrenceville (Lawrence County), and on the prairies of Sangamon County all prominently featured Methodist preachers among their officers.[37]

The prodigious rise in Methodist membership before and during the controversy made the sect an obvious conventionist target. Religious affiliation was generally down in the postwar boom years. A dejected Regular Baptist observed in 1817 that the spirit of religion was "languishing." The next year the "Circular Letter" regretted that members were still "forsaking the assembling ourselve[s] together" and prayed for "strict attention to church meetings" since "it [was] very discouraging for a minister to ride eight or ten miles to meeting, and then find his Brethren neglectful."[38]

Between 1820 and 1825, in a cycle nearly the mirror opposite of the economy's, every denomination in the state for which records were kept experienced a growth in membership. The Regular Baptists, who were almost exclusively antimission, had reached a high of 269 members before the War of 1812; by 1818 they were down to 169. In 1820, the last year of the decade for which numbers were kept, membership reached 332 and there is reason to believe it reached triple that number by 1824. The Friends of Humanity Baptists went from 149 members in 1820 to 411 in 1825. But the largest expansion of all came among the Methodists. They grew from 1,359 members in 1814 to 2,401 in 1820, and to 3,705 in 1824. Both the largest and the fastest-growing denomination in early Illinois, the Methodists were, from a political perspective, a distinct, organized group of unaffiliated voters. Confronted almost immediately with the sect's uniform opposition to the Convention Resolution, the conventionists attempted to use the Methodists' opposition by rallying to the convention side all those who disliked them and the milk-and-cider persuasion generally.[39]

Other denominations also opposed the convention, of course. Among these were the Covenantors in Randolph County; the Missionary or Bible Society Baptists such as John Mason Peck; the Cumberland Presbyterians in Bond and White Counties; and the Baptist Friends of Humanity (James Lemen's congregations) in Monroe, St. Clair, and Madison Counties. This last group came into being when Virginia emigrant James Lemen, Sr. claimed he "acted on Jefferson's plan" and "formed a Baptist church at Cantine Creek, on an anti-slavery basis."[40]

Some of the most impassioned non-conventionist writings came from Friends of Humanity pens. Their 1822 "Circular Address," written by James Lemen, Jr., summed up the Friends' point of view in a "retrospective glance." Slavery was one of the greatest evils of all time, but its special danger was that it had infected "the children of light." Although they were "in 1810, a small handful, seven in number," they "withdrew, their membership from the general union, on account of involuntary slavery." Their cause, they believed, was "just, [for it was] the cause of oppressed humanity . . . the cause which induced our forefathers to quit their peaceful homes, and go forth in martial array to meet the enemy in tented field." In addition to condemning "the sable sons of Africa . . . to be driven for pleasure like hogs and sheep to market," slavery had "defiled even the temples of the living God; causing the children of light (who have been redeemed from cruel bondage, and restored to the enjoyment of perfect liberty) to grow forgetful of the change, and to impose involuntary servitude on their brethren in the gospel, and thus becoming masters, can say to one brother, come, and he cometh, and to another, go, and he goeth; new maxims which the gospel knows nothing of."[41] Here Lemen uses the conventionist language of freedom from bondage to question their goal of "becoming masters."

In October 1823, the Friends held their annual meeting at a new church building in Monroe County. There Benjamin Ogle's "Circular" announced their opposition to "such men (not to say reptiles, in our bosom or in the bowel of state) who have exerted every nerve" to introduce slavery. These claimed to be "as much opposed to the spirit and practice of slavery as any one" and used "the borrowed (not to say stolen) cloak of humanity," yet, he asked, "is not the door threatened to be open for the introduction of an evil into our state[?]"[42] Six months later, in another Monroe County forum, Col. William Alexander gave his response to this question.

If these groups differed from the Methodists in name, they shared that denomination's Arminianism, but they also shared a cultural persuasion that distinguished them from the Regular Baptists—the most numerous religious group in the state to support the convention. By early 1824 it was common to speak of "Convention and Non-Convention preacher[s]." The classic encounter between two such preachers was staged in St. Clair County, where William Kinney and James Lemen, Jr., squared off over the Senate seat. The *Illinois Republican* claimed that Kinney's followers were "the most liberal order of men," who joined his side "without compulsion or previous concert." Lemen and his supporters, however, were divided over whether to conduct the campaign "in the Methodist mode . . . [or] the Baptist mode." It was a difficult decision, Kinney taunted, because while the Methodists had the numbers, their camp-meeting urgency was off-putting; it reminded him of "an empty wagon moving down hill." Lemen, Jr., may have had reservations about Methodist means, but he firmly agreed with their ends. Both agreed "that unmerited, involuntary, perpetual, absolute, hereditary slavery, [was] contrary to, and a violation of the principles of nature, reason, justice, policy, and scripture."[43]

The Methodists did have defenders. Hooper Warren found the attacks on missionaries and Methodists coming from Smith and Kinney's *Illinois Republican* laughable. He published a letter ridiculing their "opposi-

tion . . . to the Methodists [and] the Missionaries." The editors, the letter writer predicted, would be haunted by "the ghosts of Missionaries
and learned preachers . . . til they were fit for nothing but the strait
waistcoat and the hospital." Those sharing Warren's persuasion wanted
public rules to remain identity neutral in order to protect them from
any majority group's intrusive or restrictive demands. As another letter
writer to the *Edwardsville Spectator* put it, they feared that, although
whole-hog conventionists "always made great professions of [their] in-
tense devotion to the interests of the *public*," in fact they treated the sacred public sphere as merely "all a 'matter of moonshine.'"[44]

The disagreement between Kinney and Lemen was nicely parodied in
a "conversation" between two religious men on the subject of temper-
ance, which appeared in the columns of the *Edwardsville Spectator*. It
may serve as a primer for an imagined conversation between the two,
both running for St. Clair County senator, both Baptist preachers:

> Quaker: Now, friend, I pray thee tell me how it is that thou makest
> such a boast of thy knowledge, and opposition to intemperance, when
> thou art frequently drunk thyself. . . .
> Drinker: I am far from being a drunkard. Yet I am not one of your
> hide-bound, over-righteous men, that cannot take a dram in company
> for fear of getting drunk; nor do I have so poor an opinion of my
> neighbors.

We may assume that St. Clair voters accepted Lemen's "over-righteous"
viewpoint; he beat Kinney by 60 votes, 514 to 454, in August 1824.[45]

One final clash between the whole-hog and milk-and-cider persuasions occurred in Madison County, where three members of the Auxil-
iary Bible Society gained control over the county commissioners' court
during 1823–1824. When a sitting member died in 1822, leaving a va-
cancy on the court, Samuel Lockwood convinced Thomas Lippincott to
run as the "anti-convention candidate." His opponent was William
Jones, the county's leading Regular Baptist preacher. According to
Hooper Warren, the conventionists' selection of Jones as a candidate
was part of a plan "admirably well laid," which had succeeded "as far as
management" could be expected, because Jones was "an old settler" who
had previously served in many state offices. But most important, "few
of the opposers of the introduction of slavery" knew "that his sentiments were in favor of a convention." Further, Lippincott was "but little personally known" and "it was at a very late period when the maneuvers of the slave party were discovered." Nonetheless the
non-conventionist forces rallied and Lippincott took the office by 295
to 185 votes.[46]

Once elected to the court, Lippincott found himself in total agreement
with the other two commissioners on the problem of intemperance at

Madison taverns. This led to a decision to deny liquor licenses "to every applicant, who we believed designed to keep a mere grogshop." The result was "to turn the world upside down" in Madison County; "they stormed and threatened," he recalled of his neighbors, "but we calmly persisted and prevailed." The three commissioners, Lippincott, Hail Mason, and John Barber, "afterwards became preachers of the gospel in three different denominations, Cumberland, Methodist, and Presbyterian."[47] Each of these denominations was known to be strongly opposed to the convention movement.

Despite the attacks from Smith and Oliver, no less than eight of the eleven non-conventionist societies in the counties had Methodist officers. If the Friends of Humanity's reputed non-conventionist group, the "Illinois Anti-Slavery League," is added to these, the milk-and-cider opposition to the convention is established. The Methodists, Friends of Humanity, Cumberland Presbyterians, and the anti-slavery Daniel Parker were active in 13 counties; in none except White County did the voters give a majority to the convention, and in White County the vote was 355 in favor to 326 against. In the end, then, the attack on the Methodist preachers was not successful. Nor did the preachers ever indicate that they understood the grounds on which it was argued they should stay out of politics. "Suppose there were as great exertions now making in this state to legalize man-slaying," "An Old Preacher" wrote to Hooper Warren, "as there are now making to authorize man-stealing: would it not be the duty of every preacher to lift up his voice against it?" Benjamin Ogle wrote in a similar view: "Some tell us, that it is a political evil and does not belong to our mission. . . . But we would ask: Is it not a moral evil?"[48]

As it was, the more the *Illinois Republican* condemned the Methodists on paper, the more they strove for political righteousness from the pulpit. The main cause of the conventionists' failure in this regard was that their attack could not remain strictly religious. No matter how often they denied it, their argument amounted to a complete exclusion of clergy from politics. The preachers "have enlarged their commissions," intoned "No Church Government," "as given by heaven it was 'go ye out into all the earth and preach my gospel'; but at 'a large and respectable meeting of these reverend divines,' they enlarged the terms, by adding the words, 'and your politics'." The consequence was a dangerous usurpation: "the power is to be taken out of the hands of the people, and placed in those of the more worthy *ecclesiastics*. . . . It behooves every man to rally around the standard of his country, and preserve it from this religious crusade formed against their rights; let not their country be stained with the baneful influence of priestcraft."[49]

Why were whole hoggers so susceptible to such rallying cries? One possible explanation is that there was for them no mediator of local identity as the milk-and-cider temperament had as a result of its partial identification with the larger society. The milk-and-cider divided self still had a part of the self that remained apart; this was the part open to reason and its skepticism, which made them cautious in giving themselves over to any group identity. The whole-hog temperament had no such brakes. They made great cronies because they devoted their whole selves to their new identity, thus losing their skepticism and even their critical abilities. Whole-hog conventionists undertook many spontaneous acts on behalf of the movement that could not have been undertaken for narrowly selfish reasons.[50] What else explains why one conventionist showed so much "zeal for politics" notwithstanding, as his wife pointed out, "even he admits, a decision on the question either way, would not affect materially *our* interest."[51]

The cronyism of the wholehoggers can be interpreted in different ways. Thomas Ford considered their leaders' "tact . . . in managing the masses" a great skill. They knew how to project a local identity popular with those looking to share it. By this means, potential cronies were brought under the influence of the politicians who became "the master spirits of their several counties." Ford was repulsed by the crony mentality—he called the most rowdy elements "butcher knife boys." But it is interesting to note that even the bookish Ford understood the importance of some degree of cohesion based on familiar loyalty to democratic politics. "The best and purest mode in which leaders exercise their power, is by instruction and persuasion," as the Founders thought, and Ford readily conceded it. "This kind of government," however, "can exist only over a very intelligent and virtuous people . . . when the people are less enlightened and virtuous, the means of governing them will be less intellectual . . . [and less run according to the rules of] good government."[52]

Instead of the rule by reason, which he clearly preferred, Ford described how a sort of rule by crony operated in its place. As he portrayed it, rule by cronies was essentially localist in orientation. "There is in every county," he observed, "generally at the county seats, a little clique of county leaders, who aim to monopolize or dispose of county offices. . . . [They follow the party line of the higher-ups in order to get these offices and] they convey it to the little big men in each neighborhood, and they do the talking to the rank-and-file of the people. In this way principles and men are put up and down with amazing celerity." Realizing that many of his readers would recoil in horror from this description, he added, more by way of mutual wonderment than as relaying an inside tip: "gentle reader do not be astonished; THIS IS GOVERNMENT." He did make a concession. "The organization of men into political parties under the control of leaders as a means of government, necessarily destroys individuality of character and freedom of opinion." But even using the old standard of measuring government by "choice and reflection" as against "accident and force," the crony method was an improvement of sorts. "Government implies restraint, compulsion of either body or mind, or both," he observed dryly. "The latest improvement to effect this restraint and compulsion is to use moral means, intellectual means operating on the mind instead of the old mode of using force, such as standing armies, fire, sword and the gibbet, to control the mere bodies of men."[53]

WANDERING ISHMAELS IN THE LAND OF "TRUE REPUBLICANISM"

It is not surprising that the division between Calvinists and Arminians became politicized during the convention controversy. More surprising is the extent to which political rhetoric played a role in the overall shaping of the two persuasions. On the Calvinist side, the connection to the whole-hog political style is best indicated in the writings of Daniel Parker. Parker's remarkable theological excursus was been preserved in several of his pamphlets and his journal, the *Church Advocate*, which was published from 1829 to 1831 in Vincennes, Indiana. As a leader of the antimission movement in the West, Parker fought with western Arminians and eastern Baptists. He entered the convention battle already an experienced fighter. In the rich and detailed record of Parker's religious writings, the generally oral and illiterate whole-hog persuasion found a written outlet.

Parker's career perfectly illustrates the logic behind many of the convention controversy's "gothewhole" partisans. He did not just disagree; he fought to the death. Theology was an arena of "warfare." The "strong surges of the enemy against God's invincible Zion" were "of such an extraordinary nature . . . [that he could not] consent to sheathe the *sword* of the Lord." His dissenter's logic worked by opposition. Just so far as Calvinists were good, Arminians were bad. The way Parker presented himself on paper echoed his oppositional thinking. He always thought in twos. In autobiographical remarks scattered throughout his writings, he presented a theological self: "I am by profession a baptist, in principle and doctrine a predestinarian." This is how he introduced himself in the first volume of his new periodical, the *Church Advocate*. But he also revealed another persona, a worldly counterpart. He was also a "hunter," "farmer," and "unlearned backwoodsman." This self he described as "poor and helpless, and prone to wander." The second, worldly self prompted one commentator to dub Parker the "wandering Ishmael" of the antimission movement. Born in Virginia in 1781, he moved with his family to Georgia and later Tennessee. He moved next to Crawford County, Illinois, settling on a farm near Palestine in 1817. He remained in the state until 1833, when he wandered off once again, this time to the new frontier in the territory of Texas. Parker was a predestinarian preacher and a poor, wandering farmer; as he worked out his "system of religion" it became clear that the two identities were connected and that his Calvinism explained his wandering and justified his poverty.[54]

The debilitating realities of poverty touched Parker's life wherever he lived. "I was raised without an education," he noted, "except to read in the new Testament, but very imperfectly." During his family's journey to Tennessee, he fell under "a severe spell of sickness"; his eventual recovery did not change the fact that he had "little or no money" and no "prospect of ever owning a home for my family." At one point early in life his wife, he reported, thought the family would "certainly come to want." He replied that he "hoped not; if we have meat and bread, there is no danger of suffering, and I will try to keep that, but indeed it seemed so much out of my control to do that thing, and continue my [preaching] appointments."[55]

The problem of getting a living was compounded by low social standing. Status anxieties seem to have played an especially important role in developing Parker's outlook. He casually referred to his uneasy social position in an autobiographical narrative. He regretted, for example, that a preacher's wife was so often "spoken of as a poor trifling woman . . . when perhaps she has more than she can possibly do." Such poor women were too readily "scoffed at" for being "lazy, and slovenly." He also felt the stigma of rejection for "being rough and course in my language and manners." He frankly admitted that he "made but a poor appearance as a preacher." One time when he shared a public venue for preaching, the "Methodists appeared at first as if they thought [him] hardly worth notice."[56]

When Parker preached at the capitol in Vandalia, Thomas Lippincott was struck by his uncouth demeanor. Parker was "illiterate, uncultivated, rude in manners," Lippincott remembered 40 years later. "He would spend his hour or more, with vest unbuttoned, cravat taken off (both while speaking) laboring and sweating vehemently, tearing the English language, if not his opponent's discourse, to pieces." Nonetheless, he added, Parker "was a man of no small power . . . there was mental vigor, power of thought, if no elegance of language, in his preaching." Parker's "peculiarity was in holding, to what was called the two seed doctrine. . . . [That] every person born into the world was by his birth fixed in a class, on one side or the other of the line of character and destiny; was, in short, either a child of God or a child of the devil. As God's purposes never change, so the matter was settled from everlasting to everlasting." For Parker, salvation was so fixed, that two bloodlines had peopled the world since the days of Adam and Eve. One line, the good seed, was God's chosen progeny represented by Abel; the other line, the bad seed, was the offspring of the devil represented by Cain. From this dualist foundation, Parker evolved the antieastern, antimission position.[57]

Evidence of Parker's testy defense of his own standing appears haphazardly in the margins of his doctrinal battles. When the Washington editor of the *Columbian Star* made some demeaning comments upon refusing to print his letters, Parker responded in the *Church Advocate:* "it must be a very chilling east wind to cause a christian to become offended at religious communications, from the far distant, western wilds of Illinois, as though the east has all the wisdom." But the lowly Illinoisans were not to worry, for the source of offense was all in the East. They had "not suffered that awful smoke, which has proceeded out of the bottomless pit, [and] which seems to have so much darkened the sun & air in the east, to reach our western hemisphere." Eastern Christians had succumbed to the "bottomless pit" by promiscuously mixing church and state. They paid preachers, sent out "hired" missionaries, established Sunday schools by raising money, and attempted to win government financing for a Baptist college. These were not simply erring ways but clear signs of the presence of the Antichrist. To the head of an eastern Missionary Baptist newspaper, Parker wrote: "Sir, when you talk about men teaching and sending out well taught preachers, in this way you do, and boasting of theological institutions, and seminaries of learning, &c. You show the plain mark of the beast, and manifest the wickedness of your heart." By embracing "incorporated monied institutions, under the name of religion, and their attendance, which is at war with the first, and dearest, principles of the christian religion, and the republican government," these church leaders exposed their dark motives. Against this, the western "atmosphere is so pure from that antichristian smoke," because its Christians "have not learned to love money better than truth, nor yet the wisdom of this world better than the teachings of God's Spirit."[58]

It may be surprising that, while Parker advocated an exclusive attention to God's Spirit, he also advocated republicanism. In fact the two were closely associated in his mind. Western republicanism, as he had experienced it, was a thing of purity. It was pure because it eschewed "the world"; under that test, eastern republicanism failed utterly. Parker explicitly associated true republicanism with purity, simplicity, and equality. These worldly traits he also applied to the Christian religion. "The true christian," he remarked, was "a true republican in his national governmental principles."[59] Although the world and the spirit were rigidly separated in his view, there was one exception, one point of confluence; this was the point indicated by Jesus, a "poor illiterate fisherman," when he came to earth. Jesus lived among the poor and the lowly. The poor, plain people, "among the last choice that the world would have made," were God's one tool on earth, "his poor earthen instruments."[60] These people and their simple ways were the one sure guide to pure spirit on earth. Indeed, their very lowly status in the corrupt world was a secret indicator of their special status in God's eyes. Not coincidentally, they also pointed out their meridional opposite, the corrupted Christians and republicans who populated the eastern United States.

Republicanism was God's gift to the plain people. In this way it became a sacred doctrine. It too was founded on an absolute duality or division. Like true religion, Republicanism was either pure, simple, and egalitarian, or it was corrupt and not true. A series of absolute dualities—between good and evil, the spiritual and the natural, pure intentions and ulterior motives—drives the dichotomies. Parker divided the world into two essences or types of being, good and evil. These two essences produced marked progeny, which fight on earth in the name of their progenitors. "Is it not a fact," he asked, "that the word of Divine truth, the history of nations, and daily observation, all go to prove that there are two powers or kingdoms, with their subjects, at war with one another?"[61]

Behind these dichotomies is the absolute division between purity and corruption. In the case of each of the opponents Parker faced during his career—the Arminians, the missionaries, and the conventionists—one is struck by the absolute nature of his rejection of his opponents' views. The conventionists, for example, "practice deception" and concoct "nefarious schemes." They attempt to deceive their constituents by chaining them "down in darkness, by falsehood, and [by] corrupting the channels of public intelligence." And they did these things in the name of "one of the *blackest* causes which has ever disgraced the annals of civilized legislation." Slavery was impure and dirty; its advocates "wished to tarnish the character of our republican state." His side, on the other hand, had pursued a "course of *moral rectitude, of political virtue and integrity*"; his own motives were those to be found "emanating from a *true republican heart*." Conventionist evil was the measure of non-conventionist goodness. Slavery threatened republican equality. It was "the most irrepublican of principles—a principle which will not bear the light of reason, and whose advocates shroud themselves (as you have done in this instance) from public scrutiny, and assassin like hurl their slanderous shafts from their hiding places, at those they dare not meet in open day, on rational grounds."[62]

One of Parker's greatest foes was the missionary movement within the Baptist church. This was led by another Baptist preacher taking part in the convention controversy, John Mason Peck. The mission "system" was a particularly well-organized and persistent foe. The missionaries were involved in a "deep-laid plan to take from us our civil and religious liberties." Indeed, Parker believed that Peck and his cohorts would have felt "more justifiable in the sight of God [had they] taken my life on the high way." While he was motivated by a pure spirit, their motives were to "dethrone God; sap the foundation of the christian religion; raise Anti-Christ to his full power; exalt those Popes that are training up men to preach; establish priestcraft; and lead the public to believe that no man is qualified to preach but classical men; and thereby make them believe that those men whom god has called are fools or impostors; and by these means bring on an awful persecution (as soon as the beast has power) against the true Church of Christ." The absolute defense of purity is again at work here: Parker rarely doubts the integrity of the elect. He is willing to protect them at all costs. Just as his hatred for evil has no bounds, so his love of goodness has no bounds.[63]

In Parker's hands, male and female gender differences provide another source of distinction between good and evil. The church is the "chaste republican wife." Every opponent, and he has many, is drawn to violate this purity. The mission system, "because it is money not religion that gives membership there," is correspondingly impure and "so far as it can prevail, it will adulterate the church with the world." His image of the church as "innocent damsel" makes the rape of the slick Arminian all the more sickening. When he tried to be as "short and plain" as possible about the perfidy of the "mission system," the most ready metaphor was one of fornication and illegitimate birth: "The church of God should certainly be on her guard [during] these last times, and not suffer that woman Jezebel . . . to teach and seduce the Lord's servants to commit fornication. . . . Let those missionary adulteresses unite amongst themselves and let the bride the Lamb's wife alone." If, as Stephanie McCurry has shown among the South Carolina plain folk preachers, Parker is here shoring up his own "claims to power and authority at home," it is his whole-hog opposition to the missionaries that facilitates that power by providing it a justification.[64]

The purity/impurity rhetorical logic also influenced his argument against slavery. In his *Public Address to the Baptist Society* (1820), he forcefully associated missionary wealth with slave labor. "It is a stubborn fact," he wrote, "that through the States that hold slaves, where the mission spirit prevails very considerably, that there are numbers engaged in the mission plan who do not labor one day in a year, and yet possess great wealth and throw in liberally the support of missions." One glance at "the situation of the Negro" showed, however, that the slave-owning missionary was far from "the religion of Christ." Slaves lived in "huts . . . not fit for a work horse to stand in." The slave was not taught to "read the Bible," let alone properly dressed, yet the master was heard to exclaim, "Oh, the poor heathens! They are lying in a state of ignorance. Their direful situation so oppressed my mind that I cannot rest. O! I give my money freely to send them relief and I wonder that all the Christian world does not join in so laudable an undertaking." When Parker does have something positive to say about slavery, it is only to point out that the slave often has a fuller "experience of grace of God in the soul, than his master."[65]

Parker defined himself by opposition: he was not a slaveholder, an Arminian, or a lover of money. He dissented from all these impure things and thereby confirmed, by this opposition, his identity as their opposite. The dualist thinking this encouraged led him to formulate all-

or-nothing positions. For example, when he wrote that "education is a great common blessing," he placed the emphasis on common—it must be shared by all or there is a social imbalance. The problem with the missionary goal of educating preachers was precisely the mismatch it created vis-à-vis their congregations: "Let the learned part of the world be pleased and informed more and more, but the ignorant stay where they are." He feared that "a fraud should be practiced on them."[66] In sum, although education was surely needed, compromise and coopera-tion with the worldly big folks entailed too great a risk of corruption.

Because of this all-or-nothing temperament, whole hoggers were the most loyal friends; what they loved, they loved completely, but this love was necessarily tied to a reciprocal hatred. Parker hated easterners as the "production or instruments of the serpent" under whom "the children of God have suffered such severe bloody persecutions." He and his fol-lowers who dissented from the world learned their own identity as homeless wanderers and warriors precisely on account of this worldly persecution, for "God has suffered all these things to take place, for a purpose of his own glory, in bringing the iniquity of the enemy to view, and then by displaying his rightful power in the deliverance of his own production." Consequently, life became one long battle, for everything showed that "there is a reality in the christian warfare" against "the strength and stratagems of spiritual wicked in high places."[67]

WATCHMEN IN THE LAND OF "PURE HUMANITY"

As Parker's writings indicate the whole-hog persuasion, so his mis-sionary opponents illustrate the milk-and-cider alternative. Indeed, the opposition did not give up their claims of superiority, nor did they quit trying to instruct believers in their more socially cautious versions of re-publicanism. One of the most prominent of this group was John Mason Peck, a Free Will Baptist from Connecticut. In his memoirs Peck criti-cized that "spurious democracy . . . of popular sovereignty." During an 1823 Fourth of July speech given in St. Clair County, he argued that, un-like "the restive ungovernable spirit of ambition, bursting from the bonds of colonial subjection," which he saw in Illinois, the real cause of the revolution had been that the "fathers felt themselves justified before God and men, in appealing to arms in the revolutionary struggle. The cause was just and heaven succeeded it." In another effort at instruction, Josias Wright, a veteran of the Revolutionary War, hit at the whole-hog tendency to love the land because it was theirs. "We as Americans feel the love of country," he wrote, "not merely because of the idea that it is the land where we are born" but because of its "blessed" government. Jane Good of Madison County attacked the inconsistency of a drive for slavery in the name of the liberty of the revolution and the hypocrisy of the claims of special slave care in Illinois: "some pretend to say, he eats, he wears, he fares as I do, and has less to perplex him, and is consequently happier than if he was free. But let those who think so change conditions with the Negro, then they may be believed. If liberty is worth the blood of thousands, why withhold it from any?"[68]

The writings of Peck, Wright, and Good appeared in the *Edwardsville Spectator* of Hooper Warren. His opposition to the convention was not anti-egalitarian. A social egalitarian very much in the vein of his New Hampshire counterpart Isaac Hill, Warren simply could not join in wholesale eastern bashing. Moreover, as a "Yankee," he was not a member of the white folks' identity group. He mixed the universalism of the typical eastern-looking big folk with the compromising mentality of the localist milk-and-cider contingent. He wanted to expand social equality privately, not publicly. If negative liberty means freedom from government and positive liberty means freedom to develop one's faculties, he was for positive liberty at the private level and negative liberty at the public level—assuming the public level was free of slavery.[69]

Many preachers who followed Peck and Warren in spirit if not doctrine made the transition from religious to political righteousness. William Kinkade, whom Lippincott thought "a perfect antipode . . . in theological views" to Parker and Kinney, became a strong non-conventionist spokesman after the legislature adjourned. He was "a man of some culture, a great reader, if not more properly a student, and ingenious in argument." Lippincott found his views "peculiar" nevertheless. "Not only was he a Unitarian, but I should say humanitarian in his views of the Divine Person. I heard him preach an elaborate discourse to show that God was endowed with a human body, hands, eyes, etc., and of course occupied a specific place, from which, being very high, he could look down and see and control the world." Kinkade believed that God, who appeared in human form, was watching the American embrace of slavery with disappointment. Here was the humanist's image of the people's God. He told the "Lawrence County Society to oppose the Introduction of Slavery in Illinois," that "the storms of Divine vengeance are lowering over our devoted country, and we fear the God of justice will soon deluge the slave states in more than ten thousand horrors."[70]

In place of God's watchful eye, these religious non-conventionists assumed the burdensome but necessary role as community "watchmen." "When they see evil coming," Benjamin Ogle asked, "should they not warn the people . . . should we not be up and a doing; standing continually on our watch tower; particularly those who are called of God to be watchmen, placed, as it were, on the walls, looking out for the enemy?" In the everyday life of the counties, watchfulness could take many forms. Wherever there was a group of people intent on shaping themselves and the community to a predetermined standard, there watchmen were at work—in such organizations as the Monroe County

"Polemic Societies," the "Republican Debating Society of Morgan County," the St. Clair "society for the protection from kidnapping of free people of color," and the State Agricultural Society. The organizational skills developed under the milk-and-cider persuasion have been cited by T. Scott Miyakawa as one of the "latent functions" of Arminianism. Dissenting Arminians in "the West" were able to "maintain order and unity" in their communities and to contribute to the order of the overall community. Their "pervasive role . . . to a degree paralleled that of the New England towns in fostering responsible democracy."[71]

The instruction continued in the speeches given to hail the visiting revolutionary hero Lafayette in 1824. Three years earlier the state capital at Vandalia was placed in Fayette County, which had been named after the Frenchman. The general visited Kaskaskia where the welcoming speech was given by Governor Coles. He saw the general's contribution to the American cause as an example of a larger contribution "to the universal restoration of man to his long lost rights." The American cause, the white folks were told, was the cause of humanity and mankind generally.[72] The non-conventionists had in effect appropriated the most universal aspects of the story of the white folks and resurrected them in a new story of the people of humanity.

There is no evidence that the story of humanity was of much interest to many among the younger generation of white folks. If, in the hands of the conventionists, the cry of "the people" was used to entreat their fellow legislators to support their recently forged faction, the exceptional, universalist meaning of the term would have no appeal in the counties; for those who wanted slavery wanted, above all, to be free and independent in a particular society, though in their view its particularity was very special. By contrast, those who emphasized the historical plight of "the people" recognized that they were, like everything and everyone, ordinary parts of this world. They could not embark on an experiment in slavery without moral disintegration. Yet the explicit rhetorical message of Conrad Will's House speech in favor of limited slavery is the exact opposite of this reasoning.

If many who did find Will's plan attractive believed in Illinois's exceptional character, those who attacked it poured vinegar on the state's supposed specialness. Compare, for example, the views of "Roger" of White County and Josias Wright of Madison County. Roger considered "unlimited slavery . . . something to be dreaded." The southern plantation system he rejected out of hand. But the Illinois way was different; it offered the hope of liberty to both slave and slaveholder: "You cannot," he explained, "expect that the slave-holder will liberate all his slaves and subject himself to hard labor." The opportunity for philanthropy, for "exercising your charity and humanity" came after; for now, "you must purchase what he can spare, and give him liberty to live in this state with the balance, where he cannot fail of becoming a tender master."[73] Such talk outraged Wright, who had experience with slave-holders; he lived next to two in Madison County. He suggested that only the young and the credulous could believe anything about the new state's specialness. He was writing for the very purpose, he said, of alerting the voters to an especially sweet brand of persuasiveness fomented by William Kinney. Kinney was traveling the western half of the state, stumping in support of a convention and Will's plan. Wright was convinced of the necessity of refuting

> The sapient argument of the reverend Kinney "that slavery ought to be spread that its evil effects might be curtailed!" Such might be the case if the climate of this country, possessed the peculiar quality of rendering men less avaricious; but until he shews this to be the case, his offspring of pure humanity is but the prattle of a hypocrite or a fool. For it is not because they [the slaveholders] cannot make a sufficiency of grain for their subsistence where they are, that they [the slaves] suffer, but it is the love of money, ease, and wealth [on the part of the slaveholders], that is the cause of their sufferings, and it would be the same here; therefore fellow citizens, be not deceived by their sophistry.[74]

The young and the credulous were everywhere in early Illinois society. Will and Kinney's line of reasoning appealed to their deep need for self-worth. They believed they were the "offspring of pure humanity." Yankees and other newcomers troubled them because the newcomers were oblivious to these values. They were oblivious to the story of the people as white folks. These "Down-Easters," tied to their eastern ways and interest in the prairie, were incapable of seeing the special possibilities of the bottomland. The flood of Yankee emigrants in the 1830s signaled an end to innocence. To use Professor Dangerfield's succinct phrases: "In the shade of the forest men grew sallow and sickened, but ideals flourished; and it was not until it left the forest that the frontier lost its innocence."[75] Ironically, the bottomland forests that fostered innocence and simplicity also fostered the pro-slavery impulse. For the whole-hog support for democracy thrived among those identifying with innocence; yet the same innocence discouraged self-reflection and demonized all opposition. Whole-hog conventionists hid their contradictions from themselves and remained pure of heart. By contrast, milk-and-cider non-conventionists mixed belief in democracy with skepticism about human nature and took the reviled path of the loyal opposition. At the cost of their innocence, they secured the liberal democratic development of Illinois.

CHAPTER SEVEN

ILLINOIS AND AMERICAN POLITICAL DEVELOPMENT

When the early Illinois settlers came west, they hoped their new society would be more egalitarian than their old one. They came to Illinois to find economic opportunity but also to flee the social hierarchies of the East. Once in Illinois, they discovered that equality was easier to regulate than opportunity. By the time the conventionists demonstrated the reality of majoritarian government in passing the Convention Resolution, the Edwards and Thomas parties had evaporated, thereby fulfilling their desire for political equality. The emigrants' claim on social equality in the form of fee-simple ownership for every family in the bottomland republic also appeared within reach when the depression hit. Suddenly a market revolution that had been quietly converting yeomen into staple producers stalled, and debt payments at the land office mounted.

Faced with an economy undergoing rapid and seemingly uncontrollable change, the conventionists reacted in a predictable manner. They reasserted old values. To legitimate their movement, they drew from a rich pool of republican rhetoric in the hope of restoring in a new land what they took to be the original, egalitarian ideals of the revolution. Just as the logic of egalitarianism had worked to unseat the big folks in politics, so too it was hoped that it would work in justifying the plan for "limited slavery." With the plan, the convention leaders applied the old revolutionary logic to a new situation; this kept their movement on the offensive. The tack required, however, that the anti-slavery opposition be characterized plausibly as an opposition of the big folks, a characterization that failed to be persuasive. When the non-conventionists rallied, they proved that a local persuasion emphatically opposed to the big folks could remain popular even after arguing in favor of limits on the people's power. Their milk-and-cider persuasion became the loyal opposition within the people that the prevailing white folks' democracy had as yet failed to recognize. This episode in early Illinois features three remarkable breakthroughs in political development: the triumph of majoritarianism; the rise of an indigenous "loyal opposition" to majoritarianism; and the use of identity politics as the foundation of party ideology. In all three, early Illinois was precociously foreshadowing later patterns in the second party system and in American political development generally.

To appreciate the full extent of Illinois precocity, these developments must be viewed in the larger context of the other states and the nation. A predominantly European nation, but lacking a European aristocratic ruling class, the United States had a comparatively strong "liberal tradition" by the nineteenth century. America's liberal tradition needs a breif introduction. Liberals assume, along with Thomas Hobbes, that no objective *summum bonum* exists. Instead human life consists of a "string of appetites, one after another, that ceaseth only in death." Liberals believe that individuals must be as free as possible (consistent with the freedom of other individuals) to chose their own ultimate goods in life. This assumption limits severly the breadth and reach of government and society-level regulation over individual conduct. Michael Sandel puts the essence of the liberal tradition in a conditional phrase: "since people disagree about the best way to live, government should not affirm in law any particular vision of the good life."[1]

The liberal tradition consequently places the highest priority on protecting individuals, and liberals tend to fear the unified power of the state and society. For this reason, the Tocquevillean moment, when the authortiy of society gains an advantage over the authority of the state, has always been celebrated by liberals. Nonethless, liberal assumptions about government can combine in different ways to create a variety of social systems. All liberals hold that political authority rests on consent, that the main purpose of government is the protection of individual rights, and that to further this end government power must be limited and checked. But some emphasize public-sphere institutions and practices, while others emphasize the private sphere. To adopt the terminology of Richard J. Ellis, "competitive" individualist liberals tend to focus on the private sphere, while "egalitarian" individualist liberals stress the public sphere. J. David Greenstone understood the differences within the American liberal tradition in yet another way. In his analysis, private-sphere liberals focus on maximizing individual ends, while public-sphere liberals experiment with a diversity of individual means.[2]

Because of this internal diversity, the liberal tradition in America has been both plastic and resilient. It has been flexible enough to adapt to new circumstances without repudiating its core principles. It has, for example, countenanced slavery, an institution that violates all three of its basic tenets. Yet whenever the contradiction between liberal values and slavery was made palpable, either those in power were forced to make accommodations that did not threaten the long-term success of liberal institutions, or slavery itself was abolished. Another source of tension has been with both the majoritarian impulse of democrats and the dissenting egalitarian impulse of republicans. Public-sphere liberals who promote constitutional restraints conflict with democrats when they try to set limits on majority rule and popular will. Private-sphere liberals who promote the competitive spirit, including the spirit of market capitalism, conflict with republicans when they resist regulations controlling the concentration of wealth or when they reduce civic virtue to a calculation of dollars and cents. By and large, those advocating private-sphere liberal interests have negotiated these tensions in a way that has strengthened rather than weakened liberal values. Over the long run, however, it is clear that the interests of public-sphere liberals have generally lost out to the interests of majoritarians as republicans have lost to private-sphere liberals.

Early Illinois is a case in point. Liberal values came into conflict with both majoritarianism and republicanism, and the conflicts occurred simultaneously. The Illinois people experienced liberal institutions as limitations on majority will at precisely the same time that they experienced the pressures of shifting from a subsistence economy relying on community cooperation to a market economy driven by individual (or familial) self-help. The conventionists responded to these challenges by expressing dissent against inequality. They initiated a majoritarian challenge to the elitist politics of virtual representation. The vehicle of their democratic revolution was an identity politics that opposed old money, refinement, and eastern pretension. As a result, the tension between private-sphere liberalism and republicanism was not experienced as a problem of economic policy alone, but as part of a larger problem of political identity. When this pattern grew into a national pattern, it had its costs in terms of obfuscation of class differences, but it also had its benefits, the most important being that it made the political system safe for poor white males and their families, who had been previously excluded. From this perspective, viewed as a great engine for converting outsiders into insiders, bottomland republicanism was a success.

The move to identity politics exacerbated the tension between public-sphere liberalism and majoritarianism, at least at first. The coherency of the white folks' identity allowed its members to label all opposition as illegitimate. Characterizing the convention controversy in its worst moments, violence against political minorties was fueled by such rhetoric. In fact, it is evident that institutions limiting power were not sufficient to carry the young state through its first democratic excesses. If the politics of identity brought liberal institutions to their breaking point, however, it also provided its own resolution to the problem. The white folks was so broad a category, it quickly divided under the strain of two-party electoral competition. Whiteness became a permanent marker on the pecking order and receded into the background of political discourse, although the value of whiteness remained a presupposition shared by the entire electorate. As the convention movement dissipated, large numbers of voters migrated to a milk-and-cider republicanism, adding balance to both sides of the liberal democratic mix when they began to understand self-government as a species of self-control.

As crucial as the milk-and-cider persuasion was, it was often in the minority. Indeed, if the early Illinois case is any indicator, it suggests that political development in America operates generally in favor of majoritarians and private-sphere liberals, and at the expense of public-sphere liberals and republicans. This pattern helps one understand why African-American slavery was a possible outcome. Such an institution was not inconsistent with the prevailing winds of majoritarianism and private-sphere liberalism. When the institution did run into trouble in Illinois, part of the trouble was based on the impracticability of the state's role in overseeing the "limited slavery" plan; that is, its failure was tied to the government's underdeveloped administrative capacity, itself a result of the American liberal's fear of the state.

ILLINOIS: PRECOCIOUS CHILD OF THE UNION

How did Illinois, this frontier state, become a bellwether for the nation? When the convention struggle was over, the aspiration of political equality had been converted into the reality of majoritarian government. In 1824 this was an accomplishment that could not yet be claimed by the neighboring frontier state of Indiana. Even in an older western state such as Ohio (by 1820 the fifth-largest state in the Union), new men had only just begun to use the rhetoric of republican dissent to replace the small coterie of leading Republicans who had been ruling since 1802.[3] Why, then, was Illinois's politics so precocious and its pattern so fertile? Answers to these questions can be approached by comparing political developments in Illinois to those in other states in the Union. Any adequate answer should combine economic, political, and regional factors. It was as a result of the interactions among these factors that Illinois experienced so precociously divisions that eventually structured national politics during the second party system.

In assessing Illinois's development, the temptation to emphasize the raw physicality of the far frontier must be resisted. Too often mere physical distance from the East has encouraged the idea that the West was a new thing altogether, as if the physical environment itself changed the political culture. The West was indeed culturally distinct, but not because it was "the raw West." It achieved its distinctness through opposition; thus, the more that Illinoisans opposed the East, the more inextricably tied to the national culture they became. Those who argue that western frontier culture was unique often overlook this basic relational fact. The East haunted the West like a scorned parent haunts a child's

memory. As with slavery, so with issues like public lands policy, relations with the Native Americans, and banking: all were faced as national
problems that were professed to have local solutions.

These continuities of echo and return argue for an interpretation
stressing the interpenetration of East and West in early Illinois political
development.[4] The underlying reality of continuity complicates the answer to the precocity question. When Illinois settlers expressed their
western identity, they made sense at both local and national levels at
the same time. Announcing as "a Western man" might allow an Illinois
politician to highlight one national position (opposition to eastern privilege) while finessing another national position (sectional differences on
slavery) all for the purpose perhaps of sealing a local political maneuver.

The early prevalence of democratic expression in Illinois was unique;
the state's political culture shed the old ways of political deference sooner
than elsewhere; the ideal of social equality for the white folks was written
more deeply into the subtext of its politics. This social precocity was explained by the relative weakness of the elites, whose attempt at deferential leadership was correspondingly weak. The elite's weakness was in part
tied to the unstructured nature of the frontier; but the role that Illinois
played in the North—and that Alabama played in the South—was also
strongly influenced by economic developments in those states, and these
developments were often a result of timing and location.

Of course, local conditions along with the vagaries of timing and individual personality make all human endeavors unique at some level.
But the environmental determinism of the frontier thesis both exagger-
ates and minimizes the impact of a supposed new culture on western
politics. On the one hand, it is an exaggeration to say that the open
wilds of the West encouraged liberal democratic innovations. The dubi-
ousness of this claim is especially clear at the level of governing institutions, where Illinois's status as an ideological colony of the East is
demonstrated unmistakably. Of course, this evidence of continuity in
the constitution of 1818 is balanced by the realization that the state's
leaders were not free to experiment in making it. If Conrad Will, T. W.
Smith, and "Ames" are to be believed, the document was merely an ob-
sequious play for congressional favor. Nonetheless, Arthur Schlesinger
was surely right when he argued: "The great illusion of historians of the
frontier has been that social equality produces economic egalitarianism.
In fact, the demand for economic equality is generally born out of conditions of social inequality." Many groups in the East, such as the crafts-
men and sailors in the larger cities like New York and Philadelphia or
even in the western city of Cincinnati, held a more broadly conceived
notion of social equality than the frontier settlers precisely because they
did not have it.[5]

On the other hand, the emphasis on environmental factors mistak-
enly slights the impact of the partisan political culture brought from the

East. Donald Ratcliffe argues: "the one thing that has always kept party division alive has been memory. . . . Parties fight because they are separated by recollections of earlier fights."[6] In the Illinois case, the war against the big folks was not a new condition; it was carried there in the memories of the white folks. These memories revived when the younger generation realized that deference to Congress would be the price of membership in the Union. This produced a vehemence against the territorial elite that was new. It was then up to the vagaries of chance to magnify the conflict—and chance had its moments, as was illustrated by the attack on the unsuspecting Edward Coles.

If the open class structure of the wild frontier in Illinois had an impact on its political development, it did so indirectly. Though Illinois's republicans were not as radically democratic as the artisan republicans of New York City, they formed a larger proportion of the electorate in Illinois than the workers did in New York. The size and distribution of the yeoman class in Illinois made the state as a whole more democratic than eastern counterparts whose artisans were balanced by more influential merchants and large landholders. Again, although artisan republican minorities evinced stronger egalitarian tendencies than those typically found in Illinois, these eastern egalitarians had to face Federalists (many times as employers) and other socially conservative but politically democratic republicans. Schlesinger's thesis correctly predicted that demands for social equality would come from poeple situated like the artisans, but they had to contend with older entrenched interests in the larger, eastern states. As the Anti-Mason controversy in New York and the debate over the Virginia constitution showed, well into the late 1820s political conflict in these states still revolved around the issue of political equality; deference to authority and political "values and habits of long standing" needed to be partially cleared away and partially reinvented before the new order could stand uncontested.[7] If these struggles intensified the commitment to republicanism among the minority artisans, they slowed the development of a political system divided between two ideologically distinct paths to social equality.

In addition to the breadth of egalitarian sentiment in Illinois, its republicans also benefited from facing an elite class weakened by internal divisions. This class was soon pushed aside in Illinois, which was not the case in eastern states like New Hampshire. Certainly no prominent politician in the state compares to New Hampshire's Isaac Hill in terms of battle scars and early Jacksonian credentials, a fact directly related to the political staying power of the elites Hill faced—one thinks of Webster's defense of privilege in the Dartmouth College case. Hill's battles against them thus took longer and were more involved. An internally divided elite class made political development in Illinois distinct even from neighboring frontier republics like Indiana and Ohio, where the Jeffersonian National Republicans held the reins longer. Of course, this quick collapse meant that Illinois politics were more chaotic than else-where in the nation and that disciplined parties took longer to develop, as scholars such as Richard P. McCormick have documented.[8]

The economic instability of the territorial patrons also helped the lo-cal movement. In Alabama, which entered the Union in 1819, class con-flict caused a split in the economic and political control of the state. J. Mills Thornton has shown how the territorial elite was chased from pol-itics by the Panic of 1819 and by charges of usury against its "royal party."[9] State politics were taken over by a people's party just as in Illi-nois; here also the backcountry was in the ascendancy. But in Alabama the old elite was able to regroup quickly and, on the basis of slave prof-its, reestablish its economic influence through control over markets. In the relatively poorer Illinois, "new men" were in a position of almost complete control, able to dictate political *and economic* policy. This too added to the unique potency of the white folks in Illinois.

Or compare llinois with Indiana, states that share the Wabash and Ohio River valleys. A unified clique of wealthy men in Indiana formed a patronal web so seamless that an opposition was unable to take hold un-til the late 1820s. The three most powerful patrons cooperated by trad-ing off being senator, representative, and governor, the most plentiful patronage-dispensing positions available. By pooling their resources, they were able to control a formidable array of clients who ran the state's constitutional convention and, subsequently, its legislature. Ac-cording to Logan Esarey, "all told[,] the members of the Convention (of 1816) sat for a total of 154 terms in the legislature, thus making an aver-age of four years service in that body for each member of the Conven-tion." In Illinois, by contrast, the 31 members of the convention of 1818 won a total of 32 terms and the more representative 42 members of the first legislature won a total of only 28 future terms. This poor showing may not have been a direct effect of the patronal split, but it did result in competition between the two main factions; it caused Thomas's side to seek out the support of a wider range of clients and to appeal to the enthusiasm of those in the people's movement. This gave the younger generation leverage.[10]

The Illinois pattern was most similar to that of southern frontier re-publics like Alabama and Louisiana. What all three shared was the in-tense social envy and fear of status loss that the slavery system created among poor whites. Status under these circumstances motivated indi-viduals to fear both those above and those below them in the pecking order. In these states, Schlesinger's thesis about demands for social equality was fully realized in a nonurban setting. But in Illinois there was this remarkable difference: the "conditions of social inequality" among whites that created the drive for egalitarianism were for the most part carried around in the white folks' heads as memories of their fami-lies' exclusion from eastern society. This fact again confirms Amy

Bridges's observation that "social structure does not always have a clear and direct relation to electoral combat." Of course, in the Southwest generally, however much social equality existed in its frontier stage, unequal social structures were soon re-created by plantation slavery, which greatly increased investment in black slaves and the wealth of the big folks. This spurred even more racial antagonism on the part of poor whites and created a large forced-labor pool, which the plantation owners could use as a counterforce.[11]

Here again Illinois contrasts sharply, for its egalitarianism had no boundaries against which to define itself; the defining had to take place inside the people. Indeed, when the conventionists depicted their movement as a desperate struggle to keep the white folks' ascendancy in place, many baulked at the specter of bringing in the very slaves that threatened the white folks' status elsewhere. The same problem was faced in the attempt to use economic distinctions. While the attack on the Yankees may have been an incipient attack on merchants, no dominant merchant class was in place. Under political pressure to make distinctions within "the people," but having established race and class hegemony, convention leaders turned to divisions based on cultural style.

After 1818 when its two leading patrons were sent to Washington, the Illinois political scene was wide open. The political freedom that this granted the state's republicans helps explain the ubiquity and rapidity with which egalitarianism was ensconced in the state's political culture. Institutionally, the state's factions were still "precyclical": they had not yet developed the tight electoral discipline of the mature two-party system.[12] That system was not yet in place in 1824; nor did it fall automatically into place. But the convention controversy forced the clash of cultural styles and the redefinition of economic interests that made the ideological cleavages of the new party system possible.

Two other factors played a role in shaping Illinois's precocity, neither of which was tied to the frontier environment. The first was a matter of timing. Andrew Cayton has drawn attention to the period between 1812 and 1819 when the Old Northwest experienced a cataclysmic influx of money and emigrants. Had this "climax of a liberal society" occurred in Illinois after political equality via statehood had been achieved, as was the case in Ohio, the inevitable dislocations it brought may have been used to discredit popular sovereignty as it had in the Buckeye State. The other factor distinguishing Illinois development was the sectional division within the state's population. Here the prime causal force was not economics but geography. As generations of Illinois historians have emphasized, the early settlers were mainly from the South; only about 20 percent came from northern states. Southern emigrants dominated, but outside pressure kept the growth of slavery in check. Since neither sectional group was in complete control, they often needed to cooperate to get things done. Given this structural conflict, politicians defused the slavery bomb by displacing it with the status resentment implied in the anti–big folk rhetoric. To a large extent, the same stalemated situation characterized the national scene. Of all the contending candidates in 1824, Jackson was the only one who could take advantage of this rhetoric. The de facto compromise between the South and the West gave the Jacksonians an edge throughout the second party system.[13]

With this sectional alliance agreed to, all the other ideological aspects of the coalition fell into place, including such future longstanding American patterns as anti-federal nationalism and "pure and uncontaminated" agrarian capitalism. As Theodore Calvin Pease put the sectional calculus: "would the West accept tariff and internal improvements and yield up the public lands policy to the jealousy of her growth harbored in the East? Or would she ally herself with the South in return for free trade and favorable land policy?" In 1828 the region as a whole was undecided, but Pease explained, "so far as Illinois was concerned, the decision had been made." In the mid-1840s, just as Jacksonian symbols seemed finally to have run out of gas, the counties of southern Illinois again showed the way for the Democrats. In the currency debates of those years, cultural issues overlapped with economic ones in the name of "purity and simplicity," precisely as they had in the mind of Andrew Jackson two decades earlier.[14]

Many scholars have identified southern Illinois as a hotbed of American cultural politics during the Jacksonian era. William Gerald Shade made this argument in his masterful analysis of ideological conflict during the second party system. The bank issue was, according to Shade, "the cultural conflict that formed the basis of mid-nineteenth century politics in the Old Northwest." On this issue, he found the key division to be between the Whigs' "Puritan party" and the Democrats' combination of "combined enthusiasm for cultural pluralism with vicious anti-black racism." Shade's analysis of the vote for and against banks focused on the state of Illinois, finding it as divided on the issue as the whole nation. Banks were supported most consistently in ten of the northernmost counties of the state and were opposed with equal consistency in ten of the southernmost counties, the latter making up the area then known as "Egypt." Shade argued that in Egypt banks were seen as an "economic indicator of cultural domination" by Yankees and were opposed on those grounds. Fear of cultural domination was, he suggested, the driving force behind the Democratic vote during the second party system.[15]

What Shade implied about the swallowing of economic by cultural issues, scholars like Robert Kelley and R. Laurence Moore have argued explicitly. In their view, politics during this era was structured by the struggle between cultural (and economic) insiders, such as educated Virginians and enterprising Yankees, and cultural (and economic) outsiders, such as unlettered artisans and poor settlers. What allowed this "cultural pattern" (as Kelley called it) to continue was the ability of out-siders—first the white folks, then the Irish, Mormons, Germans, and other groups—to obtain political recognition, in spite of and in some cases because of their outsider status. This political pattern superseded a politics organized along class lines alone, one that otherwise may have swallowed all cultural divisions. By 1840 both parties in Illinois, each in its own way, was engaged in courting outsiders, such as the Mormons in Hancock County, in search of a winning coalition.[16] The pattern is more than a reinforcement of the pecking order, for it first requires a line de-marcating insiders and outsiders (whether on the basis of whiteness or other markers) and then a reorientation of political ideology in order to reflect that line of opposition. It was this pattern that the early Illi-noisans pioneered because they were in a position to pursue it without distraction from earlier divisions.

Eric Foner pointed to a similar pattern during the formation of the Republican Party. Foner's exploration of the party's roots showed it fol-lowing the trail blazed 30 years earlier by the non-conventionists: Re-publicans used the magical alchemy of "free soil" and "free labor" to de-mocratize the politically debilitating image of the passive people they inherited from the lawyers who controlled the Federalist and Whig Party leadership. Just as the non-conventionists adopted the rhetoric of plain republicanism to split the white folks, so too the Republicans used arguments about workers' independence on free soil and the "slave power conspiracy" to entice western farmers away from their Jacksonian alliance with southern plantation owners. Indeed, as the Lincoln-Douglas debates show, the strategic goal of both the Republicans and the northern Democrats in the late 1850s revolved around courting poor white male voters decades after the same game had played out, with similar results, in southern Illinois.[17]

Within this broad pattern there lie many ironies. The politics of op-position often replicates in a different form the very hierarchical struc-tures it opposes. In Illinois, those who criticized eastern pretensions the loudest ended up most faithfully replicating them. They replicated two eastern patterns in particular, that of grabbing land from the American Indians and that of coveting the financial rewards of slave labor. In fact, the exclusion of outsiders implied in western republicanism was more entrenched because it had the additional justification of furthering the cause against eastern oppression. If a new national pattern was indicated here, it was of a culture less troubled by self-doubt because it was less burdened by self-awareness. It is telling that the state most like Illinois in this period was Alabama. There the battle lines drawn in 1823 be-tween the "royal party" and the "champions of the people" remained in place throughout the second party system. There, too, political rhetoric can be said to have obfuscated more than it clarified, for the "defiant af-firmation . . . that in a democracy, numbers count" and the identity politics pleasure of electing leaders without a college education masked the state's underlying reliance on the slave plantation system.[18]

The simultaneous expression of progressive and regressive social visions has puzzled scholars attempting to make sense of Illinois politics in the early Jacksonian era. Should, for example, whole-hog Illinoisans be described as egalitarians? Was western egalitarianism the key force behind "the promotion of democracy" and "the most important effect of the frontier," as Frederick Jackson Turner argued? These questions are really just another way of asking what impact identity politics had on democracy in Illinois. For, as I have argued throughout, an egalitarian social revolution motivated the reorganization of Illinois politics. The revolutionaries did lose themselves in an impulsive sentiment of resentment. By opposing the simple and refined, western and eastern, identities, they convinced voters to support their efforts; a politics of unreason was the predictable result.[19]

One last point about Illinois's place in the development of the West is necessary. As failed past efforts indicate, no single, sovereign theory of causation explains how the West developed. Turner's emphasis on the frontier experience, for example, was potentially helpful in its focus on the way the immediate locale shaped western values. But Turner's frontier thesis pushed to the margins of the story national factors such as changes in the economy and changes in republicanism that were at its very core. In a partial corrective, the generation of progressive historians who followed Turner downplayed local nuances. This too created an imbalance, for if Turner leaned toward a determinism based on local environmental conditions, Charles Beard and his followers leaned in the direction of a national economic determinism. The paradoxical idea that local and national influences reinforced each other and were used to advance regional interests, an insight of crucial importance in the Illinois story, seems never to have been broached by either school.

Beard's approach was applied to Illinois by Earl W. Hayter. In "Sources of Early Illinois Culture," Hayter commended Turner for improving on earlier idealists who "discovered the origins of American society in the Germanic forests." By this he meant that Turner rejected the cultural determinism of the "germ theory" of democracy, the theory that the germ of popular institutions was brought to the New World by the Anglo-Saxon and Germanic peoples. This was no more than a scholarly version of the whiggish lawyers' insistence on the relevance of the "Norman Yoke." Turner improved on this approach in that he at least thought "in terms of action and interaction of environmental influences." But, according to Hayter, Turner's thesis was ultimately untenable since there were no real environmental influences in Illinois before the market developed wage labor. Until the capitalist "revolution that had begun in England nearly a century earlier . . . [made] itself felt in the frontier settlements of Illinois," the state was mired in "superstition." The people followed a traditional, fatalistic culture which held that "experimentation was dangerous."[20]

Like many hard-minded "realists," Hayter succumbed to a reductionism as simplistic as the idealism he abhorred. Real culture, he implied, is exclusively a product of developed markets. Without such markets, there can be no development. Like the peasants whose critical potential Marx decried, subsistence farmers might touch each others' lives, but only as potatoes in a sack. The problem with this view is that it overlooks the great cultural variety of traditional cultures. Some did indeed express the fatalistic perspective Marx expected. Fatalism is the predicted cultural outcome in Mary Douglas's grid/group analysis whenever high grid (hierachical) social regulations combine with low group (atomistic) social or physical isolation, such as frontier families experienced. But not all subsistence farmers have reason to be equally fatalistic, and as high grid hierarchy receded in early Illinois culture and as setlement life developed stronger social ties, there emerged the persistent strain of producer egalitarianism (low grid/high group) that runs through American rural cultures. After the democratic revolution, the lines of power and the incentives to act were quite different from the feudal system in Europe. The rural people of Illinois thought they had all "the terrible powers of a tornado."[21]

As the convention controversy unwound, the people-as-tornado image was found inoperable. Louis Hartz has shown that the same problem was encountered by Pennsylvanians in the 1820s. He observed wryly that the "unified, morally infallible entity which the age somehow visualized as the popular will, which spoke in decisive positive and negative tones, was mainly myth." Ironically, Hartz's view, while technically accurate, was typical of those who became Whigs and who focused more on the problems of governing than on the power of the people's story. Hartz proceeded to ask the hard questions that most Whigs and many Democrats eventually put to the voters: "If such an entity has ever existed in politics . . . [w]here was it to be found amid the deep-rooted sectional conflicts? Amid the factional struggles of a highly decentralized party system?"[22] But the realist's assessment takes nothing away from the reality of the drama in the minds of so many Illinoisans. The people's epic struggle against wealth and power, if a myth, was an idea that the vast majority of the state's voters carried around in their heads and on which their young leaders acted.

THE POLITICS OF POSITION IN THE LIBERAL TRADITION

Just what a reorganized politics would look like remained an open question. If a common anxiety about their uncertain social status ultimately drove the Illinoisans to rally around a pure, simple western identity, the economic concerns and interests they defined with that identity were less unified. As has been seen, the focus on clearing the bottom-land had the virtue of being promiscuously meaningful. It was able to service at least three distinct economic fears: the older generation's fear of their family's starvation, the yeomanry's fear of not obtaining the independence guaranteed by the fee simple, and the speculator's fear of failing investments. Each had a great fear of losing status, and each responded in distinct ways. Some may have been plagued by all three fears at once: individuals such as William Kinney and John Reynolds seem to have reacted to each at different points in their lives.

The younger generation, spurred on by the state's political changes, looked outward to salve their fears. When the economic depression hit, they responded publicly, not privately. Those unable to make the market work may have retreated to subsistence. Some may not have tried staple production in the first place. But under the bottomland vision, each potentially might find a meaningful role. The bottomland's plenty spoke to liberal modernizers who speculated in the market as well as to traditionalists who still lived for a "competency." From the political standpoint, this was the bottomland vision's greatest asset; as a classic "contested" ideology, it could mean different things to different groups at the same time.[23] Potentially private issues were forced onto the public agenda by the creation of a single political jurisdiction, the state of Illinois. Consolidation and reordering in the "house of power" created demand for a similar consolidation in the houses of status and capital.

The first generation of Americans in Illinois lived in isolated settlements. They showed their reliance on communal ways by sharing their labor in land-clearing, corn-husking, and barn-raising tasks. Early settlements were often self-sufficient, self-contained entities, which could be lined up side by side, one after another along the rivers, without interaction or conflict. By the time the second generation came of age, these settlements had evolved large kinship-based networks spanning entire counties.[24] This enabled the second generation to gather regularly at the church house, the courthouse yard, or the crossroads grogshop. Furthermore, the new government's sovereign jurisdiction made society and state interdependent. While young and old had their own versions of the local identity with corresponding rules of appropriate behavior, their leaders were brought together and forced to deliberate as one in the legislature at Vandalia. Land speculators and backwoodsmen, southern gentlemen and Yankee merchants, and churchgoers and cardplayers met and mixed. There Parker and Kinney and Kinkade and Peck preached; Smith, West, and Thomas Reynolds played cards and talked politics late into the night. Some did both: Kinney, a preacher, also held late night political caucuses; Reynolds, a ferocious gambler, regularly appeared at the capitol's Sunday afternoon preaching sessions.

But it is not always possible to synthesize contradictory impulses. As summarized by George Dangerfield, the western dream was "a dream that foresaw the simultaneous achievement of two dissimilar objectives: a maximum of political liberty and a maximum of material well-being; those who were possessed by it were always a little impatient of the innumerable adjustments necessary to bring those two great objectives into some kind of focus." The subsistence-surplus dream of the younger generation was from this perspective liminal. It participated equally of the world of security and the world of prosperity. An unclear resolution of the tension between safety and growth continues to this day in the region, where elements of subsistence and competency culture still persist.[25]

Adjustment to full-blown liberal individualism was complicated by the state's looser community structure. Many were fully exposed to the risks of independence, living without a safety net of community, even though they had not fully shifted to wage labor or market production. Jonathan Freeman, for example, tried in his many letters to adopt the white folks' perspective by echoing the backcountry dream of a fee-simple republic. But he stumbled over the issue of security. "Just escaped from the grip of poverty or the more horrible grip of tyranny," he pleaded, "it becomes us not to murmur because we have nothing better than liberty and plenty."[26] For many, the point of the convention controversy was that they did not have plenty. The anxieties plaguing the backcountry emigrants were not quieted by confident assertions that the white folks' millennium had already arrived. A multitude of responses were possible, then, under the broad canopy of bottomland republicanism, and the fabricators of this vision deliberately left it ambiguous.

This ambiguity encouraged the fertile Illinois political culture. A full spectrum of attitudes toward market changes left the Democratic and Whig party leaders a rich palate of cultural options from which to choose. For the most part, Democrats focused on the egalitarian aspects of republicanism; they were the most open to identity politics. Whigs focused on the social engineering potential of public reason: their individualism could spill into public reform efforts but tended to eschew group identity. Consequently, the Democrats received the lion's share of the whole-hog vote, while the Whigs did well among the milk-and-cider contingent. In one of the few studies to look at the preferences of individual voters explicitly identified by cultural traits, John Michael Rozzett found that, for Greene County Democrats and Whigs, "the variable of religion remains the strongest predictor of partisan preference." On one hand, Rozzett found that the antimission Baptists maintained a "strong partisan" preference for the Democrats, as befits their whole-hog Calvinism. On the other, he found that the missionary Baptists tended to back the Whigs and that the Methodists, as befits their milk-and-cider Arminianism, "while Whig overall, were neither weakly or strongly inclined in relative terms, but rather moderate. . . . For both the Democrats and the Whigs, the highest percentage of Methodists in any category was in the moderate range."[27]

Similarly, neither party was unmixed in its support for capitalism. As John Ashworth has shown, a "liberal capitalist consensus" cut across the moderate wings of both Whig and Democratic Parties. This consensus believed, along with Thomas Jefferson, that capitalism was—or could be made to be—a liberating, equalizing force in American society. Commercial society, for all its individualism and competition, was for these by its very nature democratic. Given this premise, one might argue that identity politics worked in a democratic direction in Illinois since it was a successful route to political importance for the white folks. It earned them a recognized status in American politics, and eventually renegotiated the social boundaries between insider and outsider. From this perspective, one could say of the white folks what R. Laurence Moore says of the Mormons: "as they made themselves, they made America."[28]

Others, those among the whole hoggers outside this consensus, might have come to a different conclusion, however. They feared commercialization either because they feared personal failure or because they believed, as was traditional, that producers could never be fully independent in a commercial society. If independence, and not recognition, is our standard of democratic success, there is plenty of evidence that identity politics was more of a hindrance than a help. For, as effective as identity politics was in furthering the political equality and recognition of the white folks, it was less effective than a frankly class-based politics might have been in furthering their interest in social equality. Jefferson's vision of capitalism as a liberating force, one in which he promised to "throw open the doors of commerce, and to knock off its shackles" relied in part on creating a fee-simple republic in the trans-Appalachian West. White folks' identity politics can be faulted for failing to foster an egalitarian reality on the ground. Those outside the liberal capitalist consensus on the Whig side, such as the abolitionists and suffragettes of the "humanitarian liberal persuasion," also judged the identity politics of the second party system a democratic failure. This was because, when the people became the white folks, an additional barrier—the barrier of whiteness—was placed in the way of a democratic recognition of the citizenship rights of slaves and Native Americans. This barrier had to be removed before the further barrier of gender could be lifted by and for women of all races.[29]

Louis Hartz argued that an American consensus had formed around a fundamental commitment to liberalism. American liberalism, he insisted, was only "one half" of John Locke's liberalism, the anti-government half devoted to negative (private, individual) liberty. In Hartz's view, Americans were all private-sphere liberals. That half of Locke's created an entire political and cultural consensus because, Hartz stressed, it was the cultural possession of a single emigrant middle class, which had been extracted from a multi-layered European class context. By establishing itself on the shores of North America, the liberal middle class

212 / DEMOCRACY AND SLAVERY

had no European opponent classes above or below to challenge it, and because of this lack of challenge, remained unaware of its own consensual nature.[30]

Hartz thus described a political culture suffering from false consciousness. Still imitating the European class pattern that had created and sustained it, the liberal right wing feared a mob, and the liberal left wing attacked an aristocracy, neither of which existed. Given this scenario, political rhetoric in America took on a "phantom" quality. Hartz's argument has continued to fascinate scholars not because it accurately describes the content of American politics but because it so accurately describes how it operated and developed. Although he never argued that classes did not exist in America, Hartz did argue that American class consciousness lacked the feudal pattern, and so never fully formed along European lines; and on this point he was simply wrong.[31] But if his starting point, the positing of a single liberal middle class, was wrong, he succeeded in concentrating attention on the fact that American political development had followed and continues to follow an unusual path. At its center was a two-party conflict whose main object was winning the votes of "the American democrat"—that is, the poor white male. Widespread white manhood suffrage meant that political power lay in courting the masses, which was not the case in Europe until the nineteenth century.

Two very different strategies for doing this developed. Whigs took the Horatio Alger approach: court the average voter by indicating the potential for social mobility under a Whig regime. The strategy worked remarkably well, attracting a huge cohort of the milk-and-cider contingent. Whig success with the Methodists was especially noteworthy because of the class gulf that it had to bridge in order to succeed. The Methodist embrace of education, the slowest but steadiest means of class advancement, ranks as one of the pivotal moments in American political development.[32] The other strategy for courting the poor white male, the Democratic approach, was to indicate how much the Democratic Party identified with ordinary folks. This approach, dominant in Illinois, discouraged class-based politics and encouraged politicians to divide the world socially, religiously, and ethnically into insiders and outsiders. Outsiders used this division to demonstrate that they were the true Americans, the pure but forsaken, real insiders. Though poorer than those living in the urban centers, they viewed city dwellers as corrupt, weak citizens who had forfeited their claim to true Americanism. Following the logic of their dissent, outsiders continued to delegitimate the worldliness and economic success of insiders by portraying them as artificially refined. Given these categories (of insider and outsider, American and un-American), self-knowledge comes about only through repeated interaction and conflict between the two groups. Hartz argued that Americans were unable to understand the class-conscious cultures of the world because they lacked the political perspective that comes from a class-based politics. But the interaction between cultural insiders and outsiders works as a rough surrogate. The middle-class consensus gains self-awareness through its contact with those dissenting from the mainstream, as do the dissenters in their contact with the mainstream. Antimission Baptist John Leland established a link with the American mainstream the day he presented the people's "Mammoth Cheese" to President Thomas Jefferson in 1802; but on that day Jeffersonian Republicanism too absorbed a piece of the antimission dissent.[33]

In Illinois, the low social status of the wandering Calvinists—lowly within both economic and religious pecking orders—prompted them to follow the logic of dissent, where dissenting from high status practices valorized the lowly. The logic became an attractive tool for social outsiders of all sorts, for it allowed them to label their opponents antirepublican devils. In fact, these opponents—Ninian Edwards, Edward Coles, John Mason Peck—were moderate republican reformers. Illinois political culture too had its "phantom" quality. If often inaccurate and illusory, the name-calling indulged in by the whole-hog persuasion was capable of generating hatred. This hatred was one of the hidden causes of violence in frontier Illinois. When the same pattern is repeated in American political development generally, the extremely reactionary quality of the logic of dissent is evidenced.

The logic of dissent was so seductive, it reached the furthest out of American outsiders: the native Americans. It was prevalent, for example, among the Shawnees, who frequently visited Illinois during this period. Tecumseh's brother Tensquatawa, known as the Prophet, began having dreams in 1805 about the white man. The "Master of Life" told him: "The Americans I did not make. They are not my children, but the children of the Evil Spirit . . . [they] grew from the scum of the great Water when it was troubled by the Evil Spirit. And the froth was driven into the Woods by a strong east wind. They are numerous but I hate them." The Prophet determined that any native contact with the whites caused contamination. His list of taboos—from whiskey to "Bread, the food of the whites," to rules against "dressing like the White man" and intermarriage—out-puritanized the Calvinists. Tenskwatawa's approach was never fully accepted by his people, the majority of whom rejected him "as a witch," but the fact that a Shawnee could find the Calvinists' logic useful indicates its potential power and reach.[34]

In short, Hartz's theory was generally right in its explanation of how political change worked in America. It worked by generating opposition (however phantom) at the level of identity: those low in the pecking order gained self-respect by opposing and dissenting from those highly placed in the order; those high in the pecking order confirmed their status by opposing and distancing themselves from those placed just below them on the pecking order (or sometimes by promoting the interests of those even farther below). Hartz's mistake was in starting with an inaccurate assessment of the substance of American values. He had miscalculated when he claimed, with Tocqueville, that Americans were born liberal. It would be more accurate to say, echoing Richard J. Ellis, that they were born republican. But republicanism was experienced as a dissenting tradition. In Illinois, republicans backed into the liberal consensus by dissenting from elitism. The white folks' numerical majority allowed leaders to pursue a politics of class resentment by other means. What was high, they made low; what was low, they made correspondingly high. They took the "Saxon people" that haunted Blackstone, the Federalists, and the Whigs and turned them into "the white folks," thereby becoming Americans. In effect, they imagined themselves into the center of the American political drama. Because of their numbers, their version of the story eventually obtained widespread recognition.

In the house of mirrors and images that the American political tradition thus became, the realities of the pecking order turn every election contest into a potential opportunity to manipulate the politics of position. Hartz's theory assumes as much, but he failed to notice that not all outsiders could define themselves or achieve recognition comfortably with this method of opposition. He missed those outsiders who defined themselves in opposition even to the opposition—slaves, natives, suffragettes. Other non-consensual outsiders included non-secularizing groups within the Jews, Catholics, Mormons, and evangelical Protestants. For these, the white folks' version of the story of the people was not lowly enough, nor did they have majority rules on their side. Indeed, these groups broke the paradigm, because at several points the story of the people—however recast—does not fit them. But even these groups' struggles have been shaped by the peculiar dynamics of dissent in America, where the definition of a particular lower-class group's interests is determined as much by its rhetorical struggles with a mainstream opponent as by an "objective" assessment of those interests.

CONCLUSION

DEMOCRATIC IDENTITIES AND
LIBERAL INSTITUTIONS

From the distance of thirty years, in the mid-1850s, John Mason Peck drew three morals from his experience in the convention controversy, one each concerning class, political organization, and party ideology. His comment on class came in the course of reflecting on Edward Coles's misfortune in being persecuted by the conventionists. Peck felt that Coles had been vindicated not only by the outcome of the contest but also by the fact that he was now "the possessor of large wealth . . . [and] the head of a most interesting family in Philadelphia" while the conventionists, "a class of men whose moral and political characters would have disqualified them for blackening his boots," had finally "destroyed themselves by whiskey and rowdyism." Looking to the political conflicts of the 1850s, Peck was also able to draw a strategic lesson from the controversy. "If I was in your *position* and in the vigor of life as I was in 1823–4," he wrote a protégé, "I would have an organization in every county and a 'club' in every precinct. Organize, organize, organize. Making stump speeches does well enough to advise the people, but quiet and private arrangements will produce votes." Finally, Peck thought he saw some support for his political favorite, Stephen Douglas, among the convention's political lessons. The whole controversy, he noted, had been caused by congressional meddling. Had the Missouri Compromise not aroused "the jealousy of the people to resist this encroachment on their rights from abroad," the struggle may very well have never taken place.[1]

Peck shows, surely without wanting to, how assumptions implicit in early Illinois politics became explicit twenty-five years later. One is the association of political insiders with upper-class status: the moral of the story, as Peck told it, was that Coles had been vindicated by his wealth; his opponents remain a class apart. Another assumption suggests that the conventionists may have earned a long-fought revenge from the mainstream. By blaming Congress and supporting Douglas, Peck envinces a bias in favor of local control that his opponents insisted upon as a first principle of republicanism. That John Mason Peck, the eastern missionary with anti-slavery sentiments, became an adherent of Douglas's "popular sovereignty" wing of the Democratic Party provides a fitting conclusion to this study of early Illinois's contradictory development.

Illinois was beset by contradictions precisely because of its democratic devotions. Democracy is a form of government under which the moral authority for deciding public policy lies with the majority. The proposition was so remarkable and flattering to most Illinoisans that they had trouble, as we still have trouble, thinking beyond it. A focus on the authority of the majority, while necessary to democratic legitimacy, leads all too easily to a politics of identity in which those outside the chosen identity of the majority are excluded. This was the case for the majority poor white emigrants to early Illinois. Democracy in Illinois failed in the same way it fails elsewhere, when a previously excluded group suddenly obtains power and uses this power to oppose those formerly high on the pecking order and to exclude other groups even further marginalized.

Some scholars, observing this endemic cycle of identity politics in democracies, have argued that democracy is essentially opposed to liberalism.[2] Since the eighteenth century, liberals have sought to limit the state's power generally; the goal of limiting power conflicts with democracy's belief in the moral authority and collective identity of the majority. Identity politics only exacerbates another tension between democracy and capitalism. The market tends to concentrate wealth, at least under its usual "imperfect" condition. It creates independence for some but dependence for many others. This tendency conflicts with democracy's aspiration of making all citizens equally free and independent. Yet democracies coexist and indeed thrive in liberal, capitalist societies.

Democracy's tensions with liberalism and capitalism are usually treated as separate issues. It is a basic premise of this study that the two tensions need to be studied together, for they developed simultaneously and influenced each other. Democrats in early Illinois confronted both at the same time, and they attempted to play the one off the other. They attempted to use the market in slave labor to fulfill the independence promised by their rights as citizens. When liberal institutions and beliefs threatened to stall the project, the movement's leaders attempted to clear all checks on their own power in the name of the people's power.

Were the triumph of liberal constitutionalism and the failure of identity politics the only morals of the convention story, it would be hard to distinguish from a lesson in the distrust of democracy, distrust of participatory democracy above all. But an important additional moral cautions against this anti-democratic lesson. The convention story also illustrates that liberal institutions are not enough to create a liberal democracy. As perfect and "more perfect" as their balancing act might be, the institutions of representative republics need to cultivate a spirit of self-government and social equality if their societies aspire to be democratic. All the enlightened schemes in the world will not produce democracy without the widespread recognition of equality. Optimally, the belief in equality will, in a cosmopolitan manner, encompass all differences. More realistically, in the American pattern, this belief only includes a respect for those recognized by the majority. Without at least this parochial recognition, however, no democracy can be established or if established can last for long. To this extent, John Adams was right in his debate with Thomas Jefferson over the nature of the "natural" aristocracy: power is concentrated in the hands of the few even in democratic societies. But there is no motor for moving the status quo away from a tendency toward oligarchy without the recognition of the needs of stigmatized outsiders. In early Illinois, it was the backcountry republicans who expressed this sentiment and initiated the process of change. That, in providing this public service, they defended their own cause is the pound of flesh required of any political system whose professed aim is perfection.

Thus it is a false impression that liberal institutions alone, by creating institutional time and space for the non-conventionist organizers, were responsible for producing a stable liberal democracy in early Illinois. Liberal institutions structured the struggle for egalitarian public policies and to some extent exacerbated it; only through this struggle did true self-government occur. In the process, egalitarian sentiment was a crucial starting point. If egalitarian sentiment, especially in its whole-hog expression, can lose its way in the labyrinth of identity politics, it still plays a crucial role in beginning the process of democratization. Democracy is self-government; self-government requires collective self-control; collective self-control has so far been possible only under the protection of liberal institutions. But the urge to define oneself communally starts the process, and it is usually a messy one involving not only mass mobilization but also the influence of an emergent set of leaders. In the Illinois case, the new leaders divided into moderate (milk-and-cider) and absolutist (whole-hog) factions, both of which supported white folks' republicanism. A great deal of the credit for the defeat of slavery must go to the contingent of moderate citizens *within* the white folks.[3] Without the active participation of the milk-and-cider non-conventionists, the institutions alone would have failed.

To the extent that the ideal of social equality is based on a sentiment, the Jacksonians were right to be suspicious of Whig abstractions and reason. Because the Whigs also professed an attachment to equality, their view remained incomplete. The Whig theory of popular sovereignty did assume a story of the oppression of the people, but, Federalist-like, it had removed the people as active players in the story. Thus, in another irony of party development, the Whigs themselves demonstrated that an emphasis on reason alone was not enough to make liberal democracy work in America. Illinoisans inherited the story of the people in the first place because they and their ancestors, having been excluded, strove to be recognized as equals; reason played the important but subsidiary role of insisting that egalitarian aspirations be placed within the larger story of humanity and that the belief in the people's virtue be limited and checked.

It should be obvious, on the cusp of the twenty-first century, that American political development is not so unique as to be inimitable. Nor is liberal democracy an oxymoron. The interaction between liberal institutions and democratic sentiments in American political development has been positive whenever it has forced egalitarians to recognize the incompleteness of communal virtues. In the Illinois case, whole-hog republicans projected a meaningful political identity as bottomland farmers that was questioned and doubted by a moderate milk-and-cider contingent. The bottomland republic was, in the eyes of its inventors, a morally pure ideal. The moderates used every liberal institution at their disposal to reject this claim, and to force as many Illinoisans as they could get to listen to confront the limitations of their backcountry social vision. Replicating this delicate balance is a difficult feat. It makes the development of liberal democracy in America and elsewhere as much an art as it is a science. The enterprise is doubly difficult because it requires collective action, and collective artistry is the most delicate of all arts. Alexis de Tocqueville wrote that "a democracy cannot get at the truth without experience, and many nations may perish for lack of the time to discover mistakes." He observed that it had been "the great privilege of the Americans . . . to be able to make retrievable mistakes."[4] By sharing our experiences, it is hoped that democratic mistakes worldwide will become less irretrievable. If so, the art of liberal democracy may become less exotic and more practiced.

NOTES

INTRODUCTION: HOW THE PEOPLE BECAME THE WHITE FOLKS

1. See the letter of an eyewitness in *Edwardsville Spectator,* December 13, 1823; *Illinois Gazette,* December 20, 1823.

2. See Coles's letter to Morris Birkbeck, dated January 29, 1824, in Clarence Walworth Alvord, ed., *Governor Edward Coles* (Springfield: Illinois State Historical Library, 1920), 150.

3. Theodore Calvin Pease, *The Frontier State, 1818–1848* (Urbana: University of Illinois, 1987), 86. Pease's work was first published in 1918 by the Illinois Centennial Commission, as volume 2 of *The Centennial History of Illinois.* For an analysis of the Centennial History series as "a historiographical landmark," see John Hoffmann, "A History of *The Centennial History of Illinois,* 1907–1920," in *Selected Papers in Illinois History, 1982,* ed. Robert W. McCluggage (Springfield: Illinois State Historical Society, 1984), 57–78.

4. For the vote totals, see Theodore Calvin Pease, ed., *Illinois Election Returns, 1818–1848* (Springfield: Illinois State Historical Library, 1923), 27. 1845 is the year Joseph Jarrot won his freedom in an appeal decided by the Illinois Supreme Court; see *Jarrot v. Jarrot* (7 Ill. 1) in *Reports of Cases Argued and Determined in the Supreme Court of the State of Illinois* (Chicago: Callaghan and Co., 1886).

5. *Republican,* April 13, 1824.

6. Anne Norton, *Reflections on Political Identity* (Baltimore: Johns Hopkins University Press, 1988), 3.

7. Christiana Holmes Tillson, *A Woman's Story of Pioneer Illinois,* ed. Milo Milton Quaife, with introduction by Kay J. Carr (Carbondale: Southern Illinois University Press, 1995), 24–25; Thomas Ford, *A History of Illinois: From Its Commencement as a State in 1818 to 1847* (Urbana: University of Illinois Press, 1995), 194. The Calhoun quotation is from George Dangerfield, *The Awakening of American Nationalism, 1815–1828* (New York: Harper and Row, 1965), 106 n. 27.

8. For an analysis of white settler states in the larger context of social contract theory, see Charles W. Mills, *The Racial Contract* (Ithaca: Cornell University Press, 1997). For the definition of "*herrenvolk* democracy," see Pierre L. van den Berghe, *Race and Racism: A Comparative Perspective* (New York: John Wiley and Sons, 1967), 18. For applications of the *herrenvolk* idea to the United States, see William W. Freehling, *The Road to Disunion,* vol. 1, *Secessionists at Bay, 1776–1854* (New York: Oxford University Press, 1990),

42. The concept of "whiteness" is discussed in David Roediger, *The Wages of Whiteness: Race and the Making of the American Working Class* (London: Verso, 1991).

9. See Louis Hartz, *The Liberal Tradition in America* (New York: Harcourt, Brace and World, 1955), 114–42; E.E. Schattschneider, *The Semi-Sovereign People: A Realist's View of Democracy in America* [1960]. (New York: Holt, Reinhart and Winston, 1983), 20.

10. Jeffrey K. Tulis, *The Rhetorical Presidency* (Princeton: Princeton University Press, 1987); Kenneth Cmiel, *Democratic Eloquence: The Fight over Popular Speech in Nineteenth-Century America* (Berkeley and Los Angeles: University of California Press, 1990); Alexander Saxton, *The Rise and Fall of the White Republic: Class Politics and Mass Culture in Nineteenth-Century America* (London: Verso, 1990); Roediger, *The Wages of Whiteness*. For the role of race in political development generally, see Mills, *Racial Contract,* and Anthony W. Marx, *Making Race and Nation: A Comparison of South Africa, the United States, and Brazil* (Cambridge: Cambridge University Press, 1998). Here I borrow a turn of phrase from Noel Ignatiev; see *How the Irish Became White* (New York: Routledge, 1995).

11. See Sloo's letter to Judge George Torrence of Ohio, "Selections from the Torrence Papers VII," in Isaac Joslin Cox, ed., *Quarterly Publication of the Historical and Philosophical Society of Ohio* (Cincinnati: Cincinnati Historical Society, 1911), 56–57.

12. David Hackett Fischer, *Albion's Seed: Four British Folkways in America* (New York: Oxford University Press, 1989).

13. The quotations in this and the next paragraph are taken from Lester J. Cappon, ed., *The Adams-Jefferson Letters* (Chapel Hill: University of North Carolina Press, 1987), 296–300. Original spelling has been altered.

14. For Douglas, see Robert W. Johannsen, ed., *The Lincoln-Douglas Debates* (New York: Oxford University Press, 1965), 28, 127. For the view that Douglas represents the utilitarian strain of American liberalism, see J. David Greenstone, *The Lincoln Persuasion: Remaking American Liberalism* (Princeton: Princeton University Press, 1993), 143; Michael Sandel, *Democracy's Discontent: America in Search of a Public Philosophy* (Cambridge, Mass.: Harvard University Press, 1996), 21–23, 8.

15. For Douglas, see *The Lincoln-Douglas Debates*, 209–10; For Lincoln, see ibid., 316 (emphasis in the original).

16. Lee Benson, *The Concept of Jacksonian Democracy: New York as a Test Case* (Princeton: Princeton University Press, 1961), 12; Arthur M. Schlesinger, Jr., *The Age of Jackson* (Boston: Little, Brown, 1945); Hartz, *Liberal Tradition;* Richard P. McCormick, *The Second American Party System: Party Formation in the Jacksonian Era* (Chapel Hill: University of North Carolina Press, 1966).

17. For "the people" as the dispossessed of Europe, see Rowland Berthoff, *Republic of the Dispossessed: The Exceptional Old-European Consensus in America* (Columbia: University of Missouri Press, 1997). Scholars crafting narratives that emphasize national trends have focused on forces as diverse as the post office, the market revolution, the northern shift to wage labor, and the public land system; see Richard R. John, *Spreading the News: The American Postal System from Franklin to Morse* (Cambridge, Mass.: Harvard University Press, 1995); Charles Sellers, *The Market Revolution: Jacksonian America,*

1815-1846 (New York: Oxford University Press, 1991); John Ashworth, *Slavery, Capitalism, and Politics in the Antebellum Republic,* vol. 1, *Commerce and Compromise, 1820–1850* (Cambridge: Cambridge University Press, 1995); Daniel Feller, *The Public Lands in Jacksonian Politics* (Madison: University of Wisconsin Press, 1984).

18. The quotation regarding state bills, from an 1827 circular referring to the original reasons for the state bank, is from Pease, *Frontier State,* 58. See the report of instructions from Wayne, White, and Gallatin Counties in *Journal of the House* (1821): 88, 109, 110. Pease, *Frontier State,* 56–59, discusses the state bank episode in the legislature; for the objections of the council of revision, see *Journal of the House* (1821): 236–39; for the attack on the objections, see the remarks made by David Blackwell, *Journal of the House* (1821): 262–71 (266).

19. Coles, inaugural address, *Journal of the House* (1821): 18–27 (21).

20. For an instance of this view, see the remarks of David Blackwell, ibid., 134.

21. For the status of northern and southern agriculture in 1815 generally, see Paul W. Gates, *The Farmer's Age: Agriculture, 1815–1860* (New York: Harper and Row, 1960), 1–50. For the "proto-industrial" developments in northern agriculture, see, for example, Thomas Dublin, "Women and Outwork in a Nineteenth-Century New England Town: Fitzwilliam, New Hampshire, 1830–1850," in *The Countryside in the Age of Capitalist Transformation,* ed. Steven Hahn and Jonathan Prude (Chapel Hill: University of North Carolina Press, 1985), 51–69. The development of southern staple production in tobacco, rice, and cotton (and the slave migration that paralleled it) is explored in Allan Kulikoff, *The Agrarian Origins of American Capitalism* (Charlottesville: University Press of Virginia, 1992), 226–63. Robert McColley, *Slavery and Jeffersonian Virginia* (Urbana: University of Illinois Press, 1964), 181, argues that the development of cotton production in the Southwest drew slave-owning settlers away from Illinois during this period. For the geological formation of the bottomland loess, see Douglas C. Ridgley, *The Geography of Illinois* (Chicago: University of Chicago Press, 1921), 25–36.

1: THE WHITE FOLKS CHALLENGE THE BIG FOLKS

1. The "swinish multitude" comment appears in a 1823 letter to James Hall at Vandalia, quoted in Theodore Calvin Pease, *The Story of Illinois* (Chicago: University of Chicago Press, 1975), 105; Cox's speech appears in the *Illinois Intelligencer,* March 8, 1823.

2. The phrase was borrowed by "John Old Times" from a "Federal editor" who "has taken a great liking to Gov. Coles"; see *Republican,* June 8, 1824.

3. Alvord, *Coles,* 41, 339. See also Thomas Lippincott, "Early Days in Madison County," *Alton Telegraph,* November 18, 1864. Warren's doubts about Coles went so deep that he wondered in a public letter whether Coles had fathered his servant's "two younger children, a boy and a girl, *mulattoes*" (Alvord, *Coles,* 362).

4. See Jefferson's August 25, 1814, letter to Coles in Thomas Jefferson, *The Portable Thomas Jefferson,* ed. Merrill D. Peterson (New York: Viking Penguin, 1975), 545–47.

5. Coles claimed to have emancipated all his slaves on the flatboat as they were traveling down the Ohio River en route to Illinois in 1819. But as his own letter to *Illinois Intelligencer,* June 4, 1822, indicates, at least seven remained in his service until 1825; see Alvord, *Coles,* 40–47, 261–63, 312, 330–31, 349, 353–54, 363; see the different introductions in *Journal of the House* (1823): 11, 18. The description of Bond is from *Republican,* April 20, 1824 (emphasis in the original).

6. See *Journal of the House* (1823): 26. Arthur Clinton Boggess, in *The Settlement of Illinois, 1778–1830* (Chicago: Chicago Historical Society, 1908), 179, tabulated that, from 1810 to 1820, "the number of slaves in Illinois increased from 168 to 917, Illinois being the only state north of Mason and Dixon's line having an increase of slaves during the decade."

7. On the indenture system, see Norman Dwight Harris, *History of Negro Servitude in Illinois and of the Slavery Agitation in That State, 1719–1864* (Chicago: A. C. McClurg, 1904). There is a brief biography of Moore in Alvord, *Coles,* 87–89. The anti-slavery address is quoted in Solon Justus Buck, *Illinois in 1818* (Springfield: Illinois Centennial Commission, 1917), 260–61.

8. For the phrase "Honest Irish," see *Republican,* June 8, 1824. Winstanley Briggs, "Le Pays des Illinois," *William and Mary Quarterly,* 3d ser., 46 (1989): 30–56. Population figures are from Clarence Walworth Alvord, *The Illinois Country, 1673–1818* (Urbana: University of Illinois Press, 1987), 415.

9. See the text of the 1787 Ordinance, in Peter S. Onuf, *Statehood and Union: A History of the Northwest Ordinance* (Bloomington: Indiana University Press, 1987), 63. All McFerron quotations are from remarks published in *Illinois Intelligencer,* February 8, 1823; "The Legitimate Power of the People," *Republican Advocate,* January 22, 1824.

10. On McFerron's anti-slavery sentiments, see Buck, *Illinois in 1818,* 257. McFerron's opinion is corroborated, from an anti-slavery perspective, by a neighbor and friend of Edward Coles in Edwardsville, Joseph Gillespie, who, in "Recollections of Early Illinois and her noted men," *Fergus Historical Series,* no. 13 (Chicago: Fergus Historical Library, 1880), 8, wrote: "The old French inhabitants treated their slaves with great kindness; slavery, with them, was a kind of patriarchal institution."

11. All quotations by Will in this and the following paragraphs are from the copy of the report presented to the House on December 21, 1822, in *Illinois Intelligencer,* December 28, 1822. 12. For the relation between Vesey and the Missouri Compromise debates, see Dangerfield, *Awakening,* 139.

13. See John W. Allen, "Slavery and Negro Servitude in Pope County, Illinois," in *An Illinois Reader,* ed. Clyde C. Walton (DeKalb: Northern Illinois University Press, 1970).

14. *Edwardsville Spectator,* March 15, 1823. On Parker's prayer motion, see *Journal of the Senate* (1823): 163.

15. See John F. Snyder, "Forgotten Statesmen of Illinois: Hon. Conrad Will," *Publications of the Historical Library of Illinois* 10 (1905): 364.

16. Douglas quoted from Robert W. Johannsen, "Stephen A. Douglas and the American Mission," in *The Frontier, the Union, and Stephen A. Douglas* (Urbana: University of Illinois Press, 1989), 78. For the Enabling Act language, see "Act of Congress, April 19, 1818," 15–19 at 17 in *Illinois Constitutions,* ed. Emil Joseph Verlie (Springfield: Illinois State Historical Library,

1919). See also Robert W. Johannsen, "Stephen A. Douglas, *Harper's Magazine*, and Popular Sovereignty," in ibid., 120–45; Harry V. Jaffa, *Crisis of the House Divided*, Phoenix edition (Chicago: University of Chicago Press, 1982), 110–31. On the attitude of the older states to slavery in the Northwest, see Onuf, *Statehood and Union*, 109–13.

17. See Richard H. Brown, "The Missouri Crisis, Slavery, and the Politics of Jacksonianism," *South Atlantic Quarterly* 65 (1966): 55–72. On the issue of planned, compensated emancipation, see Betty L. Fladeland, "Compensated Emancipation: A Rejected Alternative," *Journal of Southern History* 42 (1976): 169–86. For the American Colonization Society, see Gary B. Nash in *Race and Revolution* (Madison: Madison House, 1990), 11, 42–43 (quotation on 43); Nash (49) calls colonization the "institutional form of rampaging white racism." Ronald G. Walters, *American Reformers, 1815–1860* (New York: Hill and Wang, 1978), 78. The Ohio plan is noted in Daniel Feller, *The Jacksonian Promise* (Baltimore: Johns Hopkins University Press, 1995), 63–64; the Owenite plan is noted in Buck, *Illinois in 1818*, 277–78. For Jefferson, see William Cohen, "Thomas Jefferson and the Problem of Slavery," *Journal of American History* 56 (December 1969): 503–26 (523–24). See "Pacificus" in *Western Intelligencer*, August 12, 1818; Ferdinand Ernst, "Travels in Illinois in 1819," *Transactions of the Illinois State Historical Society* 8 (1903): 150–65, 154.

18. "Brissot," in *Republican*, March 30, 1824.

19. See W. J. Cash, *The Mind of the South* (New York: Vintage Books [1941], 1991), 3–28; Dangerfield, *Awakening*, 104–6.

20. Concerning the Senate membership, with numbers of servants: Leonard White owned two, William Boon owned four, Milton Ladd owned one, Joseph Beaird owned eight, and William Kinney owned one. For data on servants, see Margaret Cross Norton, ed., *Illinois Census Returns, 1820* (Springfield: Illinois State Historical Library, 1934), 335, 110–11, 132, 201, 265. White was government agent for the state's salines between 1808 and 1811; in 1812, he created the jurisdiction thereafter called the Saline Reservation in Gallatin County. Boon was from Jackson County where his friend Conrad Will ran the Big Muddy Saline from 1815 to 1824; see George Washington Smith, "The Salines of Southern Illinois," *Publications of the Historical Library of Illinois* 9 (1904): 249, 251. Only three other members in the eighteen-member Senate held slaves; see *Edwardsville Spectator*, February 1, 1823; for the treasurer's report, see Boggess, *Settlement of Illinois*, 149.

21. See the letter of Hooper Warren, dated December 21, 1854, in Alvord, *Coles*, 313; also Warren's comments in ibid., 363–64.

22. B. E. Hoffmann, ed., *History of Madison County, Illinois* (Edwardsville, Ill.: W. R. Brink, 1882), 132–33; *Republican*, June 15, 1824.

23. On the relation between the lack of an ideology for state action and the corresponding need for equity in state action, see L. Ray Gunn's analysis of the New York legislature during this period, in *The Decline of Authority: Public Economic Policy and Political Development in New York State, 1800–1860* (Ithaca: Cornell University Press, 1988), 141–42. By the 1840s, Smith's behavior was leading "some to believe that his mind was affected"; see Pease, *Frontier State*, 282.

24. Coles's aristocratic bearing, as a "proud Virginian," often clashed with local egalitarianism. Hooper Warren makes a special point of noting

Coles's "sporting with the Lords and Nobles" of Europe; see Alvord, *Coles,* 361, 339. Coles struck many as arrogant. A correspondent with Thomas Sloo, Jr., in Cox, "Selections from the Torrence Papers VII," 49, upon first meeting the future governor in May 1818, remarked: "He worships but one idol, and that is himself. He is a two and one half penny animal." The correspondent makes no mention of the emancipation. Coles's land purchases are noted in Robert M. Sutton, "Edward Coles and the Constitutional Crisis in Illinois, 1822–1824," *Illinois Historical Journal* 82 (Spring 1989): 36.

25. Smith cited from *Illinois Intelligencer,* December 14, 1822; "A Whiteman," *Illinois Intelligencer,* June 7, 1823.

26. Ruggles quoted in Peace, *Frontier State,* 71; Churchill in *Edwardsville Spectator,* March 15, 1823.

27. For "Aristides" and the Jefferson-Lemen Pact, see Buck, *Illinois in 1818,* 208, 319; see also Joseph B. Lemen, "The Jefferson-Lemen Anti-Slavery Pact," *Transactions of the Illinois State Historical Society* 13 (1918): 74–84. For Lemen's efforts at organizing Baptist anti-slavery congregations, see Merton L. Dillon, "Sources of Early Anti-Slavery Thought in Illinois," *Journal of the Illinois State Historical Society* 50 (1957): 39. On Coles's role in the Adams-Jefferson story, see Cappon, *Adams-Jefferson Letters,* 283–84. For the reprinted letter, see *Illinois Intelligencer,* June 4, 1822, and *Edwardsville Spectator,* July 6, 1822. The conflicted reading of Jefferson's views on slavery has persisted. For a pro-slavery reading of the Jefferson-Coles exchange, see John Hope Franklin, "Who Divided This House?" *Chicago History* 19 (1990–1991): 32–34. Coles is held up as the angel of Jefferson's better self in Paul Finkelman, *Slavery and the Founders: Race and Liberty in the Age of Jefferson* (Armonk, N.Y.: M. E. Sharpe, 1996), 166–67. For a letter praising "the immortal Jefferson" for his anti-slavery views, see *Edwardsville Spectator,* July 20, 1824.

28. Smith cited from *Illinois Intelligencer,* December 14, 1823; see also Onuf, *Statehood and Union,* 60.

29. "Compact" defenses are discussed in Onuf, *Statehood and Union,* 72–76. On the Vincennes or "Post Vinsan" legislature, see Boggess, *Settlement of Illinois,* 177–78. For an example of this language used on the anti-slavery side, see the Fourth of July oration by Theodore C. Cone, published in the *Illinois Gazette,* August 2, 1823; for Jefferson's letter, see *Illinois Gazette,* November 8, 1823.

30. *Illinois Intelligencer,* December 14, 1823.

31. Cox, in *Illinois Gazette,* March 29, 1823.

32. Eddy quoted in John William Ward, *Andrew Jackson: Symbol for an Age* (London: Oxford University Press, 1955), 133.

33. "Timour," in *Republican Advocate* (Kaskaskia), January 22, 1824; "Brissot," in *Republican,* March 30, 1824. David Waldstreicher, *In the Midst of Perpetual Fêtes: The Making of American Nationalism, 1776–1820* (Chapel Hill: University of North Carolina Press, 1997), 7, argues that the claims of "early American nationalists" were buffeted by their simultaneity with "a particular moment in world history . . . the invention of modern democracy."

34. Will cited from *Illinois Intelligencer,* December 28, 1822.

35. These are Henry Eddy's words; see *Illinois Gazette,* March 8, 1823.

36. See Martin Shefter, "The Electoral Foundations of the Political Ma-

chine: New York City, 1884–1897," in *The History of American Electoral Behavior*, ed. Joel H. Silbey, Allan G. Bogue, and William H. Flanigan (Princeton: Princeton University Press, 1978), 267.

37. For this view of "the people" in the Declaration, see Nathan Tarcov, "American Constitutionalism and Individual Rights," in *How Does the Constitution Secure Rights?*, ed. Robert A. Goldwin and William A. Schambra (Washington, D.C.: American Enterprise Institute for Policy Research, 1985), 107. One of the few discussions of American-French relations during this period is Ronald L. F. Davis, "Community and Conflict in Pioneer Saint Louis, Missouri," *Western Historical Quarterly* 10 (1979): 337–54; Kinney cited from *Edwardsville Spectator*, May 3, 1823.

38. Fischer, *Albion's Seed*, 631; Patrick Henry is quoted, ibid., 780. The role of conspiracy theories during the colonial and revolutionary periods is explored by Bernard Bailyn in *The Ideological Origins of the American Revolution* (Cambridge, Mass.: Harvard University Press, 1967) and *The Origins of American Politics* (New York: Vintage Books, 1967).

39. For Taylor's summary of the rebellions, see *Liberty Men and Great Proprietors* (Chapel Hill: University of North Carolina Press, 1990), 4–8. Alan Taylor's history of William Cooper is *William Cooper's Town: Power and Persuasion on the Frontier of the Early American Republic* (New York: Alfred A. Knopf, 1996). Sellers, *Market Revolution*. The religious basis of the conflict in Virginia is analyzed in Rhys Isaac, *The Transformation of Virginia, 1740–1800* (Chapel Hill: University of North Carolina Press, 1982). For an analysis of its economic basis, see Allan Kulikoff, *Tobacco and Slaves: The Development of Southern Cultures in the Chesapeake, 1680–1800* (Chapel Hill: University of North Carolina Press, 1986). There are many illuminating studies of the role of the backcountry in the American Revolution, but for a distinguished early effort, see Richard R. Beeman, *The Evolution of the Southern Backcountry: A Case Study of Lunenburg County, Virginia, 1746–1832* (Philadelphia: University of Pennsylvania Press, 1984). For a study emphasizing the role of dissenting religion, see William G. McLoughlin, Jr., *Isaac Backus and the American Pietistic Tradition* (Boston: Little, Brown, 1967).

40. Buck, *Illinois in 1818*, 93–96. Of the 6,020 heads of family in Illinois in 1818, Buck discovered the "birthplace or former residence of 716, or nearly twelve percent," 93. He (97) notes the predominance of Scotch-Irish names, indicating "the connection of the people with that stream of non-English immigrants which poured into Pennsylvania during the eighteenth century and then up the valleys and through the gaps to the back country of Virginia, the Carolinas, and Georgia." See also John Barnhart, "The Southern Influence in the Formation of Illinois," *Journal of the Illinois State Historical Society* 32 (1939): 363, who emphasizes the presence of lowland southerners as well as uplanders; Boggess, *Settlement of Illinois*, 112; John Reynolds, *The Pioneer History of Illinois, Containing the Discovery, in 1673, and the History of the Country to the Year Eighteen Hundred and Eighteen, When the State Government Was Organized* (Chicago: Fergus Printing, 1887), 317.

41. As Steven Hahn argues, in *The Roots of Southern Populism: Yeoman Farmers and the Transformation of the Georgia Upcountry, 1850–1890* (New York: Oxford University Press, 1983), 52, poor white economic culture included "household and fee-simple landownership," but it also involved

"communal, pre-bourgeois, [and] egalitarian proclivities [which] sharply distinguished it from that of the planters." Scholars have shown that the code of honor was only partially modified as the backcountry population moved into western states such as Kentucky; see Bertram Wyatt-Brown, *Southern Honor: Ethics and Behavior in the Old South* (Oxford and New York: Oxford University Press, 1982); Christopher Waldrep, "The Making of a Border State Society: James McGready, the Great Revival, and the Prosecution of Profanity in Kentucky," *American Historical Review* 99 (June 1994): 767–84.

42. For Birkbeck's Edwards County neighbors, see George Flower, *History of the English Settlement in Edwards County* (Chicago: Fergus Printing, 1882), 191; "Americanus," in *Illinois Intelligencer,* January 16, 1824; James Hall, "Letters from the West," *Port Folio* 13 (1821): 122; "John Rifle," in *Illinois Gazette,* June 21, August 22, 1823.

43. Daniel M. Parkinson, "Pioneer Life in Wisconsin [1855]," *Collections of the Historical Society of Wisconsin* (Madison: University of Wisconsin Press, 1984), 327.

44. Ford, *History of Illinois,* 62; Parkinson, "Pioneer Life in Wisconsin," 328.

45. Ford, *History of Illinois,* 63; "Timour," in *Republican,* March 9, 1824.

46. All quotations from Parker come from his periodical, published in a two-volume set: *Church Advocate* (Vincennes, Ind.: Elihu Stout, 1828–1831), 1:61, 17, 16.

47. Ford, *History of Illinois,* 95, 42; Marvin Meyers, *The Jacksonian Persuasion: Politics and Belief* (New York: Vintage Books, 1957), 131, rightly calls Ford's description "an invaluable account of values conversion." George Dangerfield, *The Era of Good Feelings* (Chicago: Ivan R. Dee, 1989), 108; Ford, *History of Illinois,* 19; Meyers, *The Jacksonian Persuasion,* 133. See also Reynolds, *Pioneer History,* 366. Winstanley Briggs's story of the French fall from the market, the colony's "political and economic death after 1765," is suggestive in this regard; see "Le Pays des Illinois," 52–56.

48. On this point, see David M. Potter, *People of Plenty: Economic Abundance and the American Character* (Chicago: University of Chicago Press, 1954), 121.

49. Cox, "Selections from the Torrence Papers VII," 56–57.

50. The phrase is from Ford, *History of Illinois,* 57.

51. This was the position taken by the great historian of early Illinois politics, Theodore Calvin Pease. In the introduction to *Illinois Election Returns,* xix, he writes of "the classical interpretation of Illinois party history for the first ten years of statehood . . . [in which] politics were essentially personal." McCormick, *Second American Party System,* 281, reviews Illinois factions during this time and calls them "chaotic"; see also Fischer, *Albion's Seed,* 772–76. For an attempt to tie the republican social vision to the "peasant-smallholder or artisan-proprietor outlook" of the medieval European folk, see Berthoff, *Republic of the Dispossessed,* esp. 35.

2: BOTTOMLAND FARMERS IN THE MARKET REVOLUTION

1. The phrase is from Dangerfield, *Era of Good Feelings.*

2. See Seymour Martin Lipset, *The First New Nation: The United States in*

Historical and Comparative Perspective (New York: W. W. Norton, 1979).

3. Jeremy Atack and Fred Bateman, *To Their Own Soil: Agriculture in the Antebellum North* (Ames: Iowa State University Press, 1987), 15; Sellers, *Market Revolution*, 9.

4. The term "subsistence-surplus" is used by Christopher Clark, *The Roots of Rural Capitalism: Western Massachusetts, 1780–1860* (Ithaca: Cornell University Press, 1990), 28. "Safety-first" is used by James C. Scott, *The Moral Economy of the Peasant Rebellion and Subsistence in Southeast Asia* (New Haven: Yale University Press, 1976), 4–5. Christopher Morris, in *Becoming Southern: The Evolution of a Way of Life, Warren County and Vicksburg, Mississippi, 1770–1860* (New York: Oxford University Press, 1995), 40, points out: "Even the simple life demanded that one produce something marketable, if only to purchase the items that kept life simple."

5. For the distinct republicanism of the yeomanry, see Kulikoff, *Agrarian Origins*, 1–59; for the urban version, "artisan republicanism," see Sean Wilentz, *Chants Democratic: New York City and the Rise of the American Working Class, 1788–1850* (New York: Oxford University Press, 1984).

6. The problems of "reducing culture to a mere by-product of economic interest" are considered in Sean Wilentz, "On Class and Politics in Jacksonian America," *Reviews in American History* (December 1982): 50.

7. For the settler's quote, see Tillson, *A Woman's Story*, 82; this same settler is quoted more fully in John Mack Faragher, *Sugar Creek: Life on the Illinois Prairie* (New Haven: Yale University Press, 1986), 98. For an overview of the market revolution concept and its application to the Jacksonian period, see Sellers, *Market Revolution*, 3–33.

8. John Madson, *Where the Sky Began: Land of the Tallgrass Prairie* (Ames: Iowa State University Press, 1995), 109.

9. Praise for Illinois bottomland and its fertility was widespread; see, for examples, Nicholas Biddle Van Zandt, *A Full Description of the Soil, Water, Timber, and Prairies of Each Lot, or Quarter Section of the Military Lands between the Mississippi and Illinois Rivers* (Washington City: P. Force, 1818); Benjamin Harding, *A Tour through the Western Country, 1818–1819* (New London, Conn.: S. Green, 1819). George Ogden, *Letters from the West* (New Bedford: Melcher and Rodgers, 1823), 29, writes, in a statement that can be taken as typical: "The soil in this vicinity [Shawneetown], and throughout the state is equal to any in the world for richness and durability. The prairie, or bottomland, has been cultivated in some places, for upwards of an hundred and twenty years, and still retains its original fecundity without manure" (the word "bottoms" was used more frequently than "bottomland"). For an indication of typical usage, see "Clear Creek Baptist Church Minutes," (Union County), 24–40, in *Saga of Southern Illinois* 20 (1993): 28, 32, 33; Ridgley, *Geography of Illinois*, 33–36; 153; Buck, "Lands Entered in Illinois, 1818," *Illinois in 1818*, between pages 52 and 53; Raymond Hammes, ed., "The Squatters Reports of 1807 and 1813," in *Illinois Libraries* 59 (1977): 319–82. The Report of 1807, which describes more fully the type of land entered, makes clear that almost every 320-acre parcel claimed was located adjacent to a river or a creek. See also Douglas R. McManis, *The Initial Evaluation and Utilization of the Illinois Prairies, 1815–1840* (Chicago: University of Chicago Department of Geography, 1964), esp. 62–88. Although McManis concludes that more of

the early settlers' timbered lands included prairie tracts than previously acknowledged, his detailed analysis of land entries demonstrates that "swamp
and bottomland" and "timber" were consistently entered sooner than—that
is, were preferred to—"prairie."

10. Duden, *Report on a Journey,* 55; Orr's comment is from *Republican,*
July 13, 1824; William Sewall, *Diary of William Sewall, 1797–1846* (Springfield: Hartman Printing, 1930), 129, 133; the visitor is quoted in Buck, *Illinois in 1818,* 128. Some of the local reverence for the American Bottom can
be gleaned from Reynolds, *Pioneer History,* 113: "This is perhaps the largest
and most fertile body of alluvial soil in the United States. Some of it has
been cultivated for more than one hundred and fifty years without improvement of soil, and yet it yields excellent crops."

11. Theodore L. Carlson, *The Illinois Military Tract* (Urbana: University
of Illinois Press, 1951), 28; for Menard's advice, see R. David Edmunds, *The
Shawnee Prophet* (Lincoln: University of Nebraska Press, 1983), 175. The importance of being near water and timber—but especially water—was stressed
by James Hall, who states explicitly that timbered land without water was
less valuable; see *Statistics of the West* (Cincinnati: J. A. James, 1837), 99.

12. For the tax rates, see Hoffmann, *History of Madison County,* 120.
"Brissot," in *Republican,* March 30, 1824.

13. William Oliver, *Eight Months in Illinois* (Newcastle-upon-Tyne:
William Andrew Mitchell, 1843), 39; David E. Schob, *Hired Hands and Plow-
boys: Farm Labor in the Midwest, 1815–1860* (Urbana: University of Illinois
Press, 1975), 263–64; *Republican,* April 13, 1824 ("the most fertile").

14. *Illinois Emigrant* quoted in Buck, *Illinois in 1818,* 151. Morris Birkbeck, *Letters from Illinois* (London: Taylor and Hessey, 1818), 67, estimates
the cost of a cabin built by the owner at fifty dollars. By 1832 an Illinois settler estimated the cost of house and garden at two hundred dollars; see
Schob, *Hired Hands and Plowboys,* 264.

15. Schob, *Hired Hands and Plowboys,* 263, puts the cost of a "second-
hand" farm at "$2.50 to $3.50 per acre"; see also Buck, *Illinois in 1818,*
128–29. Malcolm J. Rohrbough, *The Trans-Appalachian Frontier* (New York:
Oxford University Press, 1978), 168, records the case of three men, working
through fall and winter, who cleared sixteen acres of "small timber" and cut
enough rails to fence it. Carlson, *Illinois Military Tract,* 33, gives from six to
ten acres as an adequate amount of land to clear and survive the next winter;
Nicholas P. Hardeman, *Shucks, Shocks, and Hominy Blocks* (Baton Rouge:
Louisiana State University Press, 1981), 150, cites "about thirteen bushels of
corn per year" average consumption for one person and a hog "in the
South." I have assumed a family farm with ten mouths—human and animal—to feed; thus 130 bushels are subtracted from the total bushel yields.
The number might be lower; see Bettye Hobbs Pruitt, "Self-Sufficiency and
the Agricultural Economy of Eighteenth-Century Massachusetts," *William
and Mary Quarterly,* 3d ser., 41 (July 1984): 333–64 (345), who argues that
"thirty bushels seems a reasonable estimate for minimum family grain re-
quirements." Hardeman, *Shucks, Shocks, and Hominy Blocks,* 64, gives the following average yields: "Nonplowed new ground produced up to 30 bushels
of corn per acre the first year, a worthwhile bargain under the work pressures
of a new home site. Second-year plowing upped the yield to as much as 50

bushels. This was doubled to 104 bushels to the acre by Christopher Leaming of Ohio who resorted to deep plowing." The Massachusetts estimates are from Clark, *Roots of Rural Capitalism,* 74; the Maryland estimates from John Woods, *Two Years' Residence in the Settlement of the English Prairie in the Illinois Country, United States* [1822], vol. 10 of *Early Western Travels, 1748–1846,* ed. Reuben Gold Thwaites (Cleveland: Arthur H. Clark, 1904–1907), 10:188; the corn estimates for the South are from Gates, *The Farmer's Age,* 172.

16. For farm start-up costs, see Birkbeck, *Letters from Illinois,* 46, 67–68; Schob, *Hired Hands and Plowboys,* 263–64; and Allan Bogue, *From Prairie to Corn Belt* (Chicago: University of Chicago Press, 1963), 169. Faragher, *Sugar Creek,* 54, gives $500 as the amount necessary to "buy and fully open a farm," including a payment of $100 for eighty acres at post-1820 prices; see also Francis S. Philbrick, quoted in Rohrbough, *Trans-Appalachian Frontier,* 176. Bogue, *From Prairie to Corn Belt,* 169, puts the 1830s cost of an eighty-acre farm of government land ($100), basic farm tools, oxen and yoke, and a few cows at between $500 and $550. The "costs of flatboat trade" are discussed in Harry N. Scheiber, "The Ohio-Mississippi Flatboat Trade: Some Reconsiderations," in *The Frontier in American Development,* ed. David M. Ellis (Ithaca: Cornell University Press, 1969), 277–87. The *Sun* is quoted in Cayton, *Frontier Indiana,* 277.

17. "A Laborer" addresses those who had but "fifty or a hundred bushels of grain to sell," in *Edwardsville Spectator,* July 27, 1824. See the analysis of the added expenses and difficulties of early prairie farming, along with the differing grades of soils, in Carlson, *Illinois Military Tract,* 29–35.

18. Siyoung Park, "Land Speculation in Western Illinois: Pike County, Illinois, 1821–1835," *Journal of the Illinois State Historical Society* 77 (1984): 119; for the Madison County farmer's comment, see *Edwardsville Spectator,* August 30, 1823; on Parker, see the *Illinois Public Domain Land Tract Sales.*

19. Faragher, *Sugar Creek,* 181. For percentages on property ownership in the late nineteenth century, see Werner Sombart, *Why Is There No Socialism in the United States?,* trans. Patricia M. Hocking and C. T. Husbands (White Plains, N.Y.: International Arts and Sciences Press, 1976), 8.

20. Duden, *Report on a Journey,* 48, quoted in Buck, *Illinois in 1818,* 135. On the connection between the lack of servants and the demand for slavery, see Tillson, *A Woman's Story,* 138–41; Elias Pym Fordham, *Personal Narrative of Travels in Viginia, Maryland, Pennsylvania, Ohio, Indiana, Kentucky; and of a Residence in the Illinois Territory: 1817–1818,* ed. Frederic Austin Ogg (Cleveland: The Arthur H. Clark Company, 1906), 210.

21. *Edwardsville Spectator,* February 1, 1823; the auditor's argument is repeated forcefully by "Ames," in *Republican,* June 29, 1824; *Illinois Intelligencer,* May 24, 1823; but see the argument of "Ames," in *Republican,* June 29, 1824, where "the rent paid by the lessees of the Ohio Saline" is discussed. This estimated cost of a slave is confirmed by the records of the slave sales on June 13, 1821, when the estate of Frenchman Nicholas Jarrot was auctioned at Cahokia. Three men were sold for $550, $533, and $530; two women for $355 and $351; and a family of father, mother, and child sold for $900. See John Francis McDermott, ed., *Old Cahokia* (St. Louis: St. Louis Historical Documents Foundation, 1949), 187.

22. *Edwardsville Spectator,* July 13, 1824.

23. "An Observer," in *Illinois Intelligencer,* October 5, 1822. For a convenient review of the health of the Illinois climate from 1800 to 1820, see the *Illinois Intelligencer,* October 5, 1823.

24. Daniel Brush, *Growing Up in Southern Illinois, 1820–1861* (Chicago: Lakeside Press, 1944), 24; Charles C. Chapman, ed., *History of Pike County, Illinois* (Chicago: Charles C. Chapman, 1880), 202 (for Atlas, Pike County). Carlson, *Illinois Military Tract,* 32, qualifies Chapman's statement: "Although it must be admitted that ague and fever was very real to its victims, yet it appears as if a large number of the deaths attributed to the disease were probably due to other and more fatal complications." The most accurate view was probably supplied by Oliver, *Eight Months in Illinois,* 65: "When properly treated, ague, though often a lingering disease, and one causing much debility, is not fatal; but bilious fever sometimes assumes an aggravated character, when it speedily carries off a number of victims." For Lippincott's wives, see Lippincott, "Early Days in Madison County," *Alton Telegraph,* October 14, 31, 1864.

25. William Orr cited from *Republican,* July 13, 1824.

26. Shoal Creek farmer cited from *Edwardsville Spectator,* August 30, 1823; "One of the People," *Illinois Intelligencer,* July 20, 1822.

27. William Hubbard Brown, "Early History of Illinois," *Fergus Historical Series,* no. 14 (Chicago: Fergus Historical Library, 1881), 91.

28. Thomas Senior Berry, *Western Prices before 1861* (Cambridge, Mass.: Harvard University Press, 1943), 194; Buck, *Illinois in 1818,* 129–30, and the report of "An Old Farmer," *Illinois Intelligencer,* October 5, 1822. See John G. Clark, *The Grain Trade in the Old Northwest* (Westport, Conn.: Greenwood Press, 1980), 45–46, who tells a story of 400 barrels selling for 300 dollars; William Orr, *Republican,* June 11, 1825. For the New Orleans market prices, see the reports published in *Edwardsville Spectator,* February 8, 1823, and February 24, 1824. See also the average annual prices listed in Lewis Cecil Gray, *History of Agriculture in the Southern United States to 1860* (Clifton, N.J.: Augustus M. Kelley, 1973), 2:1039.

29. Prices quoted in Boggess, *Settlement of Illinois,* 164; Buck, *Illinois in 1818,* 130; Brown, "Early History of Illinois," 97.

30. See Joseph J. Persky, *The Burden of Dependency* (Baltimore: Johns Hopkins University Press, 1992), 6–15, 54–60; Buck, *Illinois in 1818,* 130–34, 140–42; Faragher, *Sugar Creek,* 96–103. See also, for example, Levi Coffin, *Reminiscences of Levi Coffin* (Cincinnati: R. Clarkes, 1880).

31. Christopher Morris comes to a similar conclusion in his study of Mississippi farmers during this same period; see *Becoming Southern,* 36.

32. Ford, *History of Illinois,* 24; Reynolds, *Pioneer History,* 357, 334, 376.

33. Woods, *Two Years' Residence,* 10:317, 188.

34. For Reynolds, see Rohrbough, *Trans-Appalachian Frontier,* 178; for the Lippincott venture, see "Early Days in Madison County," *Alton Telegraph,* September 2, 1864. On the many failures in the eastern half of the state, see the letters between Fredrick Rapp, leader of the German community at Harmonie, Indiana, and the merchants of Albion, Mt. Carmel, Carmi, and Shawneetown, in Karl J. A. Arndt, ed. and comp., *A Documentary History of the Indiana Decade of the Harmony Society, 1814–1824* (Indianapolis: Indiana Historical Society, 1975–1978); Thomas Hulme, "Journal of a Tour in the

Western Countries of America, September 30, 1818–August 8, 1819," in *Early Western Travels, 1748–1846*, ed. Reuben Gold Thwaites (Cleveland: Arthur H. Clark, 1904–1907), 10:46.

35. John Reynolds, *My Own Times, embracing also the History of My Life* (Chicago: Fergus Printing, 1879), 42, 52; Oliver, *Eight Months in Illinois*, 33.

36. Lippincott, "Early Days in Madison County," *Alton Telegraph*, October 28, 1864; Stephen Aron, *How the West Was Lost* (Baltimore: Johns Hopkins University Press, 1996), 164; Robert W. Patterson, "Early Society in Southern Illinois," *Fergus Historical Series*, no. 17 (Chicago: Fergus Historical Library, 1880), 106. This view of a small-scale, diversified, semi-subsistence economy is confirmed in the *Diary of William Sewall*. In the three months between April and June 1833, Sewall (148–49) noted that, besides all the while breaking prairie and planting his corn for the market, he had "cut a bee tree, and hauled it home for stock bees"; gone "into the woods to hunt . . . for my wild hogs"; "planted potatoes for early use"; "set out cabbage plants"; gone "to the bottom . . . for the purpose of getting fish"; and "sowed rutabaga turnips."

37. Alexis de Tocqueville, *Democracy in America*, ed. J. P. Mayer, trans. George Lawrence (Garden City, N.Y.: Anchor Books, 1969), 2:535–38, 551–54. The "liberal consensus" school is led by Hartz, *Liberal Tradition*, and Carl N. Degler, *Out of Our Past: The Forces That Shaped Modern America* (New York: Harper and Row, 1959). For those emphasizing the yeomanry, see the studies by Wilentz, Sellers, and Kulikoff cited earlier, and Ronald Schultz, *The Republic of Labor* (New York: Oxford University Press, 1993) and Paul A. Gilje and Howard B. Rock, eds., *Keepers of the Revolution: New Yorkers at Work in the Early Republic*, (Ithaca: Cornell University Press, 1992); Morris, *Becoming Southern*, 39 (quote). Daniel Vickers, "Competency and Competition: Economic Culture in Early America," *William and Mary Quarterly* 3d ser., 46 (1989): 28. Clark, *Roots of Rural Capitalism*, 59–155, presents a view similar to that of Vickers. One of many examples of usage is David Blackwell's defense of the "honest yeomanry of that country [New England]," whereas he writes generally of "Illinois farmers" in the *Illinois Intelligencer*, July 30, 1824.

38. Reynolds, *Pioneer History*, 330–32; Tillson, *A Woman's Story*, 135. See the *Illinois Public Domain Land Tract Sales* for Messinger's sole 1817 purchase in St. Clair County.

39. Richard J. Ellis, *American Political Cultures* (New York: Oxford University Press, 1993), 3–5, 152–54.

40. Steven J. Ross, *Workers on the Edge* (New York: Columbia University Press, 1985), 25–63; Sellers, *Market Revolution*, 17.

41. Van Zandt, *A Full Description*, 87. On Breese's relation to Kane, see Buck, *Illinois in 1818*, 266 n. 283. On Breese's authorship of the "Ames" letters, see the intimations by David Blackwell in the *Illinois Intelligencer*, July 23, 1824, and by letters in the *Edwardsville Spectator*, July 6, May 18, 1824. See also Hoffmann, *History of Madison County*, 120; *Republican*, March 30, 1824. On bottomland frontier generally, Van Zandt, in *A full Description*, 89, wrote: "The country comprised within the limits of Shawneetown and Kaskaskia districts and part of the Edwardsville district, from its being generally level, almost necessarily implies a share of ponds and stagnant water places, and, from the richness of its soil, that of luxuriant vegetation. In

some places, on the first settling, the premature disturbance of this surplus vegetable matter, together with the dampness arising from the ponds, frequently produce bilious fevers, agues, &c. Experience has, however, proven that the industrious hand of the husbandman, in suppressing the growth and removing the rubbish, and the grazing of domestic cattle, soon destroy causes of noxious vapour or miasma."

42. The "Ames" series, originally printed in the *Republican*, was reprinted in the *Illinois Republican* (see July 13, 1824) and was commented on in the *Illinois Intelligencer* (see July 13, 23, 1824).

43. *Republican*, June 22, 1824 (emphasis in the original).

44. See the reports in *Illinois Intelligencer*, February 3, 13, March 5, 1824; *Illinois Gazette*, April 10, 24, 1824; *Republican*, February 24, 1824.

45. "Respublica," in *Illinois Intelligencer*, February 13, 1824; "Vivele Convention," in *Republican*, July 20, 13, 1824.

46. "Ames," in *Republican*, July 6, 1824 (emphasis in the original). Population figures are from Alvord, *Illinois Country*, 415.

47. "Ames," in *Republican*, July 6, 1824.

48. Blackwell cited from *Illinois Intelligencer*, July 23, 1824. Admiration for the Southwest was prevalent. One example is found in the work of James Hall, the great literary "Spokesman for the West," who, in "Letters from the West," *Port Folio* (1825): 119, wrote gushingly of the "bold and adventurous military people" of Kentucky.

49. "Ames," in *Republican*, July 13, March 30, 1824.

50. For the birthplaces of the members of the Third General Assembly, see the *Edwardsville Spectator*, January 18, 1823. Blackwell's comment is found in *Illinois Intelligencer*, May 21, 1824 (he had become editor with the May 7, 1824, edition).

51. Thomas Jefferson, in his 1784 "Plan" for the territories, used a threshold of twenty thousand; see *The Portable Thomas Jefferson*, 256.

52. See "Appendix," Buck, *Illinois in 1818*, 318.

53. Emil Joseph Verlie, ed., *Illinois Constitutions*, 1:46. See also the discussion of this matter in Ford, *History of Illinois*, 11–12.

54. Edward Coles, in a letter to Nicholas Biddle, dated September 18, 1823, quoted in Alvord, *Coles*, 132 ("Atlantic cities"); "Timour," in *Republican*, April 13, 1824.

55. Blackwell cited from *Illinois Intelligencer*, May 21, 1824. The Military Tract, originally containing two million acres of land east of the Mississippi and west of the Illinois Rivers, eventually amounted to three and a half million acres reserved for veterans. See Carlson, *Illinois Military Tract*, 1–8, and Malcolm J. Rohrbough, *The Land Office Business* (New York and London: Oxford University Press, 1968), 71–88.

56. Blackwell, in *Illinois Intelligencer*, May 21, 1824. The surveyor's report is quoted in Rohrbough, *Land Office Business*, 81. Carlson, *Illinois Military Tract*, 25 n. 5, could come no closer than the general remark that "whatever the actual number was that actually settled on their claims, undoubtedly, it was only a small part of the total number who received bounty lands."

57. Carlson, *Illinois Military Tract*, 10; Ernst, "Travels in Illinois."

58. The term "Yorkers," referring to emigrants of "Dutch, Old British, Old German, Huguenot" extract, is from Ronald P. Formisano, *The Birth of*

Mass Political Parties (Princeton: Princeton University Press, 1971), 166. Charles M. Thompson, in *The Illinois Whigs before 1846* (Urbana: University of Illinois Press, 1915), 17 n. 26, states that "the northern counties did receive a considerable anti-slavery immigration between 1822 and 1824." In Morgan County, of the 130 signers to the "Constitution of the Morganian Society" (a non-conventionist group), 19 were listed in the 1820 census as living in an older Illinois county, 30 were listed in Madison County, 27 had relatives in Madison County, and 54 were new to the state. For a list of the 130, see Charles M. Eames, *Historic Morgan and Classic Jacksonville* (Jacksonville, Ill.: Daily Journal Printing Office, 1885), 12–14.

59. All quotes from William Faux, "Memorable Days in America," in *Early Western Travels 1748–1846,* ed. Rueben Gold Thwaites (Cleveland: Arthur H. Clark Co., 1904–1907), 11:262. The "amateur professors" phrase is from Morris Birkbeck's last annual address as president; his use is a telling sign that the label stung: see *Edwardsville Spectator,* December 28, 1822.

60. Birkbeck as "Jonathan Freeman," *Illinois Gazette,* August 30, 1823; Faux, "Memorable Days in America," 289; Hulme, "Journal of a Tour," 50 (emphasis in the original). On Birkbeck's decision not to seek a fifth term, Coles (cited in Alvord, *Coles,* 373), wrote: "There was another reason which he whispered to me, as having its influence in leading him to decline serving as President, and disheartening him in the cause. It was a conviction that the Country was not ripe for it, as was evinced in the want of zeal displayed in its support."

61. *Edwardsville Spectator,* January 6, 1824. Coles became president, and Churchill, already secretary of the Madison County Agricultural Society, became state corresponding secretary; the phrase "Yankee All-Town" was noted by George Churchill. See his "Annotations" on Lippincott's "Early Days in Madison County," in *Alton Telegraph,* March 24, 1865. See Coles's letter to Henry S. Dodge, dated February 22, 1821, in Alvord, *Coles,* 255–59; for the results of Coles's experiment, see Lewis C. Beck, *A Gazetteer of the States of Illinois and Missouri* (New York: Arno Press, 1975), 76–77.

62. "Jonathan Freeman" (Morris Birkbeck) cited from *Illinois Gazette,* August 30, 1823; Timour from *Republican,* April 20, 1824. The *Gazette* was the original publication in which the Jonathan Freeman letters and their respondent "John Rifle" appeared. It is the only source for the complete series; reprints in Flower, *History of the English Settlement,* and the *Edwardsville Spectator* are both incomplete.

63. Birkbeck founded the town of Wanborough. For the Federalist label, see *Edwardsville Spectator,* April 20, 1824; for Flower's quotation, see Mary Ann Salter, "George Flower Comes to the Illinois Country: A New Look at Motivations," *Journal of the Illinois State Historical Society* 69 (1976): 215–16; for "John Rifle," see *Illinois Gazette,* June 21, 1823.

64. Bogue, *From Prairie to Corn Belt,* 237; Alvord, *Coles,* 255. See also Andrew R. L. Cayton and Peter S. Onuf, *The Midwest and the Nation* (Bloomington: Indiana University Press, 1990), 39–42.

65. Richard Bardolph, *Agricultural Literature and the Early Illinois Farmer* (Urbana: University of Illinois Press, 1948), 113 n. 86. On Coles's lands, see Sutton, "Constitutional Crisis in Illinois," 36. The early settlers' fear of fire is related by Carl O. Sauer, *Seeds, Spades, Hearths, and Herds: The Domestication*

234 / NOTES TO PAGES 67-71

of Animals and Foodstuffs (Cambridge, Mass.: MIT Press, 1969), 16.

66. This is precisely what many easterners argued; see Feller, *Public Lands,* 29–35. *Edwardsville Spectator,* April 13, 1824 (poor settlers); "A Mechanic," in *Edwardsville Spectator,* July 13, 1824; Adam A. Leonard, "Personal Politics in Indiana, 1816 to 1840," *Indiana Magazine of History* 19 (1923): 8 (Indiana farmer).

3: NINIAN EDWARDS IN THE DEMOCRATIC REVOLUTION

1. The phrase "Father of Illinois" comes from John Mason Peck, "Funeral Discourse," in Ninian W. Edwards, *History of Illinois from 1778 to 1833; and Life and Times of Ninian Edwards* (Springfield: Illinois State Journal Company, 1870), 249; "one, a few, or many" is from Madison's No. 47, in James Madison, Alexander Hamilton, and John Jay, *The Federalist Papers,* ed. Clinton Rossiter (New York: Mentor, 1961), 301; "Edwards party" is from Ninian Edwards, *The Edwards Papers,* ed. E. B. Washburne (Chicago: Fergus Printing, 1884), 167; Michael Paul Rogin, *The Intellectuals and McCarthy: The Radical Specter* (Cambridge, Mass.: MIT Press, 1967), 6 (plebiscitarian democracy).

2. Amy Bridges, *A City in the Republic: Antebellum New York and the Origin of Machine Politics.* (Ithaca: Cornell University Press, 1987), 3; "Ames," in *Republican,* June 29, 1824.

3. Richard M. Young, letter dated July 8, 1825, in Edwards, *The Edwards Papers,* 237–39 (quotation on 238).

4. "Rattlebrain," in *Republican,* December 14, 1824 (emphasis in the original); Woods, *Two Years' Residence,* 317.

5. For a fictionalized account of the Illinois French custom of charivari, see "The French Village," in James Hall, *Tales of the Border* (Upper Saddle River, N.J.: Literature House, 1970), 124–25. On the role of festivities and public displays in the emergence of political culture, see Waldstreicher, *In the Midst of Perpetual Fêtes.* Anne Norton, in *Alternative Americas: A Reading of Antebellum American Culture* (Chicago: University of Chicago Press, 1986), 61–62, interprets the behavior of mobs in northern cities in a similar vein: "Those who feel themselves alienated from their social order may seek self-expression in idiosyncratic acts of irrationality. When alienation is common, displays of communal madness may evince a common desire for a new order, for new paradigms intelligible in the light of altered experience. Participants in these communal displays of irrationality express their dissatisfaction with the state as representative." See also Aristide Zolberg, "Moments of Madness," *Politics and Society* (winter 1972): 183–207.

6. Thomas Bender, *Community and Social Change in America* (New Brunswick: Rutgers University Press, 1978), 77. For a discussion of the three possible sources of political culture, see Shefter, "Electoral Foundations of the Political Machine."

7. The democratic commitment of the Anti-Federalists is stressed in Joshua Miller, *The Rise and Fall of Democracy in Early America, 1630–1789* (University Park: Pennsylvania State University Press, 1991).

8. Hartz, *Liberal Tradition,* 78. For the total population, as well as the numbers of "free people of color," see Norton, *Illinois Census Returns,* 4, 21, 30, 48, 55, 69, 70, 90, 116, 125, 134, 174, 209, 228, 252, 280, 304, 319, 352.

9. See the report of Cox's remarks in *Edwardsville Spectator,* March 1, 1823. For examples of reprinted editorials, see the "Opinion Abroad" column in *Edwardsville Spectator,* June 14, 1823.

10. Madison, Hamilton, and Jay, *Federalist Papers,* 72. On Adams's support for *"general Principles"* of government, see his discussion with Jefferson, in Cappon, *Adams-Jefferson Letters,* 326–40.

11. "Speeches by Melancton Smith" delivered in June 1788 before the New York Convention, in Herbert J. Storing, ed., *The Anti-Federalist* (Chicago: University of Chicago Press, 1985), 341, 340, 345.

12. Madison, Hamilton, and Jay, *Federalist Papers,* 70–71, 33.

13. "Speeches by Melancton Smith" in Storing, *The Anti-Federalist,* 340–41. This helps explain how the Anti-Federalists could be liberal and yet still egalitarian, contra Diggins, who assumes the two are mutually exclusive. John P. Diggins, *The Lost Soul of American Politics: Virtue, Self-Interest, and the Foundations of Liberalism* (Chicago: University of Chicago Press, 1986), 371 n. 8.

14. Madison, Hamilton, and Jay, *Federalist Papers,* 174; Storing, *The Anti-Federalist,* 343–44.

15. Storing, *The Anti-Federalist,* 341–42.

16. On artisan republicanism, see Wilentz, *Chants Democratic,* 61–103, 342; Storing, *The Anti-Federalist,* 342; On the liberal view of the public sphere, see Jurgen Habermas, *The Structural Transformation of the Public Sphere* (Cambridge, Mass.: MIT Press, 1989), esp. 27–56; also Joshua Miller, "The Ghostly Body Politic: *The Federalist Papers* and Popular Sovereignty," *Political Theory* 16 (February 1988): 99–119.

17. The view of the leading Federalist thinkers as philosophers is most clearly articulated in Meyers, *The Jacksonian Persuasion,* vii–ix, and Ralph Lerner, *The Thinking Revolutionary: Principle and Practice in the New Republic* (Ithaca: Cornell University Press, 1987), 1–38. On Calhoun, see Lacy K. Ford, "Republican Ideology in a Slave Society: The Political Economy of John C. Calhoun," *Journal of Southern History* 54 (1988): 405–24, and Vernon L. Parrington, *Main Currents in American Thought,* vol. 2, *The Romantic Revolution in America, 1800–1860* (New York: Harcourt, Brace and World, 1927), 65–78. Jackson is quoted in Meyers, *The Jacksonian Persuasion,* 19.

18. The most thorough treatment of the triumph of the "Federal Persuasion" and its liberal constitutionalist lineage is still found in Gordon S. Wood, *The Creation of the American Republic, 1776–1787* (Chapel Hill: University of North Carolina Press, 1969); Hamilton is quoted in Gordon S. Wood, "Interests and Disinterestedness in the Making of the Constitution," in *Beyond Confederation: Origins of the Constitution and American National Identity,* ed. Richard Beeman, Stephen Botein, and Edward C. Carter II (Chapel Hill: University of North Carolina Press, 1987), 90. On Hamilton as a romantic, see Forrest McDonald, *Alexander Hamilton: A Biography* (New York: W. W. Norton, 1979), 5–6. As an example of Federalist doubts: Henry Brackenridge, a member of the Pennsylvania gentry, declared in public "the people are fools"; he was never again elected to public office. In the same vein, Hamilton famously called the people a "great beast"; and Gouverneur Morris defended the "Judicial Power, that fortress of the Constitution" against "the wild wind [of] popular will." Brackenridge is quoted in Wood,

"Interests and Disinterestedness," 95; Hamilton is quoted in Parrington, *Main Currents in American Thought,* 1:305; Morris's speeches in the debate over the 1801 Judiciary Act may be found in Walter Murphy, James E. Fleming, and William F. Harris II, *American Constitutional Interpretation* (Mineola, N.Y.: West Publishing, 1986), 209.

19. Madison, Hamilton, and Jay, *Federalist Papers,* 324. The idea that the Federalists attacked democracy in order to save it is from Martin Diamond, "Democracy and the Federalist: A Reconsideration of the Framers' Intent," *American Political Science Review* 53 (1959): 52–68, and Herbert J. Storing, *What the Anti-Federalists Were For* (Chicago: University of Chicago Press, 1981), 39.

20. Madison, letter dated October 24, 1787, in Michael Kammen, ed., *The Origins of the American Constitution: A Documentary History* (New York: Penguin Books, 1986), 73.

21. Gary Wills, *Cincinnatus: George Washington and the Enlightenment* (Garden City, N.Y.: Doubleday, 1984), 99–107; Jefferson to Jay, letter of August 23, 1785, in *The Portable Thomas Jefferson,* 384; Jefferson to van Hogendorp, letter of October 13, 1785, quoted in Leo Marx, *The Machine in the Garden* (Oxford: Oxford University Pres, 1964), 134; Tocqueville, *Democracy in America,* 197. The assumption about class rivalry was widely shared in the South and was used as an argument in favor of slavery: see Hahn, *Roots of Southern Populism,* 86–133; Edmund S. Morgan, *American Slavery, American Freedom: The Ordeal of Colonial Virginia* (New York: W. W. Norton, 1975), 369–87.

22. Sir William Blackstone, *Commentaries on the Laws of England* (Chicago: University of Chicago Press, 1979), 2:2. For copyhold and socage tenures, see 2:78-102.

23. Ibid., 2:98. See also Philip S. Foner, ed., *The Life and Major Writings of Thomas Paine* (Secaucus, N.J.: Citadel Press, 1974), 382–83.

24. This story is told in bits and pieces throughout Blackstone, *Commentaries on the Laws of England ,* esp. 4:404–30, 1:66–67, 177, 227–31, 2:48–53. For a discussion of how American intellectuals viewed the Saxon and Norman past, see Trevor Colbourn, *The Lamp of Experience: Whig History and the Intellectual Origins of the American Revolution* (Chapel Hill: University of North Carolina Press, 1965). Wills, *Cincinnatus,* 115; Moses Hadas and Joe P. Poe, ed. and trans., *Livy: A History of Rome* (New York: Modern Library, 1962), 71–76.

25. William Robert Taylor, *Cavalier and Yankee* (New York: Harper Torchbooks, 1969), 85, devotes close attention to the way Henry's speech is portrayed by Wirt, who characterizes Henry's performance on this occasion as "more than mortal; it was as though the deity spoke through him." For the Puritan social contract, see Perry Miller, *Errand into the Wilderness* (Cambridge, Mass.: Harvard University Press, 1956), 147.

26. Tocqueville, *Democracy in America,* 261; *The Portable Thomas Jefferson,* 217.

27. Wood, "Interests and Disinterestedness," 90–91 (91); Drew R. McCoy, *The Elusive Republic: Political Economy in Jeffersonian America* (Chapel Hill: University of North Carolina Press, 1980), 48. See Miller, "Ghostly Body Politic," 104.

28. See Wills, *Cincinnatus,* 109–48.

29. Ford, *History of Illinois,* 24. Tillson, *A Woman's Story,* 55; Eliza W. Farnham, *Life in Prairie Land* (New York: Harper and Brothers, 1846), 234–44.

30. Ellis, *American Political Cultures,* esp. 153. For this reading of Rousseau's work generally, see Arthur Melzer, *The Natural Goodness of Man* (Chicago: University of Chicago Press, 1990).

31. For an extended argument that American republicans had much in common with modern liberals, see David F. Ericson, *The Shaping of American Liberalism: The Debates over Ratification, Nullification, and Slavery* (Chicago: University of Chicago Press, 1993), 2–26, who argues that, whereas liberals focus on liberty and happiness generally as political ends, republicans stress public liberty and happiness and pluralists stress private liberty and happiness. Ericson's thesis is persuasive for later years, but the continuities between republicans and liberals, especially between lower-class republicans and upper-class liberals, were weaker in the eighteenth century than he allows.

32. Cappon, *Adams-Jefferson Letters,* 202–3, 333–35, 387–94, 397–402, 406–9, 434–39; Robert Michels, *Political Parties: A Sociological Study of the Oligarchical Tendencies of Modern Democracy* (New York: Free Press, 1962), 342; Hartz, *Liberal Tradition,* 80.

33. Edwards's early "stranger" comment and an account of his death can be found in Edwards, *History of Illinois,* 33, 250. Helpful biographical information can be found in Michael J. Bakalis, "Ninian Edwards and Territorial Politics in Illinois, 1775–1818" (Ph.D. diss., Northwestern University, 1966).

34. Pease, *Frontier State,* 93. Charges that Edwards was aristocratic in one form or another were common; see, for example, *Republican,* April 20, June 29, 1824; for Kinney's remarks, see Alvord, *Coles,* 100–101; for "A Republican," see *Republican,* May 18, 1824.

35. Edwards, *The Edwards Papers,* 194, 195, 182, 31. In later years, Hooper Warren (Alvord, *Coles,* 340) noted that, at the time, "there was no party in the state organized on any principle of government, but . . . [rather] two rival interests." For the 1826 election returns, see Pease, *Illinois Election Returns,* 42.

36. On his education, businesses, and politics, see Edwards, *History of Illinois,* 14, 18–19, 26; on the private school in St. Louis, see *The Autobiography of Elihu H. Shepard* (St. Louis: George Knapp, 1869), 102. On his slaves, see *Edwardsville Spectator,* July 4, 1820; see also Norton, *Illinois Census Returns,* 77, 79, 86, where only Robert R. Funkhowser (with twenty-three), Nicholas Casey (with forty), and Timothy Guard (with thirty-four), all of Gallatin County, indicated owning more.

37. For Hamilton's quasi-scientific view of reason, see Madison, Hamilton, and Jay, *Federalist Papers,* 193–94.

38. The popularity of medical metaphors in "conservative thinking" about political leadership is discussed in Michael Lienesch, "Reinterpreting Rebellion: The Influence of Shays' Rebellion on American Political Thought," in *In Debt to Shays,* ed. Robert A. Gross (Charlottesville: University Press of Virginia, 1993), 167. See also Madison's physician-patient imagery in Madison, Hamilton, and Jay, *Federalist Papers,* 234–35.

39. Edwards, *History of Illinois,* 22, 21, 170. Evidence that Edwards sincerely believed in disinterested public service is found in an unaddressed letter, in which Edwards aggressively pursues the questions of "the balance of

obligations" in the faction and the role of "calculating neutrality." These comments are all the more important when it is known that the letter was sent to Nathaniel Pope; see Pease, *Frontier State,* 76.

40. For the contemporary's comment, see the letter of Gorham A. Worth to Thomas Sloo (December 15, 1819) in Cox, "Selections from the Torrence Papers VII," 26 (emphasis in the original); Ford, *History of Illinois,* 43; Edwards, *The Edwards Papers,* 128–29 (Cook letter); Buck, *Illinois in 1818,* 289–92.

41. This phrase comes from the "Governor's Objections," which Edwards delivered to the territorial legislature after it attempted to repeal the 1812 law allowing indentured servants into the state. In his objections, Edwards argues that Congress had no authority over slavery in the territory; see the text of his statement reprinted in *Illinois Intelligencer,* August 30, 1823.

42. These quotations are taken from his 1826 inaugural address, in Edwards, *History of Illinois,* 188, 107, 200.

43. Edwards, *History of Illinois,* 510, 108. On the fainting episode, see Feller, *Public Lands,* 21.

44. The "Petition to Congress by Inhabitants of St. Clair and Randolph Counties," quoted in "The Squatters Reports of 1807 and 1813," ed. Raymond Hammes, *Illinois Libraries* 59 (1977): 321.

45. Quoted by Elihu B. Washburne, *Sketch of Edward Coles* (Chicago: Fergus Printing, 1882), found in Alvord, *Coles,* 62. The exact date of this speech is unknown.

46. Judith N. Shklar, *American Citizenship: The Quest for Inclusion* (Cambridge, Mass.: Harvard University Press, 1991), 3, 46–52.

47. Edwards, *History of Illinois,* 107; Justice William Johnson in *Hawkins v. Barney's Lessee,* quoted in Paul Gates, *Landlords and Tenants on the Prairie Frontier* (Ithaca: Cornell University Press, 1973), 42.

48. Edwards, *History of Illinois,* 104. Pomeroy is quoted in Patricia Nelson Limerick, *The Legacy of Conquest: The Unbroken Past of the American West* (New York: W. W. Norton, 1987), 80.

49. "Clio," in *Illinois Gazette,* November 8, 1823. McCoy, in *The Elusive Republic,* 10, argues that the republicanism of the revolutionary generation was "an ideology in transition," which was attempting "to cling to the traditional republican spirit of classical antiquity without disregarding the new imperatives of a more commercial society." Basic to this synthesis was the combination of two factors: "personal independence," safeguarded by private property; and a political economy devoted exclusively to farming and the manufacturing of household goods. Both tended to retard the inevitable creation of "the familiar eighteenth century pattern of a stark and widening division between the propertied few and the masses of laboring, unpropertied poor" (66). Illinoisans echo both these goals.

50. Ford, *History of Illinois,* 92.

51. Ibid. The "prospectus" for Ford's new paper, the *Independent Political Censor,* appeared in each of the state's other papers; see *Republican Advocate,* January 22, 1984.

52. Ford, *History of Illinois,* 39; Edwards, *The Edwards Papers,* 255.

53. Edwards, *History of Illinois,* 207, 214.

54. Miller, *Errand into the Wilderness,* 15. For Edwards's efforts to woo

the Illinois settlers during the War of 1812, see James Simeone, "Ninian Edwards' Republican Dilemma," *Illinois Historical Journal* 90 (Winter 1997): 245–64; for Edwards's persistence as an Indian fighter, see Joseph B. Herring, "The Vermillion Kickapoos of Illinois: The Prophet Kenekuk's Peaceful Resistance to Indian Removal, 1819–1833," 28–38, in *Selected Papers in Illinois History 1983*, ed. Robert W. McCluggage (Springfield: Illinois State Historical Society, 1985).

55. Edwards, *The Edwards Papers*, 195–96, 199, 255. See also Barnhart, "Southern Influence," 358–74, who divides the Edwards and anti-Edwards groups partially on the basis of appointments, the former receiving an average 4 appointments each, the latter only 2.3.

56. See letters dated January 9, 1808, November 9, 1809, in Edwards, *The Edwards Papers*, 31–41; also Lippincott, "Early Days in Madison County," *Alton Telegraph*, November 25, 1864.

57. Edwards, *History of Illinois*, 300. The speech quotations are taken from an undated speech, but internal evidence suggests it was given sometime in the fall of 1809; ibid., 35, 32.

58. Ibid., 24–25.

59. Randolph Randall, *James Hall: Spokesman of the West* (Columbus: Ohio State University Press, 1964), 109. Also see Paul Angle, "Nathaniel Pope, 1784–1850: A Memoir," *Transactions of the Illinois State Historical Society* 43 (1936): 124–57 (141). Pope used his influence as congressional delegate to get Eddy and the *Illinois Gazette* the federal laws' publishing contract.

60. Edwards, *The Edwards Papers*, 155–59. Edwards's son notes that his father owned "no less than eight or ten stores" as well as "saw and grist mills" (see Edwards, *History of Illinois*, 242). For Pease, see *Frontier State*, 137; and *Illinois Gazette*, March 8, 1823. Cox and Enos were appointed register and receiver respectively in Sangamon County; Lockwood was appointed receiver at Edwardsville; Joseph Street was appointed Indian agent at Prairie Du Chien; see Edwards, *The Edwards Papers*, 282.

61. See the report of the voting in Buck, *Illinois in 1818*, 303–4.

62. Quotations are from Cook's letter of February 2, 1819, in Edwards, *The Edwards Papers*, 149–50.

63. *Journal of the House* (1821): 134.

64. Edwards, *The Edwards Papers*, 199.

65. Ibid.

66. See Washburne's note in Edwards, *The Edwards Papers*, 211; Hooper Warren is still using the name Calhoun on January 20, 1824.

67. On Pope's position, see the article by Hooper Warren in *Genius of Liberty* (La Salle County), December 19, 1840; on Edwards's slaves, see Thompson, *Illinois Whigs*, 16 (quoting *Edwardsville Spectator*, July 4, 1820); on Edwards's private views on slavery, see Alvord, *Coles*, 314, 329.

68. Alvord, *Coles*, 346, 362.

4: THE POLITICS OF SLAVERY IN A NORTHERN STATE

1. "Aristides," in *Illinois Intelligencer*, May 17, 1823; Alvord, *Coles*, 121–22; Birkbeck, *Illinois Gazette*, August 30, 1823; "Aristides," in *Illinois Intelligencer*, May 17, 1823 (emphasis in the original).

2. See the review of these numbers in Boggess, *Settlement of Illinois,* 179–80.

3. For the "scope of conflict" concept, see E. E. Schattschneider, *The Semi-Sovereign People,* 20; for Warren, see Alvord, *Coles,* 313, 339; Tillson, *A Woman's Story,* 49. Eugene H. Berwanger, *The Frontier against Slavery* (Urbana: University of Illinois Press, 1967), 28, argues that "racial antagonism (i.e., anti-black sentiment) was . . . a prime factor in causing the rejection of a constitutional convention in Illinois."

4. See Coles's letter to Nicholas Biddle, April 22, 1823, in Alvord, *Coles,* 120; Coles's failure can be gauged also by the fact that Thomas Sloo, Jr., revealed himself in his letters ("Selections from the Torrence Papers VII," 60, 121) to be against the institution of slavery, yet voted with the majority in the Senate on the Convention Resolution.

5. John Francis Snyder, *Adam W. Snyder and His Period in Illinois History, 1817–1842* (Virginia, Ill.: E. Needham, 1906), 29; for Thomas's experiences in Indiana, see Alvord, *Illinois Country,* 416–27.

6. Lippincott, "Early Days in Madison County," *Alton Telegraph,* November 18, 1864; Henry Barrett Chamberlin, "Elias Kent Kane," *Transactions of the Illinois State Historical Society* (1908): 168; John Francis Snyder, "Forgotten Statesmen of Illinois: Hon. Jesse Burgess Thomas," *Transactions of the Illinois State Historical Society* 9 (1904): 516 (quotation); Reynolds, *Pioneer History,* 402; Rohrbough, *Land Office Business,* 411.

7. Lippincott, "Early Days in Madison County," *Alton Telegraph,* October 16, November 18, 1864 ("pleasant manners"); Reynolds, *Pioneer History,* 401; Flower, *History of the English Settlement,* 275–76 ("public table"); Snyder, *Adam W. Snyder,* 24, 9. For Thomas's early years, see Joseph Edward Suppiger, "Jesse Burgess Thomas: Illinois's Pro-Slavery Advocate" (Ph.D. diss., University of Tennessee, 1970), 1–4. Suppiger reports that Thomas's parents were "simple farmers" (1) and that his birthplace could not be located on account of his family's wandering emigration during the years around his birth.

8. Reynolds, *My Own Times,* 34; Flower, *History of the English Settlement,* 275; Lippincott, "Early Days in Madison County," *Alton Telegraph,* October 7, 1864.

9. This phrase is from a series of testimonials reported by "a Shoal Creek farmer," *Edwardsville Spectator,* August 30, 1823.

10. The phrases come from Lippincott, "Early Days in Madison County," *Alton Telegraph,* October 28, 1864.

11. *Annals of the Congress of the United States, 1789–1824,* 16th Cong., 2nd sess., January 11, 1821, 160.

12. Briggs, "Le Pays des Illinois," 56; Hahn, *Roots of Southern Populism,* 86 ("only true aristocracy").

13. Lippincott, "Early Days in Madison County," *Alton Telegraph,* October 16, 1864; Snyder, *Adam W. Snyder,* 31.

14. Buck, *Illinois in 1818,* 291.

15. Parkinson, "Pioneer Life in Wisconsin," 325; Tillson, *A Woman's Story,* 123. The standard work outlining these cultural differences is Richard Lyle Power, *Planting Corn Belt Culture: The Impress of the Upland Southerners and Yankees in the Old Northwest* (Indianapolis: Indiana Historical Society, 1953). For a more recent effort in the same vein, see Nicole Etcheson, *The*

Emerging Midwest: Upland Southerners and the Political Culture of the Old Northwest, 1787–1861 (Bloomington: Indiana University Press, 1997).

16. Federal land sales recorded in the *Illinois Public Domain Land Tract Sales* at the State Archive (and also accessible on the Internet) can be used to verify the overall difference in wealth between the Edwards and Thomas parties. The biggest disparity is seen in the two head men: in 1817 Edwards purchased over 6,000 acres of federal land in six different counties; in 1814 Thomas purchased 480 acres and in 1817 another 547 in only two counties. Federal purchases made during the same general period by party members also indicate this same disparity: Among the Edwards partisans, Nathaniel Pope bought over 3,000 acres in five different counties between 1816 and 1818; Leonard White bought over 1,600 in three different counties between 1814 and 1819. Thomas partisan Elias Kent Kane bought 156 acres in one county in 1817; Shadrach Bond bought 97 acres in one county in 1815 and 200 acres in two counties in 1817. The only Thomas partisan to match or exceed his Edwards counterpart was John McLean. He bought over 3,500 acres in five different counties between 1817 and 1821, whereas Daniel P. Cook bought over 3,200 acres in three different counties between 1816 and 1818.

17. Edwards, *The Edwards Papers*, 155; Randall, *Spokesman of the West*, 107.

18. Ford, *History of Illinois*, 31; Edwards, *The Edwards Papers*, 155.

19. Hansen's vote was made known because of the suspicions surrounding the Pike County election; Blakeman's vote was known to Madison County voters through a public letter: see *Illinois Republican*, July 21, 1824.

20. *Illinois Intelligencer*, July 6, 1822.

21. Quoted in Buck, *Illinois in 1818*, 225.

22. Snyder, *Adam W. Snyder*, 31. For slaveholdings, see Norton, *Illinois Census Returns;* for Kane's role in the convention, see Buck, *Illinois in 1818*, 265, 266 n. 283; for the factional balance on slavery, see Barnhart, "Southern Influence," 372.

23. Edwards, *History of Illinois*, 255.

24. For the meridian law, see Francis Philbrick, *Laws of Illinois Territory*, (Springfield: Illinois State Historical Library, 1950), 25:297; Edwards, *The Edwards Papers*, 149. The eastern counties of White, Gallatin, and Crawford Counties were strongly pro-Thomas. Before the 1820 election, Cook promised Palestine (Crawford County) a land office, and to his chagrin was unable to deliver it; see Edward H. Piper to Elias Kent Kane, letter dated June 9, 1820, in the Kane collection at the Chicago Historical Society. Crawford remembered giving Kane 59 percent of the vote in 1820 and McLean 60 percent in 1822. On Thomas's promises, see *Edwardsville Spectator*, February 1, 1823. The phrase "little Cook" is quoted by Cook's contemporary, William H. Brown, in "Memoir of the Late Hon. Daniel P. Cook," found in Edwards, *History of Illinois*, 266.

25. On Warren's role in the plot, see Harris, *Negro Servitude in Illinois*, 29.

26. See Snyder, "Forgotten Statesmen of Illinois: Hon. Jesse Burgess Thomas," 320, on his "strenuous efforts" during this campaign.

27. "Timour," in *Republican*, March 9, 1824.

28. They were John McLean, Theophilus W. Smith, Emanuel J. West, Thomas Reynolds, William Kinney, Alexander P. Field, and Joseph Beaird;

see *Illinois Gazette,* March 29, 1823.

29. For a review of the roles of both Thomas and Edwards in the Missouri Compromise and the typical southern response, see Hugh C. Bailey, *John Williams Walker* (University: University of Alabama Press, 1964), 108–23; and Suppiger, "Jesse Burgess Thomas," 115. For the land office post, see Rohrbough, *Land Office Business,* 192.

30. Ronald P. Formisano, *The Transformation of Political Culture* (New York: Oxford University Press, 1983), 15–16, 22, 143–48, 375; Gilje, *The Road to Mobocracy: Popular Disorder in New York City, 1763–1834* (Chapel Hill: University of North Carolina Press, 1987), 227, 205.

31. Max Weber, *Max Weber: Selections in Translation,* ed. W. G. Runciman, trans. Eric Matthews (Cambridge: Cambridge University Press, 1978), 43, 49, 182. On patron-client relations, see John Duncan Powell, "Peasant Society and Clientist Politics," *American Political Science Review* 64 (1970): 412.

32. See Norton, *Illinois Census Returns.* See also chapter 3, note 8.

33. Weber, *Selections,* 182. See also Powell, "Peasant Society and Clientist Politics," 412.

34. Stephen Skowronek, *Building a New American State* (Cambridge: Cambridge University Press, 1982), 167. (For Skowronek the inability of a particular state apparatus to function or to appear legitimate is, in the final analysis, less important in causing its downfall than that the politicians in the existing state see an opportunity to survive and thrive in the political game set up by the new state.) The territorial system was memorably described by Francis Philbrick, *The Laws of Illinois Territory, 1809–1818,* cccxviii, as "completely ungenerous and reactionary."

35. Tocqueville, *Democracy in America,* 198.

36. On Madison's "national commercial policy," see McCoy, *The Elusive Republic,* 126.

37. Cook to Edwards, letters dated June 8, 1816, and October 2, 1817, in Edwards, *The Edwards Papers,* 122–26 and 140, 139–41. On Cook's relations with John Quincy Adams, see Philip Shriver Klein, *Pennsylvania Politics, 1817-1832* (Philadelphia: University of Pennsylvania Press, 1940), 180–82.

38. Cook in *Western Intellligencer,* December 4 and 11, 1817, quoted in Buck, *Illinois in 1818,* 231, 213; Cook to Edwards, September 26, 1820, in Edwards, *The Edwards Papers,* 165. See also James A. Edstrom, "'With . . . candour and good faith': Nathaniel Pope and the Admission Enabling Act of 1818," *Illinois Historical Journal* 88 (1995): 242–44; Edmund J. James, ed., *The Territorial Records of Illinois* (Springfield: Illinois State Historical Library, 1901), 40; Angle, "Nathaniel Pope," 143. For an analysis, in a slightly different context, of factions and the role of marriage as "the final step, the institutionalization of less tangible bonds built up gradually over a period of time," see Paul Boyer and Stephen Nissenbaum, *Salem Possessed* (Cambridge, Mass.: Harvard University Press, 1974), 183.

39. Quoted in Buck, *Illinois in 1818,* 156.

40. Edwards, *The Edwards Papers,* 199; Snyder, "Forgotten Statesmen . . . Thomas," 520 (quotation). The "Publishers' Argument" at the beginning of Reynolds, *The Pioneer History,* quotes an ad placed by Reynolds in the *Illinois Herald,* December 16, 1815, which runs as follows: "To the poor people of Illinois and Missouri Territory: To the above class of mankind whose pecuniary

circumstances will not admit of feeing a lawyer, I tender my professional services as a lawyer, in all courts I may practice in, without fee or reward."

41. See the report of Churchill's petition in the House (December 9, 1823) in *Edwardsville Spectator,* December 21, 1823.

42. For reports on both George Churchill's and Jacob Ogle's efforts, see *Edwardsville Spectator,* May 31, 1823.

43. Lippincott, "Early Days in Madison County," *Alton Telegraph,* March 27, 1865; *Edwardsville Spectator,* March 29, 1823 (Hansen quote). For Hansen's motives, see John Shaw's letter in *Edwardsville Spectator,* December 13, 1823.

44. Cox, "Selections from the Torrence Papers," 56.

45. For Lippincott's election, see *Journal of the Senate* (1823): 3, 5; *Alton Telegraph,* March 24, 1865 (quotation).

46. Norton, *Illinois Census Returns,* 252; Allen, "Slavery and Negro Servitude." Allen's survey of the records indicates that many slaves were never registered under this system, and of those who were, many were often indentured over the thirty-five-year and thirty-two-year limits, sometimes for even as many as ninety-nine years.

47. "Honestus," in *Republican,* June 22, 1824.

48. Ford, *History of Illinois,* 91.

49. William Hubbard Brown, "An Historical Sketch of the Early Movement in Illinois for the Legalization of Slavery," Fergus Historical Series, no. 4 (Chicago: Fergus Historical Library, 1876), 16–17; Flower, *History of the English Settlement,* 197–98, 206.

50. "Americanus," in *Illinois Intelligencer,* January 16, 1824; Pease, *Frontier State,* 73. See also Brown, "An Historical Sketch," 16n.

51. "Americanus," in *Illinois Intelligencer,* January 16, 1824.

52. William H. Brown, who was present during the session as a reporter, calls West a "prudent general," in "An Historical Sketch," 24; the phrase politics "out of doors" is from Henry Eddy in the *Illinois Gazette,* March 8, 1823.

53. J. Mills Thornton, *Politics and Power in a Slave State* (Baton Rouge: Louisiana State University Press, 1978), xvi; "A Lobby Member" in *Illinois Intelligencer,* March 15, 1823.

54. The information on Hansen's career objectives comes from John Shaw's testimonial in *Edwardsville Spectator,* December 13, 1823, which, by itself, would not constitute reliable evidence, but it is substantially corroborated earlier by Hooper Warren in his editorial of December 7, 1822.

55. *Republican,* June 1, 1824.

56. "Ames" in *Republican,* June 22, 1824 (emphasis in the original); *Journal of the House* (1821): 266 (emphasis in the original; Blackwell's speech is found on 261–71); "Immaculate Fourteen" comes from a Henry Eddy editorial, *Republican,* July 20, 1824. On the connection between the state bank and the convention, see the series of articles written by "Junius" to the *Edwardsville Spectator,* esp. October 11, November 1, 1823, and by Jonathan Freeman, November 22, 1823.

57. All of John Shaw's quotations are from his testimonial, in *Edwardsville Spectator,* December 13, 1823; Park, "Land Speculation," 119.

58. *Illinois Intelligencer,* February 1, 1823. Daniel Parker thought the fire suspicious and in the Senate on January 31 he moved for an investigation.

59. *Illinois Intelligencer,* May 14, 1824; *Edwardsville Spectator,* July 13, 1824.

60. The phrase "break up" is a modification of Hooper Warren's editorial, February 22, 1823.

61. William Henry Perrin, ed., *History of Alexander, Union, and Pulaski Counties, Illinois* (Chicago: O.L. Baskin, 1883), 275.

62. All quotations in this and the following two paragraphs are from *Edwardsville Spectator,* February 8, 1823.

63. *Illinois Intelligencer,* February 8, 1823.

64. The text of article 7, section 1, of the constitution reads: "Whenever two thirds of the general assembly shall think it necessary to alter or amend this constitution, they shall recommend to the electors, at the next election of members of the general assembly, to vote for or against a convention"; see Verlie, ed., *Illinois Constitutions,* 39.

65. All quotations by Kinkade are from *Edwardsville Spectator,* February 22, 1823.

66. See the remarks of Coles under the pseudonym "One of Many," in *Illinois Intelligencer,* May 14, 1824.

67. See the remarks of "A Lobby Member" who witnessed the events, in *Edwardsville Spectator,* April 19, 1823.

68. See the letter of an eyewitness in *Edwardsville Spectator,* February 15, 1823; "A Lobby Member," in *Edwardsville Spectator,* April 19, 1823.

69. *Edwardsville Spectator,* February 15, 1823; "A Lobby Member," in *Edwardsville Spectator,* April 19, 1823.

70. Ford was called a "zealot" by Churchill in his "Annotations," *Alton Telegraph,* August 11, 1865; see the reconstruction of the debate offered in the *Edwardsville Spectator,* February 22, 1823. On the Shaw-Hansen disputed election, see Pease, *Illinois Election Returns,* 206 n. 1.

71. *Edwardsville Spectator,* February 22, 1823. The December 22, 1822, edition records the vote: for Hansen were Alexander of Alexander, Alexander of Monroe, Alexander of Pope, Blakeman, Campbell, Carnes, Casey, Churchill, Daimwood, Davenport, Dorris, Emmett, Ford, Logan, McFerron, McGahey, Pell, Pugh, West, Will; against Hansen were Berry, Field, Lowrey, Mather, McFatridge, McIntosh, Moore, Ogle, Rattan, Simms, Trotier, Turney, Whitesides, Widen. See Alexander's letter reproduced in *Edwardsville Spectator,* March 29, 1823.

72. *Illinois Intelligencer,* February 15, 1823.

73. The connection between Hansen's acceptance in the House and Thomas's election has been disputed by E. B. Washburne. See also Wayne E. Stevens, "The Shaw-Hansen Election Contest," *Journal of the Illinois State Historical Society* 7 (1914–1915): 389–95. But Jess M. Thompson writes: "One or two authorities are inclined to discount reports current at the time of a bargain negotiated between Hansen and the pro-slavery majority [the Thomas group]. However, the writings of Charles J. Shellon, one-time editor of the *Springfield Journal,* in his early Pittsfield paper, 'The Radical,' containing intimate interviews with Pike County leaders of the period in question, seem to establish that there not only was such a bargain but that its terms were known and approved by Hansen's constituency in the Military Tract." See *Pike County Republican,* October 16, 1935. For details on these matters and

on the early history of Pike County, the series of articles written by Jess M. Thompson under the heading "Pike's County Seat War," in *Pike County Republican*, October 2, 1935–January 13, 1937, is invaluable.

74. *Illinois Gazette,* March 8, 1823.

75. On the disputed election of 1822, Jess M. Thompson writes: "The law required that written notice be given within 20 days of the close of the election and that taking of depositions be within 40 days. Accordingly, on August 19, 14 days after the election, Shaw gave notice of the contest to Hansen, naming the points of contest and setting August 29 as the day for taking depositions. Shaw alleged in his contest not only that the election of August 5 was illegal but also charged [that] the friends of Hansen had resorted to intimidation and bribery. . . . On August 29, depositions were taken . . . but . . . at Hansen's request Shaw permitted a postponement. . . . The House committee, before which the contest was lodged, doubtless was much disturbed by the array of evidence in behalf of Shaw . . . held that the notice of contest given by Shaw on August 19 had been superseded by a second notice given on September 4, which invalidated the first notice, and the second notice having been given after the twenty day limitation, was therefore illegal, leaving no legal grounds for a contest." See *Pike County Republican,* October 16, 1935; Field is quoted in *Edwardsville Spectator,* February 22, 1823.

76. *Edwardsville Spectator,* February 22, 1823.

77. Ibid., March 8, September 27, April 12, 1823.

78. See the extract of Churchill's speech printed in *Edwardsville Spectator,* January 4, 1823.

5: ORGANIZING THE PEOPLE

1. The number forty-five was arrived at by counting every meeting, conventionist and non-conventionist, reported in the four newspapers for which records remain: the *Edwardsville Spectator,* the *Illinois Gazette,* the *Illinois Intelligencer,* and the *Republican Advocate* (later the *Republican*). Smith and Kinney's paper, the *Illinois Republican,* has been only sporadically preserved. It is probable that, if all the conventionist meetings—often unreported in the *Spectator* and the *Intelligencer* (after May 7, 1824, when Blackwell took over)—were also counted, the number would be in the sixties.

2. See Emil Pocock, "Popular Roots of Jacksonian Democracy: The Case of Dayton, Ohio, 1815–1830," *Journal of the Early Republic* 9 (winter 1989): 489.

3. There are three crucial variables in determining turnout. The first is the population. The U.S. Census of 1820 listed the population of Illinois at 57,869 inhabitants; the state census of June 1818 listed 34,610; the state census of August 1818 (made under the pressure of reaching the 40,000 threshold for admittance into the Union) counted 40,258. Various figures have been given for the state's population in 1823. William Berry said it was "not exceeding 60,000," *Illinois Intelligencer,* January 18, 1823; Morris Birkbeck refers to "some 60,000 people" in his seventh Jonathan Freeman letter, *Illinois Gazette,* August 30, 1823; Dr. Preston Davis, in a Fourth of July oration put the number at 70,000, *Illinois Gazette,* July 26, 1823. Boggess, *Settlement of Illinois,* 188, calculates an increase of 17,655 between 1820 and

1825, giving approximately 70,000 inhabitants in 1824; the *Edwardsville Spectator,* January 4, 1826, puts the 1825 population at 71,309. Let us use 60,000 and 70,000 as our two options for the population of Illinois in 1824. The second crucial variable is eligible voters. This we know definitely since the state census of 1820 lists by county both total population and white males over twenty-one (that is, eligible voters). With total population and the number of eligible voters, we can figure the third crucial variable: the ratio of eligible voters to total population. The average ratio in Illinois in 1820 was 4.52, with no county ratio under 3.8 or over 5.6. With this figure of 4.52 applied to our two total population figures of 60,000 and 70,000, we arrive at 13,274 or 15,486 eligible voters in Illinois in 1824. Since 11,612 votes were cast in the convention contest (11,878 in the Cook-Bond race for U.S. representative), this gives either an 87 percent or a 75 percent turnout. Assuming a total population of 60,000 for the 1822 governor's race, the 8,606 votes cast give a 65 percent turnout. In 1820, with total population and eligible voters not in doubt, the highest turnout in each county (usually for the U.S. representative race between Cook and Mclean) averaged 70 percent, with a range of between 50 percent and 86 percent.

4. Ford, *History of Illinois,* 32–33; Horatio Newhall to J. Newhall, May 11, 1822, in Horatio Newhall Papers, Illinois State Historical Library, Springfield; Nathaniel Buckmaster to John Buckmaster, April 14, 1822, Buckmaster-Curran Family Papers, Illinois State Historical Library, Springfield.

5. Shklar, *American Citizenship,* 17, 1. The debate over political participation in the Jacksonian era has been recently invigorated by Glenn C. Altschuler and Stuart M. Blumin, "Limits of Political Engagement in Antebellum America: A New Look at the Gold Age of Participatory Democracy," *Journal of American History* (December 1997): 855–85, with attendant commentary.

6. Eddy is cited from Ward, *Andrew Jackson,* 134; Shefter, "Electoral Foundations of the Political Machine," 297; Formisano, *Mass Political Parties,* 59.

7. Karl Marx, *The Eighteenth Brumaire of Louis Bonaparte* (1852; reprint, New York: International Publishers, 1963), 45, 66. For a discussion of the role of the state as an independent variable in the early national period, see Richard R. John, "Government Institutions as Agents of Change: Rethinking American Political Development in the Early Republic, 1787–1835," in *Studies in American Political Development,* ed. Karen Orren and Stephen Skowronek (New Haven: Yale University Press), vol. 11, no. 2 (1997), 347–80.

8. George William Dowrie, *The Development of Banking in Illinois* (Urbana: University of Illinois Press, 1913), 24–25; on the evolution of hard money sentiments among the Democrats in this period and after, see William Gerald Shade, *Banks or No Banks: The Money Issue in Western Politics, 1832–1865* (Detroit: Wayne State University Press, 1972), 20–39.

9. Angle, "Nathaniel Pope," 158.

10. Reynolds, *My Own Times,* 153.

11. John Mason Peck cited in Peck, *Memoirs,* 188.

12. The murders are either inferred from Peck's statement or are listed in the newspapers: *Illinois Intelligencer,* July 6, November 1, 1823, May 7, 1824; *Illinois Gazette,* October 11, November 8, 1823, June 12, 1824; *Ed-*

wardsville Spectator, February 17, 1824; James E. Davis, *Frontier Illinois* (Bloomington: Indiana University Press, 1998), 7. On the murder of Smith and his first toast, see Warren, in *Genius of Liberty,* December 10, 1840, and *Republican,* February 1, 1825. On the "Rarified" and "Tammany" Smiths, see George Churchill, "Annotations," *Alton Telegraph,* March 31, 1865. For Smith's second toast, see *Edwardsville Spectator,* July 19, 1823. Flower, *History of the English Settlement,* 277–78.

13. Lippincott, "Early Days in Madison County," *Alton Telegraph,* March 31, 1865; "Citizen of Madison County," in *Edwardsville Spectator,* October 13, 1823. For the Thomas break-in, see the letters of May 8, 10, 26, 27, 1823, in the Jesse B. Thomas Papers, Illinois State Historical Library, Springfield.

14. For the first conventionist meeting, see *Illinois Intelligencer,* March 8, 1823; For the dinners and Coles's toast, see *Edwardsville Spectator,* March 8, 1823; Kinney's toast was given the next night, at a dinner presided over by Dr. John Todd: see ibid.

15. For Botsford's toast and Kelly's election, see *Illinois Intelligencer,* March 29, July 12, 1823; For Botsford's acquittal, see *Illinois Gazette,* August 30, 1823. For the eyewitness account, see Gershom Flagg to Artemas Flagg, letter dated July 20, 1823, in Barbara Lawrence and Nedra Banz, eds., *The Flagg Correspondence: Selected Letters, 1816–1854* (Carbondale and Edwardsville: Southern Illinois University Press, 1986), 33.

16. For the Bond County meetings, see *Edwardsville Spectator,* March 15, 1823; for the St. Clair County meetings, see *Edwardsville Spectator,* March 1 and 22, 1823.

17. "A Voter," *Illinois Intelligencer,* November 8, 1823. There had been the original convention meetings at the capital on February 15 and 18, 1823. After this there had been three "convention dinners" mentioned in the newspapers: at Edwardsville on March 6, at Vandalia on March 24, and at Lebanon (St. Clair County) on April 3. There is then no evidence of another conventionist gathering until the White County meeting on November 8, 1823. The first non-conventionist society was formed under the leadership of John Messinger, David Blackwell, and Rev. Samuel Mitchell at Belleville on March 22, 1823; see *Edwardsville Spectator,* April 12, 1823.

18. *Republican Advocate,* January 8, 1824.

19. Alvord, *Coles,* 133.

20. See the remarks of "A Voter," *Illinois Intelligencer,* February 20, 1824.

21. For the eyewitness account, see *Edwardsville Spectator,* December 13, 1823; for Berry's and Coates's toasts, see *Illinois Intelligencer,* March 29, 1823; for Whiteside's toast, see *Edwardsville Spectator,* March 8, 1823.

22. Coles to Birkbeck, letter dated January 29, 1824, in Alvord, *Coles,* 149.

23. *Republican,* June 8, 1824.

24. *Edwardsville Spectator,* February 17, 1824.

25. *Republican Advocate,* January 8, 1824 (Central Committee); *Edwardsville Spectator,* August 30, 1823 ("nocturnal procession"). The other meetings, at Greene County and Bond County, were also non-conventionist; for the Vandalia meetings, see *Illinois Intelligencer,* March 8, 1823.

26. *Edwardsville Spectator,* April 19, 1823; *Illinois Intelligencer,* February 13, 1824.

27. See the series of editorials, *Edwardsville Spectator,* from December 7, 1822, to February 15, 1823.

28. Alvord, *Coles,* 344. Warren compared Coles to a local black slave who was often heard on the streets of Edwardsville calling "Coming, Madam" (ibid., 347). Warren's allusion hinged on the following fact, recalled by Gillespie, in "Recollections of Early Illinois," 13: "There was this peculiarity about Gov. Coles; although he was a highly educated and accomplished gentleman, yet his talk on common subjects, when he was not on his guard, was exactly that of an old Virginia negro. Such was the force of early habits and association." These Edwardsville events were at times alluded to in editorials in the *Republican* and the *Illinois Intelligencer.*

29. *Edwardsville Spectator,* December 14, 1822.

30. The original of Smith's article has not been preserved. It was reprinted in *Illinois Intelligencer,* June 28, 1823.

31. Ibid.

32. *Edwardsville Spectator,* June 7, 1823.

33. "L," in *Edwardsville Spectator,* July 6, 1824; Reynolds to Edwards, letter dated February 6, 1823, in the Ninian Edwards Collection at the Chicago Historical Society; "L," in *Edwardsville Spectator,* July 6, 1824.

34. "Mrs. Office-hunter," in *Republican,* March 16, 1824 (emphasis in the original); "Julius," in *Edwardsville Spectator,* April 13, 1824. For Churchill, see *Edwardsville Spectator,* January 4, 1823.

35. *Edwardsville Spectator,* October 11, 1823, and February 17, 1824 ("grogshops" and "Central Committee's organization"); "A voter," *Illinois Intelligencer,* February 20, 1824; "A Conventionist," originally published in *Illinois Republican,* reprinted in *Illinois Intelligencer,* Feb. 27, 1824.

36. Eddy cited from *Illinois Gazette,* March 8, 1823; for non-conventionists and "convention fever," see "Medicus," in *Edwardsville Spectator,* July 27, 1824, and Warren's obituary for Mr. "Gothewhole Convention," August 10, 1824. See the reprint of the pamphlet under the title Morris Birkbeck, "An Appeal on the Question of a Convention," in *Transactions of the Illinois State Historical Society* 10 (1905): 147–60 (quote on 149).

37. Brown, "Early History of Illinois," 99–100.

38. *Republican,* April 13, 1824; see Thomas Perkins Abernathy, *The Formative Period in Alabama, 1815–1828* (University: University of Alabama Press, 1965), 34–35; Harding, *Tour through the Western Country,* 11.

39. See the unsigned letter in *Illinois Intelligencer,* January 18, 1823; Aristides, in *Edwardsville Spectator,* May 18, 1823. There were many attempts to identify "slavery and aristocracy" in the *Spectator;* see, for instance, March 2, 1824, September 27, 1823, and the discussion of the "slave gentry," November 22, 1823 and July 27, 1824.

40. Birkbeck writing as Jonathan Freeman, *Illinois Gazette,* October 11, 1823; the "principles" comment is from an unsigned letter in the *Illinois Intelligencer,* January 18, 1823; "Plain Truth," *Edwardsville Spectator,* April 20, 1824 (emphasis in the original).

41. Patterson, "Early Society in Southern Illinois," 113; *Republican,* March 9, 1824. The Madison County meeting was reported in *Edwardsville Spectator,* February 24, 1824, but the president is not listed. Sawyer's nativity is noted in John Shaw, "Personal Narrative," *Collections of the State Historical*

Society of Wisconsin (Madison: Wisconsin Historical Collections, 1855), 223.

42. Orr cited from *Republican Advocate,* March 2, 1824; Berry cited from *Illinois Intelligencer,* March 15, 1823.

43. For the uncovering of forgeries, see *Edwardsville Spectator,* for the month of April 1823.

44. Berry, in *Illinois Intelligencer,* February 22, 1823. See the comments made by "Impartial Justice," in *Illinois Republican,* June 22, 1824, quoted by "H," in *Edwardsville Spectator,* July 13, 1824; also "A Plain Citizen," in *Illinois Intelligencer,* March 15, 1823. Churchill's 1820 campaign speech is printed in Hoffmann, *History of Madison County,* 135.

45. See Churchill to Mr. Swift Eldred, letter dated September 9, 1818, printed in *Journal of the Illinois State Historical Society* 11 (1918): 65; see William Orr in *Republican,* July 28, 1824 (emphasis in the original); and "Convention," in *Illinois Intelligencer,* May 17, 1823. Churchill's effigy was burned once with Risdon Moore's and once with Nicholas Hansen's. The first instance is asserted in Hoffmann, *History of Madison County,* 141, and confirmed by Judge Joseph Gillespie, who related an eyewitness account in Washburne, *Sketch of Edward Coles* (see Alvord, *Coles,* 88); the second instance is simply asserted in Hoffmann, *History of Madison County,* 439. For the suggestion that Coates was responsible, see *Edwardsville Spectator,* June 28, 1823, where it is stated that the man who sought to get the "Madison county" representative to obey his "instructions," when he failed in this venture, "burnt the representative in effigy!" For the toast, see *Illinois Intelligencer,* March 29, 1823.

46. Forquer's comments were published anonymously in the *Edwardsville Spectator,* May 31, 1823.

47. For Alexander's territorial appointments, see James, *Territorial Records of Illinois;* all quotations from Alexander's speech, in this and the following paragraphs, are from *Republican,* April 20, 1824.

48. For the West brothers, see *Journal of the Illinois State Historical Society* 22 (1929): 217–19; for the Coles story, see chapter 1, note 5. Coles's own testimony indicates that he did not free all his slaves. Two old women remained in Virginia and a family of six remained with him as servants until 1825. At least ten other slaves were "officially" liberated in a public ceremony in Edwardsville in 1819. But his dramatic story of liberating his slaves as they floated down the Ohio River has remained foremost in the public memory. Two prominent reviews of Coles's actions fail to mention the details of his emancipations; see Finkelman, *Slavery and the Founders,* 165–67, and Drew McCoy, *The Last of the Fathers: James Madison and the Republican Legacy* (Cambridge: Cambridge University Press, 1989), 313–15. For Hooper Warren's interpretation, see Alvord, *Coles,* 312–13 (363).

49. Piggott, cited in *Edwardsville Spectator,* September 20, 1823.

50. Orr, in *Republican Advocate,* January 1, 1824.

51. "Spartacus," in *Illinois Intelligencer,* June 25, 1824.

52. "A Laborer," in *Edwardsville Spectator,* July 27, 1824; "Jonathan Freeman" in *Illinois Gazette,* July 26, 1823.

53. Smith and Kinney's *Illinois Republican* was particularly fond of inserting insinuating statements, unsigned and unannounced, into its columns. This culminated on July 21, 1824, with a bald statement: "Those

who want the state filled up with free negroes and to be ruled by them will vote against a convention."

54. "Vindex," in *Republican,* June 15, 1824; one "legal talent" was David Blackwell: see *Edwardsville Spectator,* April 12, 1823. Harris, *Negro Servitude in Illinois,* 58–59, notes that "the practice of assisting fugitive slaves was begun as early as 1818."

55. "Brutus," in *Illinois Intelligencer,* July 5, 1823; "A Voter," in *Edwardsville Spectator,* February 24, 1824; "A Hater of Slavery and Man-Stealing," in *Illinois Intelligencer,* January 9, 1824. Hall later led a convention meeting in Pope County by announcing "the Constitution of this state . . . is materially defective"; the meeting and resolutions are reported in *Illinois Gazette,* April 24, 1824.

56. Jonathan Freeman, in *Illinois Gazette,* June 14, October 11, 1823; Flower, *History of the English Settlement,* 260; Eddy's editorial is in *Illinois Gazette,* June 14, 1823; for the non-conventionist's letter, see *Illinois Intelligencer,* January 18, 1823; Leonard L. Richards, *Gentlemen of Property and Standing* (Oxford: Oxford University Press, 1970), 35 n. 27, found many incidents of violence against blacks and abolitionists in Cincinnati during the 1820s and 1830s. He notes that this behavior was traditionally ascribed to that town's southern persuasion. He found, however, that "less than 15% of the city's adult population were southern-born." He also found that antiblack prejudice excited violence throughout the country, including in places such as Canterbury, Connecticut, and Utica, New York; see Richards, *Gentlemen of Property and Standing,* esp. 39; *Illinois Gazette,* July 5, January 18, 1823.

57. Election results are taken from Pease, *Illinois Election Returns,* 27–29, 189–217.

58. "Americanus," in *Illinois Intelligencer,* January 16, 1824. For a discussion of "localism" as a motive for backcountry political movements in "relatively uncommercialized local economies," see Albert H. Tillson, Jr., "The Localist Roots of Backcountry Loyalism: An Examination of Popular Political Culture in Virginia's New River Valley," *Journal of Southern History* 54 (1988): 387.

59. For the justice of the peace information, see the story recounted by Jess M. Thompson from the testimony of early Morgan County settler Gen. Murray McConnell, in "Pike County History," *Pike County Republican,* January 13, 1937; the non-convetionist meeting is quoted in *Edwardsville Spectator,* March 16, 1824; for the Grammer quote, see *History of Alexander, Union, and Pulaski,* 272. The idea that the U.S. Constitution made a general pronouncement about equality seems to have been fairly common among the younger generation. James Lemen, Jr., for example, states that "the constitution of the United States . . . declares that all men are born equally free and independent"; see "A Circular Address," in William Warren Sweet, ed., *Religion on the American Frontier: The Baptists, 1783–1830* (New York: Henry Holt, 1931), 581.

60. *Edwardsville Spectator,* July 12, 1823. This same celebration is quoted by Onuf, *Statehood and Union,* 130, as evidence of the local support for the Ordinance of 1787. This was true for the non-conventionists there gathered. The point here is that even these men tended to view their political situation through a local lens. Further, it is not irrelevant to point out that Onuf takes his quotations from the toasts *prepared* for the occasion—a Fourth of July cel-

ebration but also a public dinner given in Coles and Cook's honor; my quotations are from those given on the spot by named local participants.

61. Hall's life in Illinois is well documented in Randall, *Spokeman of the West*, 81–98; for "The Pioneer," see *Tales of the Border* (1835; reprint, Upper Saddle River, N.J.: Literature House, 1970), 32-101.

62. "The Pioneer," 87, 88, 82.

63. Ibid., 84.

64. Cook, in *Edwardsville Spectator*, July 7, 1824; Reynolds, *Pioneer History*, 376, 333–35. Hoffmann, *History of Madison County*, 78, noted: "Gov. Reynolds, in his youth, was one of the best in a foot-race, and won many wagers in Randolph County, previous to his removal of the family to Madison." Success in games may have been another reason why Reynolds appreciated individual experience and accomplishment.

65. Reynolds, *My Own Times*, 74; Birkbeck is quoted from Robert C. Bray, *Rediscoveries: Literature and Place in Illinois* (Urbana: University of Illinois Press, 1982), 19; Hinde, from *Methodist Magazine* 11 (1828): 154–58, quoted in Boggess, *Settlement of Illinois*, 201; Lippincott, "Early Days in Madison County," *Alton Telegraph*, November 16, 1864. Bray, *Rediscoveries*, 34, sees a pattern of "sloughing off old-world ways and starting over with nature" in the early literature of the state. This, he argues, represents the beginnings of "a localized process of myth-making, the romantic recollection of an agricultural empire in its infancy, charged with heroism on the part of pioneers who are yet 'just folk.'"

66. See Reynolds, *Pioneer History*, esp. 316–19.

67. Bond's 1820 address, delivered in writing, is found in *Journal of the House* (1821): 15–18; his 1822 farewell address is found in *Journal of the House* (1823): 11–15.

68. Coles's remarks are found in his "To the People of Illinois," *Edwardsville Spectator*, July 6, 1824; "Aristides" in *Edwardsville Spectator*, May 3, 1823; *Republican*, July 20, 1824 (emphasis in the original).

69. Reynolds, *Pioneer History*, 324; Peck, *Memoirs*, 151; for Alexander's remarks, see *Republican*, April 20, 1824.

70. "Rattlebrain" in *Republican*, December 14, 1824; on the "quest for the primitive," see, for example, Richard T. Hughes, ed., *The American Quest for a Primitive Church* (Urbana: University of Illinois Press, 1988); for the anti-missionaries as anti-easterners, see chapter 6.

71. For an analysis of American political culture as divided between two distinct conceptions of the human personality, see J. David Greenstone, "Political Culture and American Political Development: Liberty, Union, and the Liberal Bipolarity," in Orren and Skowronek, *Studies in American Political Development* 1 (1986): 21, 28. The argument about egalitarianism and fatalism is made explicitly in Ellis, *American Political Cultures*, 3–5, 120–39; for liberalism, see Sheldon Wolin, *Politics and Vision: Community and Innovation in Western Political Thought* (Boston: Little, Brown, 1960), 286–351. For the idea as applied to the Jacksonian era, see Michael Paul Rogin, *Fathers and Sons: Andrew Jackson and the Subjugation of the American Indian* (New York: Alfred A. Knopf, 1975), 75–110.

72. Cited by "Americanus" in *Illinois Intelligencer*, January 16, 1824; "Jonathan Freeman," *Illinois Gazette*, July 26, 1823; William Orr in *Republican*,

July 20, 1824 (emphasis in the original); "Jonathan Freeman" in *Illinois Gazette*, July 26, 1823; "John Rifle" in *Illinois Gazette*, August 30, 1823; "William McCoy" in *Illinois Gazette*, July 26, 1823.

73. Wyatt-Brown, *Southern Honor*, 15, 22.

74. Richard T. Hughes and C. Leonard Allen, *Illusions of Innocence: Protestant Primitivism in America, 1630–1875* (Chicago: University of Chicago Press, 1988), 121.

6: WHOLE-HOG CALVINISTS AND MILK-AND-CIDER ARMINIANS

1. See Richard Hofstadter, *The Idea of a Party System* (Berkeley and Los Angeles: University of California Press, 1969). McCormick, *Second American Party System*, 23, notes that "the Federalists were quite ineffectual outside New England and certain of the Middle States."

2. For contemporary use of "whole hog," see, for example, *Illinois Gazette*, September 19, 1829. Tocqueville, *Democracy in America*, 257–58. Ford used "whole hog" in *History of Illinois*, 67, 69, to describe William Kinney's embrace of Jacksonian Democracy. The cultural option of communal individualists (egalitarians) is articulated by Ellis, *American Political Cultures*, 3–4.

3. "Milk and cider" is quoted in Pease, *Frontier State*, 145, and Thompson, *Illinois Whigs*, 36.

4. Edward Pessen, *Jacksonian America: Society, Personality, and Politics* (Homewood, Ill.: Dorsey Press, 1969), 58. The seminal pragmatic interpretation of the second party system is McCormick, *Second American Party System*. See also Peter D. Levine, *The Behavior of State Legislative Parties in the Jacksonian Era: New Jersey, 1829–1844* (Rutherford, N.J.: Associated University Press, 1977), and Joel H. Silbey, *The Shrine of Party: Congressional Voting Behavior, 1841–1852* (Pittsburgh: University of Pittsburgh Press, 1967). The literature on the debate over the substantive issues driving the second party system is enormous. For four important works analyzing the debate as it touches Illinois in particular, see Richard J. Jensen, *Illinois: A Bicentennial History* (New York: W. W. Norton, 1978); Rodney Owen Davis, "Illinois Legislators and Jacksonian Democracy, 1834–1841" (Ph.D. diss., University of Iowa, 1966); John Michael Rozett, "The Social Bases of Party Conflict in the Age of Jackson: Individual Voting Behavior in Greene County, Illinois, 1838–1848" (Ph.D. diss., University of Michigan, 1974); and Gerald Flood Leonard, "Partisan Political Theory and the Unwritten Constitution: The Origins of Democracy in Illinois, 1818–1840" (Ph.D. diss., University of Michigan, 1992).

5. Theodore J. Lowi, "Party, Policy, and Constitution in America," in *The American Party Systems: Stages of Political Development*, ed. William Nisbet Chambers and Walter Dean Burnham (New York: Oxford University Press, 1967), 238–76 (240).

6. This view implies that culture has two roles as an influence, one exerted on the individual and the other exerted on the body politic as a whole. On the role of culture in shaping individual and collective behavior, see Greenstone, "Political Culture and American Political Development." On the individual-shaping role, Greenstone writes: "Even though most individuals are self-interested, the way they construe their self-interest, be it political office, capitalist profits, or social prestige, is specified by their culture"

(12); whereas in the collective-shaping role, culture is conceived in such a way that, in the American case, it becomes "the major boundary condition that has severely limited the course that development took" (15).

7. James Morone, *The Democratic Wish: Popular Participation and the Limits of American Government* (New York: Basic Books, 1991), 5, argues that the image of "the people," while continually recurring in different forms, contains the "central image" of "the direct participation of a united people pursuing a shared communal interest." Mark E. Kann, "Individualism, Civic Virtue, and Gender in America," in Orren and Skowronek, *Studies in American Political Development* 4 (1990): 51, analyzes the vying claims of liberalism and republicanism as "origin stories."

8. See Nathan O. Hatch, *The Democratization of American Christianity* (New Haven: Yale University Press, 1989), 174, 173, 171, 172, 171. Hatch's reinterpretation of the Second Great Awakening emphasizes that "the most profound religious debates of the early republic followed social and class lines rather than merely intellectual ones" (35).

9. For the origin of the name "Regular Baptist" in Illinois, see Achilles Coffey, *History of the Regular Baptists* (Paducah, Ky.: Martin, 1877). Coffey maintains that the Illinois Regular Baptists were not part of the Regular Baptists who united with the Separate Baptists in 1787, for "neither all the Regulars nor Separate Baptists went into the union" (101). On the Baptist revolt during the First Great Awakening, see Donald G. Mathews, *Religion in the Old South* (Chicago: University of Chicago Press, 1977), and Isaac, *Transformation of Virginia*. The story of religious persecution may very well have been a part of Parker's family legacy. He was born in 1781 in Culpepper County, Virginia, where Baptists were severely persecuted before the Revolutionary War. For Parker's autobiography, see *Church Advocate* 2:259–88; for a recent argument stressing the continuity between the First and the Second Great Awakenings, before 1830, see James D. Bratt, "The Reorientation of American Protestantism, 1835–1845," *Church History* 67.1 (March 1998): 52–82.

10. Faragher, *Sugar Creek*, 165; George Pullen Jackson, *White Spirituals in the Southern Uplands* (New York: Dover Publications, 1965), 29, 40–41; Shirley Bean, Introduction to *The Missouri Harmony*, ed. Allen D. Carden (1820; reprint, Lincoln: University of Nebraska Press, 1994), xvi, vii, xiii.

11. For "Melinda," see Carden, *The Missouri Harmony*, 40; "Election Excludes Boasting," *Psalms, Carefully Suited to the Christian Worship in the United States* (New York: John Tiebort and Sons, 1817), 380; Carden, *The Missouri Harmony*, 71, 77.

12. See Edmund S. Morgan, *The Puritan Dilemma* (Boston: Little, Brown, 1958), 7–8. That the low-status category still prevailed in southern Illinois into the twentieth century is apparent from the memoirs of those living there. See the memoir of Edith Bradley Rendleman, *All Anybody Ever Wanted of Me Was to Work*, ed. Jane Adams (Carbondale: Southern Illinois University, 1996), 14.

13. For Badgley and Jones, see the "Circular" of the October 1819 meeting of the "Illinois Baptist Association," in Sweet, *Religion on the American Frontier,* 557; Parker, *Church Advocate* 2:23. For Peck and McCoy's work among the Native Americans in Indiana and Missouri, see John F. Cady, *The Origin and Development of the Missionary Baptist Church in Indiana* (Franklin,

Ind.: Franklin College, 1942), 33–35, 39–40, 46–47.

14. For the Regular Baptists' quotes, see Daniel Parker, *A Public Address to the Baptist Society* (Vincennes: Stout and Osborn, 1820), 9, 22; Badgley and Jones are in Sweet, *Religion on the American Frontier,* 557 (spelling updated). Sweet notes that "a fundamental Baptist tenet is the non-interference of the church in political concerns" (86).

15. One entry, entitled "Primrose," beginning the section on "plain and easy tunes" reads: "Salvation, oh! the joyful sound, 'Tis pleasure to our ears; A sovereign balm for ev'ry wound, A cordial for our fears"; cited in Carden, *The Missouri Harmony,* 21. In *Psalms, Carefully Suited to the Christian Worship,* 489, this appears as the first verse in a three-verse hymn by Methodist Isaac Watts.

16. Carden, *The Missouri Harmony,* 48. See also Tillson, *A Woman's Story,* 78, where she remembered the hymn phonetically as follows: "When I can read my titul clare, tue mansheons in the skei, I'll bid farewell to everie fear, And wipe my weeping ye, yi, yi, And wipe my weeping ye, yi, yi." The same hymn appears under the heading, "The Hopes of Heaven our Support under Trials on Earth," in *Psalms, Carefully Suited to the Christian Worship,* 470–71.

17. Sweet, *Religion on the American Frontier,* 561, 562, 557.

18. All quotes from Parker, *Church Advocate* 1:44–46.

19. Ibid., 46–47. See also Sweet, *Religion on the American Frontier,* 562.

20. Lippincott, "Early Days in Madison County," *Alton Telegraph,* March 24, 1865.

21. See the letter of "W.K." (William Kinney?), in *Edwardsville Spectator,* November 29, 1823. This letter first appeared in the *Illinois Republican* and was reprinted in the *Illinois Intelligencer,* only to be attacked by Jonathan Freeman and David J. Baker. Kinney later reputedly disavowed writing the letter; but see the rejoinder by Baker in *Edwardsville Spectator,* February 10, 1824. Eugene Genovese, *Roll Jordan Roll: The World the Slaves Made* (New York: Pantheon Books, 1974), 244.

22. Kinney's toast quoted from *Edwardsville Spectator,* March 8, 1823; Ford, *History of Illinois,* 68; Lippincott, "Early Days in Madison County," *Alton Telegraph,* March 31, 1865.

23. Quoted in William Warren Sweet, ed., *The Rise of Methodism in the West* (New York: Methodist Book Concern, 1920), 57. Parker, *Church Advocate* 1:56, viewed such meetings as veritable breeding grounds for "the Devil's religion . . . [which] operates upon the animal passions or carnal mind, converting it, not to God, but from practical wickedness to the hope of salvation by works."

24. See William James, *The Varieties of Religious Experience* (New York: Collier Books, 1961), 143, 172.

25. See, generally, ibid., 143–60; 204–9.

26. That, in early Illinois, the great proponents of reason were precisely these Methodists—the very group whose Illinois leader (Peter Cartwright) Richard Hofstadter emphasized as "a perfect embodiment of the anti-intellectualist position"—indicates a local variation that Hofstadter passed over in his national portrait, *Anti-Intellectualism in American Life* (New York: Vintage Books, 1962), 101. For an excellent summary of southern "Evangelicalism," but one that does not emphasize the local Illinois di-

visions, see Mathews, *Religion in the Old South.*

27. Thomas cited in Genovese, *Roll, Jordan, Roll,* 244; Parker, *Church Advocate* 1:62–63.

28. *Church Advocate* 1:61. For the doctrinal distinctions, see Timothy P. Weber, *Living in the Shadow of the Second Coming* (Chicago: University of Chicago Press, 1983), 9.

29. "Whitestown" in Carden, *The Missouri Harmony,* 119.

30. Bailyn, *Ideological Origins,* 234.

31. Alvord, *Coles,* 335–36.

32. Brown, "An Historical Sketch," 25. Brown adds: "By the aid of armed guards, the office remained intact, and the paper was duly published," though he left after this edition—February 22, 1823, containing another editorial attacking the legislature and the convention—was printed.

33. Smith, in *Illinois Republican,* April 19, 1823. Peck's report is from Sweet, *Religion on the American Frontier,* 97; the extent to which Peck organized the non-conventionists is in dispute. Brown, "An Historical Sketch," 27–28, wrote: "His plan of organizing the Counties by a central committee, with branches in every neighborhood, was carried out by his own exertions and personal supervision, and was greatly instrumental in saving the State. Being an agent of the American Bible Society, his duties frequently led him to Egypt and elsewhere—and he doubtless performed the double duty of disseminating the Holy Scripture and correct principles at one and the same time." But see the doubts of Merton L. Dillon, "John Mason Peck: A Study of Historical Rationalization," *Journal of the Illinois State Historical Society* 50 (1957): 385–95.

34. Since most issues of the *Illinois Republican* were lost, citations are from quotations or reprints of other newspapers. Smith quoted in *Edwardsville Spectator,* May 10, 1823, and reprinted in *Illinois Intelligencer,* July 5, 1823.

35. For the report on the Methodist preacher, see *Illinois Intelligencer,* March 22, 1823; for Lemen, Jr., see Sweet, *Religion on the American Frontier,* 587; "A Friend to Religion," in *Illinois Intelligencer,* July 5, 1823.

36. *Edwardsville Spectator,* May 3 (Randle), 24 (Smith), 17 (first attack), August 9, 1823 (Kelly). Hooper Warren, May 24, 1823, wrote that Smith had "mark[ed] out for proscription, and persecution too, at least the ministers of the Methodist society . . . [and had] attempt[ed] to intimidate them"; see also August 30, 1823.

37. Josias Randle in *Edwardsville Spectator,* May 3, 1823; For the quote from "A Friend to Consistency," see *Illinois Intelligencer,* August 23, 1823; However, Zadock Casey, a Methodist preacher in the legislature and later lieutenant governor and U.S. representative, voted for the convention.

38. Sweet, *Religion on the American Frontier,* 574, 552.

39. Sweet, *Religion on the American Frontier,* 559, 93; James Leaton, ed., *History of Methodism in Illinois from 1793 to 1832* (Cincinnati: Walden and Stowe, 1883), 104, 172, 213. Jensen, *Illinois,* 20, estimates religious affiliation at one in five during this period.

40. Diary entry reputedly made by James Lemen, Sr., quoted in Sweet, *Religion on the American Frontier,* 91. The documents Sweet had were "merely transcripts of the original papers" (88). Their authenticity is questioned by Buck, *Illinois in 1818,* 219, 319. Sweet also reprints the copy of Lemen's diary

entry on "Dec. 11, 1782," which states: "Thomas Jefferson had me to visit again a short time ago, as he wanted me to go to the Illinois Country in the northwest . . . in order to . . . oppose the introduction of slavery in that country" (88). Another entry, for "Jan. 10, 1809," states: "I received Jefferson's confidential message on Oct. 10, 1808, suggesting a division of the churches on the question of slavery and the organization of a church on a strictly anti-slavery basis" (91).

41. Sweet, *Religion on the American Frontier,* 579–80.

42. Ibid., 586–87.

43. *Republican,* April 6, 1824 ("Convention and Non-Convention preacher[s]"); *Illinois Republican,* June 16, 1824; Lippincott, "Early Days in Madison County," *Alton Telegraph,* March 31, 1865 (Kinney's empty wagon); James Lemen, Jr., "A Circular Address," in Sweet, *Religion on the American Frontier,* 579. The Friends of Humanity also appear to have accepted Methodist means; Sweet reports that "in 1830 the association gathering took the form of a camp meeting and was in session from Monday to Friday. There were many conversions accompanied by singing, exhorting, and communion services" (100).

44. *Edwardsville Spectator,* July 6 (Warren), 20 (moonshine), 1824.

45. Ibid., June 8, 1824; Pease, *Illinois Election Returns,* 208.

46. Lippincott, "Early Days in Madison County," *Alton Telegraph,* May 12, 1865; Warren, in *Edwardsville Spectator,* January 20, 1824.

47. Lippincott, "Early Days in Madison County," *Alton Telegraph,* May 12, 1865.

48. The list of counties having non-conventionist societies includes Bond, Lawrence, Madison, Morgan, Sangamon, St. Clair, White, Edgar, Greene, and Monroe; only for the last three is there no evidence of Methodist membership. Besides their presence in Monroe and St. Clair Counties, Sweet, *Religion on the American Frontier,* 95–97, notes that Friends of Humanity support was also strong in "Union, Johnson, and Edwards counties." *Edwardsville Spectator,* August 9, 1823 ("An Old Preacher"); Sweet, *Religion on the American Frontier,* 587 (Ogle).

49. "No Church Government," in *Republican,* May 11, 1824.

50. Rogin, *The Intellectuals and McCarthy: The Radical Specter,* 168, argues for a general relation between "political movements in a crisis period" and the advocation of "irrationally" broad "changes in the wider society": "in the disrupted position in which people find themselves during a crisis, they require some general explanation of the relation between narrow economic demands and their general welfare. Deprived of power, they are not likely to be motivated to act to change their situation by appeals to practical self-interest alone. Because the obstacles to surmount are so great, such appeals seem illusory and in fact often are. Therefore, some emotional appeals are essential . . . the emotional appeals of these movements transcend rationality defined in terms of Benthamite narrow self-interest."

51. "Mrs. Office-hunter," in *Republican,* March 16, 1824.

52. Ford, *History of Illinois,* 286. Ford elaborated on the techniques of popularity: popular men were "men who had made themselves agreeable to the people by a continual show of friendship and condescension; men who were loved for their gaiety, cheerfulness, apparent goodness of heart, and

agreeable manners" (282).

53. Ibid., 273–74.

54. *Church Advocate* 2:169, 1:9, 8; Parker's life as a "wandering Ishmael" is thoroughly covered in Byron Cecil Lambert, *The Rise of the Anti-Mission Baptists* (New York: Arno Press, 1980), 252–88. Parker's birth date and other biographical information are found in his autobiography; see *Church Advocate* 2:286.

55. *Church Advocate* 2:259, 263, 270, 275.

56. *Church Advocate* 2:270. His literary abilities should not be judged from his published writings, which bear the mark of editing in spelling and grammar. For the poor quality of Parker's unedited writing, see J. M. Carroll, *A History of the Texas Baptists* (Dallas: Baptists Standard Publishing, 1923), 47–50. On the social snubs of the Methodists, Parker tells the story of preaching in the same meetinghouse as them, when they did not even pretend to be listening: "it was not uncommon for a number of Bibles to be opened under my view." The lack of food because of his preaching seems to have been a sore spot, as comes out in his discussion of paying preachers: "but my family cannot eat money, and whenever the offer of a little corn, wheat, or a piece of meat becomes offensive let them alone till they get hungry enough to eat a piece of ash Poone," *A Public Address*, 30.

57. Lippincott, "Early Days in Madison County," *Alton Telegraph,* March 24, 1865.

58. *Church Advocate* 1:22; see Parker's letter to Nathan Pollard, editor of the *Family Visitor* in the *Edwardsville Spectator,* December 21, 1822.

59. *Church Advocate* 1:65.

60. Ibid., 1:17, 61.

61. Ibid., 1:41.

62. Parker, in *Edwardsville Spectator,* January 13, 1824 (emphasis in the original).

63. *Church Advocate* 2:250; Daniel Parker, *The Author's Defence* (Vincennes, Ind.: Elihu Stout, 1824), 11; *Edwardsville Spectator,* December 21, 1822.

64. *Church Advocate* 2:12, 247, 222; *A Public Address*, 24; Stephanie McCurry, *Masters of Small Worlds: Yeoman Households, Gender Relations, and the Political Culture of the Antebellum South Carolina Low Country* (New York: Oxford University Press, 1995), 147.

65. *A Public Address*, 51–52; *Church Advocate* 2:36, 42.

66. *A Public Address*, 47.

67. *Church Advocate* 2:207–10.

68. See Peck, *Memoirs*, 98; for his Fourth of July speech, see *Edwardsville Spectator,* August 16, 1823; *Edwardsville Spectator,* July 19, 1823 (Wright); *Edwardsville Spectator,* June 7, 1823 (Good); Warren appended to Good's article the following significant sociological note: "It has often been asserted, that the Ladies are almost unanimously in favor of slavery. This may be true, in a great degree, as far as it relates to the towns and cities of our state. But in the country, we presume, the case is somewhat different. The following communication is from the wife of a plain, but respectable farmer of Madison county." Actually, from the evidence, it appears that the country homes were in as great or greater need of domestic help. For the case of a Yankee household originally in the backcountry that hired servants and eventually bought

two slaves to help with the household, see Tillson, *A Woman's Story*, 131–41.

69. For Isaac Hill, see Donald B. Cole, *Jacksonian Democracy in New Hampshire, 1800–1851* (Cambridge, Mass.: Harvard University Press), 16–81. Warren might very well have followed Hill into the Jacksonian Party had the issue of slavery, not present in New Hampshire, not deterred him. Hill's defense of "religious freedom" and attack on Daniel Webster and the Anglicans during the Dartmouth College case is strikingly similar to the Illinois white folks' attitude toward big folks. Negative and positive liberty are distinguished in Isaiah Berlin, "Two Concepts of Liberty," in *Four Essays on Liberty* (London: Oxford University Press, 1969), 118–72.

70. Lippincott, "Early Days in Madison County," *Alton Telegraph*, March 24, 1865; *Edwardsville Spectator*, September 6, 1823 (Lawrence County).

71. See Ogle's comments in Sweet, *Religion on the American Frontier*, 587; Reynolds, *Pioneer History*, 374 (Monroe County); *Edwardsville Spectator*, April 27, 1824 (Morgan County), and March 1, 1823 (St. Clair County); T. Scott Miyakawa, *Protestants and Pioneers: Individualism and Conformity on the American Frontier* (Chicago: University of Chicago Press, 1964), 3, 214.

72. Alvord, *Coles*, 190. Coles's speech was typical of the many speeches made on behalf of Lafayette across the nation, such as the one printed locally, given by Pennsylvania governor John A. Shulze: "With ardent pleasure we have ever observed your strenuous exertions as the friend of man, while your great services, rendered in the cause of humanity, have commanded our admiration, the purity of your motives has insured the love and affection of Americans"; see the *Republican*, November 6, 1824. The early Illinois attitude toward the purpose of democracy is at odds with that suggested by C. B. Macpherson, in *The Real World of Democracy* (New York: Oxford University Press, 1966): "To the people at the bottom, or even half-way up, democracy was never entirely or essentially a class thing. For them it had always been not just a way of freeing themselves from oppression, but of freeing the whole of humanity, of permitting the realization of the humanity of all men" (13).

73. "Roger," in *Illinois Intelligencer*, November 22, 1823.

74. *Edwardsville Spectator*, July 19, 1823. Wright's home location is indicated by the listing in Norton, *Illinois Census Returns*, 149. The observation of Kinney was made by Joseph Gillespie in a communication with E. B. Washburne; see Alvord, *Coles*, 101.

75. Dangerfield, *Good Feelings*, 110. The phrase "Down-Easters" is used by Joseph Gillespie, "Recollections of Early Illinois," 8; he refers to it as a description of Yankees used by "our South-westerners."

7: ILLINOIS AND AMERICAN POLITICAL DEVELOPMENT

1. Thomas Hobbes, *Leviathan*, ed. Edwin Curley (1647; reprint, Indianapolis: Hackett, 1994), 57; Sandel, *Democracy's Discontent*, 4. The secondary literature on modern liberalism is enormous. A classic text emphasizing the role of passions and appetites among the liberals is Sheldon Wolin, *Politics and Vision*.

2. Ellis, *American Political Cultures*, 3–5; Greenstone, *The Lincoln Persuasion*, 53–65.

3. Logan Esarey, "Pioneer Politics in Indiana," *Indiana Magazine of*

History 13 (1917): 99–111; Andrew R. L. Cayton, *The Frontier Republic: Ideology and Politics in the Ohio Country, 1780–1825* (Kent, Ohio: Kent State University Press, 1986), 112, 133. Cayton's interpretation is supported in this regard by Donald J. Ratcliffe, *Party Spirit in a Frontier Republic: Democratic Politics in Ohio, 1793–1821* (Columbus: Ohio State University Press, 1998), 244–47.

4. Meyers, *The Jacksonian Persuasion*, 24.

5. Schlesinger, *Age of Jackson*, 209. The social egalitarianism of the "artisan republicans" of New York is well documented in Gilje and Rock, *Keepers of the Revolution*.

6. Ratcliffe, *Party Spirit in a Frontier Republic*, 248.

7. Bridges, *City in the Republic*, 61.

8. See the descriptions of frontier politics in Ohio and Indiana by Cayton in *Frontier Republic*, 129–40, and *Frontier Indiana*, 252–60. The territorial elite was overthrown in Indiana, but in *Frontier Indiana* Cayton notes that in the 1820s "the transition from the territorial aristocracy to the state aristocracy" still left the state with "a narrowly defined conception of 'the people'" (259). See also Cole, *Jacksonian Democracy in New Hampshire*, 1–9, 22–23, 47–81. Cole (78) notes that, in 1824, "Hill argued that a vote for Jackson was a vote for the spirit of 1776 and a vote against disloyalty in 1812. It was a vote for the people and a vote against the aristocracy. Hill was using rhetoric, but there was a truth in his words. . . . Even the opposition sometimes agreed with Hill." In 1824 there would have been no opposition to Hill's rhetoric in Illinois. McCormick, *Second American Party System*, 277–78, notes: "Illinois provides in an extreme form an illustration of the slowness with which politics in a new state became adjusted to the party system." This is also the thesis of Kurt E. Leichtle, "The Rise of Jacksonian Politics in Illinois," *Illinois Historical Journal* 82 (Summer 1989): 93–107, and Leonard, "Partisan Political Theory and the Unwritten Constitution."

9. Thornton, *Politics and Power*, 16.

10. Esarey, "Pioneer Politics in Indiana," 103. See Buck, *Illinois in 1818*, 280, for a list of convention members; and Pease, *Illinois Election Returns*, for subsequent election data.

11. Bridges, *City in the Republic*, 12. See also Thornton, *Politics and Power*, 442–61, and Samuel C. Hyde, Jr., *Pistols and Politics: The Dilemma of Democracy in Louisiana's Florida Parishes, 1810–1899* (Baton Rouge: Louisiana State University Press, 1996), 46–65.

12. Lee Benson, Joel H. Silbey, and Phyllis F. Field, "Towards a Theory of Stability and Change in American Voting Patterns: New York State, 1792–1970," in Silbey, Bogue, and Flanigan, *History of American Electoral Behavior*, 87.

13. Cayton, *The Frontier Republic*, 129–50. The sectional alliance within the Democratic Party is stressed by Brown, "Missouri Crisis, Slavery, and the Politics of Jacksonianism," 59.

14. The phrase "republican principles pure and uncontaminated" is from a representative of western Virginia quoted in Frederick Jackson Turner, *The Significance of the Frontier in American History*, ed. Harold P. Simonson (1893; reprint, New York: Frederick Ungar, 1963), 52. Pease, *Frontier State*, 123. See also Shade, *Banks or No Banks*, 112. Shade's quantitative analysis of the "conflict of subcultures" in northern Illinois and "Egypt"

during the later second-party-system era is still the most thorough, see especially 151–67. Robert Lloyd Kelley, *The Cultural Pattern in American Politics* (New York: Alfred A. Knopf, 1979), 165, relies heavily on Shade's work in finding the "cultural roots of economic conflicts" throughout the period.

15. Shade, *Banks or No Banks*, 252–53, 75–79, 90–92, 135–39, 151–67, esp. 252, 253, 158.

16. Ibid., 253; Kelley, *Cultural Pattern*, 160–227; R. Laurence Moore, *Religious Outsiders and the Making of Americans* (New York: Oxford University Press, 1986).

17. Eric M. Foner, *Free Soil, Free Labor, Free Men: The Ideology of the Republican Party before the Civil War* (New York: Oxford University, 1970), 11–72.

18. See Thornton, *Politics and Power*, 5–20. Thornton's argument about Alabama applies for Illinois as well: "Alabamians were preaching the substance of the Jacksonian faith long before Jackson had become its symbol." He also points out that the policies of the Jacksonian Party must be kept separate from the "fundamental social commitment" Jacksonianism represented (20–21).

19. Turner, *Significance of the Frontier*, 51; "the antithesis of feudalism and freedom" is noted as one of the key "polar dimensions which gave meaning and direction to . . . rhetorical images of the West" in Mary E. Young, "Congress Looks West: Liberal Ideology and Public Land Policy in the Nineteenth Century," in Ellis, *The Frontier in American Development*, 110.

20. *Transactions of the Illinois State Historical Society* (1936), no. 43, pp. 82, 90, 87; on the "germ theory," see Richard Hofstadter, *The Progressive Historians: Turner, Beard, Parrington* (Chicago: University of Chicago Press, 1979), 39, 66.

21. Marx, *Eighteenth Brumaire*, 124; for an overview of the "rural producers" and their egalitarianism, see Catherine McNicol Stock, *Rural Radicals from Bacon's Rebellion to the Oklahoma City Bombing* (New York: Penguin Books, 1997), 10–11, 15–54; the tornado quotation is from the first public speech by conventionist Thomas Cox
   at Vandalia, cited in *Edwardsville Spectator*, March 1, 1823.

22. Louis Hartz, *Economic Policy and Democratic Thought: Pennsylvania, 1776–1860* (Chicago: Quadrangle Books, 1968), 26.

23. Daniel Vickers, "Competency and Competition," 3–4; for the idea of contested ideologies, see Daniel T. Rodgers, *Contested Truths: Keywords in American Politics since Independence* (New York: Oxford University Press, 1988).

24. This follows Faragher's argument in *Sugar Creek*: "The riddle of backcountry community can be resolved by acknowledging the fact that two groups coexisted in Sugar Creek: a majority with high levels of mobility, who farmed for a time before pushing on and a significantly more permanent landed minority who rooted themselves in the community during the first two decades of settlement, first establishing the neighborhoods, then lived and worked together in them for many years, intermarrying and passing their improved farms on to their children" (145).

25. Dangerfield, *Good Feelings*, 106. Dangerfield's chapter "The West," 105–121, is the finest short essay on the topic. The best study of social attitudes among southern Illinois farmers is Jane Adams, *The Transformation of Rural Life* (Urbana: University of Illinois Press, 1994).

26. Freeman, in *Illinois Gazette,* August 30, 1823.

27. Rozett, "Social Bases of Party Conflict," 188, 164–65, 180–81, 182.

28. John Ashworth, *"Agrarians" and "Aristocrats": Party Political Ideology in the United States, 1837–1846* (London: Royal Historical Society, 1983), 134–74; Moore, *Religious Outsiders,* 47.

29. Jefferson is quoted by Joyce Appleby, in "The Radical *Double-Entendre* in the Right to Self-Government," in *The Origins of Anglo-American Radicalism,* ed. Margaret C. Jacob and James R. Jacob (New Jersey: Humanities Press International, 1991), 310. See also Faragher, *Sugar Creek,* 181. The humanitarian liberal persuasion, just in its infancy at this time in Illinois, is brilliantly analyzed in Greenstone, *The Lincoln Persuasion.*

30. Hartz, *Liberal Tradition,* 59–60.

31. For evidence, see Gary B. Nash, *The Urban Crucible: Social Change, Political Consciousness, and the Origins of the American Revolution* (Cambridge, Mass.: Harvard University Press, 1979). For a critique of Hartz along these lines, see Miller, *Rise and Fall of Democracy,* 75–79.

32. Evidence of Methodist respectability is prevalent throughout the West during this period. Thus, Thomas Lippincott remembers that when Lorenzo Dow, the famous Methodist itinerant, came to preach in Edwardsville, he refused to preach in the newly built courthouse, calling it a "hog pen" because it still had a dirt floor; see Lippincott, "Early Days in Madison County," *Alton Telegraph,* October 28, 1864. For other evidence, see Pocock, "Popular Roots of Jacksonian Democracy," 496–502.

33. For the mammoth cheese story, see Isaac Kramnick and R. Laurence Moore, *The Godless Constitution: The Case against Religious Correctness* (New York: W. W. Norton, 1996), 110–11.

34. Edmunds, *Shawnee Prophet,* 38, 35–37. For Tenskwatawa's being rejected as a witch, see Richard White, *The Middle Ground: Indians, Empires, and Republics in the Great Lakes Region, 1650–1815* (Cambridge: Cambridge University Press, 1991), 520.

CONCLUSION: DEMOCRATIC INDENTITIES AND LIBERAL INSTITUTIONS

1. For the comments on Coles and his detractors, see Peck's letter to Hooper Warren, March 26, 1855, in Alvord, *Coles,* 332; Peck's organization comments are quoted in Roger D. Bridges, "John Mason Peck on Illinois Slavery," *Illinois Historical Journal,* 75 (1982): 182; for his Missouri Compromise reference, see Peck's letter to Hooper Warren, March 27, 1855, in Alvord, *Coles,* 333.

2. See, for example, Andrew Levine, *Liberal Democracy: A Critique of Its Theory* (New York: Columbia University Press 1981), 3; Robert A. Dahl, *A Preface to Democratic Theory* (Chicago: University of Chicago Press, 1956), where he writes: "democratic theory itself is full of compromises—compromises of clashing and antagonistic principles . . . between the political equality of all adult citizens on the one side, and the desire to limit their sovereignty on the other," (4); and Carl Schmitt, *The Crisis of Parliamentary Democracy,* trans. Ellen Kennedy (Cambridge, Mass.: MIT Press, 1988), esp. 17, which treats "the inescapable contradiction of liberal individualism and democratic homogeneity" (17). See also Stephen Holmes, "Precommitment

and the Paradox of Democracy," in *Constitutionalism and Democracy,* ed. Jon Elster and Rune Slagstad (Cambridge: Cambridge University Press, 1988), where Holmes writes: "The existence of an irreconcilable 'tension' between constitutionalism and democracy is one of the core myths of modern political thought" (197); and Samuel Huntington, *American Politics: The Promise of Disharmony* (Cambridge, Mass.: Harvard University Press, 1981), 33: "The basic ideas of the American Creed—equality, liberty, individualism, constitutionalism, democracy—clearly do not constitute a systematic ideology, and they do not necessarily have any logical consistency. . . . Logically inconsistent as they seem to philosophers, these ideas do have a single common thrust and import . . . the distinctive aspect of the American Creed is its anti-government character."

3. The people are symbolically and actually always there, yet we do not always have a politics of social equality. Thus arise several puzzling questions. Why does the issue of social equality become a political issue at some times but not others? What explains American society's on-again off-again interest in tackling entrenched hierarchy through its political system? The search for answers to these questions has led many scholars to focus on a multitude of factors and their timing. If only one overarching cause were responsible, such as the market, or political institutions, or mass mobilization, or perhaps the charisma of leadership, one could do without the detail and sequence of history. But scholars have discovered that the timing and the interaction of causal variables matter. For this reason the study of American political development has witnessed a "turn by political scientists to history"; see the "Editors' Preface" to the first volume of *Studies in American Political Development,* ed. Karen Orren and Stephen Skowroneck (New Haven: Yale University Press, 1986), vii.

4. Tocqueville, *Democracy in America,* 225, 232.

SOURCES

ARCHIVAL SOURCES

Note: In the interest of accessibility, I have tried to cite published sources when available.

Buckmaster-Curran Family Papers. Illinois State Historical Library, Springfield.
Edward Coles Papers. Chicago Historical Society.
Henry Eddy Papers. Illinois Historical Survey, Urbana.
Ninian Edwards Collection. Chicago Historical Society.
Elis Kent Kane MSS. Chicago Historical Society.
Horatio Newhall Papers. Illinois State Historical Library, Springfield.
Daniel Parker MSS. Indiana Historical Society, Indianapolis.
Jesse B. Thomas Papers. Illinois State Historical Library, Springfield.

NEWSPAPERS

Alton Telegraph. Published at Alton by Parks and Pinckard.
Edwardsville Spectator. Published at Edwardsville by Hooper Warren.
Genius of Liberty. Published at Lowell by Hooper Warren.
Illinois Gazette. Published at Shawneetown by James Hall and Henry Eddy.
Illinois Intelligencer. Published at Vandalia by William Berry and David Blackwell.
Illinois Republican. Published at Edwardsville by Theophilus W. Smith and Oliver Kelly.
Pike County Republican. Published at Pittsfield.
Republican Advocate (later simply *Republican*). Published at Kaskaskia by William Orr.
Western Intelligencer. Published at Kaskaskia by Daniel P. Cook.

PUBLISHED SOURCES

Primary Sources

Alvord, Clarence Walworth, ed. *Governor Edward Coles*. Springfield: Illinois State Historical Library, 1920.
American State Papers Vol. 8, Public Lands. Washington, D.C.: Government Printing Office, 1832–1861.

Annals of the Congress of the United States, 1789–1824. Washington, D.C., 1834–1856.

Arndt, Karl J. A., comp. and ed. 1975–1978. *A Documentary History of the Indiana Decade of the Harmony Society, 1814–1824*. Indianapolis: Indiana Historical Society.

Beck, Lewis C. *A Gazetteer of the States of Illinois and Missouri*. 1823. Reprint, New York: Arno Press, 1975.

Birkbeck, Morris. "An Appeal on the Question of a Convention" [1823]. *Transactions of the Illinois State Historical Society* 10 (1905): 147–60.

———. *Letters from Illinois*. London: Taylor and Hessey, 1818.

Brown, William Hubbard. "Early History of Illinois." *Fergus Historical Series*, no. 14, pp. 82–104. Chicago: Fergus Historical Library, 1881.

———. "An Historical Sketch of the Early Movement in Illinois for the Legalization of Slavery." *Fergus Historical Series*, no. 4, pp. 1–30. Chicago: Fergus Historical Library, 1876.

Brush, Daniel. *Growing Up in Southern Illinois, 1820–1861*. 1862. Reprint, Chicago: Lakeside Press, 1944.

Carden, Allen D., ed. *The Missouri Harmony*. 1820. Reprint, with an introduction by Shirley Bean, Lincoln: University of Nebraska Press, 1994.

Chapman, Charles C., ed. *History of Pike County, Illinois*. Chicago: Chas. C. Chapman, 1880.

"Clear Creek Baptist Church Minutes," [Union County, 1820–1845]. In *Saga of Southern Illinois* 20 (1993): 24–40. 0.

Coffin, Levi. *Reminiscences of Levi Coffin*. Cincinnati: R. Clarkes, 1880.

Cox, Issac Joslin, ed. "Selections from the Torrence Papers VII." In *Quarterly Publication of the Historical and Philosophical Society of Ohio*. Cincinnati: Cincinnati Historical Society, 1911.

Duden, Gottfried. *Report on a Journey to the Western States of North America*. Edited by James W. Goodrich. 1829. Reprint, Columbia: The State Historical Society of Missouri, 1980.

Edwards, Ninian W. *The Edwards Papers*. Edited by E. B. Washburne. Chicago: Fergus Printing, 1884.

———. *History of Illinois from 1778 to 1833; and Life and Times of Ninian Edwards*. Springfield: Illinois State Journal Company, 1870.

Ernst, Ferdinand. "Travels in Illinois in 1819." Translated by E. P. Baker. *Transactions of the Illinois State Historical Society* 8 (1903): 150–65.

Farnham, Eliza W. *Life in Prairie Land*. New York: Harper and Brothers, 1846.

Faux, William. "Memorable Days in America." 1823. Reprint. Vol. 11 of *Early Western Travels*. Edited by Reuben Gold Thwaites. Cleveland: Arthur H. Clark, 1904–1907.

Flower, George. *History of the English Settlement in Edwards County*. Chicago: Fergus Printing, 1882.

Foner, Phillip S., ed. *The Life and Major Writings of Thomas Paine*. Secaucus, N.J.: Citadel Press, 1974.

Ford, Thomas. *A History of Illinois: From Its Commencement as a State in 1818 to 1847*. Introduction by Rodney O. Davis. 1859. Reprint, Urbana: University of Illinois Press, 1995.

Fordham, Elias Pym. *Personal Narrative of Travels in Virginia, Maryland, Penn-*

sylvania, Ohio, Indiana, Kentucky; and of a Residence in the Illinois Territory: 1817–1818. Edited by Frederic Austin Ogg. Cleveland: The Arthur H. Clark Company, 1906.

Gillespie, Joseph. "Recollections of Early Illinois and her noted men." *Fergus Historical Series*, no. 13, pp. 1–25. Chicago: Fergus Historical Library, 1880.

Hall, James. "Letters from the West." *Port Folio* (1821–1825).

———. "Letter to Thomas Sloo, Jr." [1827]. *Transactions of the Illinois State Historical Society* 16 (1911): 42.

———. *Statistics of the West*. Cincinnati: J. A. James, 1837.

———. *Tales of the Border*. 1835. Reprint, Upper Saddle River, N.J.: Literature House, 1970.

Hammes, Raymond, ed. "The Squatters Reports of 1807 and 1813." *Illinois Libraries* 59 (1977): 319–82.

Harding, Benjamin. *A Tour through the Western Country, 1818–1819*. New London, Conn.: S. Green, 1819.

Hinde, Tomas S. "Theophilus Arminius." *Methodist Magazine* 11 (1828): 154–58.

Hoffmann, B. E., ed. *History of Madison County, Illinois*. Edwardsville, Ill.: W. R. Brink, 1882.

Hulme, Thomas. "Journal of a Tour in the Western Countries of America, September 30, 1818–August 8, 1819." In Vol. 10 of *Early Western Travels, 1748–1846*. Edited by Reuben Gold Thwaites, 17–84. Cleveland: Arthur H. Clark, 1904.

Illinois Public Domain Land Tract Sales. State Archives, www.sos.state.il.us/depts/archives/data_lan.html.

James, Edmund J., ed. *The Territorial Records of Illinois*. Springfield: Illinois State Historical Library, 1901.

Johannsen, Robert W., ed. *The Lincoln-Douglas Debates*. New York: Oxford University Press, 1965.

Journal of the House of Representatives of the Second General Assembly of the State of Illinois at Their First Session. Vandalia: Brown and Berry, 1821.

Journal of the House of Representatives of the Third General Assembly of the State of Illinois at Their First Session. Vandalia: Blackwell and Berry, 1823.

Journal of the Senate of the Second General Assembly of the State of Illinois at Their First Session. Vandalia: Brown and Berry, 1821.

Journal of the Senate of the Third General Assembly of the State of Illinois at Their First Session. Vandalia: Blackwell and Berry, 1823.

Lawrence, Barbara, and Nedra Banz, eds. *The Flagg Correspondence: Selected Letters, 1816–1854*. Carbondale and Edwardsville: Southern Illinois University Press, 1986.

Leaton, James, ed. *History of Methodism in Illinois from 1793 to 1832*. Cincinnati: Walden and Stowe, 1883.

Lemen, Joseph B. "The Jefferson-Lemen Anti-Slavery Pact." *Transactions of the Illinois State Historical Society* 13 (1908): 74–84.

Lippincott, Thomas. "Early Days in Madison County." *Alton Telegraph*, September 2, 1864–August 11, 1865.

Madison, James, Alexander Hamilton, and John Jay. *The Federalist Papers*. Edited by Clinton Rossiter. 1787–1788. Reprint, New York: Mentor, 1961.

McDermott, John Francis, ed. *Old Cahokia*. St. Louis: St. Louis Historical Documents Foundation, 1949.

Norton, Margaret Cross, ed. *Illinois Census Returns, 1820*. Springfield: Illinois State Historical Library, 1934.

Ogden, George. *Letters from the West*. New Bedford: Melcher and Rodgers, 1823.

Oliver, William. *Eight Months in Illinois*. Newcastle-upon-Tyne: William Andrew Mitchell, 1843.

Parker, Daniel. *The Author's Defence*. Vincennes, Ind.: Elihu Stout, 1824.

———. *Church Advocate*. Vincennes, Ind.: Elihu Stout, 1828–1831.

———. *A Public Address to the Baptist Society*. Vincennes: Stout and Osborn, 1820.

Parkinson, Daniel M. "Pioneer Life in Wisconsin" [1855]. *Collections of the Historical Society of Wisconsin*. Madison: University of Wisconsin Press, 1984.

Patterson, Robert W. "Early Society in Southern Illinois." *Fergus Historical Series*, no. 17, pp. 102–20. Chicago: Fergus Historical Library, 1880.

Peck, John Mason. *Memoirs of John Mason Peck*. Edited by Rufus Babcock. Carbondale: Southern Illinois University Press, 1965.

———. *A New Guide for Emigrants to the West*. Boston: Gould, Kendall and Lincoln, 1836.

Perrin, William Henry, ed. *History of Alexander, Union, and Pulaski Counties, Illinois*. Chicago: O. L. Baskin, 1883.

Philbrick, Francis, ed. *The Laws of Indiana Territory, 1801–1809*. Vol. 2. Springfield: Illinois State Historical Library, 1930.

———. *The Laws of Illinois Territory, 1809–1818*. Vol. 25. Springfield: Illinois State Historical Library, 1950.

Psalms, Carefully Suited to the Christian Worship in the United States. New York: John Tiebort and Sons, 1817.

Reports of Cases Argued and Determined in the Supreme Court of the State of Illinois. Chicago: Callaghan and Co., 1886.

Reynolds, John. *My Own Times, Embracing Also the History of My Life* [1855]. Chicago: Fergus Printing, 1879.

———. *The Pioneer History of Illinois, Containing the Discovery, in 1673, and the History of the Country to the Year Eighteen Hundred and Eighteen, When the State Government Was Organized*. 1859. Reprint, Chicago: Fergus Printing, 1887.

Sewell, William. *Diary of William Sewall, 1797–1846*. Edited by John Goodell. Springfield: Hartman Printing, 1930.

Shaw, John. "Personal Narrative." [1855]. *Collections of the State Historical Society of Wisconsin*. Madison: Wisconsin Historical Collections, 1855.

Shepard, Elihu H., *The Autobiography of Elihu H. Shepard*. St. Louis: George Knapp, 1869.

Smith, Melancton. "Speeches by Melancton Smith" [1788]. In *The Anti-Federalist*. Edited by Herbert Storing. Chicago: University of Chicago Press, 1985.

Sweet, William Warren, ed. *Religion on the American Frontier: The Baptists, 1783–1830*. New York: Henry Holt, 1931.

———. *The Rise of Methodism in the West*. New York: Methodist Book Concern, 1920.

Thompson, Jess M. "Pike's County Seat War." *Pike County Republican* (Pittsfield), October 2, 1935–January 13, 1937.

Tillson, Christiana Holmes. *A Woman's Story of Pioneer Illinois* [1870–1872]. Edited by Milo Milton Quaife, with introduction by Kay J. Carr. Carbondale: Southern Illinois University Press, 1995.

Van Zandt, Nicholas Biddle. *A Full Description of the Soil, Water, Timber, and Prairies of Each Lot, or Quarter Section of the Military Lands between the Mississippi and Illinois Rivers*. Washington City: P. Force, 1818.

Verlie, Emil Joseph, ed. *Illinois Constitutions*. Vol. 1. Springfield: Illinois State Historical Library, 1919.

Woods, John. "Two Years' Residence in the Settlement of the English Prairie in the Illinois Country, United States, 1820–21." In Vol. 10 of *Early Western Travels, 1746–1846*. Edited by Reuban Gold Thwaites. Cleveland: Arthur H. Clark, 1904–1907.

PUBLISHED SOURCES

Secondary Sources

Abernathy, Thomas Perkins. *The Formative Period in Alabama, 1815–1828*. University: University of Alabama Press, 1965.

Adams, Jane. *The Transformation of Rural Life*. Urbana: University of Illinois Press, 1994.

Allen, John W. "Slavery and Negro Servitude in Pope County, Illinois." In *An Illinois Reader*. Edited by Clyde C. Walton, 102–12. DeKalb: Northern Illinois University Press, 1970.

Altschuler, Glenn C., and Stuart M. Blumin. "Limits of Political Engagement in Antebellum America: A New Look at the Gold Age of Participatory Democracy." *Journal of American History* (December 1997): 855–85.

Alvord, Clarence Walworth. *The Illinois Country, 1673–1818*. Introduction by Robert M. Sutton. 1920. Reprint, Urbana: University of Illinois Press, 1987.

Angle, Paul. "Nathaniel Pope, 1784–1850: A Memoir." *Transactions of the Illinois State Historical Society* 43 (1936): 124–57.

Appleby, Joyce. "The Radical *Double-Entendre* in the Right to Self-Government." In *The Origins of Anglo-American Radicalism*. Edited by Margaret C. Jacob and James R. Jacob, 304–12. New Jersey and London: Humanities Press International, 1991.

Aron, Stephen. *How the West Was Lost*. Baltimore: Johns Hopkins University Press, 1996.

Ashworth, John. *"Agrarians" and "Aristocrats": Party Political Ideology in the United States, 1837–1846*. London: Royal Historical Society, 1983.

———. *Slavery, Capitalism, and Politics in the Antebellum Republic*. Vol. 1, *Commerce and Compromise, 1820–1850*. Cambridge: Cambridge University Press, 1995.

Atack, Jeremy, and Fred Bateman. *To Their Own Soil: Agriculture in the Antebellum North*. Ames: Iowa State University Press, 1987.

Bailey, Hugh C. *John Williams Walker*. University: University of Alabama Press, 1964.

Bailyn, Bernard. *The Ideological Origins of the American Revolution*. Cambridge, Mass.: Harvard University Press, 1967.

———. *The Origins of American Politics*. New York. Vintage Books, 1967.

Bakalis, Michael J. "Ninian Edwards and Territorial Politics in Illinois, 1775–1818." Ph.D. diss., Northwestern University, 1966.

Banning, Lance. *The Jeffersonian Persuasion*. Ithaca: Cornell University Press, 1978.

Bardolph, Richard. *Agricultural Literature and the Early Illinois Farmer*. Urbana: University of Illinois Press, 1948.

Barnhart, John. "The Southern Influence in the Formation of Illinois." *Journal of the Illinois State Historical Society* 32 (1939): 358–78.

Barry, Brian. *Sociologists, Economists, and Democracy*. 1970. Reprint, Chicago: University of Chicago Press, 1978.

Beard, Charles A. *An Economic Interpretation of the Constitution*. 1915. Reprint, New York: The Free Press, 1935.

Beeman, Richard R. *The Evolution of the Southern Backcountry: A Case Study of Lunenburg County, Virginia, 1746–1832*. Philadelphia: University of Pennsylvania Press, 1984.

Bender, Thomas. *Community and Social Change in America*. New Brunswick: Rutgers University Press, 1978.

Benson, Lee. *The Concept of Jacksonian Democracy: New York as a Test Case*. Princeton: Princeton University Press, 1961.

Benson, Lee, Joel H. Silbey, and Phyllis F. Field. "Towards a Theory of Stability and Change in American Voting Patterns: New York State, 1792–1970." In *The History of American Electoral Behavior*. Edited by Joel H. Silbey, Allan G. Bogue, and William H. Flanigan. Princeton: Princeton University Press, 1978.

Berghe, L. van den. *Race and Racism: A Comparative Perspective*. New York: John Wiley and Sons, 1967.

Berlin, Isaiah. *Four Essays on Liberty*. London: Oxford University Press, 1969.

Berry, Thomas, Sr. *Western Prices before 1861*. Cambridge, Mass.: Harvard University Press, 1943.

Berthoff, Rowland. *Republic of the Dispossessed: The Exceptional Old-European Consensus in America*. Columbia: University of Missouri Press, 1997.

Berwanger, Eugene H. *The Frontier against Slavery*. Urbana: University of Illinois Press, 1967.

Blackstone, William. *Commentaries on the Laws of England*. 1765–1769. Reprint, Chicago: University of Chicago Press, 1979.

Bodenhamer, David J. "Law and Disorder on the Early Frontier: Marian City, Indiana, 1823–1850." *Western Historical Quarterly* 10 (1979): 323–36.

Boggess, Arthur Clinton. *The Settlement of Illinois, 1778–1830*. Chicago: Chicago Historical Society, 1908.

Bogue, Allan G. *From Prairie to Corn Belt*. Chicago: University of Chicago Press, 1963.

Bond, Beverly W., Jr. *The Civilization of the Old Northwest*. New York: Henry Holt, 1934.

Boyd, Steven R. "The Contract Clause and the Evolution of American Federalism." *William and Mary Quarterly*, 3d ser., 44 (1987): 529–48.

Boyer, Paul, and Stephen Nissenbaum. *Salem Possessed*. Cambridge, Mass.: Harvard University Press, 1974.

Bratt, James D. "The Reorientation of American Protestantism, 1835–1845." *Church History* 67.1 (March 1998): 52–82.

Bray, Robert C. *Rediscoveries: Literature and Place in Illinois*. Urbana: University of Illinois Press, 1982.

Brennan, Gerald. *The Spanish Labyrinth*. Cambridge: Cambridge University Press, 1964.

Brewer, John. *Party Ideology and Popular Politics at the Accession of George III*. Cambridge: Cambridge University Press, 1976.

Bridges, Amy. *A City in the Republic: Antebellum New York and the Origins of Machine Politics*. 1984. Reprint, Ithaca: Cornell University Press, 1987.

Bridges, Roger D. "John Mason Peck on Illinois Slavery." *Journal of the Illinois State Historical Society* 75 (1982): 179–217.

Briggs, Winstanley. "Le Pays des Illinois." *William and Mary Quarterly*, 3d ser., 46 (1989): 30–56.

———. "Slavery in French Colonial Illinois." *Chicago History* 18 (1989–1990): 66–81.

Brown, Richard H. "The Missouri Crisis, Slavery, and the Politics of Jacksonianism." *South Atlantic Quarterly* 65 (1966): 55–72.

Buck, Solon Justus. *Illinois in 1818*. Spingfield: Illinois Centennial Commission, 1917.

Cady, John F. *The Origin and Development of the Missionary Baptist Church in Indiana*. Franklin, Ind.: Franklin College, 1942.

Cappon, Lester J., ed. *The Adams-Jefferson Letters*. Chapel Hill: University of North Carolina Press, 1987.

Carlson, Theodore L. *The Illinois Military Tract*. Urbana: University of Illinois Press, 1951.

Carroll, J. M. *A History of the Texas Baptists*. Dallas: Baptists Standard Publishing, 1923.

Cash, W. J. *The Mind of the South*. 1941. Reprint, New York. Vintage Books, 1991.

Cayton, Andrew R. L. *Frontier Indiana*. Bloomington: Indiana University Press, 1996.

———. *Frontier Republic: Ideology and Politics in the Ohio Country, 1780–1825*. Kent, Ohio: Kent State University Press, 1986.

Cayton, Andrew R. L., and Peter S. Onuf. *The Midwest and the Nation*. Bloomington: Indiana University Press, 1990.

Chamberlin, Henry Barrett. "Elias Kent Kane." *Transactions of the Illinois State Historical Society* 13 (1908): 162–70.

Clark, Christopher. *The Roots of Rural Capitalism: Western Massachusetts, 1780–1860*. Ithaca: Cornell University Press, 1990.

Clark, John G. *The Grain Trade in the Old Northwest*. 1966. Reprint, Westport, Conn.: Greenwood Press, 1980.

Cmiel, Kenneth. *Democratic Eloquence: The Fight over Popular Speech in Nineteenth-Century America*. Berkeley and Los Angeles: University of California Press, 1990.

Coffey, Achilles. *History of the Regular Baptists*. Paducah, Ky.: Martin, 1877.

Cohen, William. "Thomas Jefferson and the Problem of Slavery." *Journal of American History* 56 (December 1969): 503–26.

Cole, Donald B. *Jacksonian Democracy in New Hampshire, 1800–1851*. Cambridge, Mass.: Harvard University Press, 1970.

Commager, Henry Steel, ed. *Documents of American History*. New York: F. S. Crofts, 1943.

Crenson, Matthew. *The Federal Machine*. Baltimore: Johns Hopkins University Press, 1975.

Dahl, Robert A. *Modern Political Analysis*. 5th ed. Englewood Cliffs, N.J.: Prentice Hall, 1991.

———. *A Preface to Democratic Theory*. Chicago: University of Chicago Press, 1956.

Dangerfield, George. *The Awakening of American Nationalism, 1815–1828*. New York: Harper and Row, 1965.

———. *The Era of Good Feelings*. 1952. Reprint, Chicago: Ivan R. Dee, 1989.

Davis, James E. *Frontier America, 1800–1840: A Comparative Demographic Analysis of the Frontier Process*. Glendale, Calif.: A. H. Clark, 1977.

———. *Frontier Illinois*. Bloomington: Indiana University Press, 1998.

Davis, Rodney Owen. "Illinois Legislators and Jacksonian Democracy, 1834–1841." Ph.D. diss., University of Iowa, 1966.

———. "Partisanship in Jacksonian State Politics: Party Divisions in the Illinois Legislature, 1834–1841." In *Quantification in American History*. Edited by Robert P. Swierenga, 149–62. New York: Atheneum, 1970.

———. "'The People in Miniature': The Illinois General Assembly, 1818–1848." *Journal of the Illinois State Historical Society* 81 (1988): 95–108.

Davis, Ronald L. F. "Community and Conflict in Pioneer Saint Louis, Missouri." *Western Historical Quarterly* 10 (1979): 337–54.

Degler, Carl N. *Out of Our Past: The Forces That Shaped Modern America*. New York: Harper and Row, 1959.

Diamond, Martin. "Democracy and the Federalist: A Reconsideration of the Framers' Intent." *American Political Science Review* 53 (1959): 52–68.

Diggins, John P. *The Lost Soul of American Politics: Virtue, Self-Interest, and the Foundations of Liberalism* Chicago: University of Chicago Press, 1986.

Dillon, Merton L. "John Mason Peck: A Study of Historical Rationalization." *Journal of the Illinois State Historical Society* 50 (1957): 385–95.

———. "Sources of Early Anti-Slavery Thought in Illinois." *Journal of the Illinois State Historical Society* 50 (1957): 34–56.

Dowrie, George William. *The Development of Banking in Illinois*. Urbana: University of Illinois Press, 1913.

Doyle, Don Harrison. *The Social Order of a Frontier Community*. Urbana: University of Illinois Press, 1978.

Dublin, Thomas. "Women and Outwork in a Nineteenth-Century New England Town: Fitzwilliam, New Hampshire, 1830–1850." In *The Countryside in the Age of Capitalist Transformation*. Edited by Steven Hahn and Jonathan Prude, 57–69. Chapel Hill: University of North Carolina Press, 1985.

Dunn, J. P. *Indiana: A Redemption from Slavery*. Boston: Houghton, Mifflin, 1900.

Eames, Charles M. *Historic Morgan and Classic Jacksonville*. Jacksonville, Ill.: Daily Journal Printing Office, 1885.

Edmunds, R. David. *The Shawnee Prophet*. Lincoln: University of Nebraska Press, 1983.

Edstrom, James A. "'With . . . candour and good faith': Nathaniel Pope and the Admission Enabling Act of 1818," *Illinois Historical Journal* 88 (1995): 241-62.

Ellis, Richard J. *American Political Cultures*. New York: Oxford University Press, 1993.

Ericson, David F. *The Shaping of American Liberalism: The Debates over Ratification, Nullification, and Slavery*. Chicago: University of Chicago Press, 1993.

Esarey, Logan. "The Organization of the Jackson Party in Indiana." *Proceedings for the Mississippi Valley Historical Association* 5 (1914–1915): 230–50.

———. "Pioneer Politics in Indiana." *Indiana Magazine of History* 13 (1917): 99–130.

Etcheson, Nicole. *The Emerging Midwest: Upland Southerners and the Political Culture of the Old Northwest, 1787–1861*. Bloomington: Indiana University Press, 1997.

Faragher, John Mack. "Open-Country Community." In *The Countryside in the Age of Capitalist Transformation*. Edited by Steven Hahn and Johathan Prude, 233–58. Chapel Hill: University of North Carolina Press, 1985.

———. *Sugar Creek: Life on the Illinois Prairie*. New Haven: Yale University Press, 1986.

Feller, Daniel. *The Jacksonian Promise*. Baltimore: Johns Hopkins University Press, 1995.

———. *The Public Lands in Jacksonian Politics*. Madison: University of Wisconsin Press, 1984.

Finkelman, Paul. "Slavery and Bondage in the Empire of Liberty." In *The Northwest Ordinance: Essays on Its Formation, Provisions, and Legacy*. Edited by Frederick D. Williams, 61–96. East Lansing: Michigan State University Press, 1987.

———. *Slavery and the Founders: Race and Liberty in the Age of Jefferson*. Armonk, N.Y.: M. E. Sharpe, 1996.

Fischer, David Hackett. *Albion's Seed: Four British Folkways in America*. New York: Oxford University Press, 1989.

Fladeland, Betty L. "Compensated Emancipation: A Rejected Alternative." *Journal of Southern History* 42 (1976): 169–86.

Foner, Eric M. *Free Soil, Free Labor, Free Men: The Ideology of the Republican Party before the Civil War*. New York: Oxford University, 1970.

Ford, Lacy K. "Republican Ideology in a Slave Society: The Political Economy of John C. Calhoun." *Journal of Southern History* 54 (1988): 405–24.

Formisano, Ronald P. *The Birth of Mass Political Parties*. Princeton: Princeton University Press, 1971.

———. *The Transformation of Political Culture*. New York: Oxford University Press, 1983.

Franklin, John Hope. "Who Divided This House?" *Chicago History* 19 (Fall/Finter 1990–1991): 24–35.

Freehling, William W. *The Road to Disunion*. Vol.1, *Secessionists at Bay, 1776–1854*. New York: Oxford University Press, 1990.

Gates, Paul W. *The Farmers' Age: Agriculture, 1815–1860*. New York: Harper and Row, 1960.

———. *Landlords and Tenants on the Prairie Frontier*. Ithaca: Cornell University Press, 1973.

Geertz, Clifford. *The Interpretation of Cultures*. New York: Basic Books, 1973.

Genovese, Eugene. *Roll Jordan Roll: The World the Slaves Made*. New York: Pantheon Books, 1974.

Gilje, Paul. *The Road to Mobocracy: Popular Disorder in New York City, 1763–1834*. Chapel Hill: University of North Carolina Press, 1987.

Gilje, Paul A., and Howard B. Rock, eds., *Keepers of the Revolution: New Yorkers at Work in the Early Republic*. Ithaca: Cornell University Press, 1992.

Gray, John. *Liberalism*. Minneapolis: University of Minnesota Press, 1986.

Gray, Lewis Cecil. *History of Agriculture in the Southern United States to 1860*. Vol. 2. 1933. Reprint, Clifton, N.J.: Augustus M. Kelley, 1973.

Greenstone, J. David. *The Lincoln Persuasion: Remaking American Liberalism*. Princeton: Princeton University Press, 1993.

———. "Political Culture and American Political Development: Liberty, Union, and the Liberal Bipolarity." *Studies in American Political Development* 1 (1986): 1–49.

———. "The Transient and the Permanent in American Politics: Standards, Interests, and the Concept of 'Public.'" In *Public Values and Private Power in American Politics*. Edited by J. David Greenstone, 3–33. Chicago: University of Chicago Press, 1982.

Gunn, L. Ray. *The Decline of Authority: Public Economic Policy and Political Development in New York State, 1800–1860*. Ithaca: Cornell University Press, 1988.

Habermas, Jurgen. *The Structural Transformation of the Public Sphere*. 1962. Reprint, Cambridge, Mass.: MIT Press, 1989.

Hadas, Moses, and Joe P. Poe, eds. and trans. *Livy: A History of Rome*. New York: Modern Library, 1962.

Hahn, Steven. *The Roots of Southern Populism: Yeoman Farmers and the Transformation of the Georgia Upcountry, 1850–1890*. New York: Oxford University Press, 1983.

Hahn, Steven, and Jonathan Prude, eds. *The Countryside in the Age of Capitalist Transformation*. Chapel Hill: University of North Carolina Press, 1985.

Hardeman, Nicholas P. *Shucks, Shocks, and Hominy Blocks*. Baton Rouge: Louisiana State University Press, 1981.

Harris, Norman Dwight. *History of Negro Servitude in Illinois and of the Slavery Agitation in That State, 1719–1864*. Chicago: A. C. McClurg, 1904.

Hartz, Louis. *Economic Policy and Democratic Thought: Pennsylvania, 1776–1860*. 1948. Reprint, Chicago: Quadrangle Books, 1968.

———. *The Liberal Tradition in America*. New York: Harcourt, Brace and World, 1955.

Hatch, Nathan O. *The Democratization of American Christianity*. New Haven: Yale University Press, 1989.

Hayter, Earl W. "Sources of Early Illinois Culture." *Transactions of the Illinois*

State Historical Society, no. 43 (1936): 81–96.

Herring, Joseph B. "The Vermillion Kickapoos of Illinois: The Prophet Kenekuk's Peaceful Resistance to Indian Removal, 1819–1833." In *Selected Papers in Illinois History 1983.* Edited by Robert W. McCluggage, 25–35. Springfield: Illinois State Historical Society, 1983.

Hobbes, Thomas. *Leviathan.* 1647. Edited by Edwin Curley. Indianapolis: Hackett, 1994.

Hoffmann, John. "A History of *The Centennial History of Illinois,* 1907–1920." In *Selected Papers in Illinois History, 1982.* Edited by Robert W. McCluggage, 57–78. Springfield: Illinois State Historical Society, 1984.

Hofstadter, Richard. *The American Political Tradition.* New York: Vintage Books, 1957.

———. *Anti-Intellectualism in American Life.* New York: Vintage Books, 1962.

———. *The Idea of a Party System.* Berkeley and Los Angeles: University of California Press, 1969.

———. *The Progressive Historians: Turner, Beard, Parrington* 1968. Reprint, Chicago: University of Chicago Press, 1979.

Hogan, Richard. *Class and Community in Frontier Colorado.* Lawrence: University Press of Kansas, 1990.

Holmes, Stephen. "Precommitment and the Paradox of Democracy." In *Constitutionalism and Democracy.* Edited by Jon Elster and Rune Slagstad, 195–240. Cambridge: Cambridge University Press, 1988.

Horowitz, Morton J. *The Transformation of American Law, 1780–1860.* Cambridge, Mass.: Harvard University Press, 1977.

Hughes, Richard T., ed. *The American Quest for a Primitive Church.* Urbana: University of Illinois Press, 1988.

Hughes, Richard T., and C. Leonard Allen. *Illusions of Innocence: Protestant Primitivism in America, 1630–1875.* Chicago: University of Chicago Press, 1988.

Huntington, Samuel. *American Politics: The Promise of Disharmony.* Cambridge, Mass.: Harvard University Press, 1981.

Hyde, Samuel C., Jr. *Pistols and Politics: The Dilemma of Democracy in Louisiana's Florida Parishes, 1810–1899.* Baton Rouge: Louisiana State University Press, 1996.

Ignatiev, Noel. *How the Irish Became White.* New York: Routledge, 1995.

Isaac, Rhys. *The Transformation of Virginia, 1740–1790.* Chapel Hill: University of North Carolina Press, 1982.

Jackson, George Pullen. *White Spirituals in the Southern Uplands.* 1933. Reprint, New York: Dover Publications, 1965.

Jaffa, Harry V. *Crisis of the House Divided.* 1959. Reprint, Chicago: University of Chicago Press, Phoenix Books, 1982.

James, William. *The Varieties of Religious Experience.* 1902. Reprint, New York: Collier Books, 1961.

Jefferson, Thomas. *The Portable Thomas Jefferson.* Edited by Merrill D. Peterson. New York: Viking Penguin, 1975.

Jensen, Richard J. *Illinois: A Bicentennial History.* New York: W. W. Norton, 1978.

———. "Party Coalitions and the Search for Modern Values." In *Party Coalitions in the 1980s.* Edited by Seymour M. Lipset, 55–85. San Francisco:

Institute for Contemporary Studies, 1981.

Johannsen, Robert W. *The Frontier, the Union, and Stephen A. Douglas*. Urbana: University of Illinois Press, 1989.

John, Richard R. "Government Institutions as Agents of Change: Rethinking American Political Development in the Early Republic, 1787–1835." *Studies in American Political Development* 11 (1997): 347–80.

———. *Spreading the News: The American Postal System from Franklin to Morse*. Cambridge, Mass.: Harvard University Press, 1995.

Johnson, Paul E. *A Shopkeeper's Millennium*. New York: Hill and Wang, 1978.

Kammen, Michael, ed. *The Origins of the American Constitution: A Documentary History*. New York: Penguin Books, 1986.

Kann, Mark E. "Individualism, Civic Virtue, and Gender in America." *Studies in American Political Development* 4 (1990): 46–81.

Kelley, Robert Lloyd. *The Cultural Pattern in American Politics*. 1st ed. New York: Alfred A. Knopf, 1979.

Ketcham, Ralph. *Presidents above Party*. Chapel Hill: University of North Carolina Press, 1984.

Key, V. O. *Southern Politics in State and Nation*. New York: Alfred A. Knopf, 1949.

Klein, Phillip Shriver. *Pennsylvania Politics, 1817–1832*. Philadelphia: University of Pennsylvania Press, 1940.

Kramnick, Isaac, and R. Laurence Moore. *The Godless Constitution: The Case against Religious Correctness*. New York: W. W. Norton, 1996.

Kulikoff, Allan. *The Agrarian Origins of American Capitalism*. Charlottesville: University Press of Virginia, 1992.

———. *Tobacco and Slaves: The Development of Southern Cultures in the Chesapeake, 1680–1800*. Chapel Hill: University of North Carolina Press, 1986.

Lambert, Byron Cecil. *The Rise of the Anti-Mission Baptists*. 1957. Reprint, New York: Arno Press, 1980.

Langer, William L. *Political and Social Upheaval, 1832–1852*. New York: Harper and Row, 1969.

Leichtle, Kurt E. "The Rise of Jacksonian Politics in Illinois." *Illinois Historical Journal* 82 (summer 1989): 93–107.

Leonard, Adam A. "Personal Politics in Indiana, 1816 to 1840." *Indiana Magazine of History* 19 (March 1923): 1–56.

Leonard, Gerald Flood. "Partisan Political Theory and the Unwritten Constitution: The Origins of Democracy in Illinois, 1818–1840." Ph. D. diss., University of Michigan, 1992.

Lerner, Ralph. *The Thinking Revolutionary: Principle and Practice in the New Republic*. Ithaca: Cornell University Press, 1987.

Les Benedict, Michael. "Factionalism and Representation: Some Insights from the Nineteenth-Century United States." *Social Science History* 9 (1985): 361–98.

Levine, Andrew. *Liberal Democracy: A Critique of Its Theory*. New York: Columbia University Press, 1981.

Levine, Peter D. *The Behavior of State Legislative Parties in the Jacksonian Era: New Jersey, 1829–1844*. Rutherford, N.J.: Associated University Press, 1977.

Lienesch, Michael. "Reinterpreting Rebellion: The Influence of Shays's Rebellion on American Political Thought." In *In Debt to Shays*. Edited by Robert A. Gross, 161–82. Charlottesville: University Press of Virginia, 1993.

Limerick, Patricia Nelson. *The Legacy of Conquest: The Unbroken Past of the American West*. New York: W. W. Norton, 1987.

Lipset, Seymour Martin. *The First New Nation: The United States in Historical and Comparative Perspective*. New York: W. W. Norton, 1979.

Lowi, Theodore J. "Party, Policy, and Constitution in America." In *The American Party Systems: Stages of Political Development*. Edited by William Nisbet Chambers and Walter Dean Burnham, 238–76. New York: Oxford University Press, 1967.

Lubell, Samuel. *The Future of American Politics*. 3d ed. New York: Harper and Row, 1965.

Macpherson, C. B. *The Real World of Democracy*. New York: Oxford University Press, 1966.

Madson, John. *Where the Sky Began: Land of the Tallgrass Prairie*. Ames: Iowa State University Press, 1995.

Marx, Anthony W. *Making Race and Nation: A Comparison of South Africa, the United States, and Brazil*. Cambridge: Cambridge University Press, 1998.

Marx, Karl. *The Eighteenth Brumaire of Louis Bonaparte*. 1852. Reprint, New York: International Publishers, 1963.

Marx, Leo. *The Machine in the Garden*. Oxford: Oxford University Press, 1964.

Mathews, Donald G. *Religion in the Old South*. Chicago: University of Chicago Press, 1977.

McColley, Robert. *Slavery and Jeffersonian Virginia*. Urbana: University of Illinois Press, 1964.

McCormick, Richard P. "Political Parties." In *The Encyclopedia of American Political History*. Edited by Jack P. Greene, Vol. 3, pp. 939–63. New York: Charles Scribner's Sons, 1984.

———. *The Second American Party System: Party Formation in the Jacksonian Era*. Chapel Hill: University of North Carolina Press, 1966.

McCoy, Drew. *The Elusive Republic: Political Economy in Jeffersonian America*. Chapel Hill: University of North Carolina Press, 1980.

———. *The Last of the Fathers: James Madison and the Republican Legacy*. Cambridge: Cambridge University Press, 1989.

McCurry, Stephanie. *Masters of Small Worlds: Yeoman Households, Gender Relations, and the Political Culture of the Antebellum South Carolina Low Country*. New York: Oxford University Press, 1995.

McDonald, Forrest. *Alexander Hamilton: A Biography*. New York: W. W. Norton, 1979.

McLoughlin, William G., Jr. *Isaac Backus and the American Pietistic Tradition*. Boston: Little, Brown, 1967.

McManis, Douglas R. *The Initial Evaluation and Utilization of the Illinois Prairies, 1815–1840*. Chicago: University of Chicago Department of Geography, 1964.

Melzer, Arthur. *The Natural Goodness of Man*. Chicago: University of Chicago Press, 1990.

Merchant, Carolyn. *Ecological Revolutions*. Chapel Hill: University of North Carolina Press, 1988.

Meyers, Marvin. *The Jacksonian Persuasion: Politics and Belief.* New York: Vintage Books, 1957.

Michels, Robert. *Political Parties: A Sociological Study of the Oligarchical Tendencies of Modern Democracy.* 1915. Reprint, New York: Free Press, 1962.

Miller, Joshua. "The Ghostly Body Politic: *The Federalist* Papers and Popular Sovereignty." *Political Theory* 16 (February 1988): 99–119.

———. *The Rise and Fall of Democracy in Early America, 1630–1789.* University Park: Pennsylvania State University Press, 1991.

Miller, Perry. *Errand into the Wilderness.* Cambridge, Mass.: Harvard University Press, 1956.

Mills, Charles W. *The Racial Contract.* Ithaca: Cornell University Press, 1997.

Miyakawa, T. Scott. *Protestants and Pioneers: Individualism and Conformity on the American Frontier.* Chicago: University of Chicago Press, 1964.

Moore, R. Laurence. *Religious Outsiders and the Making of Americans.* New York: Oxford University Press, 1986.

Morgan, Edmund S. *American Slavery, American Freedom: The Ordeal of Colonial Virginia.* New York: W. W. Norton, 1975.

———. *The Puritan Dilemma.* Boston: Little, Brown, 1958.

Morone, James. *The Democratic Wish: Popular Participation and the Limits of American Government.* New York: Basic Books, 1991.

Morris, Christopher. *Becoming Southern: The Evolution of a Way of Life, Warren County and Vicksburg, Mississippi, 1770–1860.* New York. Oxford University Press, 1995.

Moses, John. *Illinois, Historical and Statistical.* Chicago: Fergus Printing, 1892.

Murphy, Walter, James E. Fleming, and William F. Harris II. *American Constitutional Interpretation.* Mineola, N.Y.: West Publishing, 1986.

Nash, Gary B. *Race and Revolution.* Madison: Madison House, 1990.

———. *The Urban Crucible: Social Change, Political Consciousness, and the Origins of the American Revolution.* Cambridge, Mass.: Harvard University Press, 1979.

Norton, Anne. *Alternative Americas: A Reading of Antebellum American Culture.* Chicago: University of Chicago Press, 1986.

———. *Reflections on Political Identity.* Baltimore: Johns Hopkins University Press, 1988.

Onuf, Peter S. *Statehood and Union: A History of the Northwest Ordinance.* Bloomington: Indiana University Press, 1987.

Orren, Karen, and Stephen Skowronek. "Editors' Preface." *Studies in American Political Development* 1 (1986): vii–viii.

Park, Siyoung. "Land Speculation in Western Illinois: Pike County, Illinois, 1821–1835." *Journal of the Illinois State Historical Society* 77 (1984): 115–33.

Parrington, Vernon L. *Main Currents in American Thought.* Vol. 1, *The Colonial Mind, 1620–1800.* Vol. 2, *The Romantic Revolution in America, 1800–1860.* New York: Harcourt, Brace and World, 1927.

Pease, Theodore Calvin. *The Frontier State, 1818–1848.* 1918. Reprint, with an introduction by Robert W. Johannsen, Urbana: University of Illinois Press, 1987.

———. *The Story of Illinois.* 3d ed. Chicago: University of Chicago Press, 1975.

Pease, Theodore Calvin, ed. *Illinois Election Returns, 1818–1848.* Springfield:

Illinois State Historical Library, 1923.

Persky, Joseph J. *The Burden of Dependency*. Baltimore: Johns Hopkins University Press, 1992.

Pessen, Edward. *Jacksonian America: Society, Personality, and Politics*. Homewood, Ill.: Dorsey Press, 1969.

Piven, Frances Fox, and Richard A. Cloward. *Poor People's Movements*. New York: Pantheon Books, 1977.

Pocock, Emil. "Popular Roots of Jacksonian Democracy: The Case of Dayton, Ohio, 1815–1830." *Journal of the Early Republic* 9 (Winter 1989): 489–504.

Potter, David M. *People of Plenty: Economic Abundance and the American Character*. Chicago: University of Chicago Press, 1954.

Powell, John Duncan. "Peasant Society and Clientist Politics." *American Political Science Review* 64 (1970): 411–24.

Power, Richard Lyle. *Planting Corn Belt Culture: The Impress of the Upland Southerner and Yankee in the Old Northwest*. Indianapolis: Indiana Historical Society, 1953.

Pruitt, Bettye Hobbs. "Self-Sufficiency and the Agricultural Economy of Eighteenth-Century Massachusetts." *William and Mary Quarterly*, 3d ser., 41 (1984): 333–64.

Randall, Randolph. *James Hall: Spokesman of the West*. Columbus: Ohio State University Press, 1964.

Ratcliffe, Donald J. *Party Spirit in a Frontier Republic: Democratic Politics in Ohio, 1793–1821*. Columbus: Ohio State University Press, 1998.

Remini, Robert. *The Revolutionary Age of Andrew Jackson*. New York: Perennial Library, 1985.

Rendleman, Edith Bradley. *All Anybody Ever Wanted of Me Was to Work*. Edited by Jane Adams. Carbondale: Southern Illinois University, 1996.

Richards, Leonard L. *Gentlemen of Property and Standing*. Oxford: Oxford University Press, 1970.

Ridgley, Douglas C. *The Geography of Illinois*. Chicago: University of Chicago Press, 1921.

Rodgers, Daniel T. *Contested Truths: Keywords in American Politics Since Independence*. New York: Oxford University Press, 1988.

Roediger, David. *The Wages of Whiteness: Race and the Making of the American Working Class*. London: Verso, 1991.

Rogin, Michael Paul. *Fathers and Sons: Andrew Jackson and the Subjugation of the American Indian*. New York: Alfred A. Knopf, 1975.

———. *The Intellectuals and McCarthy: The Radical Specter*. Cambridge, Mass.: MIT Press, 1967.

Rohrbough, Malcolm J. *The Land Office Business*. New York and London: Oxford University Press, 1968.

———. *The Trans-Appalachian Frontier*. New York: Oxford University Press, 1978.

Ross, Steven J. *Workers on the Edge*. New York: Columbia University Press, 1985.

Rozett, John Michael. "The Social Bases of Party Conflict in the Age of Jackson: Individual Voting Behavior in Greene County, Illinois, 1838–1848." Ph.D. diss., University of Michigan, 1974.

Salter, Mary Ann. "George Flower Comes to the Illinois Country: A New Look at Motivations." *Journal of the Illinois State Historical Society* 69

(1976): 213–23.

Sandel, Michael J. *Democracy's Discontent: America in Search of a Public Philosophy*. Cambridge, Mass.: Harvard University Press, 1996.

Sauer, Carl O. *Seeds, Spades, Hearths, and Herds: The Domestication of Animals and Foodstuffs*. Cambridge, Mass.: MIT Press, 1969.

Saxton, Alexander. *The Rise and Fall of the White Republic: Class Politics and Mass Culture in Nineteenth-Century America*. London: Verso, 1990.

Schattschneider, E. E. *The Semi-Sovereign People: A Realist's View of Democracy in America*. 1960. Reprint, New York: Holt, Rinehart and Winston, 1983.

Scheiber, Harry N. "The Ohio-Mississippi Flatboat Trade: Some Reconsiderations." In *The Frontier in American Development*. Edited by David M. Ellis, 277–87. Ithaca: Cornell University Press, 1969.

Schlesinger, Arthur, Jr. *The Age of Jackson*. Boston: Little, Brown, 1945.

Schmitt, Carl. *The Crisis of Parliamentary Democracy*. 1923. Translated by Ellen Kennedy. Cambridge, Mass.: MIT Press, 1988.

Schob, David E. *Hired Hands and Plowboys: Farm Labor in the Midwest, 1815–1860*. Urbana: University of Illinois Press, 1975.

Schultz, Ronald. *The Republic of Labor*. New York: Oxford University Press, 1993.

Schumpeter, Joseph A. *Capitalism, Socialism, and Democracy*. 1942. Reprint, New York: Harper Torchbooks, 1975.

Scott, James C. *The Moral Economy of the Peasant Rebellion and Subsistence in Southeast Asia*. New Haven: Yale University Press, 1976.

Sellers, Charles. *The Market Revolution: Jacksonian America, 1815–1846*. New York: Oxford University Press, 1991.

Shade, William Gerald. *Banks or No Banks: The Money Issue in Western Politics, 1832–1865*. Detroit: Wayne State University Press, 1972.

Shefter, Martin. "The Electoral Foundations of the Political Machine: New York City, 1884–1897." In *The History of American Electoral Behavior*. Edited by Joel H. Silbey, Allan G. Bogue, and William H. Flanigan. Princeton: Princeton University Press, 1978.

Shklar, Judith N. *American Citizenship: The Quest for Inclusion*. Cambridge, Mass.: Harvard University Press, 1991.

Silbey, Joel H. *The Shrine of Party: Congressional Voting Behavior, 1841–1852*. Pittsburgh: University of Pittsburgh Press, 1967.

Silbey, Joel H., Allan G. Bogue, and William H. Flanigan, eds. *The History of American Electoral Behavior*. Princeton: Princeton University Press, 1978.

Simeone, James. "Ninian Edwards' Republican Dilemma." *Illinois Historical Journal* 90 (Winter 1997): 245–64.

Skowronek, Stephen. *Building a New American State*. Cambridge: Cambridge University Press, 1982.

Slotkin, Richard. *The Fatal Environment*. New York: Atheneum, 1985.

Smith, George Washington. *A History of Southern Illinois*. Chicago: Lewis Publishing, 1912.

———. "The Salines of Southern Illinois." *Publications of the Historical Library of Illinois* 9 (1904): 246–53.

Snyder, John Francis. *Adam W. Snyder and His Period in Illinois History, 1817–1842*. Virginia, Ill.: E. Needham, 1906.

———. "Forgotten Statesmen of Illinois: Hon. Conrad Will." *Publications of the Historical Library of Illinois* 10 (1905): 355–67.

———. "Forgotten Statesmen of Illinois: Hon. Jesse Burgess Thomas." *Transactions of the Illinois State Historical Society* 9 (1904): 514–23.

Sombart, Werner. *Why Is There No Socialism in the United States?* Translated by Patricia M. Hocking and C. T. Husbands. 1906. Reprint, White Plains, N.Y.: International Arts and Sciences Press, 1976.

Stevens, Harry. *The Early Jackson Party in Ohio*. Durham: Duke University Press, 1957.

Stevens, Wayne E. "The Shaw-Hansen Election Contest." *Journal of the Illinois State Historical Society* 7 (1914–1915): 389–401.

Stock, Catherine McNicol. *Rural Radicals: From Bacon's Rebellion to the Oklahoma City Bombing*. New York: Penguin Books, 1997.

Storing, Herbert J. *What the Anti-Federalists Were For*. Chicago: University of Chicago Press, 1981.

Storing, Herbert J., ed. *The Anti-Federalist*. Chicago: University of Chicago Press, 1985.

Suppiger, Joseph Edward. "Amity to Enmity: Ninian Edwards and Jesse B. Thomas." *Journal of the Illinois State Historical Society* 67 (1974): 201–14.

———. "Jesse Burgess Thomas: Illinois' Pro-Slavery Advocate." Ph.D. diss., University of Tennessee, 1970.

Sutton, Robert M. "Edward Coles and the Constitutional Crisis in Illinois, 1822–1824." *Illinois Historical Journal* 82 (Spring 1989): 33–47.

Tarcov, Nathan. "American Constitutionalism and Individual Rights." In *How Does the Constitution Secure Rights?* Edited by Robert A. Goldwin and William A. Schambra, 101–25. Washington, D.C.: American Enterprise Institute for Public Policy Research, 1985.

Taylor, Alan. *Liberty Men and Great Proprietors*. Chapel Hill: University of North Carolina Press, 1990.

———. *William Cooper's Town: Power and Persuasion on the Frontier of the Early American Republic*. New York: Alfred A. Knopf, 1996.

Taylor, William Robert. *Cavalier and Yankee*. 1957. Reprint, New York: Harper Torchbooks, 1969.

Thomas, George M. *Revivalism and Cultural Change*. Chicago: University of Chicago Press, 1989.

Thompson, Charles M. "Elections and Election Machinery in Illinois, 1818–1848." *Journal of the Illinois State Historical Society* 7 (1915): 375–97.

———. "Genesis of the Whig Party in Illinois." *Transactions of the Illinois State Historical Society* 17 (1912): 86–93.

———. *The Illinois Whigs before 1846*. Urbana: University of Illinois Press, 1915.

Thornton, J. Mills. *Politics and Power in a Slave State*. Baton Rouge: Louisiana State University Press, 1978.

Tillson, Albert H., Jr. "The Localist Roots of Backcountry Loyalism: An Examination of Popular Political Culture in Virginia's New River Valley." *Journal of Southern History* 54 (1988): 387–404.

Tocqueville, Alexis de. *Democracy in America*. Edited by J. P. Mayer. Translated by George Lawrence. Garden City, N.Y.: Anchor Books, 1969.

Tulis, Jeffrey K. "The Interpretable Presidency." In *The Presidency and the Political System*. Edited by Michael Nelson. 3d ed. Washington, D.C.: Congressional Quarterly Press, 1990.

———. *The Rhetorical Presidency*. Princeton: Princeton University Press, 1987.

Turner, Frederick Jackson. *The Significance of the Frontier in American History*.

Edited by Harold P. Simonson. New York: Frederick Ungar, 1963.

Vickers, Daniel. "Competency and Competition: Economic Culture in Early America." *William and Mary Quarterly,* 3d ser., 46 (1989): 1–29.

Waldrep, Christopher. "The Making of a Border State Society: James Mc-Gready, the Great Revival, and the Prosecution of Profanity in Kentucky." *American Historical Review* 99 (June 1994): 767–84.

Waldstreicher, David. *In the Midst of Perpetual Fêtes: The Making of American Nationalism, 1776–1820.* Chapel Hill: University of North Carolina Press, 1997.

Wallace, Michael. "Changing Concepts of Party in the United States." In *Readings in American Political History.* Edited by Frank Otto Gatell, Paul Goodman, and Allan Weinstein. New York: Oxford University Press, 1972.

Walters, Ronald G. *American Reformers, 1815–1860.* New York: Hill and Wang, 1978.

Ward, John William. *Andrew Jackson: Symbol for an Age.* London: Oxford University Press, 1955.

Watson, Harry. *Jacksonian Politics and Community Conflict.* Baton Rouge: Louisiana State University Press, 1981.

Weber, Max. *Max Weber Selections in Translation.* Edited by W. G. Runciman. Translated by Eric Matthews. Cambridge: Cambridge University Press, 1978.

Weber, Timothy P. *Living in the Shadow of the Second Coming.* Chicago: University of Chicago Press, 1983.

White, Richard. *The Middle Ground: Indians, Empires, and Republics in the Great Lakes Region, 1650–1815.* Cambridge: Cambridge University Press, 1991.

Wilentz, Sean. *Chants Democratic: New York City and the Rise of the American Working Class, 1788–1850.* New York: Oxford University Press, 1984.

———. "On Class and Politics in Jacksonian America." *Reviews in American History* (December 1982): 45–63.

Wills, Gary. *Cincinnatus: George Washington and the Enlightenment.* Garden City, N.Y.: Doubleday, 1984.

Wolin, Sheldon. *Politics and Vision: Community and Innovation in Western Political Thought.* Boston: Little, Brown, 1960.

Wood, Gordon S. *The Creation of the American Republic, 1776–1787.* Chapel Hill: University of North Carolina Press, 1969.

———. "Interests and Disinterestedness in the Making of the Constitution." In *Beyond Confederation: Origins of the Constitution and American National Identity.* Edited by Richard Beeman, Stephen Botein, and Edward C. Carter II, 69–109. Chapel Hill: University of North Carolina Press, 1987.

Wyatt-Brown, Bertram. *Southern Honor: Ethics and Behavior in the Old South.* Oxford and New York: Oxford University Press, 1982.

Young, Mary E., "Congress Looks West: Liberal Ideology and Public Land Policy in the Nineteenth Century." In *The Frontier in American Development.* Edited by David M. Ellis, 110. Ithaca: Cornell University Press, 1969.

Zemsky, Robert. *Merchants, Farmers, and River Gods: An Essay on Eighteenth-Century American Politics.* Boston: Gambit, 1971.

Zolberg, Aristide. "Moments of Madness." *Politics and Society* (Winter 1972): 183–207.

INDEX

Adams, John: on aristocracy, 17, 217; and corporate view of society, 81; on "the people," 9; republicanism of, 76

Agricultural Society, 63–65

agriculture: corn-belt, 65–66; crisis caused by traditional, 55; and New Orleans market, 47, 51–52; of North and South, 13, 221n. 21; southern "short staple," 24, 227n. 4; subsistence-surplus, 41, 210, 227n. 4, 231n. 36

Alabama: like Illinois, 206–7, 260n. 18; politics in, 203; role of, in South, 201; and use of "short staple" cotton, 24, 147

Alexander, William, 119, 127, 128, 151–53, 156, 162, 167, 184

American Bottom: fertility and size of, 42, 56, 228n. 10; and Kinney's improvement bill, 125; settlement of, by French, 36; use of, by Shawnee, 117

American Colonization Society, 23, 223n. 17

"Americanus": on convention vote trading, 119–21; on English emigrants, 34; response of, to Birkbeck, 147, 157, 163

"Ames" (Sidney Breese), 56–63, 69, 122, 135, 231n. 41

Anti-Federalists, 72–76

"Aristides": on convention movement, 97, 148; on Northwest Ordinance, 28; on reason and progress, 161

Arminians: on church-state relations, 178–80; on human faculties, 177–78; influence of, on political culture, 169–74, 195; on salvation, 14. *See also* Methodists; milk-and-cider persuasion

Ashworth, John, 211

backcountry: in Alabama, 203; and emigration to Illinois, 8, 33; and "middle-class" status, 33, 99; political culture of, 9, 69, 157, 250n. 58, 260n. 21, 260n. 24; religion of, 169–70; republicanism of, 14, 71; and white folks, 32–34. *See also* egalitarianism

Bailyn, Bernard, 180

Baptists: Free Will (Missionary), 169–71, 178, 183, 193; Friends of Humanity, 28, 182–83, 256n. 43; Regular (Anti-Missionary), 170, 172–76, 178, 183–84, 213. *See also* Arminians; Calvinists

Beaird, Joseph, 118, 124–25

Beard, Charles, 207

Belleville, 62

Bender, Thomas, 70–71

Benson, Lee, 11

Berry, Thomas Senior, 51

Berry, William, 149, 150, 181

Berthoff, Rowland, 11

big folks: Coles as, 17–18; 26, 56;

and conventionists, 37, 55, 98, 149, 166–69, 170–72; identification of, by Sloo, Jr., 8, and non-conventionists, 154, 248n. 39; status and numbers of, 71, 112; opposition to, by Thomas, 104. *See also* Edwards, Ninian

Birkbeck, Morris: and Agricultural Society, 64–65; anti-slavery views of, 59, 97, 147, 157; as English Settlement leader, 34; as "Jonathan Freeman," 65, 148–49, 154–56, 163, 210; and *Letters from Illinois,* 160. *See also* "Americanus"; "John Rifle"

Black Code: 18–19, 105, 108, 243n. 46. *See also* voluntary servitude

Blackstone, William: on "positive constitutions," 77; reading of, by Edwards, 82, 84, 92; on Saxon freedom and Norman yoke, 77, 214, 236n. 24

Blackwell, David, 59, 60, 94, 122, 136, 156, 157, 167, 181, 232n. 50

Blakeman, Curtiss, 59, 64, 105, 156

Boggess, Arthur Clinton, 33

Bond, Shadrach, 18, 100, 119, 161–62, 241n. 16

Bogue, Allan G., 65

bottomland: in backcountry mythos, 9, 32; disease in, 13, 49–50, 60, 230n. 24; excess vegetation in, 33, 59–60, 209; farming in, 13, 33, 66, 210, 231n. 41; fertility of, 42–46, 56, 227n. 9; soil types of, 42; tax rate of, 44

Breese, Sidney: as "Ames," 56–63, 69, 122, 135, 231n. 41

Bridges, Amy, 69, 203–4

Briggs, Winstanley, 102

"Brissot," 24, 31, 46

Brown, William H., 51, 52, 118–19, 181

Browne, Thomas, 95

Brush, Daniel, 50

Buck, Solon Justus, 33

Buckmaster, Nathaniel, 134

Cahokia, 99, 100, 117

Calhoun, John C., 6, 75, 95

Calvinists: on church and state, 178–80, 191–92; on human faculties, 177–78; and predestination, 169–70; on salvation, 14; wandering, 188, 213. *See also* Baptists, Regular; whole-hog persuasion

Canal Bill, 25, 119

Carden, Allen D., 170

Cayton, Andrew R. L., 204, 259n. 8

Churchill, George: and Agricultural Society, 64; anti-slavery views of, 28, 30; and conventionists, 128, 144, 150, 155, 249n. 45; election bill of, 115, 128, 130–32, 150; as non-conventionist candidate, 156

Christians: followers of Barton Stone and Alexander Campbell, 169, 173

civil society, 80, 114, 164

Clark, George Rogers, 19

Coles, Edward: and Adams and Jefferson, 28; as Agricultural Society leader, 64, 233n. 61; as Colonization Society member, 23; early career and upbringing of, 17–18, 248n. 28; Edwardsville farm of, 3–4, 26; and feud with Warren, 144, 248n. 28; as governor, 26–27; 181, 195; inaugural address of, 12, 98–99, 116, 119; as non-conventionist leader, 97, 98, 136, 138, 140, 181, 213; reasons for opposition to, 4, 26, 121–22, 130, 140–41, 202, 223n. 24; and second Vandalia mob, 130–31; slave emancipation of, 17, 153, 222n. 5, 249n. 48; and third Vandalia mob, 3, 140–41; wealth of, 26, 66

Constitution, U.S., 60, 158,

tion into, 8, 53; colonization movement in, 23; currency exchange rates in, 53; gift of, to Washington, 79; Illinois a part of, 19; influence of, on Coles, 17; state convention of, 202

voluntary servitude: in code passed at Vincennes (1805), 29, 87; in territorial indenture system, 19–21, 105, 108, 117. *See also* Black Code

Walker, Jessie, 153, 182

Warren, Hooper: animosity of, toward Coles, 17, 95, 98, 144, 153, 221n. 3, 248n. 28; attack of, by Smith, 182; and defense of missionaries and Methodists, 184–85; as Edwards's client, 93, 145; egalitarian views of, 194; and exposure of 1820 slavery plot, 108; and exposure of Madison County conventionist plot, 185; opposition of, to "slave gentry," 248n. 39; political transformation of, 143–44

Washington, George, 79, 113

Weber, Max, 111–12

West, Emanuel: as conventionist leader, 60, 119, 121, 123, 131, 156, 182; as Thomas party client, 144

Whig Party, 11, 85, 210–12, 214, 217

White, Leonard, 93, 95, 241n. 16

white folks: and claim of specialness, 195–96; egalitarian individualism of, 55, 166, 175; as Illinois backcountry population, 8, 32–38; opposition of, to big folks, 8–9, 99, 165; connotation of term, 6; and whiteness, 7, 154, 175, 199–200, 206, 211, 219n. 8; work patterns of, 53

"Whiteman, A," 26

Whiteside, William, 92

white supremacy: Douglas's explicit defense of, 10; Lincoln's implicit defense of, 10–11; as presupposition of two-party competition, 199–200, 211; white folks' assumption of, 6–7, 33–34

whole-hog persuasion: anti-slavery adherents within, 191–92; and Calvinist conversion, 178–79; defined, 166–67; and Democratic Party, 210; and logic of dissent, 191–93, 212–14; and milk-and-cider persuasion, 167, 185–93; pro-slavery adherents within, 196

Will, Conrad: as convention leader, 16, 18; House report of, 20–23; "limited slavery" plan of, 23, 150–51, 155–56, 195–97; majoritarianism of, 31; as saline owner, 223n. 20; in second convention mob, 130

Wills, Garry, 76–77

Wirt, William, 78

Wood, Gordon S., 79

Woods, John, 53, 70

Wright, Josias, 193, 195–96

Wyatt-Brown, Bertram, 163–64

yankees: and ballot voting, 150; and Bounty land emigration, 63; farming practices of, 66, 96, 161–66; Marine Settlement of, 64, 105; prejudice against, 62, 145, 149, 204; prominence of, in convention leadership, 60

yeoman farmers: and capitalists, 40–41; and class interests, 79; Melancton Smith's view of, 73–74; predominance of, in Illinois, 202; Saxon, 77; southern gentry variety of, 24; tension between independence and investment among, 52–56